THIRD REICH
1933-1945
(Maximum extent, including occupied areas)

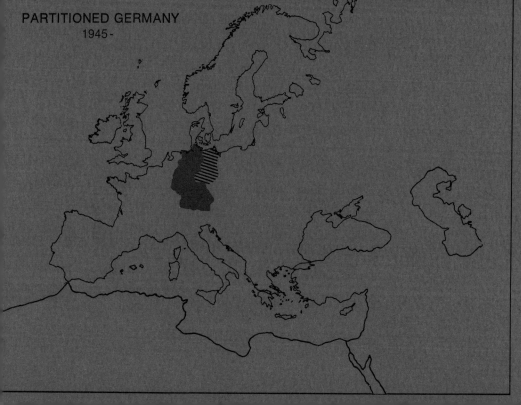

PARTITIONED GERMANY
1945 -

George Bailey is a graduate of Columbia College in New York City and Magdalen College, Oxford. He has spent almost thirty years in Europe, most of them in Germany and Austria. During World War II he served as an American army intelligence and liaison officer and as an escort officer for German generals. He was interpreter-translator in Russian and German at the surrender negotiations. He became husband, son-in-law, grandson-in-law, brother-in-law, and finally a father in a German-Jewish—Austrian publishing family (the Ullsteins of Berlin and Vienna). He is widely traveled, having gained his postwar livelihood as a liaison officer with the German police, as a literary agent, and as a journalist covering Germany and Eastern Europe for the *Reporter* and the American Broadcasting Company. In 1959 he received the Overseas Press Club's award for the best magazine reporting on foreign affairs.

The Biography of an Obsession
GERMANS

George Bailey

WORLD PUBLISHING
TIMES MIRROR
NEW YORK

The lines from "An Immortality" by Ezra Pound are
reprinted from *Lustra.* Copyright 1917 by Ezra Pound.
Reprinted by permission of New Directions Publishing
Corporation for the Committee for Ezra Pound.

Published by The World Publishing Company
Published simultaneously in Canada
by Nelson, Foster & Scott Ltd.

First printing—1972

WORLD PUBLISHING
TIMES MIRROR

To Beate

WHEN I WAS TWELVE YEARS OLD, IN THE SUM-
mer after my father died, I went to McNeil
Island in Puget Sound for the long vacation. At
that time, 1932, northwestern Washington was
said to be the wildest part of the forty-eight United
States: the Olympic peninsula was not fully sur-
veyed and charted until the beginning of World War II. In this place,
in the forest primeval, in the uncharted wilderness I met my first German
and heard the German language spoken for the first time. The German
was John Luhr, the game warden of McNeil Island. Luhr was a widower
whose three sons had left to begin families of their own. He lived alone
in a two-story wooden frame house that he had built himself. It was a
finished, professional piece of work. It had a long, spacious front porch
overlooking the straits, or "narrows" as we called them, between the
island and the mainland, and a smaller back porch. Luhr had built a
"mill" and harnessed a stream, by means of a wooden viaduct at least
a hundred yards long, to turn a lathe and generate electricity for the
house. He made his own furniture; I know because I once blew the arm
off the sofa with a blast from his sixteen-gauge shotgun: I had been trying
to flip the full shells out of the breech as I had often seen him do. Luhr
went to the "mill" and made a new arm the same day. His workshop in
the "mill" was simply but well equipped. The belts that turned the
wheels were leather straps made from deer, elk, or moose hides. Luhr
was also a well-versed electrician: he wound his own generators. In fact,
Luhr had achieved autarky; he put up in Mason jars fruit from his trees,
venison and elk meat from his hunting (this was before the availability
of deep-freeze units), and the clams he dug from the beach in front of
his house. He also occasionally smoked some of the fish he caught. All
I ever saw him buy at the store (it was five or ten miles away across the
water in Longbranch—a long way to row; Luhr did not have a motor-
boat) was coffee, salt, canned milk, and ammunition.

Luhr was a bounty hunter: he hunted cougar, gray seal, and even

[1]

crows. He was not so much interested in fishing save for spearing flounder. This he did with a long bamboo pole with three steel prongs fixed to one end. His incentive was the delicacy of fried flounder. Luhr's house was furnished after the fashion of a hunting lodge, with one exception: there were no trophies, no antlers or products of taxidermy. Except for the usual field-and-stream calendars and one or two nondescript pictures, the single ornament of the large living room was the gun rack. It was magnificent. There were eighteen guns on the rack—six slide-action or automatic shotguns, the lever-action .25–.35-caliber Remington, and the rest of them bolt-action Winchester deer rifles of various bores. There was only one side arm on the rack, the first of its kind I ever saw: a Luger. The shape of the Luger fascinated me as did its spectacular action—the triple hinge outside and on top of the magazine and barrel. The guns on the rack were all oiled and polished, lock, stock, and barrel, until they glowed with a black and blue steel dark mahogany brilliance. I have seen a great many gun collections since then, both private and in the great military museums of Europe, but I have never seen the like of the sober splendor of John Luhr's gun rack.

Then, with the capacity for wonder of a twelve-year-old, as now, looking back over four decades, the impressive thing about Luhr and his friends was their matter-of-factness. They were in paradise and they knew it. Scions of a nation of forest worshipers, they were quietly devotional in their cathedral: they took what was granted for granted. There was never any fuss. In three consecutive summers I never saw anyone approach Luhr's place by land or sea unless it was some old familiar coming as a guest. There was no other habitation within several miles. Luhr's was the only house on the narrows side of the island, a place characterized by an astonishing discrepancy between high and low tide. In the evening the sea would come up more than a hundred yards of beach and climb almost to the top of the eight-foot sea wall not more than ten yards from the porch. As night came down the sea came up and closed around you quietly and soothingly, a solicitous approach. Then in the morning the sea was gone again and in its place a great shining blade of beach naked in the sharp air and, far down, a run of water that looked brisk and narrow enough to be a river. It made for an extraordinary cycle of impressions, a brand-new deal in life every morning.

I do not know whether John Luhr and his friends, such as the rubicund Adolf Apfel, a frequent overnight and weekend guest, were bootleggers. I do not know whether the term is appropriate in any case at that time in that place. I do know that there was hard drink on the premises. The first German sentence I can remember hearing was "Das schmeckt nach mehr!" ("That tastes like more!") in answer to the question—in English—"How does it taste?" As far as I am concerned, the fact of the home brew merely shows that John Luhr, in addition to making everything else in his paradise, also made the nectar to go with the ambrosia.

When my ear became enough accustomed to the language so that I could get the drift of what they were saying, I wondered as the weeks and months went by why no one ever talked of the "old country." I asked Luhr about it. "If ever there was a homeland for the Germans," he said, "this is it." True, these were all more or less professional men of the forest, living within a double tradition of solitude, the old (German) and the new (American) frontier. In other words, "Germany is here or nowhere!" I was reminded—caught up short and reminded—of Luhr's words many years later in reading *Wilhelm Meister.* Goethe's Count Lothario, Wilhelm's patron-cum-brother-in-law, goes to America to take part in the War of Independence. Afterward he returns to Germany and fixes a large inscription over the entrance to his estate: "America is here or nowhere!" Reading Goethe over the years, I was frequently reminded of Luhr and that pristine beginning of my contact with Germans, especially when Goethe talks of the forest.

I drew my friend into the woods. While shunning the uniform fir trees, I sought those beautiful leafy groves which admittedly do not extend far and wide throughout the region but are still of such size that a poor, wounded heart can hide itself there. In the inmost deep of the forest I had sought out for myself a solemn place where the oldest oaks and beeches formed a splendidly large, shadowed area. The ground was rather sloping and rendered the contour of the trunks all the more noticeable. All around this open radius the thickest bushes merged together, through which moss-covered crags loomed in their strength and dignity and provided a swift fall for a voluminous stream.

I had hardly forced my friend to this place when he, who preferred to be in an open landscape beside a river and among his fellowmen, laughingly assured me that I had demonstrated myself to be a true German. He recounted to me in great detail from Tacitus how our forebears had delighted in the feelings with which nature inspires us so magnificently and yet so unaffectedly in such solitudes. He had not held forth long when I cried out: "Oh, why doesn't this charming place lie in some great uncharted forest, or why may we not put a fence around it in order to sanctify it and ourselves and cut both off from the world! Surely there is no more

[3]

beautiful way in which to revere the godhead than that with which no picture is needed but which simply springs from the heart when we commune with nature!"

But how awesome and terrifying it is to be utterly alone "in some great uncharted forest." Once in a while during those summers—fortunately not often—Luhr would row over to the mainland for a night's partying and leave me alone in the house. On one of these occasions while cowering in my bed I heard a cougar scream, nearby, and I was completely terror-stricken. I had heard somewhere that a cougar's scream sounded like the scream of a woman gone raving mad from some great grief. Ever since then I had dreaded the event in anticipation, and forecast it exactly as it happened—when I was alone on an island at night. If I could have, I would have fled the island then and there, but Luhr had the only boat. There was an additional danger on McNeil Island; it was also the home of the state penitentiary. This was on the other side of the island, but there were trustees said to be at large and there was always the danger of escaped prisoners.

These were distinct possibilities; their distinctness served by contrast to emphasize the nameless terrors of the unfathomable primeval. Who knew what phantoms, goblins, and monsters were lurking there? Who wanted to know? Moving through a great forest is like swimming underwater in the sea. In both there is the radial awareness that comes with complete envelopment. But it is an indistinct awareness. The solemnity of the forest, the spectral theatricality of breaking and bending light, initiates the intruder into the mystery of time, since space is relegated—confined and sorted—into sections of shadow and light. As a boy I knew a place in the great forest where, I was convinced, under the right conditions and certainly only at midnight, time could be made to stop and eternity seized. Thereafter, I was equally sure, I could recapture eternity at will merely by referring to that moment of cosmic arrest. I could remain there, if I chose, forever, in a kind of nirvana. The forest world impels nature worship; it obliges to an obsession with the symbolic suggestiveness of the elements. The lack of horizontal line trims vision upward to the O altitudo.

This was the world of the Germans. Now France, said John Luhr, had no forests. France had well-spaced stands of trees that admitted unreservedly of light, that were airy and clearly defined. But immediately east of the Rhine the big woods began, and farther east lay the Teutoburg forest of Arminius, the primordial home of the race of gods and devils, monsters and giants, riddles and runes. The forest itself is a paradox: every tree earthbound, deep-rooted, yet pointing straight upward to infinity.

When I was sixteen years old I changed the scene of my summers. I got a job as fourth cook (scullion) on the Chicago, Milwaukee, Saint Paul, and Pacific Railroad by virtue of my father's past connections: he had been a dining car steward on The Milwaukee Road. The run was between Chicago, Illinois, and Tacoma, Washington, a distance of about 2,800 miles that required two days and three nights, going or coming. It was in the galleys of the C.M.St.P.&P. that I met the European community of nations as represented by the chefs, the second and third cooks of the various crews. On The Milwaukee Road the chefs were usually, but not always, Frenchmen or Walloons; the second cooks were almost always Germans (I remember one perfectly dotty Lithuanian second cook who never said anything in English except "On time, boys?"; the only other thing I ever heard him say was "thank you," in Polish); the third cooks were usually Hungarians, sometimes Poles. I met one German chef but never worked under him. The only native American I ever met in a galley crew was a chef, Richard S. ("Dirty Dick") Richards. He always said the "S" in his name stood for "son of a bitch" and he was right. I do not know whether Dirty Dick was a good chef but he was greatly feared, and with reason.

The chef's station is at the head of a dining car galley. The chef faces a charcoal grill and has at his back a solid complex of iceboxes as high as the ceiling. Beyond the iceboxes he has a rack accommodating carving knives, one of them with a blade almost two feet long, and cleavers— an array of deadly weapons required by his function in the galley. He prepared and grilled the choice cuts of meat (he would occasionally also grill tomatoes, but I never saw a chef fry a piece of meat, or anything else, for that matter, except crêpes à l'orange). The making of consommé was also his province. The second cook was the heavy-duty cook— baking, roasting, and boiling (tongue, for instance); he also made the puddings and the mayonnaise. The third cook was the fry or short-order cook; in addition he made the coffee and the green salads. The second cook faced the stove and the ovens. I have forgotten how the range was heated but when heated its entire surface was evenly hot. The third cook had a piece of the stove and the steam table. The fourth cook, who faced the other way, had the sinks.

It is necessary to dwell on the topography of the galley because this

[5]

was the scene of my first opportunity to watch the German in the concert of nations. The chef of a kitchen or a galley is probably the only absolute monarch surviving in the Western world. It is for the others in the galley to make and keep their peace with him. It is the cook's even more than the citizen's duty to keep the peace because a fight in a kitchen is a fearfully dangerous business. Not only because of the knives, cleavers, ladles, and rolling pins to hand, but even more so because of the presence and availability of boiling water and grease and red-hot coals.

For some reason Dirty Dick had taken a scunner at the third cook, Mike, a huge Pole. Axel, the German second cook, had done his best to keep the two apart or, rather, to keep Dirty Dick from pinking the third cook with his long carving knife. On the morning of our last day out, about three hours from the end of the line, we were about an hour late coming down the western side of the Cascades. It was then that the fight broke out in full fury between Dirty Dick and the third cook. Fortunately it was after breakfast and the range had been turned off. Even so it was still hot. Dirty Dick made at the third cook with his short cleaver. The third cook snatched the top off the garbage can and held it up as a shield. Axel made way by jumping onto the stove: it was either that or the sinks, and the sinks were within the action radius of Dirty Dick's right arm. The passageway in the galley was no more than three feet wide, so that veritable lists for mortal combat were provided. I made my escape over the counter into the pantry from where I was able to watch the unequal contest. The third cook could not follow me because he was too big to squeeze through the opening between the counter and the drop cupboard. Also my escape had been covered by Mike, the third cook himself; there was nobody to cover for him. I was almost distracted by the spectacle of Axel on the stove: he was cowering and shifting from one foot to the other as the heat from the stove came up through the soles of his shoes. Dick drove his cleaver smack into the middle of the garbage can top which the third cook held with both hands by the rim. The cleaver stuck and there ensued a tug of war, each combatant holding grimly to his own. Meanwhile, Axel by turns appealed to the chef to leave off—"Dot's not a fair fight, chef, chef!"—and berated the third cook for doing what he had no choice but to do—"You must be crazy, bicking a fight vit a man who hass all de hardvare!" As the train pitched and rolled down the steep grade and around curves, Dick managed to pull his cleaver free. As he did so the third cook turned the garbage can top around much as if it were a visor, so that he could see Dick through the gaping slit left by the cleaver. "Peek-a-boo, you son of bitch!" said

Dick and set himself to have at him again. At that moment the dining car went into a curve and the roadbed dipped rather sharply—the engineer was trying to make up lost time; the door of the upper icebox swung open swiftly and caught Dirty Dick in the back of the head. He fell face down on the floor of the galley; the cleaver went into the sink. Axel jumped off the stove and knelt down to examine the chef. "He iss oudt colder zan a clam," he said.

In three years on The Milwaukee Road I worked my way up to the exalted position of third cook (every position above scullion in a kitchen is exalted), but I was happy to work my way down again. The pay was only twenty percent more than that of a fourth cook and the work was far more difficult. In short, I had no aspirations to a career as a cook; nevertheless I was fated to remain in kitchens. Even when I went to Columbia College in New York on a scholarship I applied at Alumni House for a meal job and was sent straight to the Jewish Theological Seminary to work in the kitchens as a waiter-cum-shabbas-goy. I was more than a little disgruntled at this dispensation. After all, I came to Columbia as a scholarship student. Moreover I was in the Classics Department, a student of Greek. My disgruntlement did not last long. The kitchen of the Jewish Theological Seminary of America at 122nd Street and Broadway was an extraordinary place in 1939. Like the rabbinate, the kitchen was full of immigrants of more or less recent vintage, most of them from Germany, all of them from central Europe. Most, of course, but not all Jews. The chef was a Berliner, the second cook was a huge sub-Carpathian Russian who spoke not one word of anything except Russian and his name. His name was John Adams. The third cook, in this case the pastry cook, was, as so often, a Hungarian, Samubácsi (Uncle Sam).

But the major domo of the kitchen, the man who ran everything, was a German. And what a German! He was Franz Menz of Stuttgart. He looked like a Nazi statue, a neoclassical monument to German manhood. Moreover, he had two brothers, Max and August, who were in the German army. I can see Franz standing there in the middle of the entrance hall of the refectory, his legs wide apart in the German fashion, arms akimbo, grave but not pompous, entirely self-possessed but without a trace of arrogance. Indeed, considering his background and his family connections, the very fact that he held the position he did in the seminary was a tribute to the man. It is not easy to describe Franz's situation in the seminary. In 1939 a good many of the student body, the faculty, and the service personnel were either themselves victims of the Nazis or had relatives who were or would be victims of the Nazis—or both. And there was Menz, undeniably, indissolubly German, yet above all an advertisement for himself, with all the instinctive tact, sympathy, and humor required to master a hideously difficult situation. Menz had acquired a formula for handling the Jews, perhaps without knowing it. When I met him he had been employed in the seminary for some ten years. He had stayed on by choice: Franz was one of those Germans who measured up to the traditional national ideal of factotum; he could turn his hand to anything. He once explained to me: "I like these people very much; it is pleasant working for them and working with them; they have always been very kind to me." I never heard of anybody in the seminary who took exception to Franz. On the contrary, he was respected and much liked. There were more than a few who adored him. He managed cooks and waiters with an evenness, firmness, and discretion that were exemplary.

In the spring of 1940 Franz's brother Max was killed in action in France. In the fall of the same year Franz's second brother, August, fell in Norway. I heard of both bereavements not from Franz but from students in the rabbinate who, to my astonishment, went to Franz to offer their condolences. I think that Franz's success with the Jews at the seminary was due to his straightforwardness. He tried neither to conceal nor to demonstrate anything; he was neither talkative nor taciturn, neither hearty nor lugubrious; he kept an even middle course and held just the right temper in his dealings with everyone. Those of his friends I met were of the same character, one family in Yorkville in particular that lived conveniently close to the Eighty-sixth Street pleasure strip. My fascination with anything German was my calling card. Franz and his friends would give or lend me magazines from Germany, but they were careful to tear or cut out anything that had to do with Hitler or the Nazi party. When I asked why they did this Franz said, "Hitler is no good —for anybody." At the same time Franz took some pride in the exploits of the German army in the fall of France. I remember his taking me to a Yorkville movie house to see *Sieg im Westen* (Victory in the West), the official Nazi documentary of the German conquest of France, Belgium, and the Netherlands. A police cordon had to be provided to secure thoroughfare to the box office and entrance. Of the film itself I remember the panoramic shots of the endless rows of German soldiers, standing at attention in full field pack at first light and being addressed by an invisible commander: "Kameraden, Soldaten—die Zeit ist gekommen!" (Comrades, soldiers—the time has come!). I remember the footage of the

Stukas diving with their sirens screaming. I remember most vividly the scenes where German infantry marched along French roads, singing. The song they sang began with the words "Comrades, soldiers—the time has come!" When we came out of the movie house the crowd of protesters was gone. "The Germans are good soldiers," said Franz. "They are good at anything where there are strict rules and when everybody sticks to the rules. Otherwise they are not so good."

I went to a good many German movies in Yorkville. Most of the films were harmless enough, light comedies about good-natured barflies, the sort of role that Robert Montgomery played so well. Montgomery's equivalent in the German films of the era was Gustav Fröhlich. Nomen erat omen: "fröhlich" means "happy." But somewhere—for I never attended a rally of Fritz Kuhn's "Bund" or, for that matter, ever met a German or German-American in those days who openly harbored Nazi sympathies—I had learned the "Horst Wessel Lied," the battle song of the SA, the storm troops of the Nazi party. Horst Wessel was a young Nazi thug, a platoon leader in the SA, who was killed in 1932 in a street brawl in Berlin, allegedly by Communists. It is just as likely that he was killed by his competition in pimping. The "Horst Wessel Lied" was nevertheless a rousing song; set to the tune of an old German student ditty it ran:

> The banner high, the unit in close order,
>   The SA marches with quiet, solemn tread;
> With comrades killed by Red Front and reaction
>   We march in spirit with the honored dead.

One Saturday afternoon—that is, in the quiet time of the Jewish Sabbath—I was sweeping the floor of the refectory. Without realizing it I was singing the "Horst Wessel Lied"—I hope not at the top of my voice, for I was a basso in the college chapel choir. The door burst open and in rushed Rabbi Anselm of the faculty. Rabbi Anselm was a little, kindly old scholar whose chief joy in life was singing at the meals taken on the Sabbath. He took me by the arm. "Do you know what you are singing?" he asked. Then he sat down with me at the nearest table and lectured me for a full hour on the fate of the Jews in Germany. In that hour he gave me the only motivation I ever had for going to war against the Germans.

There is a Jewish joke that serves as a good introduction to the mystery of the shabbas goy. Two Jews meet on a train in Eastern Europe. "Where are you from?" the one asks the other. "From Czernowitz." "Is that a big town?" "Oh, about five hundred souls," is the answer. "How many goyim?" "Well, let's see, there's the gendarme, the gendarme's wife and two children—that makes four goyim; where are you from?" "I'm from New York." "Is that a big town?" "Big? It's an enormous town!" "How many Jews?" "Oh, about two million!" "Two million Jews! And how many goyim?" "About seven million." "Seven million goyim!?" "That's right." "But what for?"

A shabbas goy (literally "Sabbath gentile") is a gentile servant of the Jews on the Sabbath when the Jews are prohibited by canon law from working or exerting themselves in any way. Some Jews even tie their handkerchiefs around their wrists on the eve of Sabbath so as to avoid the effort of taking it out of their pockets during the holy period. Devout Jews are thus peculiarly helpless during the Sabbath, a fact that puts the shabbas goy into a special position of trust (a shabbas goy could steal the Jews blind over the Sabbath). Probably this position of trust explains the situation of Franz Menz, who was also—to the extent that he worked on Friday evenings and Saturdays—a shabbas goy. Once, through the Columbia College Public Affairs Bureau, I obtained a ticket to the Saturday afternoon Milton Berle radio show at Radio City. Since the show began before the end of Sabbath I had to ask permission to leave the seminary early. "Permission granted," said Louis B. Finkelstein, who was then provost and later president of the seminary. "After all, this is a special occasion—goy meets Berle!"

I was Finkelstein's personal servant at the time, and Finkelstein had just been appointed by President Roosevelt to represent American Jewry on the president's committee for interdenominational cooperation. As a result he was host at many small dinners in his suite of rooms.

I received at least as good an education at the Jewish Theological Seminary as I did at Columbia College. At the former institution I learned German in the kitchen and traded lessons in German for lessons in Hebrew with Moshe Decter; also I was privy to much of the dinner conversation of the intellectual elite of America who were regularly guests at Finkelstein's table. I remember serving and listening to Van Wyck Brooks, Stephen Vincent Benét, and Christian Gauss.

I was impressed as early as the end of 1939 with the special emphasis given by students of the seminary to "a Palestinian education" as superior to anything else. It was made clear to me that there was nothing else like it and no substitute for it. I also remember the prestige enjoyed by the graduate student from Palestine in the seminary. On the basis of my seminary experience I took for granted the singlemindedness of Jews

—American, immigrant, and foreign—with regard to Palestine and the emerging state of Israel. It was a gradual deliberate procedure that did not meet the eye. What I found shocking at the seminary was that the regional barriers dividing the Jews in Europe had been transported intact to America. The Galitsianer (from Polish Galicia) was disdained by all. The Litvak (the Baltic and Russian Jew) occupied the next higher rung on the social ladder. Beyond this the precedence was difficult to sort out. It still is. But all were agreed, surely, that the Sephardic Jews (from Spain and Portugal) were preeminent. Even so, the most powerful, the most influential and, more particularly, by far the richest were the German Jews, beginning—but only beginning—with the Rothschilds who took their name from the red shield that hung out over the shop front of the narrow "street of Jews" (die Judengasse) in Frankfurt am Main. The de facto founder and first president of the seminary, Solomon Schechter, was a German Jew, as were most of the Jewish founders of museums, institutes, and newspapers in the United States—Guggenheim, Lewissohn, Schiff, Ochs, Rosenwald, et al. But I remember how shocked I was to hear a member of the graduating class of the rabbinate say, "I saw the most beautiful girl last night; I couldn't wait to speak to her. And then she opened her mouth—oh, no!—a Galitsianer!"

Most of the Jews in the kitchen were German Jews, the first wave of immigration from Europe. It struck me then that German Jews were different from the others, a breed apart: they were bigger, stockier, they were frequently blond or red-haired. They seemed to be exactly like the Germans I knew—only, as the joke goes, more so. It was the German Jews who remarked my passionate love for the German language. All Franz would say, when I asked for his comment, was "Your Deutsch is pretty good, but it ain't coming out like a Deutscher!" What attracted me to German from the first was its distinctness and clarity. It was hard, clear, and sharp as a midwinter dawn. It seemed to me the manliest of languages. There were those wonderful reinforced consonants: "Stumpf" instead of stump, "Schwert" (pronounced "shvert") instead of sword (where only the first and the last consonants are pronounced). In the pronunciation of German every letter is given a certain value and the value is unchanging. All the vowels are pure except for the mollifying influence of the umlaut. The umlaut makes for the only difficulty in German pronunciation. "Madame," said an American friend of mine to a German lady who had just criticized his pronunciation, "If you wish to speak German with me, you must bring your own umlaut." Moreover, German is a down-to-earth, nonderivative language: a telephone is a

Fernsprecher (a "far-talker"), a ventriloquist is a Bauchredner (a "belly-speaker"), and gastritis is Magenschleimhautentzündung ("stomach-mucous-membrane-inflammation") and no mistake.

In fond accordance with my grandmother's decree, I studied Greek at Columbia College. Before World War II the study of the classics was dominated by two nations, Great Britain and Germany. Before World War I, Germany had been perhaps the unquestioned leader in Greek studies. In any case it was through Greek that I came to a reverential appreciation of the German scholastic tradition. I stood in youthful awe of the great German universities whose names provided the datelines of the prefaces of so many definitive editions of classical texts: Heidelberg, Göttingen, Tübingen, Marburg, Berlin, Munich, Leipzig, and Hamlet's university, Wittenberg. At that time Columbia University quite possibly had the finest classics department in America. There were Gilbert Highet, Moses Haddas, Van Hook, J. B. Richards. Moreover, the department was headed by Kurt von Fritz, formerly of the University of Munich. Von Fritz was second only to Werner Jaeger in prominence as a Greek scholar in America. For me he was the archetype of the polyhistor. He knew French, English, Italian, of course, and he also knew Modern Greek and Russian. It was Von Fritz who interested me in the study of Russian when he acknowledged one day in class (we were three students) that the best work on the Scythians was in Russian. From this I inferred that Russian was de rigeur for a classical philologist. Von Fritz would discourse at length on the ancient Persian pantheon, the god of light, Ahura Mazda, the forerunner of Apollo, for example. He knew Arabic very well, and Hebrew. He had even studied Old Ethiopian.

Von Fritz was not a refugee. He had left Germany voluntarily with his wife and son in 1936. He had been dismissed from his post at the University of Munich simply because he had refused to take the oath of allegiance to Hitler. (All civil servants in Germany were required to take this oath; in Germany teachers are civil servants.) Six months later he was barred from the university library because he had been seen there conversing with a Jew as well as reading a French newspaper. Before very long Von Fritz became for me the personification of "the other Germany"—all that was fine and true and enduring in the heart of Europe. The general—and very hazy—idea of Europe exerted total fascination on me; I had the far-westerner's disdain for the east coast of America (and particularly New England) and his reinforced reverence for anything European—except of course politics. Outside the classroom Von Fritz would sometimes tell of the rigging and brutalizing of German elections by the Nazis. Von Fritz's formula for the solution of the Nazi problem after the war (there was never any question that the Nazis were doomed) was novel: he said there ought to be some form of "tumultuous punishment" of the Nazi leaders—thousands of them—a sort of circus maximus show execution of the chief and middling culprits. And after that all punitive policy should cease.

The only "pro-Nazi" sentiment I ever encountered in the United States was at Princeton University (and then it was pro-Nazi only in the sense that it was pro-German notwithstanding the Nazis). This was a very small group—five or six at the most—two of whom had been high school classmates of mine. The group came into being only because its leader, a highly talented instructor of Romance languages and literature at Princeton, had become intrigued with the writings of Oswald Spengler, with *The Decline of the West* particularly. In fairness I should add that the group's favoring of Germany derived solely from the Third Reich's obvious determination to fulfill the role of Caesarism proclaimed as essential to survival by Spengler. When the United States began to arm in earnest for the conflict already in progress, the sympathies of the group were transferred unqualifiedly to their own country. Even so, Spengler was a revelation to the nineteen- and twenty-year-olds from the Far West. It was hardly possible to credit the overwhelming erudition, the Faustian lore, of Spengler. Apparently we were all overwhelmed—including our instructor-leader—since we never had any really substantive discussions of Spengler's theses; significantly enough the group spent most of its time listening to records of Mozart and Beethoven symphonies and concertos from the Princeton music library. I confess I never then managed to get beyond the preface of *The Decline of the West*. But I was caught up enough to take the matter to the most highly regarded and at the same time least prejudiced teacher I had, Mark Van Doren. He devoted the better part of an hour to assuring me that Toynbee was fully as significant and far more reliable than Spengler as a historian.

The only discomfiture I suffered as a result of my involvement with the Germans in Yorkville was personal. I had been befriended by the family of a classmate at Columbia. The head of the family ("She knew her place, and it was at the head") was an extraordinary Englishwoman who had been a Red Cross nurse in France in World War I. She had spent a good deal of time (and had the photographs to prove it) with the casse-gueules, French soldiers more or less horribly disfigured by their wounds. I was too naïve to realize the incompatibility of her background with my foreground of involvement with German waiters, barmen,

[13]

cooks, and professors (the fact that most of my German friends were also Jews did not matter). In the inevitable discussions about the Nazis, and, as the war progressed, about the German war machine (so often described by that extraordinary word "juggernaut") and all things German, I was too often given to demurral in favor of the Germans. The wonderful Englishwoman finally forbade me her house. Nevertheless, when I was drafted I called her to pay my respects. "Do you know," she said, "the Germans have one expression I like very much: I think the words are so beautiful." Then she gave me her hand and said, "Auf Wiedersehen!"

In his book *Darwin, Marx, Wagner: Critique of a Heritage,* Jacques Barzun made the statement that in order to be truly European it was necessary to be anti-German. I had read the book chiefly because Barzun was one of my professors. I knew that he was a native Frenchman whose judgment had been colored with his natural resentment at the German "juggernaut's" overrunning France. Even so, the attitude expressed by Barzun had been widespread ever since World War I and continues to be so today. Yet I have never been able to understand how such an attitude could be upheld unless one were tone-deaf. With my friends at Princeton I had come to an appreciation of Beethoven and Mozart by the tortuous route of an induced fascination with Oswald Spengler. It was vastly easier to come to an appreciation of Spengler, or any other German writer, by way of spontaneous fascination with Beethoven and Mozart. I met Robert Cary Waddell, an instructor at Columbia, only because his love of German music had led him to the poet Hölderlin. Waddell's idea of heaven was eating paté de foie gras to the sound of trumpets playing Bach. Since Waddell did not know German, he asked me to translate some of Hölderlin's poems for him. Through Waddell I met other instructors at Columbia. This acquaintanceship brought me to the Metropolitan Opera for unforgettable performances of Mozart operas, *The Marriage of Figaro* and *Don Giovanni,* with Ezio Pinza in the lead roles. It also brought me to the fabulous Lüchow's on Fourteenth Street, a place which none of my German friends would have dreamed of patronizing.

It was at Lüchow's that I met the most successful waiter of my experience. This was Willy Stanger. Such were Stanger's dispatch, tact, and finesse (and his knowledge of the various German wines and their appropriateness to the courses offered) that he averaged well over fifty dollars a night in tips. His weekly take was almost four hundred dollars, the buying power of which was at least three times greater than it is now.

Of course, Stanger earned no salary; perhaps he even paid for the privilege of waiting table at Luchow's. But he made me realize for the first time that a waiter in a good establishment could become wealthy.

Jacques Barzun, along with Lionel Trilling, conducted a colloquium, a course lasting two semesters with a syllabus of perhaps twenty-five of the world's literary masterpieces. One of the questions during the final (oral) examination was, "Which of the books did you find most impressive and why?" The first part of the answer was easy enough for me: Goethe's *Faust*. But I had difficulty in explaining why. From casual sparring in our discussions of Spengler at Princeton I had come by a few tags from *Faust* (Spengler was an almost fanatic admirer of Goethe) which I found impressive in themselves but could not expand on:

> He only earns his freedom and existence
> Who daily conquers them anew.

And I knew something of Faustian man. But what really impressed me about *Faust* at the first reading was the love story of Faust and Gretchen. It seemed to me that Goethe had turned a key in the wards of the innermost human mystery with his treatment of the betrayal and abandonment of Gretchen by Faust. The last words (Gretchen's) of the First Part, "Heinrich! Heinrich!" haunted me. They still do.

Because of the languages I knew (none of them at all well, most of them well enough when at all—German, Russian, Hungarian, and Modern Greek), I was foreordained for army intelligence the moment my induction notice arrived. I had not been in basic training more than three weeks when orders arrived transferring me to the military intelligence center at Camp Ritchie, Maryland. I arrived at Ritchie in the silent company of an American soldier wearing fatigues and carrying a duffel bag. When we stepped into the guard room at the entrance of the camp to announce ourselves, to my surprise the American soldier spoke German—and it was a very cultivated German—to the corporal on duty. To my astonishment the corporal answered in German. If in the ensuing thirty-odd years Camp Ritchie has not entered world literature, it is only because the phenomenon of it has proved too difficult to grasp and transmit in any coherent way. Camp Ritchie was basically a pool—not to say "cesspool"—of language talent; it harbored every conceivable— and in some cases inconceivable—kind of immigrant: there were barracks housing Russians, Greeks, French, Italians, Spanish, Indians (American and Hindu), Icelanders, Laplanders, Mexicans, Albanians,

Ruthenians, Macedonians, Slovenians, Wends, Hungarians, Welsh, Algerians, Syrians, Montenegrins, Ceylonese, Eskimos, Tunisians, Turks, Georgians, Azerbaijani, Uzbeks, Chuvash, Cossacks, Kozakhs, Mongolians, Basques—to name but a few. Basically, nevertheless, the camp was German. Most, but by no means all, of the Germans were Jews. Of these it was said that some had been born Jewish, some had achieved Jewishness, and some had had Jewishness thrust upon them.

The catchall company for new arrivals at Ritchie was the notorious "Company H." The commanding officer (indeed the only officer) of Company H was the ill-starred Lieutenant Fasola (Bean) who was popularly described as a Sicilian peasant whose forehead had receded as a result of his having slapped it so often. It is said that proficiency in foreign languages is no real indication of intelligence. As a practitioner of the art and one who, since the age of twelve, has had to do unremittingly with linguists, I am fully prepared to accept the contention as gospel. Still, the study of languages is an intellectual pursuit. But the pursuit does not make the intellectual; the intellectual makes the pursuit. In fact, in a curious way knowledge of a foreign language tends to inhibit one from reading widely. While the linguist is able to read the original text he often can do so only with the greatest difficulty. The ability coupled with the difficulty acts as a double deterrent: it rules out reading the work in translation and discourages struggling with the original text. The soldiery and, to a considerably lesser extent, the officers' corps at Ritchie were a hodgepodge of European intellectuals. There was a high percentage of academicians, writers, poets, novelists (Klaus Mann and Stefan Heym), stage producers and directors, musicians, choreographers, dancers, singers (Sergeant William Warfield as an example of the non-European performing artist: he was in charge of the recreation hall), psychiatrists, psychologists, engineers, playboys, and sportsmen (during my time we had three erstwhile mountain climbers credited with first ascents of various Alpine peaks). During an informal inspection of barracks, Lieutenant Fasola came upon a soldier reading a book with words that were sometimes as long as the width of the page. "Can you read that?" asked Fasola. "I wrote it," was the answer. Fasola slapped his forehead into further recession. Most frustrating for Fasola were his morning pep talks to the troops: "Now I want you men to get on the ball —understand? *Get on the ball!* Any questions?" Up went the hand of Benno Frank, former producer–director–drama teacher: "Ver iss ziss ball you keep talking about, sir? Are ve to consider zat all ziss iss chust a game?"

A good many of the immigrants at Ritchie had been inducted into the American army possessing only the barest modicum of English. The impact of army lingo on their skeleton vocabularies was devastating. The factotum word in the American army is "fuck." In Company H the all-purpose slogan was "Fuck Fasola." For the German speakers confusion came with another heavy-duty American English word, "fix," because of its striking similarity to the German word for fuck, which is "ficken." And so we had Doctor Frank saying, "Ve vill fuck Fasola, boys, ve vill even fuck his vagon!"

By far the most interesting mishmash of German and English at Ritchie, however, was spoken by Captain Brandstätter, called "Brandstifter" (arsonist) by all and sundry. It was a mixture reminiscent of the French officer in Fielding's *Tom Jones:* serving in the British army he had forgotten French yet never learned English. Brandstätter was the very model of a modern Prussian officer, saber scars, monocle, and all. He was the quintessential personification of the Prussian military, an aspect that coupled with his accent made his virulent anti-Nazism and anti-Germanism broadly comical. Brandstätter was an instructor on the German army organization and with good reason: not long before he had been an instructor *in* the German army. He unfailingly addressed his classes at Ritchie as "mein trupps," a perfect compromise between the English word "troops" and the German word "Truppen." "Mein trupps," said Brandstätter on one occasion, "zese goddam Krauts hass come up vit a wery nasty tr-r-rick gegen unsere poys in Alcheria. Venn unsere poys iss comink down ze Strasse in a cheep vit de vindshield herunter zey iss taking a piece of Klavier vire und schtringing it acr-r-ross ze Schtreet. So zat ven unsere poys iss comink, zey iss dekip . . . dekop . . . dekoop . . . zey iss meeting mit a wery unfortunate accident."

Brandstätter's counterpart among the noncommissioned officers was Sergeant Knoblauch (garlic), whose career paralleled Brandstätter's. Knoblauch was another monument to Prussian manhood whose great specialties were close-order drill and calisthenics. Few graduates of Ritchie will forget Knoblauch's clarion call: "All r-r-right poys—der nächste exercise iss a Kniebeuge!" At times Knoblauch's "trupps" would request a translation after he had issued an order; at other times they would simply carry on and chaos would result. But everyone understood Knoblauch's admonition: "Don't forget, poys, I am at der tick end of de whip!"

The Post Exchange at Camp Ritchie resembled the Tower of Babel after construction had been discontinued: an Icelander reciting a saga in

Old Norse over a strawberry milkshake was a commonplace. Passages from the Upanishad in the original Sanskrit could also be heard during an informal discussion among GIs refreshing themselves after a field exercise. Those who prided themselves on the breadth of their linguistic achievements would frequent the PX merely to test their ability to identify all the languages spoken there. The Upanishad provided the inspiration for the name of a language invented solely for the purpose of confounding such people: the artificial language was called "Upmanshipad"; it boasted a vocabulary of more than two hundred words, enough for a limited conversation and just enough to pique the curiosity of overhearers to the point where they would humbly ask which language was being spoken. The avoidance of any similarities with major European and Asiatic languages set exacting requirements for the concoction and hence took time. I knew a sergeant at Ritchie, Hugh Nibley, formerly professor of ancient history at Pomona College, who spoke sixteen languages tolerably well and whose nodding linguistic acquaintanceship included twice that number.

The standards set by the extraordinary motley of talent assembled at Camp Ritchie were exacting in a great many respects. With so many ex-European producers and directors in the audience, going to the post movie theater, for example, was a new experience: cues, comments, directions, and coaching were shouted in anticipation of the screen actors' and actresses' next move. They were almost always borne out by the turn that followed. I remember the prophetic plea when Bette Davis whirled to face her tormentor in *Watch on the Rhine:* "Come on, Bette, register disdain!" The comments following the action were equally good. One stands out even today: a forgotten actress in a forgotten film turns to the warrior hero and solemnly announces: "You have forced me to become your wife but I shall never share your bed." The alto voce comment: "Merde!"

Surely the greatest event at the post movie theater was when we were all marched down in formation to see the Hollywood movie version of Stefan Heym's best-selling novel *The Hostages.* Before the movie started Stefan appeared on the stage and gave a short talk on the book. Heym, or perhaps his situation, rather, epitomized the dilemma of the American government in World War II. For Stefan was both a violent anti-Nazi and a Communist. As its most celebrated anti-Nazi he was the pride of the post. Moreover, he was a star student: his intelligence and application made him the joy of every instructor on the post. But he was also the most overinvestigated undergraduate at Ritchie and perhaps in the American army altogether. As often as not there were investigating agents—presumably FBI—on the post looking into Heym's past and present, interrogating him and his friends.

The composite Ritchie undergraduate—scientist-academician-playboy-artist-sportsman—was naturally if indulgently disdainful of most of what was native American. But it was the exuberance—the naïve enthusiasm—of the American "sabra" that taxed the Ritchie man most sorely. Take Major Applegate's close-combat course. The instructor, demonstrating the approved method of garroting a sentry: "Now, when you have thrown the piano wire over the sentry's head and pulled it tight around his neck—like so. Now! Is he going to like that?" Benno Frank, after a long, deliberative pause: "No, he iss not going to like it!" Instructor: "You are absolutely right—he will not like it!" By this time Frank and the instructor were staring at each other. Also indelible is a scene in high summer during a course in terrain instruction, map drawing and reading: here a Middle European Apollo—a clean-limbed Siegfried almost every inch of him ("almost" because he had that scintilla of Jewishness about him that heightened the whole effect; the name Siegfried or Sigismund is by no means unusual among German Jews)—here he stood, grimy, dusty, streaming with sweat, and trying to draw a map with pencil and clipboard. "And from whence," he asked, "flows this ridiculous stream?"

One of the main courses of instruction at Ritchie was Interrogation of Prisoners of War (IPW). To this purpose a cadre of fluent German speakers was cultivated to act as freshly captured prisoners of war in simulated interrogations. For the sake of verisimilitude they usually wore German uniforms (this also provided a test of the examinee's knowledge of German army rank and branch insignia) and goose-stepped around the camp in formation. They were trained to act the part of the different types of German the interrogator was likely to meet on the field of battle. Some were briefed to respond only to the subtle approach, some to the legalistic dismantling of the significance of their military oath, others would "spill their guts" only when browbeaten and hectored at the top of the interrogator's lungs. There was one, and he was famous throughout the camp, who was allowed to play it by ear—he could react to any interrogator whichever way he chose. Some of these men were professional actors. (The late Peter van Eyck was one of them. He always played a high-ranking Prussian staff officer, arrogant but correct; he would respond with extremely valuable information if the interrogator could find a way to appeal to his code of honor.) "The

Germans" were so much a part of the scene at Ritchie that an examinee, the Russian immigrant Nicholas Riasanovsky, passed a test on camp security with distinction when he pointed out that a surefire way for a German spy to enter the camp undetected would be to march through the main gate wearing the standard uniform of the German Wehrmacht with full field pack and armed to the teeth.

On one occasion the irrepressible Benno Frank was detailed to stand in for one of the acting prisoners of war. During his one and only interrogation Frank found himself confronting an examinee-interrogator with the real rank of captain and three years of college German. The captain tried the psychological approach: "How do you get along with your commanding officer?" "Splendidly!" said Frank, "Why he's more like a brother than a commanding officer—only last week he said to me, 'Frank—du bist eine Kanone!' [German idiom for *you are a great guy*], 'Frank—ich baue auf dich' [*I am relying on you*]." Of this, all the captain really understood was the word "Kanone." "Cannon? Cannon! Where is the cannon?" (The chief purpose of interrogation in the field is to find out the enemy's disposition of troops and their armament—particularly heavy weapons.) Smiling shyly, Frank tapped himself on the breast and said: "Ich bin eine Kanone!" "Du bist eine Kanone?" said the captain incredulously. "Er ist eine Kanone!" added Frank thumb over shoulder to indicate his putative commanding officer. Then, "Wir sind Kanonen!" At this point the captain blurted, "Ihr seid Kanonen?" "Sie sind Kanonen!" concluded Frank, "we have successfully conjugated the verb 'to be.' That is the end of the lesson." The next day the captain changed to a course that required only a reading knowledge of German.

But the "sabras" had more than a few ways of getting back at the immigrants. Statutorily, at least, the "sabras" ran the camp. They could confine to barracks or restrict to the post on "Ban Day" (so named after the oblivious post commander, Colonel Banfield). They could simply deny the ten-, twenty-four-, and forty-eight-hour passes. They could assign KP or "policing the area," an occupation that consisted of picking up cigarette butts and other refuse in accordance with the classic army injunction: "If you see anything that doesn't move, pick it up; if you can't pick it up, polish it! If it moves, salute it!" Down through the decades rings the stentorian voice of Master Sergeant ("Man-mountain") Dean, the huge hillbilly who won national fame or notoriety as a professional wrestler (we never knew how or why he had come to Ritchie and no one thought or dared to ask him): "Alright, you guys! I don't want to see anything but elbows and asses all day!"

One of the more refined methods of torture invented by the company commanders was the job of translating into various languages replies to fictitious letters, described as having been received by the company commander himself or by Colonel So-and-So. These replies were required almost in the form of setting an essay on given subjects. On the eve of "Ban Day" the victim was summoned to the orderly room where he was told by the first sergeant that special duty would make it impossible for him to leave the post on the morrow. When he reported on the morning of what should have been his day off he was told, for example, that the company commander had just received an invitation to a Russian wedding in Philadelphia. The duty consisted of penning four original copies of the reply—the contents of which were roughly sketched—in Russian (for the bride, the groom, and the parents of each). The hapless translator would then rush to the recreation hall, pen the translations as quickly as he could, and then rush back to the company commander in the hope that he would still have time to catch the next train for New York or Washington or Baltimore. But he was quickly disabused of his illusions: the company commander would require an oral translation of the Russian with an explanation of the rendition of every idiom and turn of phrase, one of which was "I'll be there with bells on"; he would then find them not quite to his liking and require a retranslation. By the time the company commander was finally satisfied, a perfect summer's day—as it was likely to have been—had passed. I once took it upon myself to stand up in class and announce that the officers at Ritchie would do well to weigh the wisdom of such chicanery. "There are," I said stoutly, "a good many authors and scholars of note among the enlisted men in this camp. They will certainly in future report on what is going on here and it will not be to the credit of the American army!" I was taken to task although not gigged (restricted to quarters or the like) for this piece of quixotry. When I made the statement I of course had Stefan Heym, among others, in mind. But I little realized how formidable my prophetic powers were to prove.

Perhaps an advantage but certainly a powerful distraction in learning a language beyond the pale of childhood and outside the classroom is the process of intense association of words with the circumstances in which they are encountered for the first time. I cannot hear or read the word "üppig" (luxuriant or voluptuous) without remembering my introduction to it. Liffmann, a short, underslung German Jew from Düsseldorf, who looked like the late Louis Wollheim, recounted how he had been sent away from home because he had seduced—or been seduced by

—the family maid, "ein üppiges überaus entwickeltes Mädchen" (a voluptuous, exceedingly well-developed girl), who became even more "well developed"—if less voluptuous as a result.

This was the beginning of a recurring theme in life among the Germans: trouble with the maid—or, generally, complications with the domestic help. This was my first inkling of the "Stände" (for which the English word "classes" is an unsatisfactory translation) in German social structure. "Stände" is a composite of the concepts rank, class, and caste. I would say, for example, that the German "Stände" distinctions are a good deal more deeply ingrained than British class distinctions. "So strict," as the saying goes, "are the uses" in Old Germany.

Surely the greatest surprise for the non-German immigrant soldiery at Ritchie was the abundantly documented fact that the German war machine, the "juggernaut," was moved by flesh-and-blood horses rather than by combustive horsepower. The immigrants, for their part, were duly impressed by the American army's superiority in matériel as they were by the mechanical aptitude of the native American. This they might well have been, for they had not, like the Americans, grown up with machines; few of the immigrants, although generally some ten years older than their American colleagues, could drive a car. But their attitude was not simply condescending: they acknowledged and approved of American strength, wealth, and organization while amusedly deprecating our lack of culture, our naïveté, and our psychological crudeness; we were the Romans, they were the Greeks. It was obvious, for example, that a good many of the immigrants especially were totally unsuited for the army or any form of national service. These had simply and blindly been swept in by the draft or their obvious qualifications had been judged to outweigh their equally obvious disqualifications. "I proceed after the fashion of a drunken sea serpent," said one of these unfortunates after wrecking his third jeep and severely injuring himself. "He should not be in the army at all," said Frank, "—or at least not in this part of it; if anywhere, he belongs in the WACs."

Benno was of the opinion that all Americans ought to go to Europe and all Europeans ought to come to America. The Americans in Europe would constitute a united Europe the moment they arrived; they would quickly discover how much they were one people. "Don't think the Poles would make a beeline for Poland just because their great-grandfathers lived there. Don't even think the Italians would all go back to Italy— a lot of them would head for Switzerland" (as it turned out, after the war a lot of them did, without waiting for Frank's scheme to be put into effect). "The Swedes would go south, the Greeks would go north. The Dalmations would go to Normandy, the Danes would all go to England, the English would go to the Riviera." "What about the German-Americans?" I asked. "Oh," said Frank, "the Germans in this country are not really an ethnic bloc. Except for places like Wisconsin and a few spots in Pennsylvania and maybe in Texas they are too diffuse. In any case they certainly do not represent a voting bloc. A president or a presidential candidate has to consider the Polish vote and the Jewish vote and the Italian vote but not the German vote. Some Germans would go north, say, to Denmark, some would go south to Italy, Spain, and the Dalmation coast, and some would go east to the great plains and the steppes —in other words they would scatter to the four winds." And then he chuckled.

"And over here," I said, "wouldn't the various language groups stick together and go where they had the best chance of expanding and creating new separate states? Wouldn't the French all rush up to the French-Canadian border and the Spanish all rush down to the Mexican border so you'd have Old France instead of New England and Old Spain instead of New Mexico?" "Not at all: the price of admission to America would be the undertaking to learn English, say, within five years after arrival. At that time all citizens would take a proficiency test in English. Those who flunked would be deported—to South America. After all— the language question in America has been decided, although mind you, only by one vote."

To put it rhetorically, every second German I have met since then has told me the story of how the Continental Congress voted between English and German for the national language and how German was defeated by one vote: Benjamin Franklin's. I had heard the story but in a different version, in which the language voted down by Benjamin Franklin was Greek, the classic and classical language of democracy. The eminently reasonable Franklin is quoted by H. L. Mencken as saying on this occasion, "We Americans ought to stick to English and let the English learn Greek." I am sure that Benno Frank was joking: the German version is totally implausible and the adoption of either language (or any foreign language for that matter) would have proved impractical. But the speculation—especially to a German—is nonetheless fascinating. If the Continental Congress had adopted German as the official language of the United States, the fate of Germany would have been vastly different. Bismarck said that the most important fact of the nineteenth century was that England and America had a common language. If Germany and America had had a common language the sometime German dream of world dominion could have been realized. With Great Britain it was different—the mother country was an island whose rule of the seas would make at the most for predominance, not domination, not world dominion. But with the linguistic link between the new continent and the most potentially powerful people on the old continent there would have been distinct danger of the extension of German hegemony over America by mass German immigration (a Drang nach Westen in this case would have proved far easier than a Drang nach Osten). At the very least the connection would have served to neutralize the United States in future wars involving Germany on the European continent. Perhaps it was this or like considerations that moved George Washington in his farewell address to warn his fellow citizens to beware of the Germans. It was a warning repeated by Jefferson.

I never saw Benno Frank unduly disturbed but once. This was when he had just received what must have been a truly inspired dressing down by the commander of Company A. Frank was so upset that he was almost in tears, a strange sight. He was a German Jew with a huge head, a hook nose, a massive jaw, and a Schmiss (scar). His physical structure would have been an absurdity in any uniform: one shoulder was considerably higher than the other, a peculiarity that gave him a list of at least ten degrees to the left. Moreover, he was of barely average height and of a girth which even the most sustained and strenuous physical exercise could not diminish. He was, of a truth, a first-class trencherman. On the unique occasion of his discountenancing I sought to rally his spirits by promising him in set terms that I would seek out the company commander after the war and—whether the scene happened to be a busy thoroughfare, a fine restaurant, or a solemn assembly—would stretch him full length with one well-directed blow. As a result, I became Frank's promissory protector (effective whenever circumstances in future should permit), and he became my moral preceptor and mentor. Every evening at mess call Frank would make a ceremonial point of inviting me to dinner. He even wrote out a certificate in Latin, Hebrew, and Yiddish appointing me an honorary Jew in gratitude for services rendered to the children of Israel both as a shabbas goy and a thug. In place of a signature (whose? Jehovah's?) he added the statement in quotes: "Es ist schwer zu sein a Jüd!" (It is hard to be a Jew.)

Frank had spent a year or more in Palestine teaching drama before coming to America from Germany. His wife and son were still there. In many ways Frank was a paragon of the German-Jewish dilemma: he was very much the Jew, except or including his preoccupation with Jesus Christ. He was, of course, entirely caught up in the Jewish cause, especially as manifested in the Jewish community in Palestine. But he was also quintessentially German as perhaps only someone whose life had been bound up in the German theater could be. Politically he was a left-liberal would-be socialist or had-been radical who loved to talk about the barricades and the youth of Germany and the world. He was also something of a chauvinist: his favorite German was Bismarck. He would regale me for hours on end with stories and cases in point about Bismarck. Bismarck was not only a great politician and statesman but a gentleman in the fullest sense of the word. He was a "Herr," and a "Herr" is something either more or (usually) a good deal less than a gentleman. Benno harped on Bismarck's courtesy; the prince had manners as well as a manner. Bismarck would always say (I had Benno's word for it): "Es freut mich ausserordentlich Sie kennenzulernen!" (I am extraordinarily happy to make your acquaintance).

It is not hard to see why Benno, like most Germans, preferred Bismarck. In West Germany in 1952 a public opinion poll rated Bismarck as the most popular German. This is because Bismarck remains that rarest of birds among German statesmen: he was successful. His work survived him by some three decades. To be sure, he was plagued by doubts once he had succeeded in creating the Reich. "If it should be God's will that we are defeated in the next war," he wrote late in life, "then I regard it as a foregone conclusion that our victorious enemies will use every means to prevent us from ever getting to our feet again. Recently I found myself looking at the map of Germany: one weak spot after another came to view and fell away like leaves off a tree. Everything is in flux; in time everything collapses." In order to understand the cult of Bismarck-worshipers you have to weigh the "almost factor" in German history. Except for Bismarck's half-century, German history is an unbroken chain of failures-by-a-hair, of maddeningly near misses and no cigars: the Germans *almost* reformed the Catholic Church, the Hanseatic League *almost* prevailed, the peasants *almost* succeeded in their uprising in 1527, the Hohenstauffen emperors *almost* consolidated and centralized the Holy Roman Empire, the Frankfurt Parliament of 1848–1850 *almost* created an integrated ethnic, democratic German state, and so on—frustration feeds on itself and perpetuates itself in myth. The German language failed to be adopted by the Continental Congress as the new American national language by one vote. Frederick Barbarossa sleeps in a cave under the Kyffhäuser seated at a table with his great red beard growing through its marble top. He will awake one day, arise and go forth to redress Germany's wrongs, and lead his people to the victory that is rightfully theirs. When you have missed by so little so often the conviction grows that you are bound to succeed sooner or later and probably the very next time out.

Of course there is the problem of explaining so many near misses and the nearness of the misses. The explanation nearest to hand is betrayal. It is so obvious that it runs like a leitmotiv through German history. Germans have always been accusing one another of betrayal and with good reason: betrayal consists of the refusal or withdrawal of support at the crucial moment (that is, when it is most expected or needed) by reason of the betrayer's not sharing the betrayed's conception of the national interest or the greater good or whatever. The question of whether the expectations of support were very much if at all justified is something else again. But certainly the preoccupation with the nearness of the many misses distracted attention from the adventitious aspects of the one hit: Bismarck was not only extraordinarily clever and circumspect; he was also very lucky, and his luck held.

As for Adolf Hitler, the leader of the Germans—der Führer—the only comment of Frank's I can remember had to do with casting. "If you," said Frank one day to a knot of former stage and film directors, "had to cast someone as dictator of the Third Reich in a tragedy, would you choose Adolf Hitler for the part? Certainly not! It would be hard to imagine a less likely dictator. The role that comes to mind as ideal for Hitler is that of a Heiratsschwindler (a "marriage-swindler"—a swindler who promises marriage for the sole purpose of making off with his fiancée's savings; they are very common in Germany) who operates *within the limit of two hundred marks.* He would be perfect for the Heiratsschwindler who rounds on his housemaid fiancée with eyes blazing and finger pointing and shouts: "You do not believe me!" She falls on her knees and says, "Oh, yes, Adolf, I do, I do believe you—here take the money!"

It seems highly significant to me now that the German-Jewish legion in the American army sang the rousing battle songs of 1813, the German war of liberation against Napoleon, when it took the field against the renegade fatherland in 1943: "Der Gott der Eisen wachsen liess/Der wollte keine Knechte." (The god who made iron grow/Had no desire for lackeys/Therefore he gave saber and spear/To the man who would fight for his rights/Therefore he gave him bold courage and the anger of free

speech/So that he might persist to blood and death/In making his fight.)
The beginning was soon changed to "Der Goy der Eisenhower hiess."
(The boys in the German-Jewish legion were acutely aware that Eisenhower was a German-American: Eisenhauer = iron-hewer.) Another
favorite song was "Wohlauf, Kameraden, aufs Pferd, aufs Pferd/Ins
Feld, in die Freiheit gezogen." (Up then, comrades, to horse, to horse/To
the field and to freedom advancing.)

The German-Jewish legion sang these songs as they did most things
then, with a good deal of "Schwung," the German word for élan. They
were different from everybody else. They knew exactly why they were
fighting: their morale was tremendous. They knew the langugage and
they knew the country: it was their language and it was—or had been
—their country; for them World War II was a civil war. In actual combat
they looked outlandish, as indeed they were. They sometimes looked silly
but then at times they also looked superb—and they were. The point is
that they were the only ones in the American army in Europe who really
knew what they were doing and why. As far as they were concerned the
American armed forces were colossal auxiliaries. It was the answer to
the old Jew's question in the joke: what purpose do all those millions of
goyim in New York and the rest of America serve? This was what all
those goyim were there for. As for those Germans in the legion who were
not Jews, the Brandtstätters, the Knoblauchs, and the Von Fritzes, there
was not the same clarity and limitation of vision. The German goyim
were grudge fighters like their comrades-in-arms, the German Jews, but
they were not sure that the settling of the grudge would settle anything
else. On the contrary, they had premonitions that life would be still more
complicated for Germans, and not only for Germans, after the war was
over. The German goyim were a dedicated but grim lot; the German
Jews—even the men who labored under the burden of a tremendous
personal score to settle—had a quantum of joy, they were the "happy
warriors." I witnessed countless demonstrations in World War II that
the Jew was a great fighting man. He had the "Schwung," the "Tschim-
bara-bim!," that makes the difference between a good and a very good
soldier.

THE FIRST GERMAN GERMANS I EVER SAW WERE PRISoners of war being herded onto the docks at Southampton shortly after D day. Dirty, grimy, bloody, and beaten as they were, what impressed me most was the quality and cut of their uniforms. There were a great many officers and noncommissioned officers in the group I saw. I was flabbergasted: it looked as if the German army were fighting in dress uniform. The forest green uniform of even the German privates, as compared with American fatigues or khaki, looked to me like some sort of costume, with the rimmed collars, the epaulettes (for all except privates), the silver stripes against the green background.

The next German Germans I saw—and almost the only Germans I saw for two months to come—were dead. The German dead that I encountered in Normandy and thereafter formed a pervasive impression, a sort of minor trauma, that remains with me: I cannot contemplate the Germans—even today, after having lived perhaps two decades among them—without conjuring up the thousands upon thousands of German corpses I saw in France, Belgium, Holland, and Germany. In the picture in my mind they are piled up as though in some huge, Dürer-like, apocalyptic heap. This picture probably stems from the carnage wrought by the wave of a thousand Allied bombers in laying a "carpet" preparatory to the breakthrough at Saint-Lô. Everything within the perimeter of the carpet, an area of perhaps five miles in width and two miles in depth, was dead: dogs, chickens, geese, cows and horses, and Germans. The Germans themselves had apparently evacuated the French civilians to the rear out of danger; I saw very few French dead in Normandy or elsewhere. I remember a large farmhouse that had obviously served as some sort of German field headquarters. There were thirty or forty officers and noncoms stretched out on the grass beside the house, some of them having been brought up from the cellar, all of them stone dead. In the adjacent orchard an entire company had been entrenched. Every man jack—about 130 of them—was dead. In the surrounding fields there were literally thousands of them, a congress of corpses, in every conceivable posture—some antic, some frantic. In these open-field or indoor killings there were seldom mutilation or gaping wounds in evidence. To all appearances most victims of bombing raids are killed by concussion, surprised and petrified by instantaneous death. This was not the case with the German tank crews who were the victims of direct rocket hits or whatever it took to set the tank on fire. Here death was doubly horrible because the natural agony was combined with the last desperate attempt to escape from the burning tank—often enough by utterly preposterous means, as when a tank driver would try to get out through a four-inch slit in the body of the tank between the fender and the tracks.

Armies are always made up predominantly of young men in good health and trained into excellent physical condition. This was my introduction to the youth of Germany, for the tankers we faced west of Saint-Lô were the youngest of the lot—eighteen-, nineteen-, and twenty-year-olds, their young and shining bodies burnt black or more often red and yellow. Sometimes they would have managed to get out of the tank altogether only to succumb on top of the tank behind the cupola, their bodies stretched out half clothed or often enough stark naked, the pubic hairs singed to stubs (the hair of the head had usually been protected by the tank helmet), the fine white teeth revealed by charred lips drawn back in the last scream of anguish. Because it is almost always the young who die in the front line of battle, the chief irony of war is the waste of such excellent physical equipment. It is a signal mockery to be slaughtered at the very height of one's physical powers. "Herr Stabarzt," runs the German army joke, "ich sterbe bei bester Gesundheit!" ("Staff doctor, I am dying in the best of health!")

After the breakthrough in Normandy, of course, a great many Germans were captured and a good many deserted. Significantly most of the deserters were seasoned campaigners, sergeants and noncoms who knew the war was lost and that it made no sense whatever to continue fighting. The other point was that it took a seasoned soldier to desert because desertion was technically difficult; you had to know what you were doing so as not to be caught between two fires, the one shooting at the enemy, the other shooting at the deserter. What never failed to astonish me was the last-ditch stand of so many—two or three men behind an antitank gun at some crossroads could expect to hold up a tank column for perhaps ten or fifteen minutes, certainly no more and almost certainly at the cost of their lives. But the young men—the eighteen- and nineteen-year-olds—were very often fanatics (if it is fair to call any very young man a fanatic: youth is nature's fanaticism). Once on a road in France in the race north to cut off the Germans retreating from the Falaise Gap our tank column became involved in a fire fight with a group of Germans in the forest bordering the road. We threw some grenades into the forest preparatory to going in after them but not before I gave my spiel, calling out in German to the Germans to surrender since they were surrounded and hopelessly outnumbered. Once or twice on other occasions the Germans had shouted back that *we* were surrounded and hopelessly outnumbered so that *we* had better surrender, and we had harangued each other back and forth for half an hour before engaging. On this occasion, just as one of the infantrymen had pulled the pin from his hand grenade and drawn back his arm to throw it, the sergeant in charge gave the command to move into the woods. The unfortunate infantryman was left holding the grenade, as it were; he suddenly found himself alone. His comrades had gone into the woods on both sides of the road so that he could no longer throw it in any direction. He had the pleasure of holding the grenade firmly in his hand to keep the release mechanism down while wandering up and down the road plaintively calling for help: "Hey fellows, fellows!" He was finally released from his dilemma by a sergeant who, in one of those snap decisions for which the military is famous, simply took the grenade out of his hand and threw it into the trees.

Two fragments from the explosion hit another sergeant in that portion of the anatomy where, in the wishful thinking of every enlisted man, sergeants should be hit. When I moved into the woods (very gingerly since I, as a documents expert, was armed with only a .45-caliber Colt automatic pistol), in the thick brush not four yards ahead of me there was a shot and the thud of a body hitting the ground. It was the body of a German soldier who had shot half his head away. When I opened his tunic to take his personal documents his heart was still beating. He was nineteen years old, a locksmith by trade, and a native of Ravensburg, not far from Lake Constance in Würtemberg. Rather than surrender he had stood his ground; rather than shoot me he had shot himself.

A day or two later on the same road north my lieutenant and I were ranging the countryside in search of German prisoners of war, that is to say, German soldiers who had already been taken prisoner: our job was to interrogate prisoners, not take them. The difficulty was that there was no front line at this stage of the war. The German army was streaming pell-mell back to Germany to gain the protection of the Siegfried Line.

The American and the Allied armies were trying to intercept them. My lieutenant and I were gratified at the unprecedented warmth of the welcome accorded us as we sped through each village. It simply did not occur to us that we were so rapturously hailed on all sides because we were the first Americans these Frenchmen had ever seen.

At last we sighted a truck full of German soldiers some distance ahead. I stepped on the gas so as to overtake the truck more quickly. It was rolling country so that before we finally caught up with the truck it was frequently out of sight behind the rim of a hill. We were perhaps 150 yards away when my lieutenant said, "How about that—they haven't even taken the steel helmets away from those prisoners!"

We were about fifty yards away when we finally took in the fact that the Germans were fully armed—three of them had machine guns and the other fifteen or twenty carried the usual Mauser rifles and wore hand grenades in their belts—and hence were not prisoners. My foot slipped off the gas pedal but the momentum of the jeep was such that we kept gaining until we were well within ten yards of the back of the truck. For a few moments we kept pace at that distance, staring at the Germans in dumb amazement. The Germans looked at us with impassivity. At length a German with a machine gun on the right side of the truck motioned us away or off to the side with his left arm. By this time the distance between us was growing as we began to ascend another hill. In the end the jeep simply stalled midway up the hill. We could have been picked off easily at any time after we had approached within a hundred yards. It was the only time in my life that I have been face-to-face with death and known it. The Germans in the truck were older men—noncoms in their late twenties and thirties; they were tired and running for home. The issue had been decided and they knew it. It made no sense killing a couple of gaping Americans who had blundered into pursuit of them.

On the western front the Germans were hopelessly outclassed, and not only, although conspicuously, in matériel. They were outgunned; they had no supporting air force whatever (exactly two German fighter planes strafed the beaches in Normandy on D day: there were no bombers); they were outmaneuvered (they had comparatively few troop-carrying vehicles and had anyway quite literally run out of gas; instead, they used a huge, cumbersome Rube Goldberg contraption that burned wood and generated power by inducting carbon dioxide into the cylinder chambers of the adapted conventional gas engines); wherever they went they left a trail of dead horses; they were technologically trumped (particularly in communications and in the whole field of logistics as well as in transport); in short, they were outdated.

In the abandoned bunkers we found reports of meetings built around pep talks by the commanders. The answer of troops was always the same: "Give us protection from the fighter-bombers and we will stand our ground!" But there was no protection and even if there had been, the superiority of American artillery would have kept the battle unequal. A freshly captured troop commander once asked peevishly, "We never see your infantry. Why don't you send your infantry in? Then at least we could have a fair fight!" "Why should we waste our infantry," was the answer, "when we can cut you to pieces with artillery and air power?"

There had been a famous tank battle in Normandy in which a crack German unit had fought the British to a bloody standstill. As both sides were withdrawing the German commander emerged from the cupola of his tank, bowed, and saluted.

There were a number of such incidents. They were pretty well summed up a short while later, I thought, when I heard Doctor Robert Ley, Hitler's chief of the German Labor Front, in a radio broadcast. In his speech Doctor Ley dwelt on the atrocities of Allied aerial bombings of Germany, particularly the daylight raids of the large American bomber formations. These were taking a terrible toll of human life—as had the German air raids in England before them—and were gradually reducing most of Germany's larger cities to heaps of smoking rubble. "We have conducted this war in a chivalrous fashion," he shouted in conclusion, "while you (the Americans) have conducted yourselves like gangsters! Therefore we have only this to say to you: 'Götz von Berlichingen! Götz von Berlichingen!' " Götz von Berlichingen (1480–1562) was one of the last of the German knights, half robber baron and half Robin Hood, who was immortalized by Goethe in a play of the same name. Von Berlichingen was famous for his defiance of the suzerain claims of the Bishop of Nuremberg. When his castle was surrounded by the bishop's men and he was called upon to surrender by their captain in the name of the Kaiser, Götz gave the reply that is known to every schoolboy (and girl) in Germany: "Tell your captain: for His Imperial Majesty I have, as always, due respect. But as for him, tell him he can kiss my ass!" Hence the mere mention of the hero's name in Germany is taken as a euphemism for his famous reply. One of the German tank divisions opposing the Allied advance in Normandy was the SS "Götz von Berlichingen": it was known throughout the German armed forces as the LMA [Leck' mich am Arsch—Kiss my ass] Division (the Germans are even more given to the use of initials than Americans are—if that is possible).

Götz von Berlichingen's brother-in-law (he married Götz's younger sister, Maria) was the greatest knight in German history, Franz von Sickingen. Von Sickingen was the condottiere par excellence but he was also more than that. He had his own private army and he could increase it tenfold or twentyfold if occasion, campaign, or cause warranted. He sold his services at times to the king of France and then to Charles V, whose election as kaiser he helped to secure by bringing up his troops within sight of Frankfurt where the election took place. The kaiser never paid Von Sickingen but then the kaiser seldom paid his debts; instead, Sickingen loaned the kaiser 20,000 gulden without collateral or an IOU. He never got it back.

Von Sickingen proclaimed himself the protector of Martin Luther and embraced the new faith although there is some question whether he did so chiefly to promote his own designs. For he had designs: he owned twenty-seven castles on the Rhine and was hailed as the "king of the Rhine." King he thought he might be, but king of Germany. Von Sickingen thought there was room and use for a king in Germany, which had only an absentee emperor (whose Reich extended far beyond the German lands), seven prince electors (dukes or archbishops with a vote—this was the extent of German suffrage at the time), and countless local princelings. Sickingen laid siege to the city of Worms and ravaged its territory. He even invaded the duchy of Lorraine (with the passive complicity of Charles V's predecessor, Maximilian) and forced the reigning duke to ransom the whole country. Von Sickingen's career culminated when he set himself at the head of German chivalry and attempted to lay siege to the rich and powerful archbishopric of Trier. The campaign aborted and Von Sickingen eventually paid for his first and last unqualified failure with his life. But the important thing is that these "marauding expeditions," as historians are wont to call them, were carried on with punctilious attention to the full form of the code of chivalry. Ample warning was given: a "Fehdebrief" or formal challenge in writing was sent, as were manifests explaining and justifying the action to the local inhabitants. When Von Sickingen lay dying of his wounds after he himself had been besieged by the archbishop of Trier he was called to account. "Franz," admonished His Eminence, "what reason can you give for attacking me and my poor people in the diocese?" In reply Von Sickingen spoke his last words: "About that we could talk a long time

—nothing without cause." Franz said a mouthful: "Fehde" is the German word for feud; a "Fehdebrief" such as Von Sickingen sent to His Eminence was the proclamation that a state of feud existed between the two parties. It was the Teutonic equivalent of "Garde-toi, je me garde!" The Germans were passionately given to feuding. "Nothing," wrote Goethe, "could still the chivalric feuding spirit [Fehdegeist] of the Germans."

In the area around Mons, Belgium, late in August there was a vortical convergence of pursuer and pursued. We succeeded in cutting off the German retreat, but they succeeded by the same token in cutting us off temporarily—separating the spearhead from the shaft of the spear. We were surrounded as though on a traffic island while the enemy traffic flowed around us for three days. To put it technically, we were in a blocking position across the path of retreat of at least five German divisions, one of them a parachute division.

We captured five German generals and killed one; among our prisoners was the commanding general of the parachutists, Rüdiger von Heyking. He was the first German general I had ever met, an older man probably in his late fifties. He was very mild of manner and indeed almost jovial. He was shortish and on the heavy side—not at all my idea of a German general, whom I expected to be a sort of super Brandstätter. Von Heyking looked more like the family doctor except that he was perfectly groomed. I was—as always—fascinated by the uniform, the excellence of cut and cloth. He wore the blue-black leather greatcoat prescribed for Army field officers and the dove-gray leather gloves much affected by German officers. In fact, the higher the rank in the German army the more leather there was in the prescribed and affected wear that went with it. Germans love leather. Adalbert Stifter's Witiko, chivalric hero and model for "rectitude of conduct and righteousness of life," is called the "leatherman" because of his dress: leather hat-helmet, leather doublet, leather trousers, leather boots. But it is a very old love. Pagan German warriors wore a leather harness laced together with thongs for armor; this was called a "Schirm" (protection) and the wearer a "Schirmmann," a word that according to some sources was later Latinized by Tacitus into "German."

I had about an hour, most of it alone, with Von Heyking. Our general refused to see him. There was reason for his aloofness: our general was a Jew, Major General Morris Rose, the son of a Denver, Colorado, rabbi. Now Rose—*he* looked like the very model of a Prussian major general: thin-lipped, sharp features, closely cropped hair, a ramrod of a man whose legs drove him forward like twin pistons—Rose was the toughest looking officer I have ever seen. Appearances were not deceiving. Rose was a troubleshooter who had been brought in to take over the division in Normandy because the commanding general had been relieved of his command. There was not a man in division headquarters who did not fear Rose. I saw staff officers, full colonels, standing at attention before Rose, the sweat pouring off their faces, visibly shaking in their tanker's boots. And yet Von Heyking, for all his Gemütlichkeit, had a considerable reputation in the German army; he had been one of the commanding officers of the parachute operation that took Crete. I tried to picture the family doctor jumping out of a Junkers over Crete in battle dress; I gave it up. I went through Von Heyking's personal documents and found some old photographs of him in uniform as a lad. "How long have you been a soldier?" I asked. "I have always been a soldier," he said with a chuckle. "Always? You can't have been born in uniform?" "Not quite," and he beamed at me, "but I put on my first military uniform when I was eight years old." (I gave it up again.)

While Von Heyking was with us in our isolated blocking position —cut off as we were by those we had cut off—four young Germans in an armored car tried to break through on the road we were guarding. They never had a chance. The gas tanks on the back of their car riddled by .50-caliber machine gun bullets, it burst into flame, crashed into a tree, and exploded. The four Germans were quite literally blown to pieces. One of them had been cut in two at the waist and had lost both his legs just above the knee. The mutilated trunk looked like a piece of broken· statuary. "Ein tolles Unternehmen" (a mad undertaking), said Von Heyking. I was reminded of Klopstock's "Ode to Hermann and Thusnelda": "demanding the supreme effort of his sons, over thousands of young bodies shall his triumphal car roll on."

On that same night quite a few of our officers went out to try to make contact with other American units and never came back. Lieutenant Hüni, a Swiss-German immigrant, was found dead the next morning not far away from the barn where we were all holed up; Lieutenant Peterson was likewise found dead nearby next morning. Lieutenant Nolte, a German-American, had the good fortune to be taken prisoner by the Germans. We were all pretty much huddled together in the barn, the "German legion" of the American army with their German prisoners of war. One of the "legion" present was Sergeant Werner Neu, a short, stocky—not to say fat, because he was very strong—German-Jewish refugee-immigrant. Neu had fled Germany in the mid-1930s to escape the concentration camp where most of his relatives were ultimately doomed to die. He had found haven in France, and although he was later forced to flee France in turn, he remained forever grateful for the hospitality and graciousness of his first host country. Whenever anyone shouted "Vive la France!" during our triumphal passage, Neu would unfailingly add: "—et les colonies!"

As the night wore on and the sounds of battle quieted we would hear the groaning and sobbing of the German wounded around us outside the barn. One of our prisoners was a German staff doctor. "Will somebody come out with me and help me bring in the wounded? Maybe I can do something for them," he said. It had to be one of the Americans, of course, because the doctor and a German helper might simply take the opportunity to escape. On the other hand an American volunteer would be running the risk of a ruse by the German doctor once they were outside in the dark. There were several more or less round rejections of the appeal. Then Neu said, "I'll go out with you," and out they went— the handsome, blond German doctor and the little (but very strong) German Jew who looked almost like a Nazi caricature of a Jew. They brought in four or five German wounded that night. Neu was a man of vast, apparently boundless, good humor. He had a fine tenor voice and he loved to sing German folk songs with anybody who would sing them with him. For himself he often sang a snatch of a song. It went:

Tschim-bara-bim-bam-beh! Na, denn vorwärts—fromm, diel
    und munter—
A koscher Jüd geht niemals unter!

[Tum-tara-tum-tum tah! well, then, forward—true, pious, gay—
A kosher Jew will make his way.]

According to the division album Neu's residence was in Saint Louis. He was a butcher by profession. I assume he ran a kosher shop.

Although their military value was nil, the personal documents of the generals we had captured or killed were highly interesting. The dead major general's papers contained a number of family photographs from his home in Hildesheim, among them a picture of his daughter, who was either a beautiful girl or extremely photogenic. I resolved to go to Hildesheim as soon as I could and present her my compliments and condolences.

I got to Hildesheim exactly twenty-five years later coming from Berlin. A bit late for condolences or compliments, I thought. Approaching Hildesheim from the east the traveler is startled to encounter on a plumb line with the road the index finger of some huge mailed fist slowly rising over the horizon in absolute admonition. The finger is an exceedingly tall church tower with a sharp spire. It is an arresting sight and appropriate to a town drenched in the history and blood of the Thirty Years War.

But then, in the high summer of 1944 as I daydreamed of the dead general's daughter, Hildesheim and the Thirty Years War were barely remembered names from a college course on European history. The most interesting in our bag of German generals was the only brigadier of the lot. Both his official and his personal correspondence (he kept carbon copies of all his letters to his wife) dealt voluminously and exclusively with the fact that he had been passed over for promotion to general for almost five years. As time dragged on, the then-colonel became increasingly apprehensive that he would not make general before the war was over; this, regardless of the war's outcome, would have been the ultimate catastrophe for a careerist of such advanced standing. One of the colonel's superiors, the commanding general of an army, explained to him at length why he had been overlooked for promotion the year before. "You will remember," wrote the general superior, "that morning in the lobby of the Hotel Crillon in Paris when Herr Reichsmarschal Göring came in and we all gave the German salute (actually the Nazi salute, more actually the ancient Roman salute) and said, "Heil Hitler!"—all except you, that is. You gave the military salute and then proffered your hand to the Herr Reichsmarschal and said 'Guten Tag' (good day). I found your conduct on this occasion absolutely revolting!" It was clear from this and similar castigations that the colonel simply could not or would not accustom himself to the Nazi forms. Even so he finally received his promotion—just one week before he was captured. Of course he had had the appropriate uniform and insignia ready and waiting for years. His letter announcing the news to his wife was ecstatic. He signed it "Dein Generälchen" (your darling little general). When I talked to him he was—despite a painful arm wound—still riding the crest of euphoria: he was a general; that was all that mattered.

Rose, too, had his share of the vagaries that appertain to general rank. When one does the grand tour of Europe as a member of the headquarters of an armored division one stays in the very best places— châteaus, castles, villas, and the like. Of course, there is some military sense to this: castles and château-forts are by definition strong points, fortified prominences of some sort. The best places also qualify by their size for the honor of being commandeered as the command post of a general: the shelter must be large enough to accommodate the party. Even so, generals gravitate to aristocrats because generals are themselves aristocrats in the most direct sense of the term. In wartime at least, generals do not get to the top and, above all, they do not stay at the top unless they belong there.

Rose once put up for the night on the country estate of Baron de Rothschild in the north of France—and my, how the armored vehicles, the tanks, and assault guns churned up the grounds of the estate! What a mess we made of the front lawn! We put up with another baron—or rather *baronne,* as the Belgians call a baroness—in Namur. The baronne was very old but she had a very pretty granddaughter. The baronne also spoke excellent German (which made my task easier), having been educated at the court of some German prince or duke even before the founding of the Second Reich. She had met Bismarck and all three kaisers. She regaled me for hours with stories, historical tittle-tattle that was somehow boring and amusing at the same time.

Morris Rose had the honor—and he certainly had the motivation —to lead the first Allied division into Germany in World War II. In our sector the retreating Germans did not have the time to man the Siegfried Line or even to lay mines in front of its fortifications. So we did "hang our washing on the Siegfried Line." The Third Armored Division simply rolled through the ghost fortifications and kept on rolling until it ran out of gas southeast of Aachen (where Charlemagne was crowned emperor and lies buried) in a small town called Kornelimünster. It was here I met my first German civilian on German soil, a six-year-old boy standing in the middle of the road. He looked hungry. I gave him a chocolate bar which he bolted. His mother came up and I bowed and greeted her: "Gnädige Frau" (a set form of greeting, literally "gracious lady"). She looked at me wide-eyed and said with emphasis: "Gnädiger Herr!" ("kind sir" or "merciful sir," not the set form of greeting, which is simply "mein Herr").

Kornelimünster was our first command post in Germany and there were some curious incidents. The most bizarre of these concerned a crucifix. The Rhineland is solidly Catholic and a good many black or dark brown wood crucifixes were in evidence in the rooms of the houses we commandeered. In the room that served as our operations center the chief of staff of the division, a Texan named John Brown, discovered what he described as an SS insignia at the base of one of the crucifixes. It was a skull identical with the death's head worn just over the visor of the cap of the SS uniform. The good rural Catholics of Kornelimünster were horrified at the idea of associating the SS with the crucifix. They explained that the skull fixed at the foot of the cross was a memento mori, an admonition to remember and pray for the dead. Nevertheless the identical symbols were insidiously suggestive: I was haunted by the idea of some sort of association—however perverse—between the cross and the SS skull insignia. I did not know that the skull had been the insignia worn on the hats of German hussar units ("Death's Head Hussars") for a hundred years and more. The insignia was adopted by the SS and given a new and utterly sinister significance: the SS "Death's Head Formations" were the concentration camp guards.

Although it was part of my job, I suppose it was inevitable, given my overriding interest in Germans, that I should be reprimanded for fraternizing with them. Rose had seen me talking on more than one occasion and suspected (rightly) that I was putting the largest possible interpretation on my assignment. Since I was the only one at headquarters who could talk to the Germans, I considered it my duty to find out as much about them as I could. Rose called me in and told me flatly not to talk to Germans unless I was specifically ordered to do so. I did not reduce my contacts with the Germans: I merely took care that I was covered by somebody or other's order. He who serves many masters has an easy time playing them off against one another.

Our next command post, which was to mark our furthest advance into Germany for the next three months and more, was Villa Waldfriede just outside Stolberg. This—a huge four-story château—was the residence of the "zipper king" of Germany. The factory, in which the greatest single portion of Germany's zippers had been made, was just down the hill. At Villa Waldfriede, as far as I was concerned, the nonfraternization law went by the board. The caretaker of the villa, Franz Wagenknecht, and his wife Phillipina were allowed to remain in their two-room apartment in the basement. Since I was the only liaison contact with the caretaker, I had the run of the place, and since my bunkmate ground his teeth in his sleep, I brought my sleeping bag into the Wagenknechts' kitchen and slept on the floor. As the weeks drew into months I came to know the Wagenknechts very well. Phillipina would cook me her specialty—Rhein wine pudding—and Franz would instruct me on the workings of the villa's power plant, the heating system, the virtues and foibles of the former kitchen and household staff (I had gravitated to the kitchen again) and life in general. He had been a machinist in a submarine—the notorious U-boat—crew in World War I.

"Thank God," he said more than once, "all I had to do was take care of my machine—thank God I didn't even have to take care of a machine in this war!" Franz Wagenknecht was and still is an utterly honest, able, and resourceful mechanic, a model husband, and—if there is such a thing —a model father, a typical German in the traditional sense of that term. He knew and filled his place, which was, when things were going badly, in the engine room of a submarine, and when all went well, in the basement and tool houses of a large estate or institute.

I spent a good deal of my spare time listening to German radio broadcasts, aware as we all were that the Third Reich was entering its final agony. Much of the programming was devoted to music, of course; most of this was light opera, operetta, and "Schlager" (hits): "Tum-tatta-tum-tum-tum-tum-tum! It sounds over seven hills:/And everyone knows who will soon arrive—the little postillion!" One quarter-hour program was entitled "Alsatians, Listen Here!" Another was devoted to the German "Landser" (GI) and featured as narrator the meister of meisters, Hans Sachs ("Hans Sachs sends you greetings, lads"), who in his homey way encouraged them to keep fighting by citing examples of bravery from German folklore. Between programs there was invariably an announcement: either "Über dem Reichsgebiet befindet sich kein feindlicher Kampfverband" (over the Reich's territory there is no enemy battle squadron) which was the more usual, or, if Allied bombers were active, "Starker Kampfverband mit Spitze auf Hannover" (large enemy battle formation headed toward Hanover). When the war was over Germans would sometimes say, "Yes—under the battle squadron there is no enemy Reich's territory!"

There were a few—I thought surprisingly few—speeches by German political leaders. I also heard Doctor Ley again. This was the most terrible speech I have ever heard (excepting possibly some of the speeches of the Arab foreign ministers and ambassador-delegates to the United Nations immediately prior to the Six-Day War): Ley described an incident in which an eleven-year-old German boy had asked a patrolling American soldier for a bar of candy. While the soldier searched his pockets for the candy bar the German boy pulled out a pistol and shot him in the stomach, a death wound. Ley relished the incident ("Hey Ami, do you have a candy bar for me? Ha, ha.") for the purpose of popularizing resistance even after the war was over. This was the notorious but stillborn "Werewolf movement." I also heard Doctor Goebbels addressing a formation of the Volkssturm in Berlin on the occasion of the last levee of troops. The Volkssturm was the bottom of the barrel, the age group from fifty to sixty-five. "I do not have the impression," said Goebbels, "that you are all on crutches!" This drew a big laugh. On New Year's Eve during the Battle of the Bulge and after we had been thrown back out of Germany I heard the führer speak. It was a very solemn speech, but he sounded robust and he was determined to keep fighting. "I appeal to the German youth," he said. He always had—very much so—but I wondered how much of the German youth was left. I had seen more than a few youngsters of seventeen years of age in the front line and there had been talk of whole formations of Hitler Youth (ten to eighteen years old) being committed.

One day we were visited by several British and American officers from higher—much higher—headquarters. They were from Army Group or perhaps even SHAEF (Supreme Headquarters Allied Expeditionary Force). The reason for their visit had been a sensational discovery. Someone had found that the zipper factory down the hill had been producing, in addition to zippers, jet turbines. There was a good deal of excitement. I was detailed to the group of investigators for the length of their stay. They brought in the scion of the zipper king, a man in his late thirties who had actually headed up the factory. He had known that a special department set up within the factory had been producing turbines but he had not known anything more than that.

It was the first time I consciously heard the German phrase "Nehm' ich an" (so I assume). This was hardly because I had never heard that particular word order before; most probably it was because "so I assume" was the zipper prince's answer to most of the questions put to him by the investigators.

The great distraction in learning a foreign language—and this holds truer the older the student—comes from the fact that it is done consciously. There is a natural tendency to associate words and phrases learned with the attendant circumstances and especially with the people from whom they are learned. The student takes a mortgage on his powers of attention if he uses a "walking dictionary" or a "dictionary you can take to bed with you." I once met a crusty old American professor who purported to be busy on a translation of *Faust* into the American vernacular. He volunteered the information that his idea of foreign relations was to sleep with as many foreign women as he possibly could. If he learned his German in this way it would explain why I have never seen nor heard of the finished product of his scholarly labors. If Lothario is a would-be-linguist and has an associative turn of mind (he need not have a heart), he will find himself too often adrift and adream at the turn of a phrase.

When one learns a language outside the classroom, words become mnemonic devices for personalities and events: they make it easy to recall the attendant people, places, and times but impossible to banish them; they are there whenever the magic word or phrase falls. "And many a dear shadow," as Goethe sang, "rises up." Fortunately the undear shadows are not quite so quick to rise.

While at Villa Waldfriede I was detailed to help evacuate a group of Ukrainian girls who had just been liberated from the German families to whom they had been allotted as "Ostarbeiterinnen" (eastern laborers —these were civilians of the Eastern European countries overrun by the Nazis who were pressed into service in Germany). My job was to explain to them in Russian that they were to be transported in trucks to the rear preparatory to their return to the Soviet Union. I wrote out a short speech in my best Russian. "We are giving you," I said (I remember by the mnemonic device of having used the phrase for the first time), "the longed-for opportunity of returning to the Soviet Union!"

My announcement went over, as they say in the American vernacular, like the discovery of a turd in the champagne punch. At first I thought that the young ladies had misunderstood my Russian. I soon realized that they had understood my speech all too well. The lot of them stood there for a moment in perfect dejection. Then came the excuses: they had no clothes for the trip (this was quickly disproved by the bringing in of their luggage), the war was not yet over and they did not want to stay in refugee camps, etc. When I made it clear that they had no choice, they all insisted on being allowed to go back to their old quarters to pick up additional belongings. This we allowed them to do and it immediately became apparent that they simply wanted to say their final good-byes. Without exception these were copiously tearful. The girls for the most part said that they had been treated like daughters (there is in fact in Germany the tradition of the "Haustochter," the maid who is more or less treated like one of the family); two of the German families protested that they had long wished to adopt their Ukrainian maids (who were war orphans) but had been prevented from doing so by the Nazi regime. It also became clear during the drive to the trucking point that the girls' apprehension of returning to the Soviet Union was still greater than their affection for their German keepers. I was astonished. This was the first unmistakable evidence I had encountered that the Soviet Union was not the beloved homeland of all its citizens. A Soviet pilot whom we had found hiding out in the Hürtgen forest had been laconic in his talks with me. He had merely said that he hoped the Soviet government, having conquered its enemies, would now open all the churches and keep them open. I took this with a grain of salt, assuming that there were perhaps as few atheists in cockpits as there were in foxholes.

One fine Sunday morning in October I went down into Stolberg or, rather, the western half of it (the eastern half was still held by the German army) to find a young German soldier and take him to prisoner of war camp. We had had word that he had simply gone home, since his home happened to be in Stolberg, when his unit—or what was left of it —straggled through the town. I found him sitting at breakfast with his mother. "I have been expecting you," he said. He was in civilian clothes, having hidden or, more probably, burned his uniform, as I gathered: when I asked him if he would prefer going to camp in his uniform he said, "I'll never put on another uniform—not even a bus driver's!" I assured his mother that he would be well off in the prisoner of war camp. Of course, I didn't know what I was talking about except for one thing. I knew that the food in the American prisoner of war camps was better than the Germans in Germany were getting or would get for a long time to come, so I emphasized that. His mother believed me; she had seen how lavishly generous the GIs were with their K rations.

Once and only once, in November I think, we came under enemy artillery fire at Villa Waldfriede. It was a barrage consisting of some ten rounds laid down with great precision and so unexpected that it seemed like an act of God at the time. What had actually happened was obvious enough. We had been holding the line desultorily in Stolberg for more than six weeks. During this time information—perhaps nothing more complicated than a telephone call across the front line—on the exact location of division headquarters had passed into the hands of the German army. Some German artillery officers had consulted their grid maps, plotted trajectories, and sighted their guns. Thirteen of our men were wounded, two of them very badly.

After our own artillery had silenced the German guns with counter-barrages, the wounded who could still walk lined up outside the division surgeon's office for treatment. Rose came up and talked with them all until the last man had been treated by the surgeon. Then he stepped up and said, "All right, doc, now you can take care of me." No one had noticed it but Rose had taken shrapnel in both shoulders. They were light wounds that had not bled enough to show on the outside of his uniform. There was a good deal of discussion afterward as to whether Rose's waiting for the last man to be treated before going himself was done for effect: whether he was merely taking advantage of an opportunity to impress the troops. Notwithstanding the discussion, Rose's performance impressed everybody.

On December 6, 1944, I was commissioned a second lieutenant in the field. I think I know from the transformation that overtook me with the granting of the commission how "your darling little general" felt when he finally received his general's commission. It was a watershed. After that nothing was ever the same—especially the food. As an officer I ate in the officer's mess. For me this was very important: cooks eat well and my memory was good.

But the biggest change was with the Germans; I was now "Herr Leutnant" whereas before they hadn't known what to call me. I wore no insignia of rank on the consideration that a military man who interrogated German generals would be better off if he could pose as or at least allow the inference that he was some sort of highfalutin specialist if not a commissar. I also had the pleasure, and my heart beat high with it, of having Rose walk over to shake hands with me. "Congratulations," he said, "your new unit's gain is our loss." When I went to say good-bye to Franz and Phillipina, Franz snapped to when he saw me and said in only half-mock military manner: "Melde gehorsamst, Herr Oberleutnant!" ("Report most obediently," the set form for reporting for duty in the German armed forces). Phillipina cried. (Once when we were all huddled together in the basement during a German air raid on our headquarters, the percussion of a very near-miss propelled Phillipina into my arms and she stayed there for the three-minute duration of the raid while I comforted her—and myself.) Later the same day I left for my new unit. It was the day the Battle of the Bulge began.

My orders transferring me to the 90th Infantry Division read that I was to proceed by rail. The nearest rail-head in operation at the time, that is, before Hitler began the Ardennes offensive, was Namur. When I arrived at the Rail Transport Office in Namur I was confronted with the news that the Germans had mounted a major offensive and had broken through on a fairly broad front. As a result there would be no trains running out of Namur until further notice.

Quite naturally I bethought myself of the old baronne in her big empty castle all alone except for her pretty granddaughter. I found her at home—she was really, I think, almost too old to go anywhere—but with a different granddaughter. I was greeted with "Herr Leutnant!" again as I was admitted to the baronne and asked to be her guest for as long as I liked. It was a strange, ambiguous atmosphere in Namur those first few days of the Ardennes offensive when it was still just possible that the Germans would break through. As for me, I was delighted to be out of artillery range. There was no real likelihood of danger for Namur but there was the possibility of it. The possibility was small enough for comfort and large enough for excitement. Once in the morning and once in the evening I'd go down to the Rail Transport Office and inquire about trains. I was in no hurry. It was four days before they put a train together going south.

At that time I had a song I often sang or whistled or hummed. It was a Hungarian folk song, almost a nonsense rhyme set to a sprightly tune. After my first night in the château I was awakened by the sound of this song. At first I didn't know where I was. Then I couldn't understand where the singer was. I was enchanted, in a spell cast by someone's singing. When I realized that the sound was coming up through the dumbwaiter, I jumped into my clothes and ran down to the kitchen. The singer was the baronne's other granddaughter, Pierrette. She told me that she had heard me singing the song the day before. With that she captured my imagination. For a long while after, always lurking in the back of my mind was this other granddaughter and her gentle piracy of my song.

Just before Christmas I managed to join the 90th Infantry Division under Major General James Van Fleet (who later made a name for himself in Greece and in Korea) in Thionville. When I arrived the division was in reserve, but in less than a week we were on our way to relieve the 101st Airborne Division which had been surrounded by the Germans at Bastogne. In their chivalric fashion the Germans had called a truce after they had surrounded the 101st. They sent forth emissaries to treat for the surrender of the completely surrounded and hopelessly outnumbered American unit. In answer thereto the American commander, General McAllister, said "Nuts!," a reply that mightily confused the Germans. But the translation is simple: Götz von Berlichingen! The Germans got the idea when the weather cleared and they were slaughtered by American fighter-bombers.

While still in Thionville I sat, as interpreter, on the board of a court-martial of a German, a native of Lorraine, or Lothringen as the Germans call it (about one-half of the Lothringer, or Lorrainiens, as the French call them, are German-speaking). The defendant was charged with stealing state property. There was a good deal of confusion because the identity of the proprietor-state had changed (back) from Germany to France. In the scramble to evacuate the area before the onrushing Allies, some German official or other had authorized the defendant to deal thus and so—or so he protested: there was no one left to corroborate his story.

The American court-martial found him guilty and sentenced him to five years. When sentence was pronounced the German did not understand it and was obliged to wait for my translation. In terms of the psychological effect, then, it was I who was pronouncing sentence. He was optimistic and my words hit him full in the face: "Five years imprisonment." I could see, for a split second, the significance of my words in his eyes, although the expression on his face did not change. Then his head dropped to his chest as if some invisible knife had cut the tendon holding it erect. I thought the sentence unusually severe: I had expected something like six months, a year at the most, if the court found against him; I had thought that there was an even chance it would not. I resolved then and there that I would not sit on any more courts-martial if I could possibly avoid it; especially not on those sitting in judgment of foreign nationals. For me, taking active part in the judgment instead of merely parroting the finding and the sentence in another language would have been still worse. I have always abhorred passing judgment on anyone for anything. As far as I am concerned the passing of judgment (except on oneself) is an arrogation—the assumption of a right over another or others that is unwarrantable, even or especially by law; more especially when one set of laws suddenly displaces another. The American court-martial in Thionville sat in judgment of the Lothringian by right of conquest. In moral terms the right of conquest is a technicality.

In the barracks at Thionville, which a few weeks before had housed the headquarters of a German division, I found a large, leather-bound, illustrated (with engravings) book of pornography. Its date of publication was before World War I. The style of the drawings (there was little text beyond the subtitles) can be bracketed, I think, with the terms "fin de siècle," "belle epoque," and "Jugendstil," like something Aubrey Beardsley might have done had he been constrained to adhere to the tenets of Socialist Realism. I remember a picture entitled *Stehaufmännchen* (Roly-poly) which showed a penis erectus balanced upright as a separate entity on its testicles before an admiring group of female spectators. Another showed a winged penis erectus flying into a women's dormitory. Still another, entitled *Die Freundinnen* (The Girl Friends),

GERMANS

depicted two middle-aged lesbians at work with each other (or play, as the case may have been.) Finally I remember a Rabelaisian drawing of a peasant woman lifting her skirts to display her shaggy pudendum. It was entitled *Die Hauptsache* (The Main Thing). Characteristic of these illustrations and all the other German "erotica" I saw during and immediately after the war (folders with full brush illustrations of the sequences of the sexual act—mostly between husband and wife) was the Biedermeier or Victorian spirit that informed them. The men were always imperially slim, the women inevitably of a fleshly abundance à la belle of the Policemen's Municipal Ball.

All in all it was about as sexy as Milton's description of the prelapsarian connubial dalliance of Adam and Eve in *Paradise Lost.* There was a strong puritan streak in the Nazi movement. According to the party propaganda, "the German woman does not smoke, the German woman does not drink," and she made love primarily, if not solely, for the purpose of increasing the German race, with strict regard for its purity. This explains the old-fashionedness of the erotica in the Nazi period. The examples I saw were either pre–World War I editions or new editions of the same.

I made my first acquaintance with a border people when the 90th Infantry Division moved into Luxembourg in the course of the American counteroffensive in the Battle of the Bulge. We set up the division intelligence headquarters (G–2), consisting of two field telephones, a situation map and a typewriter in the living room of the mayor's house in Wilwerdingen (Wilwerdange in French), a village of some twenty-five houses then, in the northern tip of the duchy. Once in the mayor's house I immediately noticed a strikingly pretty dark-haired young woman dressed entirely in black. I asked her if she were in mourning. "No," she said, "I am the mayor of Wilwerdingen." And so she was and what a delightful apparition withal. The pleasure of her company was so great that she made me forget—except for brief flashes of curiosity—the baronne's other granddaughter in Namur.

The mayor of Wilwerdingen was Leonie Schroeder. Like all Luxembourgers she spoke both German and French in addition to Letzeburgisch, a dialect which all Luxembourgers insisted was not German but which I had no difficulty understanding from my knowledge of German. The Luxembourgers had the great but also highly dubious honour of being included in the Third Reich as Germans. This was part of the Heim ins Reich (home into the Reich) policy of the Nazis whereby border territories harboring Germanic populations were simply incorporated into the Reich. Leonie complained that instead of bringing her home into the Reich, the Nazis brought the Reich into her home: they were and remained interlopers. Luxembourg was quietly annexed just after the fall of France. The same honor was not accorded the Dutch who were also considered Germanic but apparently not quite ready for the league. The Nazis planned to bring the Dutch in after a suitable period of instruction and processing.

The Allies, however, did not consider the Luxembourgers a part of the Third Reich or even German in the sense that the Germans had been formally declared an "enemy people." The Luxembourgers were officially regarded as "liberated" along with the French, Belgians, and the Dutch. Nonfraternization, for example, did not apply to the Luxembourgers. The result was "fraternization" of which I have never seen the like before or since.

It is a fact that the American as an ethnic type—and it is well to consider that the Greek word "ethnos" denotes a group of people who are accustomed to live together—the American as a product typical of the customs and usages common to the continent of North America is naturally more congenial to the Germanic than to the Latin peoples. In no small measure, of course, this affinity is due to the Anglo-Saxon base of the nation in combination with the largest minority in America which is German. But in immediate terms it comes to the way of doing things, backslapping or bowing, shaking hands or shaking fists. Generally, American troops did not get along well with the French, who are a reserved people with an abhorrence for backslappers. Thus the love feast I witnessed between American troops and the Luxembourgers was the politically uncomplicated side of the coin struck from the continuing history of German-American relations.

The Luxembourgers were in a euphoria only somewhat sobered by the threat of a German comeback. Time and again I heard them say: "It is only a military question now"—all very well for anyone who is not in the military. But even if the Germans had come back again it would not have shaken the conviction that the Third Reich had run its antic course. Its death throes were indeed less antic than its triumphs. The only dignified thing the Third Reich could do was die. Leonie and those of her fellow countrymen I met thought the Nazis were silly—especially Goebbels and Von Ribbentrop. The Nazis were hamfisted, uncouth, and uneducated. Those who were well educated, at least formally—like Goebbels—were hopeless fanatics, or fools—like Von Ribbentrop. But the gay disdain of the Luxembourgers for the Nazis covered a deep revulsion from the Germans. When I arrived in Luxembourg in 1945 the "Letzeburgers" spoke French with a German accent; now the "Luxembourgeois" speak German with a French accent.

My attempts to fraternize with Leonie were encumbered by her magisterial eminence and the new dignity thrust upon me by a spontaneous lieutenancy. I did not know how to act as an officer except that I was supposed to set an example for the enlisted men. I knew it would not do to have everybody making passes at the mayor.

After three or four days in Wilwerdingen we moved some thirty miles down the road into Germany. I was made a liaison officer between division headquarters and corps, which had moved up within a few miles on the other side of Wilwerdingen. In shuttling back and forth I made a point of stopping off at Wilwerdingen to pay my respects to the mayor. The mayor made a point of cooking breakfast for me. The mayor's house was like many farmhouses in Europe; that is, both house and barn were sheltered under one roof. The kitchen was particularly pleasant. It was large with a low ceiling and when the barn door was closed it was warm and full of good smells. (In my mother's house the kitchen was the largest and most pleasant room. We seldom went into the living room and never used the dining room except for Sunday dinners.)

One morning the mayor turned to me while she was scrambling eggs and asked: "Do you like eggs?" I said yes, I liked eggs very much. "I don't," said the mayor. "I like meat." Now I was doing my best to read a romantic meaning into this exchange and so I missed the obvious fact that the mayor liked meat because meat had been scarce for some five years. So when the mayor said she liked meat I said yes, I thought she would. "What do you mean?" she asked rather quickly. I said I didn't know, I just thought that she would probably like meat. (A year and a half later by way of making conversation I asked a young lady in Bremerhaven what her favorite food was. She answered, "Meat, meat!") A few minutes later when I had eaten the scrambled eggs and the mayor had seated herself across from me at the table, a cat walked into the room. "Do you like cats?" asked the mayor. I said that I liked cats very much —as a matter of fact, was terribly fond of cats. "I don't," she said. "I like dogs." I asked if she liked big dogs. "Yes," she said. So I said that I thought she would. "Why?" she asked. I said I didn't know but it just seemed to me that she might be the kind of person who liked big dogs. I might have added that I hoped she did because I was very big (I am bigger now). But I thought it better left unsaid and understood. Anyway bigness is advertisement enough for itself.

I have a remembrance of a road, from a trip I made once during the war with three Kameraden from the German-Jewish legion. It is a remembrance that I cherish because it has no beginning and no end, just a long stretch of some unknown, unidentified road. I know where we were going—to Paris—and going to Paris for the first time is a dream in itself. But I cannot remember how we actually got there. That is why I like the remembrance so much: it hangs forever in an abeyance of anticipation, in a mood of great, quiet joy—to be going away from the war and toward Paris.

I append a dream to the remembrance. I returned to Wilwerdingen on a very high trajectory from Paris to Mainz, rolling up to the mayor's house in the middle of a storm around midnight. The house was dark; so I honked the horn. A couple of minutes passed and a light went on. Then the front door opened and the mayor came out. When she approached the jeep I called out greetings from Paris. She said, "Come in, you must be hungry." After a very early breakfast the mayor and I went into a little back room off the kitchen and talked. At one point the mayor leaned forward and said very distinctly: "You bastard." I protested that I did not know why she should call me a bastard. "No," she said, "but you were pretty sure I would like big dogs, weren't you." Then she gave me her hand. "Here," she said, "you can start with this." Then, or shortly thereafter, a little old woman came in and hustled us off to bed —to separate beds. Hours later, after another breakfast, I took my leave with the whole family front and center to see me off. I wondered if the old woman had turned out just to make sure I left. I made many trajectories thereafter between the front and the "Zone of the Interior" (as the American army calls everything inside the continental United States) since the war ended and the front became the Iron Curtain and I was demobilized but the world was not. But no trajectory carried me through Wilwerdingen.

The only thing I remember distinctly about my first trip to Paris was its purpose: to arrange for my transfer to the Officers' Liaison School (Russian). When it became clear that the meeting between the Western Allies and the Russians in Germany was imminent, the American army belatedly began to look around for Russian speakers within its ranks. These were—they had to be—for the most part Ritchie men. Since I belonged to that confraternity I had no trouble finding out the officers in charge and arranging for my transfer to the Russian Liaison Group. I had several reasons for desiring the transfer but the main reason was to get away from the front. There was also a strong pull in the opposite direction: the Officers' Liaison School was in Le Vésinet, the garden spot among the banlieux of Paris.

I had had enough of the war; I reckoned nine months at the front was long enough. I was sick of the carnage and destruction, of prowling like a ghoul among the German corpses looking for documents. Just before my trip to Paris my division had entered Mainz. The spectacle of Mainz was stupefying. The city had been bombed until it was nothing more and nothing less than a huge pile of rubble. Almost every street in the inner "city" was blocked with huge chunks of granite piled sometimes two stories high from the buildings blasted to pieces on either side. When I saw Mainz I wondered what was meant by the term "leveling a city." Instead of being leveled Mainz was a mountain of ruin, a monument to its own destruction. I watched the inhabitants of the city—those left were all living in cellars—skulk down to the river for water. They had literally been reduced to the condition of rodents. It was appalling.

There was also the highly repulsive business of commandeering houses, of turning people out of house and home. In Germany we commandeered houses as often as we stopped for the night. I knew a Scotsman, Captain George McGhee of the British army, who, because he spoke flawless German, was often saddled with the onus of commandeering houses. He began his speech to the lady of the house invariably as follows: "Gracious lady (gnädige Frau), on behalf of the silly, silly government I represent . . ." Once a house was commandeered it stayed commandeered; troops that vacated a house were quickly followed by troops of the next echelon who had no desire to scout the area for new quarters and go through the doleful charade of commandeering. Even so I was struck by the matter-of-fact German acceptance of the practice. I remembered that my uncle had fought in France in the AEF (American Expeditionary Force) and served in the American army of occupation in 1919, but I did not realize that there was a German tradition of being occupied that went back a thousand years. Only once did a housewife approach me after she had loaded her personal belongings onto a cart. "Please remember that we are poor people," she said and repeated, "poor people." On another occasion—and only one other—a teen-age girl burst into tears when I asked her who had ransacked the bedrooms. "Not I," she sobbed, "not I!" I should add that I saw very little ransacking done by American troops. But troops do not have to ransack or willfully destroy to leave a place looking as if it had lain in the path of a tornado.

One absurd episode remains an irreducible salient in my memory. It was an argument I had with a lieutenant from another division over whether his unit or mine should occupy a certain house for one night. "I cannot possibly let you have this house," he said. I asked him why that was, since there were plenty of houses in the next town to which his division had moved on the night before. "Because we hold this village by right of conquest," he said. "We must protect and preserve our glory —we can't let anyone usurp the glory we have won here!" To make matters worse this *miles gloriosus Americanus* spoke with a heavy Brooklyn accent. I asked him whether withholding the house from us would make any difference to the division historian. But he was adamant. I asked him if he had read Clausewitz. "You bet I have!" he said.

N LATE MARCH I WAS TRANSFERRED TO THE RUSSIAN LIAISON School at Le Vésinet. I was just three weeks among the "droshky drivers" as they were called when I was transferred to SHAEF (Forward) at Reims. I was given this assignment simply because I was the only officer at the school who spoke both Russian and German. Once at SHAEF I was detailed to the German Army Section (intelligence) under British Colonel John Austin. I had not been in the section three days when Austin called me in. "Your records show that you speak German," he said. "Do you think your German is good enough to enable you to act as General Bedell Smith's interpreter in negotiations with the Germans?" I gulped and said I thought it was. Austin sent me to Major General Kenneth Strong of the British army, who was chief of SHAEF intelligence. Strong handed me a captured German army report and asked me to translate it as I stood. "I think you'll do," he said when I had finished. "Now report to General Eisenhower's train at ten o'clock tonight."

In the dining car the next morning (I did not know where we were going or why), I met General Walter Bedell Smith for the first time. "Where did you learn your languages?" he asked me. I told him that I had majored in Classical Greek at college and branched out. This set the general off on the subject of archaeology (it is a subject that seems to fascinate generals as a guild). During breakfast he enlarged upon the archaeological treasures of Sicily. A little while later the Russian General Ivan Susloparov came in and we went through the same routine, Susloparov enlarging on his favorite subject: artillery. He was a major general of artillery and he talked a fine bombardment. He did not neglect to lob in some politics: "The Communist system comes down to this— if you work well, you eat well." Susloparov had obviously worked very well; he was a huge, round-faced, jovial man. In fact he was one of the few really big Russian generals I have met. It was a standing joke among liaison officers that Russian generals had been cut down to size since they were almost invariably small, while full colonels were usually large and bulky.

The negotiations we were about to undertake concerned the projected parachute drops of supplies to the starving Dutch population behind the German lines. They took place on May 1 in a red-brick church in Nijmegen, which had recently been captured by American troops. In addition to Bedell Smith, Susloparov, and General François Sevez, who as a deputy chief of staff represented the French army, Prince Bernhard of the Netherlands took part. Every time Bernhard stepped outside the church for a breather, the assembled townsmen, either waving or wearing orange streamers, ribbons, and sashes, would strike up the national anthem. Bernhard was in high spirits, but as the day wore on he grew careful not to show himself out of doors. He took great interest in the Russians; I spent the conference breaks interpreting between him and Susloparov. Bernhard was particularly interested in the Soviet partisans. He emphasized to Susloparov that he was prepared to put his squadron of planes at the partisans' disposal for food and medicine drops, flying out wounded and the like. Susloparov expressed his gratitude but explained that the partisans were so well organized that they could take care of themselves. "Anyway," said Susloparov after Bernhard had fled indoors to escape another rendition of the national anthem, "the war's almost over—what's with him?"

Though the German army of occupation in the Netherlands was now cut off, it refused to surrender as long as German troops elsewhere were still fighting. But the Nazi high commissioner, Arthur von Seyss-Inquart, former chancellor of Austria (for a few weeks), had agreed in principle to allow the Allies to parachute food and other supplies into German-held Holland, provided the Allies agreed to a local and unofficial cease-fire. Seyss-Inquart was in Nijmegen to negotiate the details. I was thrown off at the beginning of the conference by Bedell Smith's toughness toward him. "I do not mean to insult you," he told Seyss-Inquart, "but I want to make it clear that you and your immediate subordinates will be held strictly accountable to an Allied military court for the effective and fair distribution to the Dutch population of all supplies that are dropped." I was both astonished and fascinated by Seyss-Inquart. Here was one of the top Nazis, Hitler's proconsul in Holland, the Reich had just been cut in two by invading armies from the west and east, and he sat there across the table from us utterly unruffled, as coolly, as calmly as if he were conducting a routine board meeting in some dusty, dim Viennese bank. I could not see his eyes because his glasses reflected the light from the windows behind us.

Bedell Smith also mentioned accountability for any crimes committed by the Germans against the Dutch. When I instinctively tried to take the edge off his language as I rendered it into German, Smith interrupted, ordering me to translate literally. A British staff officer then set forth the Allied plans for the drops. Seyss-Inquart, who knew the situation in German-occupied Holland in minute detail, quietly and methodically refuted the feasibility of all the planned drops, pointing out in a number of cases that the proposed target areas were or soon would be under flood water. He then suggested alternatives that were promptly accepted by Smith. On the way back to SHAEF in Reims, when the general expressed his satisfaction with the results of the conference, I expected him to comment on Seyss-Inquart's masterful performance. But he did not so much as hint at it. The attitude of the Allied generals toward the German group throughout the conference had been cold but correct—except for Smith's opening statements. Bedell Smith regarded Seyss-Inquart not only as a Nazi politician, as distinct from the German military officers in Seyss-Inquart's entourage, but also as a de facto war criminal awaiting trial and sentence.

General Strong, who was now my immediate superior, had been a military attaché at the British Embassy in Berlin for several years before the war. He therefore knew a great many German generals personally. A day or two after my return from Nijmegen he asked me to act as escort officer to a German general whom he described to me as an old friend of his. This was Colonel General Count von Schwerin, until his capture the week before commander of the 101st "Windhund" (Greyhound) Division. Von Schwerin had been punitively transferred to the Russian front three years before after some anti-Nazi remarks he had made were reported to the führer. The Allies (not only Strong) regarded him as a more or less active opponent of the Nazi regime. My mission was to take Von Schwerin to Paris where he was to meet Wild Bill Donovan, the head of the Office of Special Services (the forerunner of the Central Intelligence Agency). During the four-hour drive, I asked Von Schwerin, who was in his mid-fifties and a fine figure of a man, a gray-haired charmer, why he hadn't realized from reading *Mein Kampf* what was in store for the German nation and Europe if Hitler ever came to power? "I never read *Mein Kampf*," said Von Schwerin, "and what is more I don't know of anyone who has."

For the most part we talked about his experiences at the Russian front. He said that in more than a few cases Russian army and partisan units, when surrounded by the Germans and out of food but not ammunition, had resorted to cannibalism to keep alive and continue fighting. Later, after their ultimate capture, when asked why they had done this, the commissars invariably replied, "It was necessary." Von Schwerin did not add and I did not then know that Hitler had issued orders that all commissars were to be summarily shot. The Russians of course knew of this order. Even if they hadn't they would have assumed and propagated as fact the existence of such an order. As we entered Paris through the Porte des Lilas about noon of a fine day in May, Von Schwerin exclaimed, "Ah, Paris, Paris! I have so many friends here!" Then he turned to me and added, "And they are not collaborators either!"

A few days later I was detailed to act as escort officer and interpreter to Colonel General Alfred Gustav Jodl and his party who had arrived at SHAEF to negotiate the surrender of the German armed forces. I was immediately struck by the contrast between Jodl and Admiral Hans Georg von Friedeburg who had preceded Jodl to Reims as the envoy of Admiral Karl Doenitz, Doenitz having succeeded Hitler as reichskanzler (chancellor) and commander in chief of the German armed forces. Jodl seemed utterly crushed: he acted throughout like a man in a trance. Von Friedeburg, in contrast, was effusive. His first words to me were: "They are charming, charming, your generals—why, the Allies are absolutely delightful people!"

Then he asked me, as the use is—it is the obvious conversation piece when talking with interpreters—where I had learned such wonderful German. I gave my stock answer: in "Little Germany" (Klein Deutschland). Von Friedeburg reacted to this as Germans always did: "You mean in 'Great Germany' " (Gross Deutschland). I then gave the stock explanation that "Little Germany" was Yorkville, the German quarter of New York. No German I ever met thought this was funny or otherwise meaningful. I gave up after a while. What I had been trying to do was make a play on "big" and "little" as adjectives describing Germany. "Gross Deutschland" was an official Nazi term for Germany. I sought to suggest to my conversation partner that there was another Germany in another place, that it was small, and that it had had something to do with cutting "Great Germany" down to size. I did not realize that the undertaking was categorically hopeless because "Little Germany" and "Little German" were extremely important terms in German history, referring to the "small solution" of the German Problem (the solution implemented by Bismarck to the exclusion of the German-speaking territories of Austria; the inclusion of these territories constituted the "Great German" solution). Proficiency in a foreign language presupposes the fairly comprehensive knowledge of the history of the language area.

Von Friedeburg's delight with the Allies was built entirely on the German group's meetings with Smith and Strong. I do not know what Smith told the Germans when they arrived. But the impression of the meetings I gained from Von Friedeburg was confirmed by Jodl later, when, apropos of nothing, he suddenly approached and told me that he would never forget the kindness and gallantry of Bedell Smith.

When I was not with the German party, I spent most of my time shuttling between General Smith's office in the "red schoolhouse" and Susloparov's headquarters in the Hotel Lion d'Or, coordinating agreement on the articles of surrender. The Allies, of course, were pressing the Doenitz government to empower Jodl to sign the surrender forthwith. The Germans had tried previously to surrender on the western front alone and were still doing everything possible to avoid surrendering individual units to the Russians. Even though it was made clear to Jodl at the outset that no partial conditions whatever would be discussed by the Allies, Doenitz played for time.

Meanwhile the surrender negotiations, such as they were, consisted in stipulating technical measures for the securing of communications and supply lines and the physical safety of the Allied troops in Germany. The only negotiations worthy of the name were those carried on between Generals Smith and Susloparov, or rather, between Smith and Moscow with Susloparov acting as intermediary. Susloparov was himself merely a liaison officer who could do nothing more than send and receive signals to and from Moscow on the radio transmitter the Russians took with them wherever they went. Whenever I appeared at the Lion d'Or with questions or answers for Susloparov, he would begin by saying: "I have just sent a telegram to Moscow." But he never once said that he had received a message from Moscow. I began to think that his receiver had broken down and that he was too proud to admit it.

Smith and Susloparov haggled all of May 6 over two points: the definition of "property," particularly "government property," the Russian plumping for the widest possible definition with an eye to reparations (but this was not the only reason for Russian concern with the definition; property plays a far greater role in communism than it does in capitalism); the other question was whether Susloparov was or could be empowered by Moscow to sign the articles of surrender.

The first point was settled pretty much in the Russians' favor; the second point is a story in itself. On my last visit to Susloparov at about nine in the evening, he had still not received an answer to his request for empowerment. I happened to be the duty officer in General Smith's office that night. On that night at SHAEF we were waiting for two empowerments, the German and the Russian. At about two in the morning of May 7, the long-awaited signal empowering Jodl to sign came in from Doenitz's headquarters (the signal empowering Susloparov to sign never came). I took the message off the ticker and alerted the general's secretary. I was filled with apprehension because I was sure that Susloparov had still not heard from Moscow and hence would not be able to sign, and I was equally sure that the job of producing Susloparov in the war room for the signing would fall to me. It did not. To my astonishment, in hardly more than half an hour the signatories—including Susloparov —and their parties were assembled in the war room.

The signing itself was perfunctory, lasting scarcely longer than it took Jodl to scan the articles of surrender. When General Sevez, who was the last to sign, had finished, Jodl stood up and announced that he wished to say something. In a prepared statement he said that the German people were now at the mercy of the Allies; he said that the German people had achieved more and suffered more than any other people in the war. He finished by saying that he hoped the victors would treat the vanquished with generosity. The speech was left in the air. Nobody translated Jodl's words or even moved to inquire whether a translation was desired. Major Oxenius, Jodl's adjutant, who had been a schoolteacher in Wales before the war, did not move to do so; neither did General Strong; neither did George Reinhardt, the other American interpreter in German; and neither did I.

To me the statement seemed somehow improper, particularly the reference to the sufferings and achievements of the German people. These, as the instruments of the Nazis, had caused and inflicted untellable suffering upon several hundred million non-Germans. Why point out their own sufferings and even their achievements? I could not appreciate at that time that it was fitting for Jodl to do so, that he was speaking strictly as a soldier and a patriot and a German. At the same time I felt dismay that the statement, untranslated, would be lost to the record. My apprehension of course was unfounded: Jodl made the statement solely for the record and had obviously cleared it in writing with Smith. Smith's acceptance of the statement was another evidence of the distinction he drew between German soldiers and Nazi war criminals, a distinction the judges of Nuremberg did not allow when they lumped Jodl and Field Marshal Keitel with Seyss-Inquart.

After Jodl's statement we filed through several corridors to General Eisenhower's office. This was the only time I ever saw Eisenhower. Perhaps because of the drama and significance of the event I was subjected to an optical illusion: Eisenhower was seated at a table in an alcove whose floor was a step higher than that of the room. He appeared to be of gigantic stature. It was as if his physical presence had become symbolically commensurate with the size and power of the Western Alliance. The impression of massive size was increased when Eisenhower turned his head and shoulders to face Jodl, who stood forward on the lower floor like a truant schoolboy about to be disciplined. Through General Strong, Eisenhower asked Jodl if he had understood the terms of the surrender. Jodl answered "Ja" and the German party was dismissed.

The next morning I was relieved as duty officer in General Smith's office only to go on duty again as escort officer to the Germans. When I arrived in Jodl's quarters he took out his copy of the surrender document and asked me whose signature was at the bottom. On the German copy there was no title identifying General Sevez's minuscule signature. When I told Jodl whose it was, he asked, "Who is he?" When I explained, Jodl merely shook his head and, looking more miserable than ever, walked away. Even Von Friedeburg was somewhat subdued that morning, though still buoyant and chatty. I took this contrast between the two men away with me, for it was the last time I saw them together. I was all the more surprised a short time later to learn that Von Friedeburg had committed suicide by poisoning himself. Jodl had looked entirely capable of suicide: I should not have been surprised if he had shot himself at any point in the surrender proceedings. But it never occurred to me that Von Friedeburg's effusive cheeriness was a form of hysteria.

The mystery surrounding Susloparov's empowerment to sign the surrender was compounded later the same day when the Soviet government repudiated the Reims agreement and insisted that the surrender ceremony take place the next day in Russian-occupied Berlin. The Soviet High Command did not even bother to recall Susloparov. There was no need to. Susloparov flew to Berlin with the Allied signatories the next day and disappeared from the moment he stepped off the plane. Inquiries directed by SHAEF officers to the Russian military concerning him were met with apparent incomprehension.

I learned of the Soviet repudiation at five-thirty in the afternoon when General Smith asked me if I could provide him with a Russian translation of the articles of surrender in seventeen typewritten fair copies by eight the next morning. The problem was the typing. The only

Russian typewriters I knew of were in Paris at the Liaison School. The general gave me his car, his driver, and a block of foolscap.

We made excellent time until we entered the outskirts of Paris, where we encountered human roadblocks every foot of the way: the good people of Paris were already celebrating V-E Day. Every last street was full of jubilant, jostling, dancing crowds through which we could only thread our way at a speed of three or four miles an hour. I was obliged to get out of the car on a number of occasions and plead for thoroughfare, trying to explain (and feeling like a fool doing so) that, technically, the war was not yet over. It took two hours to drive from Reims to Paris and three hours to cross Paris. We arrived at the Liaison School billets around eleven at night. Of course we found them empty. Like everyone else, the officers and men of the school were out celebrating. It took me almost three hours of frantic scurrying from bar to bistro to boudoir to track down five of them. At this point another problem loomed. The five "droshky drivers" were all fluent in Russian, but two were drunk and none could type. In the next three hours, in a sequence of seek-it-and-sock-it pandemonium, we used up some two hundred sheets of typing paper but managed to produce the seventeen fair copies.

Thoroughly shaken by the ordeal, I stepped into General Smith's car at five in the morning, gave the driver instructions, and fell bluntly asleep. I had gone forty-six hours without sleep. I awoke at about seven to find that we were in Châlons-sur-Marne, the driver having missed the turn for Reims. We doubled back at top speed and arrived at SHAEF twenty minutes late but just in time to catch the general before he left by plane for Berlin. There was one last obstacle. I had lost my garrison cap in the melee in Paris. (A daughter of France had whisked it off my head and danced away waving it as a trophy.) I was immediately called to account by an RAF wing commander for being out of uniform. I sought to impress him with the importance of my mission so that he would stop nattering and let me pass: I announced that I was carrying seventeen fair copies of the articles of surrender in Russian. "You are?" he said. "Well, you're not a very 'fair copy' of an officer, are you?" Then he made way. My rejoinder was in Russian.

The Reims version of the articles of surrender served as a basis for negotiations with the Russians in Berlin. But the official Soviet account of World War II did not even mention Reims until 1963 when the six-volume *History of the Great Patriotic War of the Soviet Union* was published. Here it was called the "protocol of surrender" (as distinct from the "General Act of Surrender" signed the next day in Berlin) and characterized as an abortive piece of perfidy on the part of the Western Allies, with the implication that it was part of the attempt to conclude a separate peace so as to combine forces with the Germans and make common front against the Soviets. The Soviet fear of a common cause developing between the Western Allies and the Germans was based on the Communist theory of a natural affinity between capitalism and fascism. But this version contains one obvious flaw: it omits any mention of Susloparov. The reason for the omission is clear enough; if the Reims surrender was separate, perfidious, illegal, and unauthorized, then what was Susloparov doing there?

An answer was provided to this question twenty years later in the July–August 1965 issue of the Soviet publication *History of the USSR*, in an article signed by the chief marshal of artillery, Voronov. Susloparov's signature under the articles of surrender, writes Voronov, was a mistake. Voronov adds that Susloparov "did it on his own initiative and without authorization." He recalls receiving a phone call from Stalin who inquired if Susloparov had ever distinguished himself ("For what is he famous?"). Voronov apparently answered that Susloparov had never distinguished himself much. "Then how dare he sign a document of such tremendous international importance?" asked Stalin. Stalin then directed a number of "salty words" at Soviet artillery and concluded by demanding that Susloparov be "severely punished." Voronov says that he was deeply troubled by the whole business: "I did not know how or why Susloparov had turned up at Reims."

I do. Before moving to SHAEF toward the end of 1944 Susloparov had been the chief of the Soviet Military Mission to Allied Headquarters in Italy. His role at Reims has to be regarded against the background of another, previous surrender, that of the German armies in Italy. The refusal of the Western Allies to allow three Soviet officers to participate in the talks concerning the surrender with SS General Wolff in Berne, Switzerland, almost disrupted the Alliance, Stalin virtually accusing Roosevelt—to his face—of treachery. The Anglo-American desire to maintain maximum security in the discussions with the German command in Italy inevitably smacked of a separate peace with the Germans. After that both the Soviet High Command and the Western Allies insisted that a Soviet representative be present at any and all negotiations conducted by the Allies (hence Susloparov's otherwise unnecessary presence at the Nijmegen conference with Seyss-Inquart). When Eisenhower was taken to task by the Soviet High Command for proceeding with the Reims surrender without specific approval from Moscow, he pointed out that the Soviet protest had arrived too late and that he had kept the agreement not to make a separate truce because Susloparov, the Soviet representative at Supreme Headquarters, had been present at the ceremony and had signed the surrender document. Susloparov was caught squarely between the Anglo-American and the Soviet supreme commands. He not only had the duty, he also had the formal assignment to participate in all negotiations conducted by the Allies with belligerents.

But at the same time he did not have—and it is clear now that he could not hope to receive—the authority to sign "a document of such tremendous international importance." But neither could Susloparov hope to receive a refusal of such authority, much less orders not to sign the surrender document. Such a move would have made the Soviets look like separatists. What looked like a free choice for Susloparov was in reality a foregone conclusion.

For years I thought that Susloparov, awakened at two o'clock in the morning by the call of destiny, had signed the surrender document in a fit of magnificent whimsy. It is clear now that he never had the chance for such an extravagance. Susloparov was the historic fall guy caught between the two systems connected solely by common enmity during a global conflict.

The two surrender ceremonies and the two surrender documents were preordained by the fact that there were two fronts, two supreme headquarters, and two supreme commanders, neither one of whom was willing to take part in a ceremony on territory conquered and held by the other. This was all the more so in the sequence of events imposed by the Germans, who chose to sue for peace in the West rather than in the East. When the Russians sharply protested the Reims surrender and demanded the Act of Surrender take place in Berlin, Eisenhower informed them that he "was more than ready to come to Berlin the next day, in the place designated by Zhukov, to sign a formal ratification." In the event, he was not. He was prevailed upon by his advisers not to go to Berlin because "it would tend to distract from the importance of the Reims ceremony and might lower his own prestige," in the words of General Strong.

What was the importance of the Reims ceremony? The simple fact of the surrender. The advice Eisenhower received from his staff was sound. The war was over; the surrender had been negotiated and signed by all the chief belligerent powers. Having taken place the Reims ceremony also took precedence. Eisenhower could not then go along to Berlin and repeat the act as though nothing had happened or, rather, as though he had tried to pull a fast one, had been called to account by the Soviets, and required to repudiate it.

But in the Soviet Union World War II had always been referred to as the Great Patriotic War. For the Soviets the surrender of the Wehrmacht had to be made to *the* Soviet military representative (Zhukov) in the capital of *the* agressor nation (Berlin) conquered by *the* army (the Red Army). I cannot think what would have happened if the Western Allies, instead of the Russians, had taken Berlin. Probably the Soviet leadership would have gone stark raving mad. The fall of Berlin to the Western Allies would have ruined the whole show for the Soviets. It would certainly have robbed the war retroactively of the sense they had given it. For this reason the Soviets must have taken every conceivable precaution to prevent anything of the sort happening: almost certainly they made the Soviet Union's readiness to join the United Nations contingent upon the Red Army's taking Berlin. For this reason I have never believed that Eisenhower's famous or infamous decision not to press on to take Berlin was really his. Stalin must have extracted the strongest possible assurances from Roosevelt that the conquest of Berlin would be reserved to the Russians—as indeed it was in the London Agreement of September 1944.

In the end two documents were drawn up: the first, the "Act of Military Surrender"; the second, the "formal ratification" (with the curious title "Undertaking Given by Certain Emissaries to the Allied High Command"). The two documents were a brace designed to accommodate the duality of the situation, a device allowing each side of the alliance to put its own interpretation and its own titles on the two acts and their sequence. This the Soviets did by simply ignoring the Reims ceremony for eighteen years and then by referring to it as the "protocol of surrender."

I think it is necessary to go back to that night in May 1945 when we waited at SHAEF for the two empowerments, the German and the Russian. The German empowerment came because the Germans wanted to surrender to the West. The Russian empowerment never came because the Russians did not want the Germans to surrender to the West but to the East. The Central fact of World War II in Europe is that there were not only two fronts but two wars: the war between the Anglo-American Allies and the Germans in the West and the war between the Soviet Union and the Germans in the East. The connection between the Western Allies and the Soviet Union was not an alliance in any meaningful sense of the term but a liaison that was dictated solely by the exigencies of the situation.

This accounts for the Russian attitude to the Berlin problem. The Soviets would never have allowed the Western Allies to occupy the western sectors of Berlin if it had not been necessary to do so in exchange for Thuringia and Saxony-Anhalt which were essential to make the Soviet zone a viable politico-economic unit. This was their rightful share of the conquest of Germany by virtue of the sacrifices they had made even if they themselves had not conquered it. It was for the same reason that the Soviets never gave any thought to the access routes from the West to Berlin. Basically the Western Allied occupation of Berlin was regarded as a temporary measure, a provisional indulgence.

Thus it is inaccurate and misleading to say that the Germans lost the war: they lost two wars. In World War I the Germans lost the war on the western front but won the war on the eastern front. The loss of both wars on both fronts was a novum in German history. The loss of the two wars in itself sealed the division of Germany.

Here again what looked like a series of free choices—the Western Allies' decision to arm West Germany, the Soviet decision to arm East Germany, the Soviet decision to build a wall through the middle of Berlin and the Western Allies' decision to accept it, for examples—was in reality a progression of foregone conclusions stemming from the central fact of Germany's loss of two wars in 1945. When the two fronts of the opposing world systems, capitalism and communism, united only in their opposition to Germany, came together in the center of Germany in the historic "Meeting on the Elbe" the result was not a meeting but a confrontation: it had to be—by definition. When the two fronts met they automatically coalesced into the Iron Curtain, this by simple virtue of the fact that the opposing systems had succeeded in destroying the only thing that had forced their association in the first place.

The corollary of this fundamental situation is that Germany must side with either one or the other of the two systems in order to regain its unity. Until the construction of the Berlin Wall the Germans, in East as well as West Germany, actively or instinctively sided with the Western Allies. After the Wall many Germans began the slow, tortuous process of transferring their effective allegiance from the Western Allies to the Soviets. This development was inevitable in the sense that it is not in the nature of Western culture to lend itself to ideological trench warfare: the capitalist system is too diffuse to muster the resoluteness necessary to maintain a formal, continuing enmity without the clear-cut prospect of a solution—military or otherwise. It is far more feasible to make front against an enemy by siding with the singleminded Soviet system, a system that specializes in and thrives on ideological warfare.

I remember coming off the LST boat onto Omaha Beach in Normandy on D-day-plus-eight to the accompaniment on the public address system of Nelson Eddy's singing "For I've Known One Night of Love." The trouble was I hadn't. But when we stopped fighting in May 1945, it seemed to me that it behooved us to start loving. In that splendid spring of 1945 Germany lay in ruins. It was the quiet after the storm.

In the long, clear evenings in Frankfurt, Goethe's hometown (to which SHAEF had moved at the end of May), I was reminded time and again of the work of another poet, Browning. The poem "Love among the Ruins" seemed to offer a prescription for convalescence: "Where the quiet end of evening smiles . . . Miles on miles," and ending with the simple "Love is best." I thought there ought to be a lot of loving, and among the ruins, which were not only symbols but proof that everything else was gone anyway, blown up, destroyed—shot to hell. I thought that after so much killing and dying there ought to be an awful lot of living, that people ought to be able to do what they liked—what they hadn't been able to do for so many years. I did not think that there ought to be much work done unless somebody really wanted to work. In France, in Belgium, in Holland, in all the liberated countries, there was jubilation and exhilaration. After the long night all of a sudden came the dawn— a new life opened up. It was a beginning. In Germany it was the end, the "quiet end of evening" after a terrible, all-destroying storm. It was the peace that comes with utter exhaustion—"all passion spent." But the night was coming.

LIEUTENANT FRED LENHARDT, WHOSE IMPERFECT KNOWLEDGE of English idiom alone betrayed him as an immigrant— instead of "run of the mill" he would invariably say "run *in* the mill"—asked me one weekend whether I could take him to nearby Mainz to visit someone (as a liaison officer I was assigned a jeep). We threaded our way among the colossal debris of Mainz's inner city—spring weeds were beginning to grow through the ruins—to a building whose huge granite blocks had been jumbled over the surface of the earth like a throw of dice. On one of these blocks written in chalk was the legend "Family Braun bombed out, moved to such and such an address," "Family Fuhrmann bombed out, moved to . . . , etc." We proceeded to the address given only to find another forwarding address chalked on a similar pile of rubble. The family Lenhardt was looking for had been bombed out three times; we finally found them far out of town, living in the upstairs of a farmhouse among the vineyards near the Rhine. When Lenhardt knocked on the door an old lady answered. When she took in Lenhardt's physiognomy she unceremoniously fainted. Lenhardt caught her and broke her fall. It was his mother. A good while later, after they had exchanged endearments and gossip, the mother turned to her son and said: "How wonderful that you are an officer! Now you can do something for your homeland." "No, mother," said Lenhardt, "*my* homeland is over there." And he pointed west.

SHAEF Frankfurt was housed, fittingly enough, in the I. G. Farben building. Around the spacious grounds of the I. G. Farben complex (complete with casino) a triple barrier of barbed wire was strung. We were prisoners: the unoriented victors were surrounded by the apathetic vanquished. And then there was the nonfraternization rule, always more honored in the breach than in the observance. The behavior of the enlisted men under the rule was best summed up by a soldier's soldier, George S. Patton, when he advised his troops, "Don't talk to 'em—just fuck 'em!" But for officers and ranking noncoms appearances had to be upheld at least to some extent. So there was a great deal of skulking to and fro.

One afternoon my sergeant, an enterprising Portuguese-American, burst into our section shouting, "Lieutenant, I've just discovered 6,000 Polish girls!" These were former "East workers" who had been liberated from German families or factories, had been rounded up in what later became known as a Displaced Persons (DP) Camp, and were awaiting repatriation. These girls, being non-Germans, were on limits. The exodus from SHAEF to the Polish girls' camp precipitated by my sergeant's announcement provided me with the pleasant but innocent acquaintanceship of a Polish damsel from Lodz-Wodz, as she called it. She had been away from home so long that she could no longer make an effective choice between the German and the Polish pronunciation of the name of her hometown.

Two months before when I first arrived in Le Vésinet I wangled a week's leave, went straight to Namur, and laid siege to the baronne's other granddaughter. I found her among the roses in the château's garden and asked her if she would like to go for a walk. We walked up the hill behind the château. This was a sort of forehill or first step to the much larger hill whose top accommodated the citadel of Namur. For some reason I was in a hurry to get to the top. Pierrette wasn't. About halfway she stopped and turned and said: "Look at the Meuse—isn't it beautiful!" I said yes, yes, and hurried her on. When we finally got to the top I tried to kiss her. To my astonishment she repulsed me violently. So we went right back down the hill again, Pierrette leading this time: she was very angry. Halfway down the hill—at exactly the same spot where we had stopped on the way up—I tried to draw her up by pointing to the river. "Isn't it beautiful!" I said.

After that it was difficult. It took me two days to get my arm around her when we walked. I wanted to kiss her very much but she wouldn't have it. Finally, on my last night, I managed to kiss her forehead just at the hairline. More than that I could not achieve. When I broke down and actually asked her to let me kiss her she refused point blank. I gave up in dejection and went to my room. I hadn't been in the room five minutes when the door opened and Pierrette came in. She stood with her back against the writing desk and looked at the floor. Then she said, slowly and quietly: "Vous voyez, Bailey—on a l'habitude de s'embrasser sans s'aimer. Un baiser ne signifie rien. C'est pour ça . . . je ne veux pas que vous m'embrassiez parce que je vous aime." And then she translated into English word for word what she had just said in French. I don't know why. We had never spoken anything but French with one another. "You see, people kiss without loving one the other. A kiss means nothing. That is why I not want you to kiss me . . . because I love you." Then without another word she turned and walked out. I left early the next morning.

Pierrette had a brother who had been carted off to Germany some two years before. Her family had his address and had corresponded with him regularly; he had been assigned to work on a stud farm, an estate called Rosenhof north of Jena in middle Germany. The family was naturally concerned because communications with Germany had been interrupted ever since the Western Allies had liberated Belgium in August 1944. I undertook to find the brother. Equipped with his address, I drove up the autobahn at the end of May and turned north at Jena.

At that time the whole of this area, as far east as Leipzig and beyond, was occupied by the American army. There were no roadblocks or checkpoints to impede my progress and I had no trouble finding the place. I drove into the courtyard at high speed, skidded to a halt in a geyser of loose gravel, jumped out of the jeep with my hand on the holster of my Colt .45, and shouted: "Where is the baron?" A large, blond, rather florid man of about fifty stepped into the courtyard and said quietly that the baron had left for home the week before. I asked to be shown the baron's quarters. He had had a room to himself—a pleasant and a large one on the second floor of the main house. Germans are as caste-conscious as any people in Europe and more so than most.

During my impromptu tour of the farm I noticed a very pretty white-blond dairymaid who seemed to be lurking within earshot. "She misses the baron," said the estate owner. I convinced myself within a few minutes that the durance of the baron had not been vile.

The estate owner was tortured by the rumor that the Americans were about to vacate the whole area to make way for the Russians who would be the permanent occupying force. I had heard the rumor before, but I had never seen or heard anything at SHAEF concerning the exact delineation of the zones of occupation. I assumed that American and British troops had gone as far east as prearranged at Yalta (as they had in Czechoslovakia), no further and no less far. So I sought to rally his spirits as best I could. "If the Russians come here," he said, "it will be a catastrophe."

On my way back I stopped in Weimar, the national shrine of German culture by virtue of Goethe's fifty years of residence there at the court of Duke Karl August of Sachsen-Weimar. I had just inspected

Goethe's town house and was about to visit his country estate when an American lieutenant accosted me. "If you are interested in German monuments," he said, "then you really ought to see the one about four miles up the road here." Which was that? "Buchenwald," said the lieutenant. I had heard of Buchenwald, of course, but I was thunderstruck to learn that it was practically on the outskirts of Weimar—of Weimar! And yet there it was, situated on a plateau just north of Weimar at the edge of a beech forest ("Buchenwald").

The camp had been liberated by the American army perhaps a week or ten days before my arrival. The American unit in charge of the camp had left things pretty much as the combat troops had found them. The Americans had taken to forcing the Germans from Weimar and the surrounding countryside to tour the camp and witness the handiwork of the Third Reich. One of these "conducted tours" passed through the camp while I was there. As the group came into view of the huge open mass grave, several of the women fainted and two or three of the younger women vomited with convulsions of horror at the sight. In the grave were perhaps two thousand bodies thrown in every which way and piled upon one another as they fell in various antic poses. The open grave was truly apocalyptic, the maw of the inferno.

For the rest, the surprising thing about the camp was the lack of horror. Presumably awaiting burial or some other disposal, there were several thousand naked cadavers stacked neatly in rows like cords of wood. But the cadavers were so emaciated that they did not look human: they were no more than skin-covered skeletons—life-sized puppets discarded by the puppeteer, their guide-wires cut away. The dead in Buchenwald had been systematically reduced by hunger to the point where they looked like what they in fact were, the discards, the rejects of National Socialist society.

I found the sight too grotesque to be horrible or touching—indeed, too grotesque for comprehension. The victims had been dehumanized. Actually they had all been murdered long before. These puppets stacked high in neat rows were the end result of a slow, harrowing process. The victims had been gradually stripped of every shred of human dignity and, almost, of human semblance. The only part of the cadavers that still looked human were the feet. These, rather than emaciated, were swollen. The skin-covered skeletons we saw were hardly more than tokens of the murderous deed.

The most striking aspect of Buchenwald was its matter-of-factness. The "business (of murder) as usual" atmosphere was what made the totality of the impression incomprehensible. There was, for example, the building in the back of the guards' camp called the "horse stables," in reality a slaughterhouse. A truck drove up to the front door and unloaded the "death-candidates" who entered the large windowless front room where they undressed and placed their valuables on a table. At the opposite end of the building was the so-called doctors' room which opened to the left into the actual abattoir. This was complete with a bullet-absorptive wall (covered by a curtain), a sluice to run off the blood (this was done, in the best Chicago slaughterhouse style, with a water-hose operated by an SS man stationed behind a wooden wall on the far left). In the center of the rear of the building was the space for the stacking of the corpses; this opened directly to the outside where a truck was waiting. On either side of the stacking area were rooms containing sawdust and straw. The building also contained a rest room and a dining room for the execution squads.

It was not mere happenstance, I learned, that Buchenwald came into being hardly more than four miles from Weimar. In the mid-1930s the führer and the reichskanzler frequented the theatre in Weimar. Spending as much time as he did in Weimar, Hitler conceived the idea of establishing a camp for his elite bodyguard, the SS, nearby. Himmler carnifex carried out his führer's wishes by using the area provided by the city council not for a regular SS camp but for a unit of his newly created "Death's Head Formations" instead. These were the concentration camp guards: the prisoners followed the guards and Buchenwald was the result.

But there was another connection. The proximity of Buchenwald with Weimar was the ultimate blasphemy to culture, obscenity on the altar, the Holy Grail brimfull with blood and shit. But it was also entirely fitting. The proximity epitomized the system that produced it. The SS was the elite of the Nazi elite. But it was a distorted elite, based on a confusion of basic concepts. The distortion was phantasmagorical. In an almost casual way—he was speaking of eighteenth-century French literature—Goethe put his finger on this phenomenon. "Refinement," he said, "is really rejective." Whatever is too exclusive deforms as it forms. It is latently denunciatory, a process of discarding that produces the great discard, the corpse, as its end result.

As a documents expert I had come across a mass of Nazi "literature." Not long before arriving in Buchenwald I had read a classic Nazi anti-Semitic novel, *Sins Against the Blood*, by Artur Dinter. In the novel a Jewish financier, who had been awarded the title councilor of commerce by a grateful government, dies suddenly in the arms of three blond maidens in a love nest he had set up and maintained, along with five other such establishments in as many cities: Munich, Breslau, Dresden, Hamburg, and Frankfurt. Since the young concubines did not know who the financier was (he had taken great pains to keep his identity secret) they were obliged to inform the police of his death.

As a result a devilish plot was exposed. For the Jewish financier specialized in seducing and getting with child young, blond virgins. At the time of his death the councilor of commerce had fathered well over a hundred half-breed bastards (most of them boys who looked exactly like their father). He provided all the mothers with pensions to enable them to bring up their children. But from the time of their accouchement he never saw his victims again, going on to virgin fields and pastures new. His operating principle (and the author's leitmotiv as made explicit in another episode) was allegedly based on broad experience in animal breeding: namely, that one impure pregnancy rendered a thoroughbred Aryan woman forever unfit to bear racially pure offspring regardless of the purity of the subsequent partner. The woman remained forever defiled and could only produce children who were the expression of that defilement. This was the financier-villain's life work: the programmatic pollution of the German race.

I was also reminded of a curious interview I had had back at the stud farm, Rosenhof. I had met a German prince of the blood or "hereditary prince," the term that was included in his complicated title. I also gathered that the prince was of the Uradel ("ancient aristocracy"), that is, his family's rank and title predated the thirteenth century. The prince gave every appearance of having been genetically refined to the point of reversion. He seemed to me to be a finely featured, beautifully groomed animal, but an animal nevertheless, an animal that could talk. To be sure he could not talk much: like the talking dog in the Ilf and Petrov story (whose trainer has to keep reminding the audience that the talking dog is still, after all, only a dog) he commanded but a few words. The prince looked like his thoroughbred horses, like a Houyhnhnm, so noble, so beautiful an animal, and so perfectly trained, that one expected him to be able to talk—not much but a little.

When I returned to Namur weeks later, the news that I had appeared in Rosenhof had preceded me (either the estate owner or the milkmaid had written the brother about it). The brother confirmed that his two years in Rosenhof had been as pleasant as they possibly could have been under the circumstances. A light came into his eyes when I

[71]

mentioned the milkmaid. As for me and the light in *my* eyes, it wasn't long before Pierrette was in my arms and when I kissed her—this time full on the mouth—I fairly exploded with exultation. "La citadelle est prise!" I almost shouted. The citadel of Namur, the extensive outworks of which figure so largely in the narrations of Uncle Toby in *Tristram Shandy*, had become for both of us a kind of symbol of Pierrette's resistance.

But the citadel had not been taken. The first thing Pierrette did after we kissed was to tell me that everything between us was impossible. At first I thought this was histrionics, putting on airs. But I soon realized that she was utterly serious: "C'est inutile," she said. It was no use: we could never marry. But she refused to tell me why. She said she couldn't tell me. She did say that it wasn't my fault, that there was nothing I could do about it. Try as I might, I could not get it out of her. I hectored, I cajoled, I made indirect approaches to the subject. I even tried some of the interrogation techniques I had learned at Camp Ritchie. Finally I began to think that perhaps it had something to do with her. I thought there might have been insanity in the family (too much inbreeding in the Walloon aristocracy). I even thought of congenital syphilis (a result of my overindoctrination on venereal disease in the American army but also because she had once—in desperate mummery in lieu of explanation— pointed to the veins in her arms). But both of these suppositions were ruled out: her sisters were normal enough and the old baronne had lectured me on the family history for hours on end. My speculations brought me nowhere.

Our last night together Pierrette and I spent in the attic of the château. It was innocent but all the more intense because we understood this to be our final leavetaking—the last good-bye. She talked about her family and about me, how I would go back to America and choose a city or an area of the country to live in. She talked about her past and my future, like a mother taking leave of her son. She kept saying, "You will work hard and be a good man."

One night is not a very long time for two lovers to compose themselves for an eternal separation. I suppose it takes a lifetime of lovemaking to do it properly. I was horrified at the idea that the eternal separation (an how much more solemn the words sounded in French—la separation éternelle!) was to begin with a lifetime. Till life do us part: a pseudo-suicide pact as a scheme for living? I told her about a buddy of mine who was killed in Normandy and whose last words were, "What about the great, rich years ahead?" With any luck the two of us could reckon with another fifty years of life. Why anticipate by fifty years or fifty minutes a separation that was bound to come anyway? Lovers conspired to stay together or plotted to reunite. It took me all night to make my plea but she was not to be moved.

The next morning just one hour before I left I met Pierrette's elder sister in the garden. She asked why I seemed so dejected and I told her. "You mean," she said, "that Pierrette won't tell you why she can't marry you?" I told her that was what I meant. "Well," she said, "if Pierrette won't tell you, *I'll* tell you." I had the sense of an all-important caesura, a crucial pause, a turning point: I had the sense that this was a crux of my life and of life in general. "It is because you are a Jew." I looked at the sister for some while without comprehension. Then came a tidal wave of incredulity. I finally asked what made them think me a Jew. "That was easy," answered the sister; "you remember one Sunday a few weeks ago when we had some relatives over for tea and we talked about Jews and someone asked you what you thought of them—and you said, 'They are a very brave people.' Then we knew that you were a Jew. One of our cousins told Pierrette: 'Il est juif, ton boy!' "

I was relieved and amused at this sudden unveiling of the dark, terrible secret: that I, the shabbas goy, should have been taken for a Jew struck me as supremely funny. I told the sister that if Pierrette had not raised objections on such flimsy circumstantial evidence I could have proved my non-Jewishness to her in the normal course of events. I informed Pierrette in much the same vein, and the entire problem was dissolved in laughter. We parted on the understanding that I was to write and she was to wait.

But the more I pondered the whole story after my departure the more unpleasant it became. I began to regret that I had said I was not a Jew; it seemed to me that I had sonehow acted dishonorably. The only personal document I carried with me was Benno's certificate appointing me an honorary Jew. I had met the baronial family only because Maurice Rose, the son of the rabbi of Denver, Colorado, and the commander of a tank division of the American army, had liberated Namur and selected the château as his command post. Rose, the Happy Warrior, was dead, killed in action in Germany, on the last day of March fighting for what? There was never any question about what Rose was fighting for. I had seen what Rose was fighting for in the apocalyptic prosiness of Buchenwald.

The baronial family had marveled at Rose, le beau général. I doubt very much that the family even knew Rose's name, let alone that he was a Jew. At that fatal Sunday tea in Namur I had not enlarged upon my opinion that the Jews were a brave people. And if I had I should almost certainly not have mentioned Rose. There were plenty of other examples of Jewish bravery I had witnessed in the German-Jewish legion. That was just it. I felt that I had let the side down.

The baronial family, like all the European aristocrats I have ever met, were given to poking fun at or simply deploring the petty-bourgeois, philistine mentality. In German the Spiessbürger—literally the "pike-(bearing) citizen," the foot-slogger of the local militia—is the bane and also the all-important foil of the aristocracy's existence: in Austria it is the strongest term of opprobrium extant. The sisters baronial were free with the term "esprit d'étroit" (narrowness of spirit or narrowmindedness) as the chronic moral epidemic of the Belgians, themselves by implication excluded. I had spent more than enough time in New York to know that anti-Semitism was by no means restricted to the Germans. But I was, as I gradually discovered, shocked to find it at that time, in that place, anchored in the psychic makeup of otherwise seemingly delightful people.

My relationship with Pierrette was ruined by the episode. I could not bring myself to write, even in answer to her letters, although here, too, I felt I was wrong in not at least trying to set forth the problem to her. But, in the phrase of Laurence Sterne, "I could not write this self-same letter." I suspected, as I still do, that I was at last merely using the moral consideration as a pretext to shuffle off a liaison in which I was no longer very much interested, that Namur and its citadel were at base hardly more to me than Wilwerdingen.

But the suspicion was, and remains, perfunctory. The sense of guilt remains. If Rose hadn't just been killed, if six million other Jews hadn't just been killed, if many more millions of non-Jews hadn't just been killed it would have been different. A great many people who are anything but murderers, who are decent, upstanding citizens in other countries and in other, "normal" times, are more or less anti-Semitic. Is philo-Semitism or the lack of anti-Semitism the hallmark of moral sanity? It surely is not the hallmark of what passes for taste in the Anglo-Saxon world. The problem of anti-Semitism is, of course, complicated enormously by the attitude of the Jews toward themselves.

I might have taken it upon myself to lead Pierrette up out of the nether regions of blind prejudice. But I have always found it difficult to distinguish between moral position and moral posturing. Moreover, I was new to old Europe and aware only that there were hidden forces at work, age-old feuds still to be fought out or reconciled, problems so encrusted with tradtion that the Europeans themselves did not clearly perceive them. Andy Hardy meets Beowulf: how could I presume to pose as moral preceptor (a role I have never liked anyway) at that time in that place? I was thrown off course permanently by the discovery some time later that the "hereditary prince" I had met in Rosenhof, the aristocrat of ancient lineage who looked and acted like a thoroughbred horse, was in fact the Erbprinz Josias zu Waldeck-Pyrmont, obergruppenführer (lieutenant general) of the SS and commanding officer of the SS Administrative District Fulda-Werra. As the higher SS and police authority of Military District IX Weimar, the "hereditary prince" was the de jure and de facto head of Buchenwald. In addition to these duties the prince dedicated himself to the "Office for the Breeding of Thoroughbred Horses and Race Horses."

I could not help but remember the desperate mummery of Pierrette's pointing to the veins in her arms in explanation of why we could not marry. She had said it was not my fault. It was not her fault either. But there it was. I couldn't see any essential difference between Dinter's Nazi dread of racial pollution based on experience in animal breeding, and the Belgian baronial fear of having a Jewish sprig grafted onto the family tree. The difference is one of degree. Admittedly the degree is great, but what continued to gravel me was the idea, common to both positions, of reducing the human race to the norms of animal husbandry. In the end I thought it might be a good idea to march the baronial family (and how many others like them?) through Buchenwald on a tour of inspection such as we had forced the Germans from the surrounding countryside to undertake.

To call the whole of Germany during the twelve years of the Third Reich a vast concentration camp, as one is constantly tempted to do, is begging the question. But there is one sense in which the comparison holds true. The corruption—both conscious and unconscious—was so widespread and so virulent that it infected the mores of the people much as the camps corrupted the psyches and mortified the flesh of the inmates.

Certainly the domain of German creative art was entirely destroyed. During the war a good many people, Germans and non-Germans alike, expected to be presented with the fruits of the German "literary underground"—manuscripts of literary value, it was thought, would be brought to light from their hiding places. But there were no such manuscripts, no secret gardens had flourished the while: there had been no

[75]

"literary underground." Indeed, for almost fifteen years (Günter Grass's *The Tin Drum* appeared in 1959) the only literary works of note produced by writers of German were the plays and stories of Friedrich Dürrenmatt and Max Frisch, both of them Swiss.

Expectations of achievements in other artistic pursuits during the war, say in music or painting, were likewise unfounded: there was nothing. After the war the Germans were exhausted, disillusioned, and numb from the bludgeonings of both their masters and their enemies. They were in mass psychological shock from which they are only now beginning to recover. Germany's war generation became Germany's postwar generation of the broken backs—the poor, disoriented citizen-convict, the moral cripple who cringed before the prospect of his son's inevitable question: "Papa, what did you do during the war?"

Because the great majority of Germans either actively or passively supported the Nazi regime, the Western Allies propagated the theory of "collective guilt": each German was to be held generally responsible for the crimes committed under the Nazi regime in the name of the German people. "The term 'collective guilt,' " wrote Theodor Heuss, the first president of the West German Federal Republic, "and what stands behind it, is . . . a crass simplification; it is actually a reversal of the way in which the Nazis were accustomed to regard the Jews: that the fact that one was a Jew supposedly carried with it the phenomenon of guilt. But something like collective shame grew out of this (the Nazi) time and has remained. The worst thing that Hitler did to us is surely this, that he forced us into a sense of shame for bearing, in common with him and his minions, the name 'German.' "

The central fact of the Nazi period for the Germans is that the German people largely discredited itself *to* itself. This was far worse, far more crippling to any form of political or cultural activity than the quarter-century and more of pariahdom that followed the war. Because of this paralysis of the will, inertia prevailed in every field of national life except economics, a pursuit left open to the Germans and taken up by them out of sheer necessity.

It was inevitable that this huge moral debt would be exploited—individually and collectively—by outsiders posing as creditors. The assumption of the right to pass judgment is more harmful to those in a position to assume the right. This applies nationally as well as personally. What happened to Germany after the war was an extension of what happened to the German we court-martialled in Thionville when we brought in our own moral, judicial, and political criteria and applied them rigorously—and wrongly. All parties suffered and still suffer from the occupation of Germany, but the most terrible aspect of the whole terrible mess is the fact that German guilt served to confirm Germany's conquerors and neighbors in the practice of those crimes of which the Germans stood convicted. It was as if all non-Germans had achieved expiation in advance by proxy.

When I arrived in Czechoslovakia in midsummer 1945 (having come directly from my last and final stopover in Namur) the Czechs and Moravians, in a prolonged fit of ethnocentric vindictiveness, were in the process of deporting the entire Sudeten-German population, most of whose families had lived in the area for at least three hundred and fifty years—at twelve hours notice. The number of deportees numbered almost three million. Each of them was allowed to take with him as much of his belongings as he could carry. I was astonished at the number of lares and penates among the luggage, particularly hunting trophies, mounted stag antlers and wild goat horns. The Czechs showed no consideration whatever to the women and children. One of the chief organizers of this merciless business was a man with the common Czech name of Svoboda (freedom). Three years later, shortly after the Communist coup in Czechoslovakia, I met the same Svoboda in a Bavarian camp for Czech refugees.

During this time one of our liaison group, Lieutenant William Sloane Coffin, Jr., acted as escort officer to Andrei Vishinsky, chief prosecutor of the Soviet Union, on his trip from Prague to the War Crimes Trials at Nuremberg. As they passed by one of the scenes of mass deportation in which Czechs were herding Germans into boxcars much as Germans had herded Jews and other "Untermenschen" ("subhumans") into boxcars in their time, Coffin asked Vishinsky what he thought of the operation. "Well," said Vishinsky, "the Czechs are a small people." Coffin was aware of some of the irony, at least, of asking the chief prosecutor of the Soviet Union and particularly Vishinsky, of all people, for his opinion of a mass deportation action.

"The mechanism of destruction of West European humanity," wrote Vadim Rosanov, who was a prophet, "will consist in its indifference to injustice." The simple fact of the guilt-shame of the Germans rendered them—as a people, as a national entity—incapable of indignation: he who has lost his dignity cannot become indignant; it is not in him. There is no basis for the registry of outrage or even affront. The loss of German dignity which, in its operative sense, is the capacity for indignation, was an untellable loss to the civilized world. More grievous still was the collateral loss of shame by the victors in dealing with the German vanquished, as demonstrated in this instance by the Czechs. The loss of dignity of the vanquished culprit (only the *vanquished* culprit, be it noted) is commensurate with the loss of shame by the victors in their dealings with the vanquished.

For me the most disgusting and dismaying result of World War II and its aftermath is this: that the exposure and universal condemnation of the moral insanity of the Nazis ministered to the reinforcement of the moral insanity of the Communists, particularly the Communist party of the Soviet Union. The Germans were fair game in the eyes of the world and, far more important, in their own eyes. Surely the most deadly sin of the Germans, in their own eyes as in the eyes of the world, was their largely successful attempt to exterminate the Jews of Europe. During the Nuremberg War Crimes Trials, the case against the Germans for their treatment of the Jews was made on all sides. But it is thus all the more extraordinary that on the heels of this evidence the Soviet Union should have mounted and maintained to this day a campaign both at home and abroad against the Jews—witness the trial of the doctors in Moscow, the Rajk show-trial complex in Hungary, and the Slansky show-trial complex immediately following in Czechoslovakia by way of a beginning. The steadily increasing Soviet communist preoccupation with the Jews on grounds largely identical with those of the Nazi preoccupation (cosmopolitanism, greed for gold) for me posed the question whether there is not an underlying general identity of the two movements.

There were other evidences of connections not so subterranean. I traveled frequently to a small town east of Prague. This was Milovice, the headquarters of the Russian army occupying Czechoslovakia. Milovice had the necessary buildings, motor parks, and other facilities for an army headquarters. It had until shortly before our arrival served as a German army headquarters. (It now serves again as the headquarters of a Russian army occupying Czechoslovakia.) In Milovice I walked into a Soviet noncommissioned officers' barracks. There were some thirty beds in the room. Over each bed hung a framed picture of Stalin. The thirty pictures were identical. I walked out of the barracks a good deal faster than I had walked in.

Not long after we arrived in Czechoslovakia my sergeant liberated a Tatra, a Czech touring car with an eight-cylinder air-cooled engine in the rear, from an SS standartenführer (colonel)—or so my sergeant said. This, painted over in olive drab, became my official (and unofficial) liaison car. One advantage, among others, of the Tatra was that the baggage space behind the rear seat would accommodate eight five-gallon Jerry cans; these with a full tank in addition provided enough gas for a thousand miles of "Tatraing," as the Czechs called it. There was also time enough for "Tatraing": we were not kept so very busy. The Russians, so far as liaison with the Americans was concerned, pursued a policy of live and let live.

This meant that Prague was open to us, the liaison officers; Prague, "zlata Praha" (golden Prague) as the Czechs call it, "die goldene Stadt" (the golden city) to the Germans. Almost a third of the Czech lands, Bohemia and Moravia, were inhabited by Germans from time immemorial. Prague of the hundred towers had a double nature: it was a German as well as a Czech outpost. The seat of the first German university, founded by Kaiser Karl IV in 1348, Prague was a great German cultural center as well as the captital of the Czech nation. The German colony in Prague was thirty-five thousand strong on the eve of World War I. Everybody in Prague spoke German, the official language of the empire, either as a second language or with native fluency. Prager Deutsch, Prague German, is regarded to this day as the finest specimen of the spoken language.

The Czech lands, Bohemia and Moravia, had been infiltrated racially and culturally as had the local Jewish minority: the native language of Franz Kafka was German. The Czechs are Germanized Slavs. In front of the statue of King Wenceslas in the center of Prague there are twenty-six stone pilings sunk deep into the ground to commemorate the noblemen executed by the Habsburgs after the catastrophic battle of White Mountain in the Thirty Years War, which ranks as the great national disaster of the Czechs. Sixteen of those noblemen were German. Prague was the point of pause and consolidation of both the German and the Czech cultures.

The friction of this tangency, in which the two peoples alternated in the position of minority, generated excellence as well as fanaticism on both sides. *The Good Soldier Schweik* is a masterpiece in both the Czech original and the German translation. Schweik is unthinkable without the assimilation as well as the confrontation of Czech and German forces. So is the poet Rainer Maria Rilke on the German side. And so is Arthur von Seyss-Inquart. The latter-day German minority position in Bohemia and Moravia and environs generated the fanaticism that was the spiritual cradle of Nazism. The history of Europe is the story of European minorities. The most unerring prophet of the European apocalypse, Kafka, was a member of a minority (Jewish) within a minority (German) within a minority (Czech) of the Austro-Hungarian Empire. His situation made for triple exposure rather than threefold isolation. When I arrived in Prague, I was carrying a copy of Kafka's *The Trial.* I set myself to read the novel because I enjoy reading the works of an author on his home ground.

A more compelling reason to read *The Trial* was the approach of the greatest trial in human history at Nuremberg. Kafka's novel begins with the beginning of a trial—in a double sense: "Someone must have slandered Josef K because without his having done anything bad, he was arrested one morning." (As so many people were in Hitler's Germany and continued to be in Stalin's Russia.) It ends when sentence is passed (actually sentence is never passed: Josef K is told that the trial will gradually merge into a sentence) and Josef K is executed in a fashion reminiscent of the German Vehmic murders. The knife is plunged into his heart and turned twice. He dies, in his own last words, "like a dog." On the way to the execution ground (a vacant lot in the outskirts of Prague) he and his two escort-executioners are almost stopped by a suspicious policeman. Almost. But there is no justice—not really—and they are allowed to pass unquestioned. Kafka is the arch-practitioner of the ethic of lucidity as handed down from Plato and tempered by Immanuel Kant. His working thesis was that mankind is too weak to perceive the true world steadily. Truth can be caught only by glimpses. "It peeks through the fissures of so-called reality," as Kafka's friend and biographer, Max Brod, put it.

The words lucidity and hallucination come from the same root. They are the opposite sides of the same semantic coin, the "hal" of hallucination embodying the alpha privitive or negation of the root meaning. A hallucination is the dark interval of a sane man as opposed to the lucid interval of a madman. But in a world of shifting criteria, opposing value systems, and mutually exclusive moral codes, which is which? Like his home country Kafka was in a border situation. He moves along the seam, the line that at once divides and connects the real and the unreal, the dark and the light, the East and the West, the Slav and the German, the individual and the collective. His aesthetic habitat is the no man's land between the warring factions that make up the duality of the human condition. This is the region of contingent truth, of truth dependent on the extent and kind of knowledge, where for lack of a point of reference, a doubt expressed or a reservation implied can blow up a whole section of the landscape, where a direct question can cause an earthquake that invalidates an entire traditional category of experience.

This was the fabric of Kafka's apocalyptic vision of the future. "When Gregor Samsa awoke one morning from uneasy dreams he found himself metamorphosed into a giant cockroach." The metamorphosis is the story of the affliction of a member of a small family with a hideous and mortal disease. Samsa spends months trying to adjust to his deteriorating condition and is finally swept out with the rubbish by the maid. He ends up in the ash can like an emaciated concentration camp inmate.

The heroes of *The Trial* and *Metamorphosis* (as of so many other Kafka stories) awake into a nightmare—as Europe did in 1933. It is a nightmare created by the gradual, inexorable extension of the discretionary powers of the state. Kafka comments in his letters that his stories "do not serve the state" in any conceivable way. For thirty years of his life Kafka lived in the absolutist Habsburgian monarchy, one of the two German states in which insulting an official (Beamtenbeleidigung) was —and in their various successor states still is—a serious offence. Kafka caught the system at the historical moment of transition from late feudal collectivism of the absolute monarchy to the neo-feudal collectivism of the totalitarian state. The breathing space was short: it lasted less than a generation in Europe and, during the Kerensky government, less than six months in Russia.

We came at another moment of transition. We came to dance on the extinct volcano, the volcano we Russians and Americans had worked to extinguish, not together but each working his side of the Magic Mountain. The dance was short. We danced—four or five of us, American liaison officers with as many Czech girls, perhaps ten in all—alone in the huge White Ballroom of the Imperial Palace in Prague, the Hradicany, in celebration on V-J Day. The dance was short. The two Czech girls I danced with were dead within five years: the one, Ludmilla Lobkowicz, threw herself under a train in the Prague main railway station à la Anna Karenina; the other, Dušana Pitteova, died as a result of a nervous breakdown in London in the late fall of 1948—after the Communist putsch in Czechoslovakia and just after the British Home Office had refused to extend her residence permit.

It was indeed the briefest of intermissions. In fact the new war began before the old one had ended; for those who could read the omens this was clear from the nature and manner of the liberation of Prague. According to the terms of the Yalta Conference, the liberation of Prague was to be reserved to the Russians. For this reason the American troops, who were on the scene long before the Russians, pulled up just beyond the town of Rokycany some thirty-five miles short of Prague. But the fall of military positions does not depend on schedules. Prague was ready for the taking by mid-April. The only armed force there to take it from the hopeless motley of SS and German army troops was the renegade Russian army, the so-called Russian Army of Liberation of General Alexander Vlassov. The RAL had been put together by the Germans from Russian defectors and prisoners of war (like Vlassov himself who had been captured during the battle of Moscow in 1941–1942) to provide a rallying point for anti-communist Russians and the various national minorities of the Soviet Union. Its military purpose, ostensibly, was to take the field against the Soviet army.

Actually the RAL was involved in only very few minor skirmishes against Soviet troops. Its one major action was its last, the defeat of the Nazi German defenders of Prague and the liberation of that city. It made for a bewildering situation. The Czechs did not know how to conduct themselves vis-à-vis a Russian armed force which was anti-Soviet. They did nothing but accept the surrender achieved by the Vlassovites. The fate of the Vlassovite army proper was reserved for the aftermath of the war. But the Vlassovite army was merely the articulate expression of the general disaffection within the Soviet Union. It was an antibody of the Soviet system.

The phenomenon of such resistance did not cease with the end of the war. On the contrary. Defection within the Soviet army was widespread in Eastern Europe even before the war was formally ended. I had not been two weeks at American occupation headquarters near Pilsen when the first Soviet defector came in and announced that he was surrendering to the American army. "But we are your allies," we protested, "how can you surrender to your allies?" "That is just it," was the answer, "while the war was on I could not surrender to the enemy. But now that the war is over and the Germans have been defeated and I have done my duty to my country I can with all honor surrender to my country's allies." They came across the demarcation line between the Soviet and American occupation areas, two or three of them every week. We were constantly involved with Soviet defectors because we did not know what to do with them. The orders we received from Third Army headquarters were clear: turn them back. Yalta again. But there was natural reluctance to do so. It took time to discover the real motivation for desertion. When, as was almost always the case, no crime had been committed except the act of desertion itself, it was an excruciating business to bind over prisoners to the nearest Red Army post with the certain knowledge that they were being sent to their doom. The penalty for desertion in the field is death. Moreover, the Soviet Union was still technically at war, as we were in bitter reality, with Japan.

It was still more difficult to bind over a Red Army soldier who was not a Russian. One afternoon in August a Red Army first lieutenant with several medals for bravery on his tunic walked into our headquarters and "surrendered." His name was Bari Hairulin. He had been wounded three times. He had taken part in the defense of Stalingrad and fought in every campaign thereafter. He was a Turkman. He had hated the Germans but they were now defeated. Next to Germans he hated the Russians. He was a quiet, reserved man, a man of natural dignity who, as a devout Moslem, prayed very frequently. We kept him three days and then turned him back to the Russians. When we were obliged to inform Bari Hairulin that he was being escorted back to the Russians, he broke down. He threw himself on the ground and begged in Russian, "Shoot me" and then in German, "Bitte, erschiessen Sie mich!" He repeated this incessantly all the way, sometimes shouting, sometimes imploringly, "Bitte, erschiessen Sie mich!" Until we came in sight of the Red Army guard post. Then he straightened up, composed himself, and met his fate with dignity.

We came to dance on the extinct volcano. The dance was short but antic enough while it lasted. On October 12, 1945, the commanding general of the Twenty-second Corps of the American army decorated some twenty officers and men of the Fifth Russian Guards Assault Army in a solemn ceremony followed by a banquet (which was anything but solemn) in the Hotel Continental in Pilsen, Czechoslovakia. I have no idea why General Ernest Harmon, the corps commander (widely known as the "pocket-Patton" because of his arrested vertical growth and his affectation of ivory-handled pistols), conceived the idea of decorating the Russians with American medals for bravery. Ostensibly his purpose was to promote good relations between the two commands. The Russians, and especially those singled out for the honor, suspected that the whole thing was a ruse to collect biographical information on Red Army officers and noncoms (those to be honored were respectfully requested to furnish their biographies—particularly their war records—for inclusion in the citation). As a result no such information was forthcoming. All we got was the name and rank (but not the serial number) of the Russians concerned.

Nevertheless the occasion did represent a major test for the liaison group if only because of the demand on interpreters posed by the banquet. We were a group of eight men and four officers, only one of whom, William Sloane Coffin, Jr., had been to Officer Candidate School. By far the best interpreter in the group was Prince Alexis Scherbatow, whose name was famous in Russia. ("Are you by any chance related to Prince Scherbatow?" General Lebedenko asked of him. The answer: "Himself.")

Scherbatow ("Alyosha") was duly attached as General Harmon's interpreter. The trouble here was twofold: Scherbatow was a Russian emigré prince who had little use for generals but he was also—I think I should say "technically"—a sergeant in the American army although there was no way of discerning this from his dress; Harmon, while certainly a good soldier, was a vulgarian. During the decoration ceremony Scherbatow stopped to chat with a Russian general while General Harmon moved on to another group of Russians standing at attention waiting to be decorated. Suddenly finding himself without an interpreter, Harmon turned around and saw Scherbatow in conversation some distance behind him. "Come over here, you son of a bitch!" Harmon shouted. Scherbatow complied, informing the general in an even tone that he was not a son of a bitch. I am sure that Harmon did not know who Scherbatow was. Had he known he might just possibly have paused to consider that the aspersion carried by the epithet as applied to the illustrious lineage of Scherbatow would be far more grievous than in ordinary circumstances.

Scherbatow never forgave Harmon. Later when all had taken their places at the banquet table Scherbatow sustained another rude shock: he found himself obliged to stand behind the general throughout the banquet. When dessert was finished, Harmon stood up and tinkled his wine glass for attention. "Gentlemen," he began, "Mr. Murphy here" (gesturing at American Ambassador Robert Murphy) "is Irish." Scherbatow looked at Harmon, shrugged his shoulders and translated. Harmon went on, "General Bull is Irish" (indicating General "Pinky" Bull, the chief of staff at SHAEF). Scherbatow translated. "*I'm* Irish," continued Harmon. Scherbatow translated, and then, before Harmon could go on, addressed himself to the general: "And my wife is Irish." Harmon was not sure he had heard aright. "What did you say?" he asked, turning around to Scherbatow. "I said my wife is Irish, too, General," beamed Scherbatow. "Look here," said Harmon, after pausing to consider again whether he had heard aright, "you keep your kith and kin out of this: who's makin' this speech—you or I?" "Both of us, General," said Scherbatow leaning forward confidentially, "both of us." He spoke true. From that point on Harmon made one speech and Scherbatow made another. Harmon would say something perfectly commonplace like "When I came into town this morning I noticed a monument to those who fell fighting for freedom." Scherbatow would render this in Russian as follows: "When I came into this brothel this morning I wondered where all the good-looking whores were." The Russians exploded with laughter. "What are they laughing at?" asked Harmon, turning to Scherbatow. "I've no idea," said Scherbatow. It was not long before the Russians, who had two interpreters of their own, were fully aware of what was happening. Russians are full of fun (among other things). They took the prank in the spirit in which Scherbatow intended it and laughed uproariously. Moreover, Scherbatow, although an American citizen, was Russian; as far as the Russians were concerned he was *their* prince, and so indeed did they refer to him—as "our prince." The fact that he was in—or rather, out of—American uniform was for them a mere technicality. Only the commanding general of the Fifth Guards Army, Zhadov, managed to contain himself and look gravely at Scherbatow who fleshed his wit outrageously at Harmon's expense. At last Harmon realized what was happening, proposed a toast, and sat down.

There was near tumult for the next few moments until an American division commander stood up and made a speech in which he protested over and over again, "How in hell can two peoples who have fought so bravely side by side and shed so much blood as the Americans and the Russians have in this war . . . how in hell can we even dream of ever fighting each other?" The general did not realize that the two peoples had not fought side by side but from either side to the center where they then stood opposing each other: they came from the East and the West, the glacier flood and the lava torrent, and they met and contended over the wreck of the Nazi empire. Not that it would have made all that much difference if they *had* fought side by side; alliances are ordinarily short-lived, containing the seeds of their own destruction. But the oppositeness of the approaches and the separateness of the efforts (despite American aid to the Soviet Union) foreordained the immediate air and sense of confrontation as much as did their annihilation of the German state.

After Scherbatow's performance I expected, as senior officer of the liaison group, to be court-martialed for fomenting insubordination or some such thing. But all that happened was that next day Harmon informed us through his adjutant that he never wanted to see Scherbatow again. Scherbatow was satisfied with the arrangement, or so he said. A few days later Scherbatow encountered Harmon in the chief of staff's office. "General," he said promptly, "what's this I hear about your not wanting to see me again?" "What's that?" said Harmon and then added, "Nonsense, nonsense!" and hastily withdrew.

None of us could understand the strange hold that Scherbatow seemed to have over the general. It was not until years later that the mystery was solved. After the Americans and the Russians withdrew from Czechoslovakia, General Harmon became commander of the Constabulary, a large force of American soldiery who, wearing bright orange scarfs to distinguish them from the rest of their fellow countrymen, patrolled and policed the American zone of Germany. One evening some two years later after another banquet Harmon's adjutant asked him if he remembered Sergeant Scherbatow. "Did you say '*Sergeant* Scherbatow'?" asked Harmon incredulously. The adjutant affirmed that he had indeed. "Good God!" exploded Harmon, "and I always thought he was a civilian!"

It was Scherbatow who told me that there were three German princesses on the post one autumn day in Czechoslovakia. They had been brought all the way from Landshut in Bavaria as witnesses—and in the one case as plaintiff—in the court-martial of an American captian who had been charged with stealing the Von Hohenlohe jewels. The youngest "princess" proved to be a commoner connected with the princesses Von Hohenlohe through the marriage of a close blood relative. She was nineteen years old and the most beautiful woman I had ever seen. I very soon found myself smuggling Von Hohenlohe jewelry from a castle in Bohemia to another castle in Bavaria. The culprit captain had presumably begun the same way and for the same reason—out of attraction for the young "princess." There was no problem at the Czech-German border; the Czech guards merely saluted American army vehicles going either way. Nor were there all that many jewels to smuggle. No more than enough to fill a chamois-skin bag the size of a large pear: a few rings, a necklace, two or three brooches, and a small tiara.

My destination was Schloss Isar-Eck outside Moosburg near Landshut, a castle belonging to the Graf de la Rosée—despite the name a German count. Schloss Isar-Eck served as a camp for displaced aristocrats, a DA camp, as it were. Most of these were from the Sudetenland and still suffering from the shock of summary deportation. Some of the deportees—the older ones who had been cossetted all ther lives, like an eighty-year-old baron I met there—admittedly felt better physically than they had for many years. The very privations and rigors imposed upon them had done them good. My on-the-ground education in the subject of the Third Reich began with the old baron. He told me how he had awaked one morning in 1939 to find himself a member of an auxiliary organization of the National Socialist party: his hunting club had simply been incorporated into the party hunters' association.

Because it was a haven for homeless aristocrats, Schloss Isar-Eck was crowded. One afternoon I sat on a couch in an antechamber with my "princess," whose affection I found embarrassing just then because the privacy we enjoyed was bound to end abruptly and immediately, the traffic in the Schloss being what it was. Just as my fay had put her arms around my neck and rested her head against my campaign ribbons, in stepped the old Princess von Hohenlohe. She took in the tableau at a glance and epitomized it: "Hmmph!" she sniffed, "—Bottom and Titania!" I affirmed that the old princess knew Shakespeare rather well. "Everybody in Germany knows Shakespeare," said my princess, who didn't think her step-grandmother's remark was funny.

This was my introduction to the German cult of Shakespeare. Probably even today the most famous translation in world literature is the Schlegel-Tieck translation of Shakespeare into German. "They made Shakespeare a German poet," as Goethe said. Over the last three hundred years there have been more productions of Shakespeare in Germany than in England. At the beginning of the thirties Max Reinhardt directed a production of *A Midsummer Night's Dream* in Berlin that made theater history. It was basically the same production that Kortner, as a German-Jewish immigrant, directed in Hollywood with James Cagney in my role as Bottom and Mickey Rooney as Puck. The Schlegel-Tieck translation is not always absolutely accurate; nevertheless the achievement, in terms of a faithful, true, and feeling rendition of the original, is stupendous. The German-Jewish poet Heine knew English well, but it was from his acquaintance with the Schlegel-Tieck translation that he pronounced the corpus of Shakespeare's works "the secular New Testament." Thus the Germans, without having to know English at all, were the only non-English-speaking people in the world with something approaching a full appreciation of Shakespeare.

In 1945 there were very few Germans with a useable knowledge of English. The owners of Schloss Isar-Eck spoke French beautifully but their English was so faulty they were obliged to ask me for the correct legends for "no trespassing," "private property," and "off limits" signs. It was hoped that these would discourage American army units from settling on Schloss Isar-Eck as a place to set up shop. Presumably the signs turned the trick: I never heard any complaints.

ARRIVED IN NUREMBERG THE DAY AFTER AMERICAN AND Soviet forces withdrew from Czechoslovakia and just in time to hear Lord Justice Lawrence, the president of the International Military Tribunal, introduce the proceedings: "The trial which is now about to begin is unique in the history of the jurisprudence of the world and it is of supreme importance to millions of people all over the globe." I looked upon the trial—or the complex of trials that made up the Nuremberg Judgment—as an elaborate ritual punishment. I had only the most general grasp of law. But the very magnitude of the proceedings revealed the flaws in the foundation of the structure designed to support the ritual. I sensed, as I am sure a great many people did, that what purported to be the jurisprudential basis of the proceedings was in fact largely if not merely the trappings of a mass emotional need. The legal aspects of Nuremberg were a form of disguise.

Now this was very strange because much of the effort of the prosecution at Nuremberg was taken up with trying to penetrate the disguise of the state as such and particularly, of course, the Nazi state, the state as manifested in the Third Reich. What was so baffling to all concerned, prosecution and defense and spectators alike, was the paradox involved and the terrible power the paradox had unleashed: a comparatively few individuals had managed to capture the machinery of government and house themselves in the "majestic ethical edifice" of the state, as Kant called it. What was more they had managed to place themselves at the levers of power, of the tremendous power that is generated and channeled by the modern industrial state. "The prosecution," said one German defense counsel, "is based upon the conception of conspiracy to conquer the world on the part of a few dozen criminals.

"The German state, if one looks upon things in this way, becomes a mere shadow or tool. But this state has long been in existence; no one could set aside the enormous weight of its history. A number of facts in its history, domestic and especially foreign, accounted for Hitler's rise to power and facilitated it for him, while there were other things in this history that guided, urged, limited, or restrained Hitler in his choice of aims and means, and helped decide the success or failure of his measures and undertakings."

The defense of all the "major war criminals"—except Speer who entered a partial plea of guilty—was based on the principle of state sovereignty and the absolute and binding validity of the orders derived from its supreme authority. This is the "act of state" plea according to which immunity exists for acts committed on behalf of the state. The defense contended that if the leaders of a defeated nation could be tried and punished, such action would be in violation of the "fundamental principle of international law prohibiting the unauthorized interference by force of one national legal order in the jurisdictional sphere of validity of another national legal order."

The trouble was that this defense was ultimately based on the contention that the German state was personified by one man whose every order, decree, instruction, directive, and regulation—whether written or oral—had the validity and binding power of law. "Why, these people don't even know what a state is!" exclaimed Ulrich von Hassell of the Nazis shortly after their takeover. Neither did the prosecution at Nuremberg. The Third Reich was the monocracy of a monomaniac. But this wouldn't do as a comprehensive explanation of what had actually happened, as the following section of a speech by a counsel for the German defense indicates.

Hitler combined in his person all the powers of issuing legislative and administrative orders of a supreme character, orders which could not be questioned and were absolutely valid; but immediately below him the power of the state was divided up into a vast mass of spheres of competence. . . . Every department was jealously watching to see that no other trespassed into its field. Everywhere it was prepared [to counteract] tendencies of other departments toward expansion. Considering the great mass of tasks which the so-called totalitarian state had heaped upon itself, cases where two or three departments were competent for the same matter could not be avoided. Conflicts between departments were inevitable. If a conspiracy existed, as the indictment assumes, the conspirators were remarkably incompetent organizers. Instead of cooperating and going through thick and thin together, they fought one another. Instead of a conspiracy we would seem to have had more of a "dispiracy." The history of the jealousy and mistrust among the powerful figures under Hitler has still to be written. . . . In the relations between all departments and within each department, people surrounded themselves with ever-increasing secrecy; between departments and within each department, between ranks and within the various ranks, more and more matters were classed as "secret." Never before has there been so much "public life," that is, nonprivate life in Germany as under Hitler; and also never before was public life so screened off from the people, particularly from the individual members of the hierarchy themselves, as under Hitler.

The International Military Tribunal rejected the "act of state" plea: acceptance would have made prosecution impossible since the former agents of the state could not then have been held responsible because they had acted on behalf of the state and the state would have remained immune—except for fines and reparations—by virtue of its sovereignty. But in order to prosecute either the agents or the state successfully the prosecution was forced to contend that something vaguely like a codified body of international penal law existed prohibiting and setting penalties for planning and waging aggressive war. As evidence of this the prosecution adduced protocols and resolutions of the League of Nations branding wars of aggression as international crimes, the centerpiece being the Kellogg-Briand Pact.

The technical flaws in this evidence were as various as the documents presented. In the Kellogg-Briand Pact, war was not designated a crime nor was the renunciation of it reinforced by a sanction. Moreover, while none of these documents had been ratified, all had been defied and made a mockery of by one of the victor nations sitting in judgment of the Germans in Nuremberg: the Soviet Union. Nobody was so acutely aware of this as the Germans. The Soviet Union had shared the aggression against Poland (the Von Ribbentrop-Molotov Pact), had waged aggressive war against Finland, and annexed three Baltic states with which she had concluded nonaggression treaties. The tribunal at Nuremberg was made up of the four prosecuting nations—the victors over the Germans—who drew their authority to prosecute the vanquished from the Charter of the Tribunal (which the victors had drawn up in London for the purpose). In denying the individual defendants immunity because they had acted on behalf of the state, the "act of state" plea, the prosecution was obliged to proclaim that "individuals have international duties which transcend the national obligations of obedience imposed by the individual state. He who violates the laws of war cannot obtain immunity while acting in pursuance of the authority of the state, if the state . . . moves outside its competence under international law."

Here the unbridled (and so negative because unbridled) idealism of the Germans had been answered by the indomitable naïveté of the

Americans. "We must never forget," said Chief Justice Robert H. Jackson, "that the record on which we judge these defendants today is the record on which history will judge us tomorrow. To pass these defendants a poisoned chalice is to put it to our own lips as well." This admonition was spelled out in the Weizsäcker Judgment, a subsidiary trial at Nuremberg:

> We are here to define a standard of conduct of responsibility, not only for Germans as the vanquished in war, not only with regard to past and present events, but those which in the future can be reasonably and properly applied to men and officials of every state and nation, those of the victors as well as those of the vanquished. Any other approach would make a mockery of international law and would result in wrongs quite as serious and fatal as those which were sought to be remedied.

And so they chattered on, little realizing that by demanding the unconditional surrender of Germany and denying the existence of the German state they had split the world in two. In attending some of the sessions of the trial against the major war criminals and in reading the reports of its progress, I was reminded again and again of the passage at the beginning of the *Odyssey*: "Fools! who slaughtered the cattle sacred to the sun-king; behold, the god deprived them of the day of homecoming."

In destroying the German state by refusing to recognize the authority of German law (so as to be able to prosecute German leaders as individuals retroactively under a new criminal law) the victors at Nuremberg invoked an international authority that did not exist and for whose creation they undertook no measures. The victors at Nuremberg undermined the concept of the state in breaching its defined local authority by proclaiming a higher responsibility to an abstraction called "international law." Along with the noble rhetoric went a lunatic disregard for reality. According to the statute of the International Court of Justice, "Only states may be parties in cases before the court." Moreover, it was clear to the German defense counsel that the victors "had not bound themselves in any way . . . to have the law of the Charter apply against themselves also."

Most glaring, of course, was the ostensible absence of any attempt to establish the Charter as generally binding for the community of nations. "It would take," as an American professor of law noted, "a drastic revision of the United Nations Charter to bring it into harmony with the principles of the Charter and Judgment of Nuremberg." In fact the Charter and Judgment of Nuremberg was expressly rejected by the

United Nations. I am not a historian but in the course of my general reading I have yet to encounter a spectacle of slovenly thinking on the part of professional intellects comparable to that of the prosecution at Nuremberg—excepting always the Soviet contingent who certainly had a clear notion of what was being done, namely slaughtering the cattle sacred to the sun-king.

Precisely because of their experience in the Third Reich the Germans were visited by awesome forebodings of the true significance of the trial. "It means a change of incalculable importance," wrote the Berlin lawyer Kurt Behling, "when the laws against war crimes now demand the punishment of individuals. Above all, it is in contradiction to the famous passage in Rousseau's *Contrat Social* according to which war is not a relation between men but only between states, and therefore can justify only a liability of the state."

The Nuremberg Trial was gigantically Kafkaesque: the proceedings involved Kafka's ethic of lucidity weighted over into an ethic of hallucination. The jurists of the Western Allies blundered into the region of contingent truth, of truth dependent on the categories and forms of perception sanctioned over the span of human history. By shifting the point of reference from the traditional to the abstract-utopian, by mistaking the pinning of their hopes for the positing of a valid thesis, they proceeded on the false premise of the immanent feasibility of creating an international court with the power and authority to apply unified and normative penal law across national boundaries. They did not pause to consider that such a judicial authority presupposed the existence, in effect, of a supranational world government. The presupposition attracted the support of the world's first world citizen, Gary Davis, and instilled the widespread illusion that the United Nations Organization is the organization of the United Nations. As Doctor Carl Haensel, a counsel at Nuremberg, pointed out: "Today it is perhaps more important to the development of international law that international law be given validity under the authority of the American flag rather than that an international group pronounce legal principles for which the American world power does not feel responsible."

The Western victors at Nuremberg mined the whole landscape of traditional legal sanctions and norms. In one sense, at least, they kept their word and visited the vengeance of their method upon themselves: the theory that the higher responsibility of the individual is to an undefined international law sabotaged the authority of the conventional state and replaced it with an abstraction that can be manipulated to justify the arbitrariness of the victors. "Proceedings of this kind," wrote the defense counsel for Admiral Doenitz, "have been and in the near future will be, conducted against members of defeated nations only!" In the *near* future? The above statement was published in 1950.

One aspect of the tragedy of the Nuremberg Judgment is that the Western Allies were reacting emotionally to what the Germans had done. They were allowing themselves to be provoked into headlong reaction by the dead leader of the Germans. "The concept of the nation," said the Austrian poet Hugo von Hofmannsthal, "must not be overexerted." Hitler overexerted the concept of the nation with his gala Wagnerian production of the Third Reich. It was too much, I suppose, for anyone to bear. The provocation was too great. With his excesses he succeeded in goading the Western Allies into destroying the German nation. And not only the German nation. Knowingly or instinctively, most if not all the defendants in the main Nuremberg Trail tried to protect and preserve the basic substance, the essential elements of the German nation. They were all struggling, I gathered, for the continuity of the German state—despite the unconditional surrender.

This half blind and muted struggle was exemplified for me in the line of defense and attitude in court of Seyss-Inquart. He confined himself painstakingly to clarifying and justifying the part he played in the Anschluss—the annexation of Austria by Germany in 1938. The Anschluss was the high point of Seyss-Inquart's career: for three days— from the resignation of Schuschnigg to the proclamation of the Anschluss—he was chancellor of Austria. I made a point of attending sessions of the trial in which Seyss-Inquart and Jodl took the stand. It had been eight months since I had last seen them. The physical appearance of Seyss-Inquart exercised a fascination over me. When I had seen him close up at Nijmegen before the negotiations there had actually begun, I had thought him the personification of evil: the smooth, fleshy face had a watery yellow cast to it which was heightened by blotches of red in the cheeks. About his thick but finely drawn lips there was the expression of restrained disgust, as though he was constantly suffering from slight nausea. There was an aura of putrefaction about that face with its blind mirror-eyes, reminiscent of the legions of German corpses I had seen.

No doubt this was a subjective impression. It was largely, but not entirely, dispelled when Seyss-Inquart began to speak. He spoke at his trial as he had at the Nijmegen negotiations, calmly, evenly, in a quiet, matter-of-fact tone of voice. "You can rest assured," he told the French prosecutor, "that I will say all I remember. Should I forget something please tell me. I shall not deny it if it is true." Very much to my surprise Bedell Smith appeared at the trial to give testimony that the flooding in Holland in the spring had been strictly confined by Seyss-Inquart to the extent justified by military necessity. I was also surprised by Seyss-Inquart's admission that he was an anti-Semite:

> I will say quite openly that since the First World War and the postwar period, I was an anti-Semite and went to Holland as such. . . . I had the impression, which will be confirmed everywhere, that the Jews, [as a matter] of course, had to be against National Socialist Germany. There was no discussion of the question of guilt as far as I was concerned. As head of an occupied territory I had only to deal with the fact. I had to realize that, particularly from the Jewish circles, I had to reckon with resistance, defeatism, and so on.

This statement impressed me precisely because I knew something of the Jewish side of the question. It was almost as if Seyss-Inquart was proclaiming that the Nazi-German persecution of the Jews was something like a fair fight. Or if not, then somehow or other justified and at the very least necessary. That suggestion of nausea in the expression around Seyss-Inquart's mouth began to take on a new significance. It began to look like revulsion, the revulsion of a man who had found himself propelled to the top of a very unpleasant business by his ability, his sense of duty, and the momentum of his original misapprehension of National Socialism. Like so many others he had mistaken the nature of the beast.

The prewar Vienna police chief, Anton Skubl, testifying in Seyss-Inquart's behalf, gave this account of the defendant's first meeting with Hitler: " 'I am,' said Seyss-Inquart to Hitler, 'an Austrian minister sworn to defend the Austrian constitution. I am a practicing Catholic and will have no truck with any prosecution of the Church. I come from a country unwilling to submit to any totalitarianism.' " Skubl insisted that Seyss-Inquart had been profoundly disillusioned by what had happened after the Anschluss and especially with the disappearance of Austria—"and all that she had stood for"—within the Reich.

Seyss-Inquart had been overtaken by events, events which no individual could grasp in their entirety, much less control at will. Nevertheless he had gone on to do his duty, however distasteful his duty had become for him. He had done his duty in conscience and according to his lights. When he learned that Dutch Jews were to be deported to Auschwitz he had a committee formed and sent to Auschwitz to examine and report on conditions there. A report was returned that the commission had been shown a camp with decent living quarters, excellent sanitary facilities, and factories nearby to keep the inmates profitably occupied. But there was, of course, no question but that he was guilty as charged on all counts except the first and second—planning to wage aggressive war and waging aggressive war.

Unlike Jodl, Seyss-Inquart had no illusions about his fate. He was quoted by a fellow-defendant, Hans Fritzsche, as follows: "Whatever I say, my rope is being woven from Dutch hemp. All I can do here—and I consider it my main task—is to clarify the background of the Anschluss. I am not interested in anything I am accused of having done elsewhere. Anyway, all this will count for nothing as soon as new conflicts appear in the world and people cease to see my actions through a distorting glass of hatred." He was wrong there.

Jodl's conviction that he had always acted honorably as a soldier was never shaken. He went to the scaffold with it. At the end of his cross-examination he was asked: "Do you still claim to be an honorable soldier and a truthful man?" Said Jodl, "The evidence has given further proof of it." When I saw Jodl in the Nuremberg dock he had lost some fifteen pounds and looked it. All the defendants at Nuremberg were on short rations. The reason for this was that the whole of Germany was on short rations.

The most damaging piece of evidence in the opinion of the court was Jodl's handling of the Commissar Order. This was Hitler's order, issued at the beginning of Operation Barbarossa, which was the code name for the invasion of the Soviet Union by the German armed forces. According to the order all commissars that fell into the hands of the Germans were to be summarily shot. This was flat: the order admitted of no exceptions and no discretion on the part of commanders. Jodl, according to creditable sources, was extremely unhappy about the order and tried as best he could to circumvent the issuance and implementation of the draft. He added the comment "Man zieht es am besten als Repressalie auf." For the tribunal this comment had been mistranslated as, "It is therefore best to brand it as a reprisal." Jodl's defense counsel, Doctor Exner, pointed out that the actual import of the comment was "It is best to handle it as a reprisal." In sum, instead of trying to conceal the viciousness of the order in a relatively acceptable disguise, Jodl was actually trying to suggest that the order be carried out only as a reprisal. That is, only when the Red Army set the precedent by committing an equally savage act.

Jodl applied the same consideration to the Commando Order which directed that all commandos were to be executed without exception and regardless of their actions. As Benno Frank had pointed out in the close-combat course in Camp Ritchie, no sentry is going to like being sneaked up on and garroted by a commando—anybody's commando. It really isn't in the nature of the enterprise: a commando's job is not a happy one. As Jodl put it—and he was putting it mildly—"many of the British commandos were acting in an illegal fashion and thus placing themselves outside military law." But then who had put commandos *inside* military law? By their very nature commandos constitute a borderline case. They are partisans in uniform or, rather, uniformed and highly trained troops acting as partisans.

The Germans have always had trouble with borders and borderline cases. Hitler was acting entirely in character when he condemned the innovation out of hand, outlawing the commandos a priori. His reaction was very "German." Jodl refused point blank to draft the Commando Order. He was obliged to distribute the order, as he had, or resign. But he took steps to limit its application to troops who had acted "in an unsoldierly fashion." Jodl was also acting very much in character. He accepted the innovation of commandos per se but at the same time attempted to circumscribe it by insisting on the strict adherence to formal rules. I would describe Jodl's reaction as German without quotation marks.

And yet Jodl was a National Socialist. Jodl the upright, honorable and unerringly correct professional soldier firmly and avowedly believed in the Nazi movement, its methods—at least as broadly outlined in party propaganda—and its goals. In other words, Jodl, who at Reims had seemed to be the soldier's soldier—at the other end of the scale from the Nazi party boss (which was what we had taken Seyss-Inquart to be)— Jodl, the chevalier sans reproche, was the convinced Nazi, heart and soul with the movement. "My aims," said Jodl to the Operations Staff of the OKW (Supreme Command) on July 24, 1944 (four days after the abortive Von Stauffenberg putsch), "were by and large the aims of the movement, since my thinking was always nationalistic, social, and anti-Catholic."

And yet, this impression, too, was deceptive. I remember seeing the great Swiss-German clown, Grock, a few years later in Berlin. He came out into the center of the circus arena and did a juggling act, keeping three balls in the air. After a minute or so the spectators gradually realized that Grock was not really juggling the balls but only pretending to do so. After another full minute there came the second realization that pretending to do the juggling was actually a better trick—and more difficult of accomplishment—than the juggling itself would have been. The illusion that is more difficult to create than the reality it pretends to represent—is this the cause or the result of the German passion for mechanistic abstraction? A great many Germans have sacrificed their lives and the lives of a great many other people, fellow countrymen included, because the illusion was more important to them than the reality. Indeed, because they were convinced that creating the illusion was the only way to the ultimate achievement of the reality, of the higher, better reality. As Hölderlin put it: "We are nothing; what we seek is everything."

I will not pretend that I grasped the significance of these events when they occurred or before a good deal of time had passed. These were inklings that were provided, sometimes in great flurries of direct evidence as during the course of the Nuremberg Trials. But that was just the difficulty. The Nuremberg Trial was too much, too soon, and all at once. Seyss-Inquart and General Jodl were not the only ones who were overtaken by events. Almost everyone—even a good many cadre Communists—were as unready as Ethelred for Nuremberg. We were all presented with a perfectly bewildering panorama of national and international tragedy.

And as the details suddenly came to light and the background began to emerge from behind the screens of official secrecy, the confusion only increased. Bedell Smith, who had jumped all over Seyss-Inquart at Nijmegen, testified in his behalf at Nuremberg. Nuremberg made Jodl look bad in the first analysis, better in the second analysis, and better and better in the subsequent analyses. Professional Allied military men saw the truth or rather sensed it from the first. Soldiers understand each other, at least instinctively. "Soldiers are soldiers," runs the Russian proverb, "only the color of the buttons varies." They also—at least instinctively—understood what Jodl stood for (in a way that Field Marshal Keitel did not). They recognized at least one of the main issues involved. Jodl himself made it clear enough: he was a solier bound by oath to obey; he had not been allowed to resign; he could protest, as he had, but then he was bound to obey. He made the point that the prosecution could thank its own obedient soldiers for being in a position to prosecute. Jodl was condemned to death and executed as a war criminal. I met more than a few American and British officers at Nuremberg who swore a blue streak when they learned of the sentence. One major I knew said, "We are going to pay for this piece of stupidity ten millions times over!" It was generally agreed that if Jodl had been tried as little as two years later he would have got off with fifteen or twenty years at most. There is really little doubt of it: my horse-faced, thoroughbred, horse-breeding acquaintance from Rosenhof—the hereditary prince, SS gruppenführer, and master of Buchenwald zu Waldeck-Pyrmont—was sentenced to life; his sentence was then commuted to twenty years. In the event he was released after seven years' imprisonment on grounds of poor health. He died on his estates at the age of seventy in 1967.

But for the "droshky drivers" in Russian Liaison there was a conflict of conscience that paralleled the main issue at Nuremberg. Just when the "civilized world" was sitting in judgment of the major war criminals whose crime consisted in failing to disobey the orders of the führer, we in Russian Liaison were plagued by our consciences for obeying the directive to turn back all Soviet defectors to the Red Army. Our liaison work had provided us with a great many unwelcome insights into the nature of the Soviet system. Familiarity with the system bred not only contempt but also dismay: under Stalin Soviet communism was obviously far more effectively totalitarian than National Socialism had been under Hitler.

Time and again we swore that we would not turn back another defector. But we couldn't figure out how to avoid turning them back. At that time, unfortunately, turning back defectors was one of the major functions of Russian Liaison. Orders were orders. Time and again we protested to Third Army Headquarters against the directive concerning defectors. To what avail may be imagined. It is all very well to pontificate about the moral obligation to refuse to obey an "illegal" or inhumane order. But the problem is not least a technical one. As a purely practical matter, how does one go about refusing to comply with an order, particularly an order affecting so sensitive an issue as the return of deserters to an Allied army?

I do not know of anyone in Russian Liaison who had illusions about our "great Soviet ally" after as little as three months' duty. Moreover, there was no denying the fact that liaison, by its very nature, encouraged defection on the part of the Soviets. Acquaintance with the Western Allies tended to disprove Soviet propaganda about Westerners generally and the contact with Western officers and officials provided or seemed to provide the practical possibility for making an arrangement to defect. By way of counteraction, Stalin issued a directive to the Red Army in September 1945 prohibiting all but the most strict official contact between all Red Army personnel and all foreigners. By November the liaison "honeymoon" was over.

[98]

But all such considerations only complicated matters. Circumventing the order to return Soviet defectors would have required an apparatus—at least a skeleton staff of some sort. It is extremely difficult to set up an apparatus of any sort within an organization so disciplined as an army. It is impossible to do so without its eventually becoming known. The only successful sabotage of the order in my experience was the operation conducted by the Polish liaison officer (of the British-sponsored Anders Army), Captain Lyssowsky, at American Corps Headquarters in Czechoslovakia. Lyssowsky was ostensibly engaged in the repatriation of displaced Poles. Over the weeks we noticed that Lyssowsky's charges were invariably young men of military age and bearing: they snapped to whenever an officer appeared. One night four Soviet officers with drawn pistols cornered Lyssowsky in a cul-de-sac in Prague. The Russians were out of luck: Lyssowsky was a crack shot. He killed all four of them on the spot. As a result of this incident Lyssowsky abruptly departed Corps Headquarters. In the investigation that followed it was discovered that Lyssowsky's Polish repatriation specialized in channeling Polish deserters from the Red Army into DP camps in France.

It may seem inappropriate and even melodramatic to make the comparison of American army officers engaged in Russian Liaison with the defendants in the dock at Nuremberg; but the comparison forced itself upon us. Like the prisoners in the dock at Nuremberg we were acting as the agents of the state in an enterprise that meant death or life imprisonment for those affected. And we were "privileged" to be in a position to discern unmistakably that this activity was morally wrong. There was no mistaking—especially among Red Army men and those as close to them as we were—what Stalin was. Knowing the Soviet system for what it was, it was no solace to spend long hours talking with these doomed "enemies of the people" and "people's parasites" for whom we provided armed escort to the nearest Red Army receiving point. The Soviet terms "enemy of the people" and "people's parasites" had their exact equivalents in the official jargon of the Nazis and were indeed identical political manifestations. An "enemy of the people" is no more and no less than an enemy of the people's leader. The Greeks had a word (a literal translation) for the people's leader—demagogue. In short, we in Russian Liaison were involved, as the defendants in the dock at Nuremberg had been, in suppressing by force the various forms of resistance to the demagogue. As far as I am concerned this applies also to the tens of thousands of Vlassovite troops whom we repatriated by the trainload to the Soviets during the first two years after the war. These mass bindings over were always accompanied by suicides or escape attempts that proved to be suicidal. Jumping off a fast-moving train almost always resulted in a smashed skull. Quite naturally we consoled ourselves with the fact that we were soldiers and officers doing our duty —even though we knew that "our duty" in this case was wrong. It was altogether an heroic deed for which many of us received medals and citations. This experience coincided with the Nuremberg Trials in a way that was for me uncanny and ominous. It gave me a certain sympathy with a good many of the prisoners in the dock.

My sympathy with many of the prisoners in the dock at Nuremberg went so far as to include the unconscious repression of unpleasant if not shameful acts. My revulsion at the binding over of the Turcoman Bari Hairulin ("Please shoot me!") was so great that over the years I had gradually and subconsciously fabricated my own protective myth. This was to the effect that after the Hairulin incident I—and my comrades in liaision with me—"never returned another Soviet defector," which was the statement I originally wrote in this account when I described the Hairulin incident. But my own records prove that this contention was merely the cautery of self-deception: of course we continued to turn back Soviet defectors—by the hundreds and, if one accepts (as one should) the Vlassovites in the category, by the thousands. And this for as long as the order remained in force—namely, until the Berlin blockade when Soviet defectors suddenly and officially became most welcome.

There was another compelling reason for the change in the Western Allied attitude toward the German military, particularly those accused or suspected of war crimes. When the Soviets tried to blockade West Berlin into submission in 1948 in became clear to the Anglo-American military leadership (and to the upper echelons of the American and British civil service generally) that Germany would have to be rearmed in order to form a new Western Alliance against the Soviet Union. So we had the utterly grotesque situation of the Allies who had condemned the German military out of hand "for all time" and declared the German General Staff to be a criminal organization, reversing themselves within less than two years after Nuremberg and requesting the Germans to rearm in order to make front against the Soviet Union. In short, part of the prosecution was asking the defendants to join it against another part of the prosecution. Germany could not be rearmed without the help of the German military. In return for their willingness to cooperate, the German military demanded that the Western Allies desist from further prosecution of the German military. This new contingency put a bull-dozer to work in the landscape of contingent truth. Even without the new contingency the sentences already meted out to various members of the German military would almost certainly have been commuted. With the passing of time passions waned and cooler heads prevailed.

Here was another linguistic mnemonic device, the German word "schnöde." Definition: contemptuous, disdainful, inconsiderate, shameless, base, vile. The only time I have ever heard the word spoken or seen it in print was during the war when we, the Western Allies, used it in our harangues to the Germans on the other side of the firing line: "Never in the history of the world has a people been so schnöde—shamelessly —betrayed as the German people by its leadership." That was certainly the way the great bulk of the German people felt during the Nuremberg Trial. When the sentences were announced, four-fifths of the letters that came into the court were protests against the mildness of the nondeath sentences.

Von Fritz was right: the people wanted a form of "tumultuous punishment"—the circus maximus show-execution of all the putative culprits. And they were encouraged in this attitude by Allied (including Russian) propaganda. The unprecedented singling out of individuals regardless of their agency for the state was itself an invitation to foist the burden of the guilt on key personalities of the Reich. So, too, of course was the charge of conspiracy. But was the Nazi leadership solely and entirely responsible for the Third Reich? It takes two to tango. One man does not make a leader. Did the German nation break down into a small percentage of cosmically sinister con men and a vast multitude of innocent dupes?

The coverage of the Nuremberg Trials and the immediate postwar German scene was hate-ridden, calculating, or merely opportunist. Often enough it was all three. Almost the same characterization is true of the book literature on the Nazi period that appeared during the first few years after the war. There was the same impulse to rush into print on the basis of scanty evidence and unsound premises. Moreover, the German newspaper and radio reportage out of Nuremberg was restricted by paper and power shortages. German newspapers, for the first postwar year, appeared only three times a week. At the end of the trial of the major war criminals a book was published which all Germans were exhorted to read. Of this book ten thousand copies were printed. I never saw it in a German home; I never heard it discussed by anybody, German or foreigner. As for me, I managed to attend perhaps half a dozen sessions of the trial since I did not have the good or bad fortune to be stationed in Nuremberg but in towns more or less close by. By and large I lived then as I have since—like a student of the crime on the scene of the crime, studying forward and backward, living and observing history in the making among the Germans, and delving into the Nazi and pre-Nazi German past when I could and as best I could. The Nuremberg Trials raised gigantic problems while providing only partial or cryptic answers that were too often misleading.

Of course the most stunning discovery of the trial was the deliberate, cataclysmic destruction of six million Jews. Nobody could believe that the prisoners in the dock at Nuremberg had not known at least something of this incredible slaughter. More significant, the prisoners themselves were incredulous—or steadfastly claimed to be so. Only Göring refused to believe what he saw in the film coverage of the extermination camps. The grounds he gave for his disbelief were that it was the evidence produced by the enemy whereas he had no way of checking it. He also said (to other prisoners) that it did not square with what he knew of the situation. He admitted, however, that he had no idea of what was behind the term "final solution."

The "final solution of the Jewish problem" was the great watershed of Nazi crimes and of all crime. Short of the "final solution" as it was revealed in Nuremberg in films, documents, and the oral testimony of witnesses (particularly the commanders of the Auschwitz and Belsen concentration camps), everything that happened in World War II was somehow or other explicable, at least from the German point of view. The various invasions—the Third Reich's "aggressive wars"—were explainable (to soldiers and politicians at any rate) as contingent necessities for the forestalling of similar attacks by the enemy against the Reich. This was certainly the case for the invasion of Holland and Belgium (as it was in World War I) because of the nearness—across about twenty miles of river flat—of the industrial heart of Germany, the Ruhr, to the Dutch border. It was also the case with the invasion of Norway in which the Germans anticipated the British by no more than a few hours; this was admitted by the British at Nuremberg. Even the invasion of the Soviet Union could be—and was—represented by the prisoners in the dock as a preventive strike: the Soviet "mobilization" on the eastern border in Poland, the Soviet invasion of Finland, and Molotov's demand that the Soviet be given control of the Skagerrak as well as the Dardanelles were usually cited among other indications of Soviet aggressive intentions against Germany. But the deliberate extermination of the Jews according to a carefully conceived and implemented plan—"the final solution"—was and remained totally inexplicable. On this one point alone there was consternation among the prisoners in the dock at Nuremberg: no one could deny—no one (not even Göring) dared attempt to deny—that the "final solution" was a crime.

In his testimony in his own defense Seyss-Inquart referred the prosecution to his speeches for an explanation of his attitude and specifically his policy as reichskommissar regarding the Jews. Seyss-Inquart was reichskommissar for the Netherlands for five years almost to the day. In those five years he did *his best* to assure optimal conditions for the cooperation of the Dutch population with the Reich. Most of his speeches in Holland are taken up with explanation—explanation of the Germans to the Dutch and of the Dutch to the Germans. "We Germans," he said in his first speech as reichskommissar,

> have been placed willy-nilly in a geographical area which has rendered us defenseless to the attacks from East and West by whoever happened to be more powerful at the moment. For centuries we were exposed to the booty-wars of the French; for centuries onslaughts from the East broke in upon us, onslaughts which we time and again fended off to the salvation of the Occident. The German blood in our veins gives us the same initiative and spirit of enterprise which made such able seafarers and merchants of the Dutch and which made us Germans in our struggle for the right to live the best soldiers in the world. But we Germans still have ringing in our ears the saying of that man whose life work has fallen apart under the blows of the German armed forces—the saying that remains as the last legacy of hate: "There are twenty million Germans too many!" May every nation that is moved to set itself up as a judge vis-à-vis Germany today keep in mind what it means to have a saying thrown at you that reflects the goal of a political credo to be implemented in order to bring about a just and eternal peace: every fourth living member of this nation is too much for the earth to bear and must be destroyed.

Seyss-Inquart's reference here is to Clemenceau's "vingt million de trop" statement made by the "tiger" just after World War I and known to every educated German. It had a curious parallel after World War II in a statement attributed by SS Standartenführer Peiper to Heinrich Himmler and made known at Nuremberg, namely that forty million Slavs would have to be slaughtered in a military campaign. (It finally developed that Himmler, in this particular instance, had been estimating the casualties in an eventual Russian campaign: Clemenceau's statement was a dramatic way of putting the problem of Germany's numerical superiority over France. Both statements were subsequently interpreted as threats.)

In the same speech by Seyss-Inquart there is—for me—a striking passage:

> In this most distressing and utterly desperate moment of German history, fate sent the führer, who for four years as a combat infantryman in the foremost line of battle had cherished his great mission. There came the years of struggle, there came the resistance, the protests against the occupation of the Ruhr by the French, so that the whole German people would be alerted and made aware, there came the march of November 19, 1921, and again fate protected the führer, as party member Graf threw himself into the path of the seven bullets that were aimed at the body of the führer. Then there awakened in German people the faith in Germany, and the symbol of the hooked cross [swastika] on the banner that has become sacred to us is the symbol of the struggle and the promise of victory. Unwaveringly, making no compromises, scorning all attacks, the führer led his faithful followers, who had become the army of a politically conscious German people, to power. . . . From now on the decisions of the führer are events of truly international consequence.

This is hagiography. It is one thing to find a devotional strain in Nazi party propaganda or the would-be belles lettres of party hacks. It is quite another thing when it appears in the inaugural address of a political leader to a nation under military occupation to which he has just been appointed high commissioner. It seemed to me that this had to be taken seriously. This devotional strain runs through all Seyss-Inquart's speeches. "Looking back," he says,

> the way traveled by the German people is unbelievable; from the most profound disruptions, on the very edge of the abyss and the destruction of its existence, it was alerted through the unique greatness of one man to its greatest power and glory. We are traveling a road on which the Lord has guided and to this day visibly blessed us. It is the grace accorded by Providence that we are able to take part in this as co-workers and comrades-in-arms of the führer.
> The path of the New Order is the path of the unification of the German Reich. It leads through the wars of liberation to the years 1866, 1870–1871, 1914, to 1918, and achieves the breakthrough to its perfection in just that moment when the enemies of this order —above all the British and the internationally directed forces of Jewry, of the Freemasons, and of capitalism—thought to have achieved the definitive destruction of this core [of Germanness].

[104]

Fate evidently required the catastrophe of the year 1918 and the indignities and destruction-bent malevolent treatment of the following years in order to move the entire German people to break out into its maximum effectiveness, carried by the faith and spirit of enterprise of National Socialism—a faith and spirit that have seized peoples and individuals only in those epochs that we have come to know as turning points in history.

"It may be," says Seyss-Inquart in another passage, "that Dutchmen see in the German an eternally fomenting, agitating, provocative, expanding element, never to be satisfied, always growing, never ending. The geographically unprotected borders of the German nationhood, borders open on almost all sides and exposed to the impact of populations of alien blood, forced the German to become a fighter, to become a man who is eternally seeking and striving." I found this putative Dutch description of the Germans uncannily similar to the German description of another people. As he indicated at Nuremberg, Seyss-Inquart's speeches contain a number of expository references to this people. Here is one from a speech he gave during his first year as reichskommissar:

Here in the Netherlands we have had student strikes at the universities of Delft and Leiden. These strikes were accounted for by directives concerning the continued presence of Jewish professors in the universities, said directives allegedly being infractions of the freedom and moral foundation of Dutch life. I take this incident as an occasion to address myself to the Jewish problem in the Netherlands. I affirm that my promise "We do not want to pressure the Dutch nation nor impose our convictions upon it" to be as valid as ever, but it is valid only for the Dutch people. Jews are not regarded by us as a component of the Dutch people. For National Socialism and for the National Socialist Reich, Jews are the enemy. From the moment of their emancipation their influence was directed toward the destruction of the folk and moral values of the German people. Their purpose was to replace the consciously nationalistic philosophy of life with an international nihilism. The fatal significance of Jewishness for the German people became perfectly clear during the World War. Why, they were actually the ones who whetted the dagger whose thrust into the back of the German armies broke the resistance of the Germans. From 1918 on they were the ones who wanted to dissolve and disintegrate all the traditional folk, ethical, and religious values in the German people. For us the Jews are not Dutchmen. They are those enemies with whom we can conclude neither armistice nor peace. This will be valid here, if you please, for the duration of the occupation. Don't expect any directives from me—except orders to the police—regulating these matters. We shall

[105]

smite the Jews wherever we meet them, and whoever chooses to be in company with them will have to bear the consequences.

This attitude has nothing to do with tolerance [sic]. I have long pondered the principle of tolerance such as William of Orange made the platform of his domestic policy. It is clear to me today that the deeper sense and purpose of this principle and the categorical imperative of its enforcement was the welfare of the Dutch people. Tolerance had to be made an article of faith. It was dictated by concern for the people as the highest good in order to prevent the Dutch people from tearing each other apart. For this reason the concern for the ethnic welfare of the people was the carrying and determining principle, tolerance as an article of faith within the body politic was an imperative ethnic duty. Tolerance for its own sake is an emanation of the already mentioned Dutch inclination to an idyllic, lotus-eating existence. I believe that we find today we are likely to meet with much more division and negation in the Dutch people than real tolerance.

Here was the aspect or the idea of the "fair fight" or at least the necessary fight, the war without quarter to the bitter end, the fight to the death between two peoples, the Germans and the Jews. Seyss-Inquart did not get the idea of the war to the death between Germans and Jews from Adolf Hitler. It was in the air he breathed after World War I. The rabid anti-Semitism of most of the Nazi German leaders—most of them, not all of them—was born of the disaster at the end of World War I, but it had been conceived long before. I had no idea how long before. In this connection I found the Nuremberg testimony of Julius Streicher (of all people), the editor of the notorious anti-Semitic newspaper, *Der Stürmer* (The Assailant), most interesting:

> DR. MARX: The so-called Racial Law was promulgated at the Reich Party Day in Nuremberg in 1935. Were you consulted about the planning and preparation of the draft of that law; and did you have any part in it, especially in its preparation?
> STREICHER: Yes, I believe I had part in it insofar as for years I have written that any further mixture of German blood with Jewish blood must be avoided. I have written such articles again and again; and in my articles I have repeatedly emphasized the fact that the Jews should serve as an example to every race, for they created a racial law for themselves—the law of Moses, which says, "If you come into a foreign land you shall not take unto yourself foreign women." And that, gentlemen, is of tremendous importance in judging the Nuremberg Laws. Those laws of the Jews were taken as a model for these laws. When after centuries, the Jewish lawgiver Ezra discovered that, the law notwithstanding, many Jews had

[106]

married non-Jewish women, these marriages were dissolved. That was the beginning of Jewry which, because it introduced these racial laws, has survived throughout the centuries, while all other races and civilizations have perished.

DR. MARX: Herr Streicher, this is rather too much of a digression. . . . Apart from your weekly journal, and particularly after the party came into power, were there any other publications in Germany which treated the Jewish question in an anti-Semitic way?

STREICHER: Anti-Semitic publications have existed in Germany for centuries. A book I had, written by Dr. Martin Luther, was, for instance, confiscated. Dr. Martin Luther would very probably sit in my place in the defendant's dock today, if this book had been taken into consideration by the proscecution. In the book *The Jews and Their Lies,* Dr. Martin Luther writes that the Jews are serpent's brood and one should burn down their synagogues and destroy them. . . .

[At this point Streicher was interrupted by Dr. Marx and then taken to task by Justice Jackson for answering unresponsively. A bit later in the testimony Streicher's illustrious predecessor was mentioned again.]

DR. MARX: Now I come to the picture books which were issued by the *Der Stürmer* publishing house. You know that two picture books were published, one with the title *Trust No Fox in the Field,* and the other with the title *The Poisonous Toadstool.* Do you assume responsibility for these picture books?

STREICHER: Yes. May I say, by way of summary, that I assume responsibility for everything which was written by my assistants or which came into my publishing house.

DR. MARX: Who was the author of these picture books?

STREICHER: The book *Trust No Fox in the Field and No Jew under His Oath* was done and illustrated by a young woman artist, and she also wrote the text. The title which appears on the picture book is from Dr. Martin Luther.

I do not know whether the judges and prosecution at Nuremberg took the trouble to read Seyss-Inquart's speeches. But I doubt it. If they had they would have discovered a striking similarity between what Seyss-Inquart told the conquered Dutch in 1940 and what they, the Western Allies, were telling the conquered Germans in 1945. In both cases the conquered peoples were adjured to recognize and accept a new order: for the conquered Dutch it was the Nazi New Order for Euope; for the conquered Germans it was a new world order based on a higher responsibility to international law. In 1940 the Germans were quacking about a new dispensation to cover the whole of Europe and indeed the world

[107]

once the German Reich had been recognized and taken rightful place in paramountcy or co-paramountcy with the great powers among the nations of the world.

Exactly the same thing happened at Nuremberg when the Western Allies proclaimed a new order of international law. That is what the Nuremberg Trials were all about. They were the attempt to establish a new order. It is hard to say which attempt was sillier: the Germans' attempting to establish a new order by conquest and simply dictating it, or the Allies' trying to establish a new order in a coalition of sovereign powers whose ideas on almost anything one cares to name were and still are as different from each other as night from day. It is obvious that after every great, world-shaking victory—a victory that makes so much difference to so many—it is obvious that there should be this compulsion to proclaim a permanent change in the way of man, in the regulation of life, of national life and international life. But it is also obvious that such a juncture in the affairs of men, while emotions run high and griefs go deep, is the worst possible time to attempt to bring about a permanent change.

But these glimpses behind the scene of the crime were for me no more than that, glimpses, as the trial ran through the first postwar year and on. They were inklings registered and then set aside for future reference. I thought it significant that Göring managed to commit suicide despite all the stringency of security the Americans could muster and maintain (not all that much by European standards: the Americans were short on experience in that particular discipline). But not very significant. It was a sign that there was something still left—enough to foil the Allies in their attempt to hang the chief war criminal. But no more than that.

For the rest I was impressed by the apparent disproportion between individual contribution—except in Albert Speer's case—and general results. All the major war criminals, able (as some were) or mediocre (as most were), were propelled upward and outward by events the generation of which was mystery. The mystery had a name: Adolf Hitler. But the name did not really provide a clue to the mystery. To the contrary: it had a diversionary effect. For the first few years after the war, when the memory of the man was still fresh—or, rather, when the sound of that voice still rang in the ears of the Germans—the name was the patent explanation for virtually everything that had happened: "Der Führer ist an allem schuld!" It was all the fault of the führer! That was, after all, the consensus of the prisoners in the dock at Nuremberg. Even Himmler's agency in the extermination of six million Jews was apparently just that: Himmler had repeatedly avowed that he had never, in so much as a single instance, determined the life or death of human beings except on express orders from the führer: "Führer befehl!—wir folgen" (Leader command!—we obey). In time the memory inevitably became a myth—a myth of evil, and the name Adolf Hitler in common parlance became the synonym for absolute evil.

Even so, this posed the question of how the Germans could have given themselves to the service of absolute evil. For the Germans there were too many conspicuous contradictions involved to make any sense of their situation. At the war's end and for a long time afterward they were literally thunderstruck: they did not know what had hit them. Fifteen years after the war, during the Tenth Congress of Cultural Freedom held in Berlin, the German publisher Joseph Caspar Witsch stated that no one yet knew how it was that Nazism had come about. They had been betrayed, of course: what had happened to the Germans no people could wish upon itself. They had been hoodwinked, spellbound: Hitler was a sorcerer whom they had mistaken for an oracle. But this version still left the sorcery to be explained; at best the Germans were a nation of unprecedented dupes. Whatever the version of the past was, there was unanimous agreement on one point: the past had to be surmounted. This self-admonition has been coined negatively: "die unbewältigte Vergangenheit"—the unsurmounted past—is the most hackneyed phrase in German life. Everybody uses it. Nobody knows what it means. For in order to surmount ("bewältigen" actually means to master, to bring under control) the past, the past must first be identified and defined. But for the first few years the Germans were so benumbed by the impact of the debacle, and so occupied and preoccupied with keeping themselves alive by foraging for food and fuel that the past was eclipsed by the present.

The year that marked the end of the "Thousand-Year Reich"—1945—was known in Germany as Year Zero. An apt name, for it came after the end but was not yet a beginning. This period of nothingness and need, of great physical distress might have ministered to the psychic welfare of the Germans had it not been for the deaths of countless innocents—children, the infirm of all ages, those who were not shrewd or hard enough to fend for themselves in a world dominated by the black market—who took sick from sheer undernourishment and died. The food rationing for the Germans, at 1,500 calories a day, was officially admitted to be at starvation level. In Berlin, a city governed by a council made up of the Four Powers during the first winter, a German woman lived two months in one room with her dead husband because the admission of his death would have deprived her of his ration card. Subzero temperatures and the lack of fuel combined to preserve the body as though it had been placed in a deep freezer.

MY EXPECTATION OF LOVE AMONG THE RUINS was disappointed. There were plenty of ruins but very little love. It was never demonstrated. It did not prevail as I had thought and hoped it would. When there was love, it grew in private, hidden gardens. There was, of course, a great deal of physical love: in an economy of extreme scarcity, physical love comes under the heading of "the simple pleasures." In most cases, indeed, moral considerations were simply thrown to the winds. During a brief period when I was stationed in Bamberg, my sergeant came to me and asked why I did not take part in the nightly forays to the surrounding villages to pick up women. These forays were known in GI parlance as "the meat run." I said that I would gladly join the party but I couldn't face the conversational ping-pong that decorum required as a prelude to intimacy. "What conversation?" asked my sergeant; "there's no conversation—all you have to do is give 'em a bar of soap!" A French lieutenant I knew was simply enchanted with German women. "Mon dieu," he said, "you tell a German woman, 'Meet at such and such a street corner at eight in the evening and we will fuck,' and she will meet you at the corner at eight in the evening and she will fuck you to a frazzle! C'est magnifique!" I gathered that he was most impressed by the directness and—again—the matter-of-factness of the procedure. But my French friend was forgetting that the German women he met just after the war were all forced to calculate the material advantages that were likely to result from the bestowal of their favors.

More valid observations were made by French prisoners of war in Germany. "At first," one of them told me, "we French prisoners tried the typical French approach to German women—with courtoisie, flowers, playing the gallant, that sort of thing. It didn't work well at all. We learned the efficacious approach from a German farmhand who for some reason or other had been exempted from military service. He just stepped up behind a girl I'd been courting unsuccessfully for two weeks and slapped her firmly on the rump. She didn't even look around but raised her arms above her head and shouted, 'Donnerwetter!—Noch einmal!' [Thunderation!—Do it again!]."

This, of course, was a farm girl and, in any case, it is caricaturing the German woman. But a caricature is an exaggeration, not a distortion of the truth. The amatory passions of German women are relatively easily inflamed. There is, indeed, a directness, a matter-of-factness; an attitude and approach to the act and significance of sex that is relatively unencumbered (and unprotected) by social conventions. The incidence of illegitimate births among the Germans—and among *Germanic* peoples generally—has always been very high. The German woman's attitude to sex—without the pill—was pretty much like her more westerly sister's attitude to sex *with* the pill. This is due not only to the absence of any puritan ethic such as the Anglo-Saxons have been saddled with but also and rather more significantly to the prevalence of a special relation of the Germans to nature. The Germans live very close to nature. They are nature lovers par excellence—even nature idolaters. This love and understanding of nature includes particularly the natural functions of the body. The Germans consider sex a natural function of the body. They tend to regard sex not only as good clean fun but also as healthy. "Women need physical love," said Franz Wagenknecht in the cellar of Villa Waldfriede one day—apropos of I can't remember what, "if they don't get it they become irritable and acquire complexes." The Germans' love of nature and the natural functions of the body is the legacy of their forest-dwelling ancestry; they manage to combine the legacy with the area of its origin: love in the woods or the open fields is a national pastime.

On a brief trip to Paris after the war I was invited to a dinner party given by George Gribbel, a septuagenarian British expatriate writer. The guest of honor was Jacques Delarue, novelist as well as nonfiction author specializing in the study of murder, member of the Sûreté, and, as we understood (erroneously) at the time, chief of the vice squad of Paris. Madame Gribbel, who was a Frenchwoman and almost as old as her husband, was fascinated by the dark, handsome, sinuous Delarue who looked like a Corsican, appearances being especially deceiving in his— Norman—case. After dinner and after approaching the subject and shying off again half a dozen times, Madame Gribbel screwed her courage to the sticking point and addressed Delarue directly: "Monsieur, I should like so much to know . . . ah, how should I say it? . . . ah, hmm . . . Monsieur . . ."

DELARUE: Madame?

MME GRIBBEL: Monsieur . . . la prostitution . . . how is prostitution conducted as a business?

DELARUE: Ma foi, madame—it is conducted like all other businesses.

MME GRIBBEL: Certainly, monsieur—but what is the current price—how shall I say it?—of love?

DELARUE: That depends, madame, on the area—the section of town.

MME GRIBBEL: And which and where is the highest price, monsieur?

DELARUE: Without any doubt between the Opéra and the Madeleine, where the price is about five hundred francs.

MME GRIBBEL: Oh, how terrible! [Quelle horreur!]

DELARUE: Madame?

MME GRIBBEL: But that is very little!

DELARUE: But, madame, what do you expect? [Que voulez-vous?] It is a question of ten minutes—maximum.

MME GRIBBEL: O, quelle horreur!

DELARUE: Ah, oui, madame, c'est l'abattoir de l'amour! [It is the slaughterhouse of love!]

To be sure, Madame Gribbel was a very old, rather provincial French lady. To be sure, there was more than a little coquetry in her performance. But such a conversation is unthinkable in Germany; not even the oldest, most provincial German lady could or would ever put questions like Madame Gribbel's nor react as she did to the answers had some foreigner put the question, let us say, to the chief of the morals police (Sittenpolizei) of any town or city in Germany.

The difference between the Gallic and Teutonic attitudes to sex is well illustrated in an anecdote about the French and (federal) German soldier on maneuvers together. Pierre: "I have a forty-eight-hour pass and I am going to go to my apartment in Paris, buy a bottle of champagne, undress my mistress, and pour it all over her. Then I am going to lick it all off." Hans: "My God, how wonderful! Say, could I do that with beer?"

Madame Gribbel steeled herself to put another question to Delarue: "Monsieur . . . what happens when . . . ah . . . the client is not satisfied with the services rendered? I mean, what recourse does he have in such a case?" Delarue: "Madame, I know of only one case that actually came to court. In her own defense the young lady testified that although she had done all in her power [malgré tout ses efforts]. . . . The judge threw out the case."

The only discussion I have ever heard in Germany on the same general problem was in Sankt Pauli, Hamburg's famous and notorious honky-tonk pleasure strip and sex mile. Here, one of the brothel–night club owners discoursed on the eventuality of a "client's" discovering too late (after paying his money) that he had come to grips with a transvestite (in either direction). The owner's views on the subject can be summed up as caveat emptor. Here again as so often in Germany the problem is one of identification and the confusion of concepts.

With this admonition in mind, then: there was a woman like the earth. She had a strong clear, melodious voice. (Madame de Staël noted that German women characteristically have pleasant voices.) We often sang together. More often my mouth was on hers. Her upper front teeth were slightly irregular. The irregularity gave a hint of the animal in her when she smiled—it was almost as if she were showing fangs. We met every night after dark for many months in a grove of birch trees at the top of a hill in Bavaria. We would talk and sing and then we would make love—with or without preliminaries and always on the ground either in the grove or in the open fields. She made love as naturally as she breathed but with something like quiet, persistent abandon. Adagio. At times when she approached the climax she would say, "I am going mad" or "I see everything" or "You bastard!" or "Give me the seed: I am like a flower," and "Maybe I'll get five head." (What she actually said was "five pieces"—"Vielleicht kriege ich fünf Stück"—but I felt it was almost as if she were talking about livestock.) She was strong and our lovemaking was delightfully strenuous—a decathlon of sexual acts. Once she bit me in a place where I had least expected to be bitten. When I yelped she said: "I'm sorry—do you suppose it will show?" We were occupied and preoccupied with the love-feast. We sat there, lay there, stood there night after night after night quietly, earnestly devouring each other. There is a steady, grate-glow passion about such a business that sits well in the soul: we were licking beer off one another, as it were—not champagne. As part of the beer rather than champagne—perspiration instead of perfume—approach to sex I would include the observation that a good many German women do not shave their legs. My mother-in-law once asked one of them why this was so and was told that most men prefer hairy legs to clean-shaven ones. There is something to this.

German men are apparently—but perhaps only apparently—romantics in love. Like most men everywhere, only more so, Germans see a new life in a woman's face. When a German sees a new life in a woman's face, the woman becomes eine Frau für das Leben—a woman for life—that is, a woman with whom he can build a new and far better life (than the one he is building with the woman he happens to be with at the time). This sight of a new life in a woman's face is an expression, I have heard tell, of the fact that a woman will do anything for the man she loves. I am convinced that this was what Goethe was getting at when he concluded *Faust* with the words "Das Ewig-Weibliche zieht uns hinan"—"The Eternal-Womanly leads us on!"—and on and on. A woman who is worth having is very difficult to get—or if not, very difficult to keep; or if not, very difficult to get rid of. That is the problem in a nutshell. For those who can afford it, it is not all that unusual to marry three, four, or five times before finally finding "the woman for a lifetime" or giving up the quest. For the great majority there is a rather elaborate system of liaisons. As the old German hit tune has it:

> Every fellow has a little lady friend,
> For a little lady friend is needed now and then.

German men often keep at least one mistress, often enough two or even three concurrently. Setting aside the amatory exactions of such polygyny, what impresses American men (I have this from colleagues who have spent years monitoring the tapes of telephone intercepts in Germany) is the sheer logistical load and the demands on conspiratorial technique involved. It is extraordinary—again, by American standards —how many Germans in public life keep mistresses (it is particularly surprising of German politicians). Clearly, general tolerance of such a situation is fairly high, otherwise they would not exist. There is a famous case in postwar Germany in which the correspondence of a prominent politician with his mistress was published as a book with the title *Once Upon a Time There Was a Girl.* The book was suppressed before it reached the stands for sale. Even so, a good many many copies are in private (and political) hands. Often enough—too often, however—the strain proves to be too great: one hears again and again of cases where the enterprising German male, caught between his mistress and his wife, or in the middle of a triangle of mistresses and wife, is so torn by the opposing attractions that he puts a bullet through his head.

It is striking that in German nightlife the stripteasers and assorted exotic dancing girls (they are called Schönheitstänzerinnen—beauty dancers—in German) often confuse sex with obscenity, the erotic with the fecal, going through motions that are suggestive not of copulation but of defecation. It is as if the German woman, under assignment to come up with something wicked, naturally and instinctively turns to the excremental since the act of sex in her esteem is not wicked at all. It is often pointed out that German profanity relies heavily on the fecal—Scheisskopf ("shithead") and Klugscheisser ("smart-shitter") for "wise guy"; a situation is "beschissen" ("shat upon")—and the scatological to the almost total exclusion of the sexual. Dirt, and particularly human excreta—shit—are opprobrious in the German cult of cleanliness, which has theological and demonological as well as tributary hygienic origins. The German word that has got me into trouble more often than any other (because it has always proved to be far more powerful than I have assessed it) is "Schweinerei," literally "swinery," filthiness, obscenity; more literally "piggishness." One of the chief characteristics of the German language is that its words—even in combinations—almost always retain their original, direct, nonderivative meanings. The Germans have never had a ban, religious or other, on the eating of pork. If the pig is as big a bogey to the Germans as it is to the Jews, it is because of its habits as far as the Germans are concerned. The Germans' morbid preoccupation with feces reminds me rather of the joke about the sex-mad anonymous telephone caller who has the bad luck to find himself talking to a five-year-old girl: "Get this, kid—peepee, potty-potty, poo!"

To me the German confusion of the sexual with the fecal connotes infantilism. As for the alleged conspicuous paucity and "brutal crudeness" of expressions for sexualia, these charges seem to me to rest on an ignorance of South German profanity and slang, some of whose terms (like the Austrian "Wischerl" for penis) are quaint and comely enough. In any case I think C. S. Lewis's assertion holds for German as well as most languages: "To describe the act of love in detail without resorting to allegory," he once told a television interviewer, "one is restricted to three choices: the language of the nursery, the language of the gutter, or the language of science—all are equally unsatisfactory."

A few days after the war, in a resort hotel in the Rhineland, a young German woman appealed to my second in command for protection against another American lieutenant whose advances had left her fuming with indignation. The unwanted suitor had been crude enough to offer her some chocolate bars in exchange for her favors. Protection was quickly afforded. In gratitude the rescued damsel liberally bestowed her favors on her protector, a reaction not uncommon in chivalric lore. According to the recounting of it, there ensued a night of love that involved several great sexual passages. In the midst of these, a good while after midnight, the young woman announced that she was ravenously hungry. It was too late to buy food or go foraging. My lieutenant bethought himself of the chocolate bars he carried in his overcoat pocket. (In this respect the American army in Europe was made up of "chocolate soldiers.") Without a word he got up and presented the bars to his companion, who bolted them with great relish and without the least reproach. The two lovers then readdressed themselves to their occupation.

This night was unforgettable to my lieutenant for several reasons, among them the fact that the German girl recited poetry throughout. "What sort of poetry?" I asked. "Only one poem—again and again: it was Schiller's "Ode to Joy." I think a translation of the first few lines of the "Ode to Joy" is appropriate.

> Joy, beautiful divine spark,
>   Daughter of Elysium,
> We enter, fire-drunk
>   Heavenly one, your holy temple.
> Your magic binds together again
>   What fashion so sternly divides;
> All men shall become brothers
>   Where your gentle pinion glides.
>
> *Chorus*
> Be embraced, millions!
> This kiss to the whole world! . . .

Apropos of "this kiss to the whole world" and the charge that German women are generally too free with their favors, there is the following story. Just last year a former U-boat officer complained ruefully of his wartime girl friend (a complaint, after all, that was at least a quarter of a century old). Every time he was on leave, he said, and his submarine's home port was attacked by an allied bomber, his girl would say, "Do you think the pilot is a good-looking fellow?" "Now how the hell do you like that?" the former submarine officer asked me. Submariners are superpatriots with a marked incapacity for appreciation of fine impartiality vis-à-vis the stern divisions of fashion.

For me, the model of German womanhood in just this point of fine impartiality was the blonde beauty photographed on the Kurfürstendamm in Berlin surrounded by grinning Nazi storm troopers and wearing a large placard held in place by a string around her neck. The placard read (with the inevitable rhyme):

> I am the greatest swine, I own,
> I give myself to Jews alone!

That photograph has gone around the world time and again; it has appeared in dozens of books about the Nazi period. Next to the beautiful blonde girl, almost a head shorter than she, stood her ugly-looking little Jewish boy friend. This was the public humiliation of two German citizens not by an official organ of the state but by members of a political party's paramilitary organization—while members of an official organ of the state, the police, looked on.

The date of this particular piece of racist example-making was August 13, 1934, a Sunday. The date sticks in my mind because it was the thirteenth, because it was a Sunday, the Lord's day, and because it was in August, a fine month in Berlin—hot, but not too hot, and clear. Finally and mainly, the date sticks in my mind because twenty-seven years later on the same date, August 13, 1961, a Sunday, the East German Communist armed forces strung barbed wire along the length of the twenty-six and a half miles of sector boundary between East and West Berlin, thus sealing off one half of the city from the other. It was the beginning of the construction of the Berlin Wall which still stands and is, to my mind, an affront to human dignity without precedent. Except that there was a precedent: the coincidence of the two dates in 1934 and 1961 moves me, even against my will, to regard the construction of the Berlin Wall as being somehow an act of retribution for the affront to human dignity (and to the simplest idea of polity) that took place in Berlin on Sunday, August 13, twenty-seven years earlier.

But there is a love that abides among Germans, a love that could not be displaced by the ravages of war or misplaced as the result of shocks to the nervous system. This is the German's filial devotion to Mother Nature and especially his fraternal love of animals. It is always a pleasure to see a German communing with animals in park, farmyard, or forest. I am tempted, as others have been, to assert that the honest Teuton has more feeling for and understanding of his fellow animals than he has for his fellowmen. Indeed, Heinrich Himmler went so far as to infer the right of Germans to lord it over Europe from the claim that they were the only continental Europeans who treated animals humanely. (Note the qualification "continental": even Himmler would not have dreamed of disallowing the Saxon cousin, the Englishman, in this regard. The only safe way to cross the street in England, so runs the cockney joke, is to take a dog with you; no Englishman would run over a dog.) I was first made aware of this grand passion in the early fifties in Berlin. Frau Scheel, who lived nearby, bought a live gosling in midsummer for the express purpose of fattening the bird for the kill on Christmas Eve.

The gosling was specially fed with milk and white bread—a diet calculated to make its flesh abundant and tender—and given the run of the garden. As the months went by the bird—inevitably, as I now realize—became the pet of the entire family. Came the day of reckoning, the paterfamilias discovered that he could not bring himself to kill the goose. At the same time all concerned were loath to abandon the prospect of a fine goose dinner on Christmas Day. So they decided to do the deed humanely. They soaked a handkerchief with chloroform and gently wrapped it around the pet's head. When the goose keeled over, Frau Scheel plucked it and put it on the pantry shelf, meaning to clean out the entrails the next morning. But when the family came down for breakfast, there was the goose, more naked than the day it was born, walking somewhat dazedly about the kitchen. This was too much. The survival of the goose was taken as a sign. No further attempt was made on the life of the bird, by stealth or otherwise. Instead Frau Scheel knitted a green pullover "gooseneck sweater" to protect the pet from the cold until its feathers grew back in. The goose's name was Oscar.

The proverbial friendship of every German for all animals (Jeder Deutscher ein Tierfreund!) has been borne out in my experience. Germans will go to considerable lengths to keep an afflicted pet alive. A friend of mine had a dachshund ("badgerdog") whose entire hindquarters became incurably paralyzed, a disaster that frequently befalls the species because the extreme length of the body and the shortness of the legs put inordinate pressure on the spinal column. So complete was the paralysis of Pumml, as he was called, that there was no question of his lifting a hind leg. Pumml could neither urinate nor have a bowel movement. His owner induced urination by laying Pumml on a table and gradually pressing his fist against the dog's bladder. Bowel movements were induced by enema. The entire procedure lasted about four minutes and was undertaken twice a day, mornings and evenings. This went on for more than three years and ended only when Pumml contracted another disease. Thereupon his owner reluctantly shot him.

As with fauna so with flora. The German passion for flowers, gardens, and parks is altogether remarkable. It is no great exaggeration to say that every streetside window in Germany has a box garden of flowers in it. The most beautiful gardens I have ever seen are in the green boroughs of Berlin. Berlin has a vast amount of land set out in parks, over eight thousand acres, perhaps the largest area for parks of any city in the world. According to a statistic for 1970 Berliners spent an average of 14 marks per capita during the year for flowers. I suspect that in any international comparison of per capita flower buying, the Berlin figure would prove to be extraordinarily high. If so, it would be largely due to the German custom which dictates that every male guest should bring flowers to the lady of the house (a box of candy is a permissible but infrequent alternative). We had a friend in Berlin who had fallen on evil days. We therefore made a practice of inviting him to dinner once a week so as to reduce his outlay for food. We were forced to discontinue the practice because our guest invariably brought a bouquet or a pot of flowers that cost him far more than the food and drink we provided saved him.

The German's relationshop to nature is as direct and therefore as mystical as that of the American Indian. A major aspect of the "German problem" is the dogged, often desperate attempt of the German to maintain his ties with nature and all that is natural in the face of the industrial and technological revolutions. It is a dilemma that is epitomized for me by Alfred Krupp who established the great industrial empire that bears his father's name. Krupp had an air hose installed into his sanctum sanctorum (located in a tower high above the din and soot of his factories) so that he could reach for the tube and take deep whiffs from the pile of cow dung to which the hose led.

Certainly one of the main links connecting the German with the innermost workings of nature is the use of animal intestine as the natural casing for ground meant: the sausage link. This is not to contend that the sausage is a German invention. But it is the most typical German form of victual. The Germans have perfected the invention beyond the dreams of any other nation. There are some fifteen hundred different kinds of sausage currently produced in Germany. Germans would not be Germans without sausage. Es geht um die Wurst (literally, "The sausage depends on it") is a much used German idiom meaning that everything depends on it, that the issue is crucially important. The existence of another idiom, Mir ist alles Wurst ("It's all sausage to me"), with the exact opposite meaning ("I couldn't care less") merely attests to the ubiquity of sausage in German life.

The connection also manifests itself in the general cultivation of the natural sciences. I suffered for years from the inevitability of the scientific documentary film's immediately preceding the main attraction in German movie houses. These films were almost always about insects. The only memorable insight I ever achieved during these interminable sessions was in speculation on the moral difference between the praying man and the praying mantis. Then, too, every self-respecting German bourgeois who owned a library was sure to possess the thirteen volumes bound in half leather of Brehm's *Tierleben* ("Animal Life"), subtitled "General Information on the Animal Kingdom." Each volume averages 600 pages and the entire set contains over 3,500 illustrations, 279 of them in color. The first edition of this tour de force (in six volumes) appeared in 1869 and was largely based on the observations of the widely traveled Alfred Edmund Brehm. In his preface Brehm acknowledges debt (for information stemming from the classics) to one man only: "If then mistakes should be noticed with regard to such accounts, let Oken answer for them."

Lorenz Oken, who came of age at the turn of the eithteenth century, was a naturalist, a professor of zoology, and a natural philosopher. Oken instigated the first joint convention of German naturalists and physicians (in 1822). More important to my purpose, Oken is listed in the standard German encyclopedia, *Der Grosse Brockhaus*, as "the most important natural philosopher of the romantic period." According to the account, "He regarded natural philosophy as 'the science of the eternal transubstantiation of God in the world. It has to do with the manifestation of mathematical ideas. All things in nature are moving numbers that reduce themselves to the absolute unity. The ether is God's body, matter is thickened ether, light is the stretching of ether. Organisms developed from bubbles [cells] in the primordial slime.' "

This is an example of the typical German fusion of science and religion, of the material with the abstract, within the terms of an abounding love of nature.

J UST BEFORE CHRISTMAS IN 1945 I WAS POSTED TO THE town of Hof an der Saale, a strange corner of the German world—again, on the seam. Hof lay on the demarcation line between the Soviet and American zones of occupation in Germany, just ten miles from the Czech border. We were to act as a liaison group with the Eleventh Russian Guards Assault Army under General Chuikov in Weimar. I say "we": "we" were Lieutenant William Sloane Coffin, Jr., Sergeant Alexander Rusanovsky, Corporal Ivan Chysefsky, and myself—Americans all. Except for the highly unpleasant business of turning several thousand Vlassovite Russian soldiers over to the Red Army, our "liaison" with the Soviets had already been reduced to perfunctory contacts. Russians traveling to and from Nuremberg or as members of repatriation teams (trying to find and persuade reluctant Russian DPs to return home) would call for help whenever their transportation broke down, which was often enough. Otherwise the Soviets had already sealed off their zone of occupation and kept to themselves. There were no more American-Soviet parties. For the most part we lived quietly and carefreely and our liaison was with the Germans. We lived in a three-story, so-called three-family house at 9, Robert-Koch-Strasse. We occupied the first two floors, leaving the third floor to the earlier occupants. As we found them, these were three housewives, Frau Grass, Frau Klarner, and Frau Peez, all of whose husbands were either missing in action or known to be prisoners of war in the Soviet Union. There were three children from two families: two Klauses and a girl named Hedwig. But there were also sisters, brothers, cousins, uncles, friends. We were authorized to run our own mess and drew double the rations we needed since the liaison group was seldom at more than half strength. Moreover, neither Coffin nor I was a smoker and we gave our ration of cigarettes away. I find it difficult to believe now that either one of us really knew what he was doing: cigarettes were literally worth their weight in gold. For these reasons—quite apart from

Coffin's native charm—we were very popular. Knowingly and unknowingly we fed at least half the neighborhood.

Coffin was somewhat given—as so many of us were—to lecturing the Germans on the sins of the Third Reich. It was always interesting to see him corner an incredulous garbage collector or meter reader and harangue the statutory suspect for a quarter of an hour on the evils of the "führer principle" and absolute obedience and collective guilt. Although a fine linguist, Coffin had never bothered to study German, an omission that did not in the least discourage him from speaking the language with great gusto and to surprising effect. Indeed he was guilty of the biggest clinker I have ever heard in German. I had taken him down to Schloss Isar-Eck to meet my princesses. When Coffin was introduced to their highnesses, he bowed, smiled broadly, and said, "Verzeihen Sie, wenn ich Sie zerstöre." What he meant to say was "Forgive me if I disturb you" (. . . Sie störe). What he did say was "Forgive me if I destroy you." There was an extended pause until the consternation evaporated.

In the Robert-Koch-Strasse we were initiated into the German ceremonial expectation of holidays. I had never seen anything like this: the Germans have a heightened sense of holidays. There are a great many holidays in Germany, both Protestant and Catholic. The Germans measure time by them and the course of life hinges on them. There are holidays clearly in prospect at all times. Four Sundays before Christmas Advent begins. An Advent wreath with four candles is hung from the ceiling or placed on a table and a candle is lit on each successive Sunday. Also an Advent calendar is pinned to the wall. This is a picture of some Christmas scene with twenty-four numbered doors cut into the cardboard. With the beginning of each day the appropriate door is opened to reveal another picture.

December 6 is St. Nicholas's Day. On the eve of St. Nicholas's Day the children put their shoes before the doors of their bedrooms to find them filled with presents in the morning (but only so much as to fill the shoes). Or St. Nicholas appears himself on his day. In Austria he is always in company with the Krampus, bogey man of early childhood, generally of fearsome aspect, with a brown fur-edged surcoat. When St. Nicholas appears he distributes presents from his bag to all good children. For all bad children the Krampus is armed with a sheaf of willows bound together at one end to make a switch. This is the only time St. Nicholas or the Krampus appears. On Christmas Eve, when the presents are invariably opened under the fir tree (Tannenbaum), attention is concentrated on the birth of Christ, either, as in Catholic areas, by going to midnight mass, or by admiring the crèche—the cradle scene—home-made or in an elaborate model in some public place. On December 25 begin the twelve days of Christmas. These end with Epiphany on January 6, the feast of commemoration of the appearance of the Magi before the Christ child.

The Fasching or Carnival season among the Germans lasts from two to three and a half months, depending on the area. In the Rhineland, for example, Carnival begins as early as November 11 and ends—as it does everywhere—with the first day of Lent: "On Ash Wednesday," as the song goes, "it is all over!" Carnival for the Germans is a protracted period of revelry, hilarity, license, licentiousness, and general misrule. During Carnival the Germans indulge their passion for wine, women, song, and dance, and above all for disguising themselves in exotic or period costumes. Ninety-five percent of all Carnival balls are costume or masked balls.

The ball calendar for Vienna for any year will list some 250 balls, beginning with New Year's Eve and ending with Shrove Tuesday. Here is a representative list: Pharmacy Ball, Ball of Chemistry and Economy, Viennese Doctors' Ball, Opera Ball (in Vienna the grand occasion of the season), Viennese Coffeehouse Owners' Club Ball, Ball of the Viennese Cartel Group, Ball of the Viennese Lawyers' Association and Law Students' Group, Ball of the Construction and Wood Workers, Annual Festival of the Pharmacist Employees of Austria, Ball of the Association of Jewish University Students, Pathfinders League Ball, Twelfth Night Ball of the Noncommissioned Officers of Vienna, Ball of the Sons and Daughters of Butchers and Meat Smokers, Ball of the County Guild of Furriers, Glovemakers, and Tanners, County Guild of Wallpaper Hangers Ball, Bonbon Ball of the Central Federation of Candy Store Owners, Ball of the Athletic Association of the National Bank, Ball of the State Guild of Sheet Metal Workers and Coppersmiths, Viennese Gas and Electric Meter Readers Ball, Sociability Association of the City Sanitary Engineers Ball, Ball of the State Guild of Gas and Water Pipes Installers, Ball of the Association of Customs (Guard) Officials, Ice Factory Sport Club Ball, Transylvanian Saxons Ball, Costume Festival of the Glee Club of Austrian Railroad Officials in Vienna, Ball of the Association of Viennese Retail Coal Merchants, Ball of the Union of Floor Tilers and Pipe Layers and Their Assistants, Bad Girls' Ball, Traveling Salesmen's Ball, Chemical Cleaners Guild Ball, Children's Ball of the Austrian

People's Party (conservative), Red Chrysanthemum Ball of the Social Democratic Party of Austria, Czechs' Ball, Simmeringer Gardeners' Ball.

At a costume ball during Carnival in Linz, Austria, in the late 1960s a young man met a young girl, danced with her all night, and fell madly in love with her. After the ball was over and the young man sought to consummate their passionate attachment (as is the use during Carnival), his beloved stepped back, took off the wig she had been wearing, and revealed herself to be a seventeen-year-old boy, a plumber's apprentice. The frustrated lover killed the impostor with his bare hands.

During Carnival adultery is licensed and copulation thrives. A great many of the divorces in Germany and German-speaking countries have their origin in the infatuations that come (and go) in the gaiety and intoxication of the Carnival season. During Carnival, as the unofficial German proverb goes, in case of extreme need one can always go to bed with one's own wife. A favorite Carnival joke is the situation in which mummers at a masked ball go to bed only to discover that they are man and wife. Despite or perhaps because of the pagan beginning of Carnival (there is a direct line of descent from the Roman saturnalia) the custom is observed with more persistent and premeditated abandon in Catholic areas such as Austria, Bavaria, and the Rhineland than in the Protestant North and East. But the difference is only one of degree.

Easter and Whitsuntide are major holidays in Germany, as is May Day, another pagan derivation (the immemorial celebration of the rites of spring in all three cases). The latter was adopted by the German labor movement as the traditional first holiday of the workers. Perhaps the most unvarnished pagan holiday in Germany is Johannistag (Saint John's Day), the celebration of the summer solstice when, in some regions—particularly Westphalia—a burning wheel (the sun wheel) is rolled down a hill. The Feast of Thanksgiving at Harvest (Erntedankfest) in September, which found its way via England to the United States to become Thanksgiving Day, is of course another primordial pagan rite which has become so Christianized in Germany that there is no longer a traditional feast connected with it. Rather church altars are decorated with the produce of orchard and field. Saint Martin's Day in November is a feast day on which the Martin's Goose, led with a string around its neck, takes part in the parade headed by Saint Martin on horseback, wearing a gorgeous cloak and a sword to cut it with (in conformance with the legend in which the saint cuts his cloak in two to share it with a beggar). The procession is generally made up of children dressed as beggars or in various garish costumes. During the day the children go begging by threes and fours to all the houses in the neighborhood and sing songs for the occasion, among them:

We are in the house of a rich man
Who'll give us gifts as best he can!

Not long after the war I met Benno Frank again. He was stationed near Frankfurt in the headquarters of Psychological Warfare. His chief was a man named Tombs. Nomen est omen: Mr. Tombs took a grave attitude to everything—or so it seemed. He was not averse to repeating himself; "I don't trust these Germans" was his favorite catchphrase. One of the things Psychological Warfare did in Germany was to arrange for more or less prominent Germans to give talks and lead political discussions at public gatherings. I attended the first of these evenings with Benno. There were only three speakers; it was hard to induce Germans to take part in public political discussions then. One of the speakers was a Diplom-Ingenieur (a graduate of a school of engineering) who was very definite, as becomes an engineer, and whose message was "Wir haben uns vermessen!"—We have misjudged ourselves, miscalculated ourselves, or, more generally, made a botch of surveying our situation, our substance, and our potential. At the time this attempt at an explanation struck me as a macabre, ludicrous "Oops! Our mistake!" And yet the Third Reich was a mistake, a mis-take (German "Fehlgriff"), a misapprehension: the Germans, explained the engineer, had made a false measurement, they had gauged themselves to be something they weren't, gauged their situation to be something it wasn't and, for that matter, gauged the world to be something it wasn't. The whole hideous business had been based on a wildly inaccurate survey of reality.

It was just before Christmas 1945 and Benno also introduced me to a German idyll in Königstein near Frankfurt am Main. The idyll consisted of a German family with four children, three girls and a boy, all of whom with their parents were highly accomplished amateur musicians. They made Hausmusik—music played in the home, often chamber music—with piano, violin, cello, and flute. They specialized, of course, in sextets. On that evening they played a sextet by Schubert to enchanting effect. The surroundings, too, were idyllic: they lived in a large, chalet-style house built of fir and cedar, its interior paneled with stained and polished oak. The oak paneling caught the points of light from the candles on the Christmas tree and on the Advent wreathes and sent them glinting on the taffy-colored hair of the three daughters of the house. The daughters all wore their hair in the Bavarian "goosegirl" style, parted in the middle and combed hard away from the part to be twisted taffylike at the nape into two thick braids hanging down the back. They were all, with their mother, dressed in Bavarian dirndls, the South German peasant costume with voluminous skirts, ceremonial apron, and wide, square, deep décolletage. They were all neat as pins and scrubbed till they shone, reflecting as much light as the oak paneling. The room was full of glancing light and sinuous sound. I was enchanted. "These," said Benno at one point in the evening, "are the 'other Germans.' Can you imagine their having had anything to do with the gas chambers and the cremation ovens of the SS? Well, they *did*: they had their part to play." I put that down to the rhetoric of the time and place. Naturally enough, everybody suspected everybody.

Benno's greatest contribution to my experience and general well-being was his introducing me to "Tante Hanna," Frau Hanna Geuer, the widow of the first, last, and only president of the Rhenish republic. This was a very short-lived, French-sponsored "separate state" on the left bank of the Rhine after World War I. "Tante Hanna," said Benno, "is my aunt and now she is your aunt." Actually, Frau Geuer was the aunt of Benno's best friend, Franz. Tante Hanna lived in a glittering white four-story villa in a beautifully cultivated, hilly suburb of Wiesbaden. The villa itself was almost flush with the street, but behind it—invisible to the passerby—was a very large, luxuriant, but carefully trimmed garden. The villa was furnished and appointed like a palace. All the rooms and the huge stairwell with its broad, shallow steps were also luminously white, the walls hung with tapestries and oil paintings. There was always plenty to eat, excellently cooked. We usually had tea when we went to see Tante Hanna and the pastry was baroque in its elegance and as sweet as fresh cider. I attributed this elegant sufficiency to the good offices of Benno until I learned that Franz was an employee of the French military government.

Tante Hanna was well over seventy then but she looked as smooth, high-colored, and ageless as a doll of Dresden china. She had obviously been a beautiful woman in her youth and middle age. She was always in excellent spirits; she was one of those creatures endowed with an inexhaustible capacity for wonder and enthusiasm. Johanna Geuer was born in 1870 in Essen, in the Ruhr, the only daughter and second child of a professor at the city Gymnasium (high school). At the age of nineteen she married one of her father's students. But what a one! At that time in the city of Essen there were two exceedingly rich men: Krupp, the factory owner, and Piekenbroek, the house owner. Tante Hanna married the youngest son of Piekenbroek.

Within a year she was a widow, young Piekenbroek having fallen victim to what they used to call "galloping consumption." But Johanna was also a very wealthy widow; her husband had left her several million marks. She removed to Wiesbaden, which she preferred to the only other notable spa in Germany, Baden-Baden. She bought the four-story gleaming white villa in the Hilda-Strasse on the side of a hill overlooking the casino. In 1895 she married Privy Councilor (Geheimer Regierungsrat) Clemens Caesar, who was at least twenty-five years her senior.

It was as Frau Geheimer Regierungsrat that fourteen years later she met the man of her life, Doctor Hans Adam Dorten, a dashing young fellow (younger than Hanna) with a monocle and a fine head of close-cropped curly hair. An excellent horseman (he became a Rittmeister, or captain of cavalry, during the war), he was also a very devout Catholic as befitted a native of Cologne, "the holy city on the Rhine" in whose cathedral the remains of the three Magi lie buried. Because of this, a dispensation for the annulment of Hanna's marriage to the privy councilor—permission to take away from Caesar what was Caesar's , as it were —had to be obtained from the pope. So it was not until 1910, when Hanna was already forty years old, that she married her dashing Doctor Dorten.

They were divorced in 1925, after the debacle of the movement for an independent Rhineland. Some of the leaders of the movement (or movements) were assassinated by Prussian special troops, others were imprisoned. All were denounced as traitors generally. Dorten removed to France where he was registered as a resident of Nice when the divorce became effective. But there was no talk of any of this when I arrived on the scene. I left Wiesbaden and surrounding area with the impression that Tante Hanna had long been the widow of an exemplary man who had done—or tried to do—a noble deed.

N JANUARY 1946 I REMEMBERED SOMETHING THAT MY IM-
mediate superior at SHAEF, Colonel John ("Stiffy") Austin had
said to me when I took leave of him six months before. "If," he
said (and I was much surprised that he said anything: not for
nothing did we call him "Stiffy"), "when you are mustered out you
find yourself at a loose end, come and see me." I was curious: I
hadn't the faintest idea of what he had meant. So on my first long leave
after the war I went to England and looked him up at the address in
Abingdon he had given me. I asked him what he had meant by his "loose
end" speech. "Ah," he said, "I am a philosophy don at Magdalen College, Oxford, and I am the chairman of the Board of Admissions and if
you like, I shall tell Sir Henry Tizzard that you are a good fellow and
we'll get you in." So he did, and so I was.

I had—or had had—two scholastic ambitions. One was to go to
Oxford as a Rhodes scholar (necessarily as a Rhodes scholar: how else
did an American get to Oxford?). The other was to teach Greek or
English at a German university. The Rhodes scholarships did not take
up again until 1947. I decided on the spot against waiting a full year and
then taking my chances before a Rhodes selection board. I had more than
a year's pay as a second lieutenant in my back pocket and the GI Bill
of Rights, which at that time afforded the recipient seventy dollars a
month for some four or five years, depending on the length of service.
I chose to read English instead of Greek because I already had a degree
with a Greek major and because I did not want to do a postgrauduate
course at Oxford. I wanted the full treatment. Above all, I wanted to be
"smoked at" by a tutor. The tutor in this case was the problem. The
English tutor at Magdalen happened to be the most famous Oxonian in
residence—Clive Staples Lewis, he of *The Screwtape Letters*, *The Problem of Pain*, and *The Great Divorce*. Even at that time, *The Screwtape
Letters* alone had gone through twenty British and fourteen American
printings. As a celebrity of unparalleled magnitude, Lewis had far more
undergraduates than he could conveniently handle in a college already

overcrowded with the backlog of the war years. If I persisted in my intention of reading English, my final acceptance would depend on Lewis. My first meeting with Lewis was inauspicious enough: just as I was leaving, Lewis turned to me and said, "Are you aware, sir, that your fly is open?" I assured him that I had not been and fled. Lewis had questioned whether, as. an American, I had sufficient background in English literature to undertake the course. But in the end he accepted me.

Unlike the content, the form of the Full Honours Course of English Language and Literature at Oxford is simple: one essay a week on a set topic, or the undergraduate's selection from a set series of topics— usually an author or a period of English literary history—which is read aloud to the tutor during an hour's tutorial. Ordinarily the reading of the essay takes up the first fifteen minutes of the hour. In the remaining time the tutor attacks the essay's argument, and the undergraduate does his best to defend it.

But this was only one part of the Full Honours Course. The other part was language: Anglo-Saxon, Middle English, and etymology. The "Anglo-Saxon tutor," as he was called, was J. A. W. ("Jack") Bennett. The staple of the Anglo-Saxon course was and probably always will be *Beowulf*; those of Middle English were *Sir Gawain and the Green Knight* and a far more important though later work, *Piers the Plowman*. I took to Bennett immediately: he was a kindred spirit, a New Zealander. Also, my knowledge of German was of great help in studying Anglo-Saxon, which was a branch of West Germanic. With Lewis I had some little trouble from the start. During my first tutorial, to illustrate some point Lewis mentioned Mozart's *The Marriage of Figaro*. "You have these pauses," he said, "even in opera when the story goes on without the music—like the recitative in *The Marriage of Figaro.*" "Sir," I interrupted, "there is not one unmusical moment in *The Marriage of Figaro!*" I had only a few months before spent many hours in the Kurhaus in Wiesbaden as Tante Hanna's guest listening to Mozart operas. For me, Mozart's recitative was music. To my surprise (because I wasn't sure) Lewis conceded the point. But he was anything but happy about it.

Not long afterward I concluded an essay with a long quote in the original German from one of Thomas Mann's critical essays. I took this liberty because Lewis in his critical essays (which everyone reading English studied assiduously) quoted German as well as Greek, Latin, French, and Italian. When I had finished reading the essay, there was a long, unusual silence. Finally Lewis said, "Will you translate that

German passage for me, please?" (It was not until some years later when he wrote the autobiographical *Surprised by Joy* that Lewis publicly admitted that he had never really learned German.) At that time I was very much surprised, and not by joy.

But my most grievous surprise with Lewis came some time later when, during the reading of my essay on Shakespeare's *Merchant of Venice*, I commented that because of what had happened to the Jews in Germany and German-occupied Europe during the war it would be impossible to present *The Merchant of Venice* for perhaps many years to come. This, it seemed to me, was far from contending—as the German-Jewish philosopher and academician Theodor Adorno had after the Nuremberg exposé of the "final solution"—that "no one will ever be able to write a lyric poem after Auschwitz!" But to present the character of Shylock, the medieval archetype of the money-grubbing, blood-sucking usurious Jew after Auschwitz struck me as something like a ritual repetition of the Nazi execration—at least until Auschwitz and the "final solution" altogether had receded into some sort of historical perspective. "Not at all," said Lewis. "All you have to do is add a quarter of an inch to Shylock's nose. Just a bit of putty and the problem is solved!" As it turned out, it was not until 1969—almost a quarter of a century later— that *The Merchant of Venice* was presented in Germany in a production by the German Jew, Fritz Kortner. Kortner himself played Shylock and gave a superbly sensitive performance. Immediately following there was a panel discussion of the play chaired by Günter Grass and including the rabbi of Cologne. It was and was meant to be a significant occasion; it marked a turning point or, rather, a point of return.

This is not to belittle Lewis as a scholar or brand him as nothing more than a scholar, however great he may have been within the confines of the definition. Lewis was a medievalist. The roots and trunk of his learning were Greek and Latin; its branches were Old French, Provençal, and Italian. He knew Old Norse, but it was not a speciality—even though the *Edda* was one of his favorite works. He read it in translation. He all but ignored German and did indeed ignore all Slavic languages, including Old Church Slavonic. Some case perhaps (but not much of one) can be made for the medievalist's slighting German to favor French and Italian to the extent that Lewis did. In this connection Latin covers a multitude of commissions. In Germany the end of the Middle Ages coincides with the end of Latin and the almost magical appearance of Luther's German.

Obviously Lewis's learning was weighted heavily to the West. But here his preferences were typical of the Englishman and part and parcel of the national cultural development. (After World War I—more than forty years after and not long before his death—Lewis crossed the English Channel only once.) For the Englishman as for Lewis the original German connection was exchanged for and obscured by Old Norse. The display of Old Norse as an important component in the formation of the English language and literature is something very like a historical card trick. It is used to camouflage the German foundation laid by the three German tribes who invaded the huge Celtic island just offshore from the continent. The Angles or Angul, the Low German tribe from Holstein, gave their name to the new country—Angul-land: England. The English language is a Latinized, Gallicized German.

The essential characteristic of Anglo-Saxon literature, as of all Germanic literature, is the omnipresence of gods and demons. The old Germanic world was the pagan world par excellence. For me *Beowulf* was not the cornerstone in the foundation of the English language and literature. For me *Beowulf* was the door to the dim, remote German past that had been startlingly foreshortened by the sudden, entirely unexpected havoc-wreaking eruption of the primordial Germanic hero into modern industrial life: "Be-Adolf." When Beowulf comes to Denmark to rescue Hrothgar's kingdom from the ravagings of the man-monster Grendel, he greets his royal host with the words, "Waes thu, Hrothgar, hal!" (Be you, Hrothgar, hale!) In other words—with the same original meaning—"Hail Hrothgar!" Heil Hitler! When Beowulf guards Hrothgar's great hall through the night, he mortally wounds the marauding Grendel by tearing off the monster's arm in a tremendous battle. The next night Grendel's mother (an even more horrible monster) avenges his death by making off with one of Hrothgar's most eminent kinsmen. Beowulf then pursues Grendel's mother to her lair at the bottom of a swamp. Beowulf descends into the swamp fully armed (in full field pack and equipment) and slays the monster-mother. At this I, the superannuated schoolboy, could not help but see Adolf as the symbolic hero of the German nation, descending fully armed into Pripet Marshes in pursuit of the monster Bolshevik bear—unlike Beowulf never to re-emerge.

Beowulf is himself a sort of Hermann, the German Hercules, the mythical half-god who combines supernatural physical strength with unremitting valor in the service of his clan or his clan's friends. Beowulf originally meant "fearsome wolf." Cynewulf, the name of another Anglo-Saxon hero, means "royal wolf." Wolf and Wolfgang (he of the wolf's gait—as in Mozart) are still popular German "Christian" forenames. There is the warrior-hero Wolfdietrich in the epic *Ortnit* who is the archetype of the old German "Recke," a word that denotes a half savage warrior-hero-giant who fights like a beast of prey, who is crude and terrible. Wolfdietrich's battle harness steams when he is angry. In *Ortnit* the women are coarse, foul-mouthed furies devoid of shame. Everything is huge (like the führer's architectural conceptions): there are vast, gaping wounds (but no wound ever gaped like Grendel's when Beowulf tore off his arm). Untellably large numbers of men and animals are involved in battles.

I see from the notes I took on Professor Wrenn's lectures on *Beowulf* that "magic was widely practiced in the Germanic pagan world and was a long time dying. It was reintroduced into England by Norwegians." (The Nordic-Germanic axis again). *Beowulf* is "full of demons and elves and evil spirits. In Old English elves are definitely evil. In the 'Anglo-Saxon Charms' arrowheads are 'elf-shots,' 'the invisible darts of the elves.' " *Beowulf*, like all Germanic heroic poems, is also full of corpses, particularly corpses from the lower world; the Old Germanic peoples are very much given to necromancy, the divining of the future by means of communication with the dead. Mention is made of "helrunan," the necromancers, who are "creatures of mystery," "rūn" (rune) being a mystery. The "hel" of "helrunan" is our "hell," the word the Old Germans used for both the pagan and the Christian notions of Hades. Originally in Germanic languages hell was a place of concealment (from Anglo-Saxon "helan": compare the modern German "hehlen," to hide).

Since my introduction to the Germans on their home continent was inseparably associated with hillocks of corpses, gaping wounds, dismembered bodies, and coagulated blood, I was ready to read all sorts of significances into the exegesis of *Beowulf*. It seemed to me that the Germanic-German preoccupation with carnage and corpses came close to necrolatry and necrophilia, the worship and physical love of corpses and carnification—the production of corpses for the sake of the production of corpses. There is at least some truth in this: it is impossible to separate the hero (Held) from the hero's death (Heldentod)—the hero works with death, as the special troops of the SS had their own strange device: "to give death and to receive death." The physical product of death is the corpse.

And yet the old Germans had a remarkably matter-of-fact way of dealing with murder and the act of killing. "When you killed a man in Anglo-Saxon times, you owed to the family the value that they had lost through your deed. There must therefore exist a blood-feud until either you paid them the necessary 'wergild' or you were slain by their hands or they by yours. Such a feud existed between Grendel and Hrothgar" (Wrenn's lectures). In the German paradox, the obsession with life, the "of-the-earth earthiness" is coupled with the fascination with death and its mysteries, with "the very German thirst for death" (Todessüchtigkeit) that blends into a proneness to martyrdom. The coupling link is the corpse. The corpse is the symbol of the transition from life to death, the evidence of the connection between the two. The German attitude to death is and apparently always has been signally matter-of-fact.

The familiarity with corpses and the attitude to death as a practical matter are aspects of the German passion for mechanistic abstraction. The value of the phrase rests on the balance of equal emphases between the words "passion," "mechanistic," and "abstraction." In the German approach to life (and death) there is always something of the artisan, the handicraftsman. There was always this striving to pin the abstract down —and pretty much on a do-it-yourself basis. According to Wrenn it is wrong to translate "haerg," the West Saxon place of worship, as "temple": the Germanic people did not have temples; what they had was rather like a "tabernacle," a more or less makeshift shelter built to contain the image and holy objects of worship. In Jewish history the Tabernacle was the tent that contained the Ark of the Covenant during the wanderings of the Jewish people. The Old Germans put together a tabernacle wherever they could and whenever there was need. Not only was the head of the clan chief and priest in one (dux et sacerdotus), every head of a household was a priest as well, leading his family and retainers in worship at the altar set up in the home. In this sense Luther's reformation of the church, making every man his own priest, is a return to a linear development from the Old German practice.

There are a great many pretty girls in England. But in my time there were very few in Oxford. As far as I knew, the only really pretty girls in Oxford were foreigners, for the most part Danish and French, who worked in private homes as housemaids or governesses. There were even a few German girls in this group although most of them gave themselves out to be Danish or Swedish; it was a good deal more fashionable at the time. Once again we had the phenomenon in England of the Teuton masquerading as the Scandinavian.

One of these young German governesses-cum-maids was conspicuous for the rarest of attributes among all the creatures that walk erect

—a beautiful stride. This attribute is so rare in the English-speaking world that there is no set or apt way of expressing it: "gait" is for horses. "They said a light came from her when she moved," sang Tennyson. And indeed, this young lady trod the earth so lightly that she literally seemed to be walking on air—I judged about half an inch or perhaps only a centimeter above the ground. (A German poet would be more likely to *hear* a comparison than *see* it: in praising his heroine, Christian Dietrich Grabbe singles out "the music of her movements.") Not knowing she was foreign, I assumed she was British. Assuming she was British, I further assumed that she was nonresident and simply visiting Oxford over the weekend as was the use among pretty girls in England. My false assumptions led me to the false conclusion that she would be gone forever on the morrow. My false conclusion drove me to the desperate measure of making the approach direct—"I stepped right up and said 'Howdy' "— at high noon at the corner of Cornmarket and Broad Streets.

The result was a fiasco. The German girl took fright (which seemed uncharacteristic somehow), umbrage, and my heart on the occasion and kept all three. When I learned, as I soon did, that she was German and resident in Oxford, I undertook to make amends. By so doing, of course, I only aggravated the situation. One attempt at a public apology boomeranged so badly that I kept to my rooms for two whole days. Now Oxford is a small town, in area and otherwise; in a very short time we had an intolerable situation. In the course of our normal rounds, hers more or less domestic, mine more or less academic, we were bound to meet. When our rounds became abnormal owing to our efforts to avoid one another —when, indeed, the two of us were catfooting it around Oxford like two frontier western gunfighters stalking one another on the strength of a reciprocal ultimatum expiring at sundown—the only consequence was that we met all the more frequently and under still more embarrassing circumstances.

On one particularly fine late spring morning the situation came to a head. I was in great spirits. I stepped outside the lodge into High Street and turned straight into the German girl. It was a bona fide collision. For an instant we found ourselves staring cross-eyed at one another, nose to nose. Reaction was reflexive and violent on both sides: spinning on the heels and taking precipitous and unashamed flight in opposite directions. My day, as the saying goes, was ruined and I assume that hers was too. In my share of the discomfiture I decided that matters had gone far enough. So I indited the following letter:

Sehr geehrtes Fräulein Trauenstein-Schöningen:

It is as certain as anything in this life that I shall spend the coming weekend in London. I plan to leave Oxford early Friday afternoon and return not before Monday morning. I take the liberty of informing you of this because I thought you might like to make the most of an opportunity to visit Magdalen during my guaranteed absence.

It is a matter of regret to me that because of my presence here you regard—and understandably so—the entire southwest quarter of Oxford as a danger zone. I lament this particularly because it cuts you off from the river. May I therefore suggest that we arrange some sort of schedule which will preclude the possibility of a chance meeting? I seldom have recourse to the river (I always use the punts moored behind Magdalen) before seven o'clock in the evening. The mornings and the afternoons, then, are open to you. As a further precaution you could go downstream from Magdalen. I always go upstream.

It seems to me that a similar arrangement could be employed on land, especially since my goings and comings during the day are parochial. I leave Magdalen by the Long Wall gate every morning at exactly ten-thirty and proceed in a beeline up High Street as far as the Ross Café. I am always back within the walls of Magdalen before eleven-fifteen. Thus you could conduct your morning shopping before or after this time with complete impunity. Even if you choose to disregard these time limits, once you have reached the Cornmarket you are in the clear. You could then return home via Broad Street and Holywell without fear of untoward incident.

I must warn you in closing that there is one time during the week—on Sunday—that I use Long Wall–Holywell–Broad Street and part of St. Giles both going and coming. I usually leave about two-thirty in the afternoon and return about seven. I hope you will find it convenient to arrange your Sunday excursions accordingly. Trusting, then, that we do not meet in the near future,

auf nicht Wiedersehen,
George Bailey

I will admit that I thought this letter witty enough to be ingratiating. Within a week or so I wrote a second letter to Fräulein Trauenstein-Schöningen inviting her to dinner. I received this answer:

Dear Mr. Bailey,

I should perhaps be ready to consider your invitation favorably were it not for the letter which you sent me last week and the fact that we have not been previously introduced. I hope you realize that any further attempts on your part to establish an acquaintanceship will likewise prove futile.

Yours,
Ursula Trauenstein-Schöningen

This was one of those occasions when my reliance on the German sense of humor disappointed me. I closed the exchange as best I could:

Sehr geehrtes, etc.

I would not unwrite my letter of last week if I could; and though I boast many talented friends there is none of them quite so talented as to be able to introduce us previously.

For this relief much thanks.

Hochachtungsvoll,
George Bailey

Everything about Oxford is extraordinary, as befitted the incubator of a world elite. To begin with, there was the atmosphere of the place. The first person I met when I stepped into the Magdalen College quadrangle in September 1946 was a former naval officer—he looked like the ruddy, bearded "tar" on the Player's Cigarettes package—who accosted me with this address: "Ah, you're Bailey, are you? Well, now that you're here I suppose you're wondering what to do with yourself. Let me give you some advice. Get yourself a bit of supper, a jug of beer, go down to the river, and punt off into the twilight." In a sense I spent the next three years punting around in the twilight. Twilight—" 'tween-light," from the older Germanic "light between bright and dark." "Where bright and dark meet each other," wrote Julius Langbehn, "there the spirits delight in gathering: they love the twilight." In Oxford the play of light on stone wreaks the magic of twilight at all hours. For the stones of Oxford, the "dreaming spires" and tessellated parapets, break up the light, half absorb it, modulate it, trick it. The domes and steeples tint and stain the perception and beget dreams. In the medieval town of Oxford I dreamed of "Old Germany."

A second thing about Oxford—like any university but far more so —is the truly extraordinary, unique collection of books. The chief significance of being at a university is the access to books. Even in the Magdalen College Library I found and read Freiherr von Eichendorf's *From the Life of a Good-for-Nothing* and a volume of his verse and Gottfried Keller's *Green Henry, Clothes Make the Man*, and *A Village Romeo and Juliet*. And in the Magdalen Library I also found Doctor Faustus himself—there, poring over huge, hand-printed, and curiously painted old books, with his green visor fixed low on his forehead, was Charlie Onions, CBE, FBA, MA Lond.; MA, Hon. Litt.D., Oxon.; Hon. Litt.D., Leeds; Hon. LL.D., Birmingham; Hon. FRSL; Fellow of Magdalen College; Reader in English Philology in the University of Oxford, Editor of the *Oxford English Dictionary*. Here was a man who knew German —and Russian—and Hungarian. He could go as far as the fourth synonym (if there was one) of any word in the Russian dictionary.

A third extraordinary thing about Oxford—and, indeed, about England altogether in those days—was the food: it was extraordinarily bad. The British are miserable cooks at the best of times. My sojourn at Oxford fell in the midst of the postwar "austerity" of strict food rationing. At college we were regaled with one egg on every fourth Sunday of the month. When a new dish appeared on the menu, "whale and pigeon pie," the president of the college made a short introductory speech: "Gentlemen," he said, "the British cuisine is renowned as the worst in the world save only the Eskimo. Now the Labour government has imported several thousand tons of whale meat to bring us abreast of the Eskimos. In honor of this feat we present you today with a new dish— 'whale and pigeon pie.' As you will, I am sure, immediately discover, gentlemen, the ratio of the ingredients is one whale to one pigeon." The Yorkshire pudding smelled like a wet dishcloth. Fortunately it had no taste at all. The appalling "bubble-and-squeak," an overcooked, cooked-over mess of cabbage and potatoes, was the daily fare at the British restaurant so no refuge was to be found there.

I dwell on the rigors of the British cuisine because they provided me with the incentive to make the most of another extraordinary thing about Oxford: the university was in session only twenty-four weeks of the year. There are three terms, each lasting eight weeks. These are separated by two vacations, each of six weeks' duration, and the sixteen-week "long vac" in the summer. During vacation undergraduates must leave their rooms in the university. Thus compulsion was combined with inducement to spend twenty-eight weeks of the year abroad. For me "abroad" meant the Continent and the Continent meant Germany or at least Switzerland.

Now Switzerland is another march, or border area, of Germany. It was not always so: under the Hohenstauffens the Holy Roman Empire of the German Nation included Burgundy, Italy, and Sicily; Switzerland was the hub. Barbarossa set up his headquarters in Lugano. About eighty percent of the Swiss population is German. Of course, the Swiss Germans founded the Helvetian Confederation, the French, Italian, and Romansh cantons subsequently acceding. It was interesting to see how the Swiss Germans did what they could to alleviate the sufferings of the German Germans. In Switzerland, Germany is often referred to as "the Great Canton," as though it were merely another canton of Switzerland, a notion not unlike the New Yorker's map of America.

Yet the solicitude and sense of responsibility among the Swiss Germans for "the Great Canton" is genuine. For about five years after the war Zurich was the greatest theater town in Europe because a good many of the best German actors, unable to work in occupied Germany and Austria, found refuge and livelihood in Switzerland. For at least fifteen years after the war the *Neue Zürcher Zeitung* was the best and only good German-language newspaper (it is still the best), not least because it performed very important advisory and monitory functions on a political level for the German Germans. This it was in an excellent position to do since its editor-in-chief, Willy Bretscher, was the chairman of the National Council's Committee for Foreign Affairs. A comparable situation would exist in the United States if Senator William Fulbright were the editor of the *New York Times*. On a more material level, many a German fortune was saved by timely deposit in a Swiss bank. True, it is far from easy to become a Swiss citizen: there is a residence requirement of a minimum of twelve years and character and financial qualifications are strict; it is even difficult to acquire a residence or work permit. And yet thousands of Germans and German Jews survived the war in safety and comparative comfort in Switzerland. A good many of both groups became Swiss citizens. There are German and German-Jewish colonies in all large Swiss cities.

I found myself in the midst of the German and German-Jewish colony in Geneva at the end of a chain of circumstances that had its beginning in Oxford. A South African Jewish classmate at Magdalen had flown from London to Geneva to join the rest of us who were proceeding by train. On the plane he made the acquaintance of a German-Jewish immigrant girl who was on her way to visit her cousin in Geneva. This was the Christmas vacation and so my friend was invited to a Christmas party at the cousin's and invited to invite his Oxford friends.

In this way I met the cousin, who was the granddaughter of Antonie ("Toni") Ullstein. Toni Ullstein was the widow of Hans Ullstein, the eldest of the five sons of Leopold, the founder of perhaps the largest publishing firm in Europe—the House of Ullstein. I knew nothing at all about the Ullsteins and I did not understand the Viennese connection. Nor was I enlightened by the granddaughter of Toni Ullstein. In fact I was impressed and intrigued by the granddaughter for that very reason: she was the first female of the species I had ever met who, on closer and even lengthy acquaintance, had nothing whatever to say about herself, her family, and her home. It was only several months later, when it became obvious to both of us and all interested bystanders that I was courting her, that she made a statement in this regard. She said: "I belong to a very strange family." In the beginning what little I knew about the Ullsteins I learned only from Toni and from Jewish classmates who had Continental connections.

Toni was almost eighty when I met her in 1948. She remains the grandest *grande dame* of my experience. She was a Berlinerin, born the daughter of Gustav Heymann in Grunewald, the millionaire's suburb of Berlin. Born into wealth, she had also married into great wealth at the age of nineteen. Her husband, Hans Ullstein, was U-1 (that is, the first child of the original Leopold Ullstein—see Ullstein family tree on page 142), at the top of the scale of the Ullstein filial seniority that ranged from U-1 to U-5. A widow since 1934, she had lived in Berlin until 1939 when her escape to Switzerland was arranged by Hjalmar Schacht. The relationship between Hjalmar Schacht and Toni Ullstein was the most natural in the capitalist world: her money in his bank. Toni's eldest child, (Mat)Hilda, had married an officer in the Imperial Prussian army in World War I. The officer was a Viennese who had the option of enlisting in the Prussian army because his father had been a Prussian citizen. The Viennese Prussian officer's great-grandfather was a Scotsman of Clan Ross. He wore the Ross tartan tie and waistcoat as long as he lived. This then was the Viennese connection. Ross, like his father-in-law Ullstein, had four children, three of them daughters, Jutta, Helga, and Beate. I married his youngest daughter, Beate.

As I have indicated I had not the faintest notion of what I was getting into. My education began immediately. Of course I appreciated the fact that my wife was half Jewish or, in family parlance, a "zebra." For the Nazis, Ross was rather like a frontier scout who married the daughter of an Indian chief: his character was as unquestioned as her status, but the union of the two made him a squaw-man, demeaned her to a squaw, and left their children half-breeds. But this was only the beginning of the complication. The Ullsteins were very German German Jews. Ross was an Austrian citizen, a native Viennese, but all his children had been born in Berlin in the colossal mansion of U-1 in the Bettinastrasse in Grunewald.

Also, to my astonishment I discovered that my wife's Austrian citizenship complicated my own status. I got a whiff of what was to come when I went to the Standesamt (registry office) to apply for a marriage license. In the marriage bureau I found a very old man perched on a very high stool at an equally high desk with a sloping surface. He was writing with a quill pen in an enormous registry book. This was my introduction to the suffusive Austrian cipher, "k. und k."—literally "kingly and caesarly," royal and imperial—the atmosphere, the ambiance, the tradition, the "being" of the Habsburg Empire. When I crossed that threshold I stepped fifty years into the past. Fifty? Make it a hundred, two hundred, three hundred—it is of no import: the empire is timeless. From his posture, the old fellow might have been Uriah Heep, but he had a fine old, if scrawny, eagle's head and he wore a pince-nez and the highest starched white collar I have ever seen. "I must have," he piped, "a certificate from your legation to the effect that there is no objection to your marrying an Austrian national." I protested, to no avail. An inquiry at the American legation resulted in the information (from the sergeant on duty) that the United States government "don't care if you marry a gorilla." I trotted back with the news to my ancient official. "Then," said he, "I shall require a negative certificate." "You don't mean . . . ," I began. "Yes: a negative certificate is a certificate certifying that you don't need a certificate." And the old boy would not budge until I produced the "negative certificate."

Fräulein Ross, with her Prussian-Jewish-Scottish ancestry, was of course Protestant and insisted on a church wedding. For my part I was determined that my best man should be an American. Coffin was too far away, at Yale Divinity School. So I traveled to Darmstadt in Germany, to the editorial offices of the European edition of the American army newspaper, *Stars and Stripes,* to find an American best man. This was Phil ("Filthy") Taylor, the sports editor. When I explained the situation to him, he said, "Well, I'm not so sure I approve of your marrying a Kraut." "She is not a Kraut," I said, "she is Viennese." "Well," said Filthy, "then she's a Kraut in three-quarter time."

Taylor's remark proved to be prophetic; for while Austrians were not considered—as Germans were—to be "enemy aliens" by the Western Allies, their status in this regard was more than a little suspect. It was not as if I had married a Frenchwoman. There were various reasons for this official tendency to equate Austrians with Germans. For one thing the Sudeten Germans had been Austrians until the the end of World War I when they were irresponsibly included in the new Czechoslovak state; they became "German" with the Munich Accord which dismembered Czechoslovakia in 1938; many of the Sudeten Germans moved to Austria during or immediately after World War II and there remained a sizable Sudeten German colony in Austria. For another thing the "Inn quarter," which included the birthplace of Hitler, Braunau, had been annexed by Austria from Bavaria during the War of the Bavarian Succession in 1778. As a result of these developments and other factors

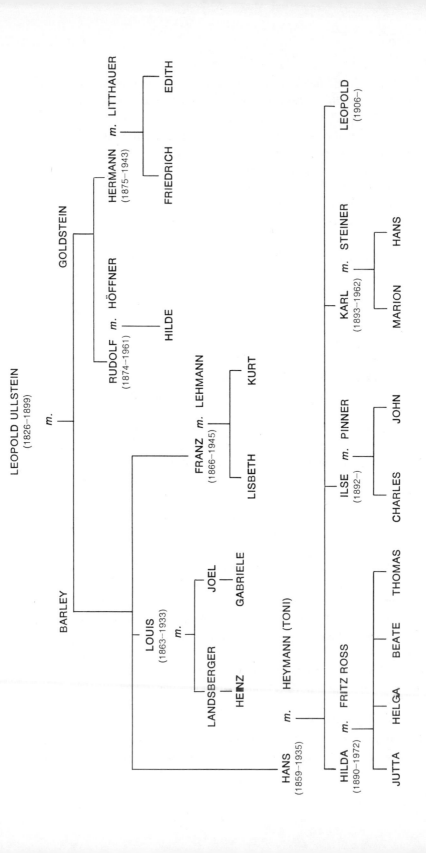

there were literally millions of family connections between Germany and Austria. There were countless cases of double residence and—at least in effect—double citizenship. The notation "Berlin" as place of birth in my wife's Austrian passport was merely an added fillip to the statutory equation of Austrian with German.

My prospects of a lectureship in English at the University of Munich—at a salary of seven hundred German marks (less than $170) a month—became nonsensical the moment I took a wife. I then turned to the Education Department of the American High Commission. My application was received with enthusiasm until it was discovered that I had married an Austrian national. I was politely told that my marital status in effect disqualified me because it would complicate my security clearance beyond all bounds.

The complication of the security clearance disbarred me from acceptance by all American government offices—including the Central Intelligence Agency (although I did not know at the time that I was being interviewed by the CIA)—except my alma mater, the American army. I was still a reserve officer and the American army had no qualms whatever about my newly created labyrinthine foreign family connections. I was taken on as a Department of the Army Civilian (DAC) in the capacity of resettlement officer. Of course the branch of service was Intelligence, and the work was intimately connected with intelligence activity since my job was to resettle Eastern European defectors, and particularly Soviet defectors (more particularly Red Army deserters), in the West. In short, I was taking up where I had left off, dealing with defectors, but with the signal difference that instead of turning them back I was to "aid and abet" them in the achievement of their purpose— settling in the West. Of course all defectors were interrogated or "debriefed," if one will, at considerable length, sometimes for months on end. From the nature of this phase of the work the unit to which I belonged was officially known as "Collation and Evaluation." My wife, when asked for her husband's unit designation at the Post Exchange, promptly replied, "Collusion and Devaluation."

As a description of my activity her malapropism was more accurate than the official designation. When a defector had completed his course of interrogation and security screening, he was turned over to our section for resettlement—by no means necessarily in the country of his choice (his choice was almost always the United States). Security screening was imperative: since the Soviet Union and its satellites were unable to prevent the flow of refugees and defectors from their borders they did the next best thing and made use of it as a channel for the introduction of espionage agents into Western countries. For this reason security was of the first priority: everybody's security was involved—not least that of the defector himself. In order to protect the defector against detection and pursuit by the intelligence agencies of his former country, a new identity complete with personal history had to be invented and drummed into him. Still more important, the defector had to be furnished with a set of appropriate documents. These included a Kennkarte (identity card), the basic German document, which contained date and place of birth, profession, and a number of highly important stamps such as the residence permit (for foreigners) and the local police registration.

The registration with the police of any change of address is common to all European countries; in Germany it was introduced during the reign of Frederick the Great. Thus the resettlement team—my superior, my assistant (both of them German-American Jews), and myself—was obliged to cultivate police and magisterial officials in various localities; the smaller the locality the better for our purpose. At times we would descend like protection-selling gangsters on the mayor of some remote mountain village, glad-hand him, stick a cigar in his mouth, fast-talk him, and run our nondescript charges through his entire administrative apparatus. And this on the basis of nothing more than a general statement affixed with the all-important "official stamp" and signed by a fictional lieutenant of infantry, Stanford J. Valpack, as administrative officer of a fictional unit of the army of the United States.

Of course the army of the United States was not fictional and neither were we: the German officials concerned all acted under a form of duress. What I found interesting was the way they all instinctively adapted themselves to the fact of duress. This was another manifestation of the very considerable experience the Rhinelanders have had over the centuries with occupation armies. Whenever I was too frank about a case with a German police official, he would say, "I didn't hear that!" or more often, "I do not wish to have heard that!" But very seldom if ever was there a murmur of reluctance; never an attempt or a shift at an attempt to refer to some higher headquarters, theirs or ours. Any one of these officials could have made no end of trouble for us simply by refusing to cooperate and by making the incident known to the authorities in the American High Commission.

It is interesting to speculate what would have happened if someone had officially denounced our activity. For we were, in fact, operating "against all flags"—except the small hidden regimental standard of military expediency. I was detained and my credentials scrutinized on more than one occasion by Counter Intelligence Corps (CIC) agents at the request of various offices and agencies in the DP camps. Those most suspicious of our activity were the American consular officials in the camps. Not the least reason for this was the fact that—although the American government was sponsoring and implementing the resettlement of the defectors (through the American army)—the United States was, in effect, the one country to which these unfortunates could not go. At the same time America (meaning North America, including Canada as a poor but acceptable alternative to the United States) was the passionately desired destination of *all* defectors, except the various groups of Middle and Eastern Germans.

It was our duty to hornswoggle everybody (including ourselves) on any and all aspects of a resettlement candidate's past history, his character, and his qualifications. We were body-and-soul salesmen, intent on packaging our human product as attractively as possible. Since our fabrication of the new personality was restricted only by the candidate's ability to learn and play his role, we were generally able to equip him with almost ideal character, qualifications, and background. These could be revised if necessary in accordance with changes in the immigration quotas and categories of the various countries. I once tried to pass off a Kuban cossack as an experienced dairy farmer before the Canadian Immigration Commission. Unfortunately, the chairman of the examining board that day happened to be the Canadian minister of immigration. He, in turn, happened to be a dairy farmer. I had assumed that any self-respecting cossack would be able to milk a cow. To my dismay the cossack denounced the milking of cows as beneath the dignity of the Cossack Brotherhood, which had never been known to milk anything except mares, and then, preferably, wild mares.

If it makes sense, as it does, to call the whole of Germany during the Third Reich a vast concentration camp, then it makes fully as much sense to consider the whole of West Germany in the first postwar decade, at least, a vast displaced persons camp. There were more than three million foreigners in Germany at war's end. All but a very small percentage of these were forced labor from Eastern Europe—from Poland, the Baltic States, and Russia. There were also perhaps as many as one hundred thousand Eastern European Jews who had been brought into the Reich—and kept out of the concentration camps—as skilled labor. As for German refugees, defectors, and "displaced persons," in general there were these degrees and descriptions: those from the various ethnic German (Volksdeutsche) colonies in Eastern European countries, those from East Prussia and East Germany, those from Middle Germany (the Soviet zone), and those who had been bombed out one or more times and found shelter with relatives or friends in another part of West Germany.

The total number of such Germans was perhaps twenty million. For the first three or four years after the war marauding bands of DPs roamed the country, murdering and pillaging. Over this period the victims of these bands (who were, like the deserters, uprooted peasants and other castaways who plagued the countryside during the Thirty Years War) numbered in the thousands. I remember how dismayed my old friend Professor Von Fritz was when an acquaintance of his, a young farmer, was attacked, robbed, and killed by a band of Polish DPs in the French zone in 1946.

There were 22 concentration camps and 165 labor camps in the Third Reich. As often as not these camps were used as DP camps out of sheer necessity: upwards of twenty percent of all German housing had been destroyed or severely damaged during the war. Until 1951 the Russians used Buchenwald as a concentration camp for enemies of the East German communist regime and other "undesirables." Thus the function of Buchenwald remained generally the same although the tables of the former relationship were turned: now the inmates were German —sometimes indeed former concentration camp guard personnel—while the guards were Russian soldiers. Similarly the Americans used Dachau as an internment camp for Germans—including former military— charged with war crimes and awaiting trial.

Indeed, Dachau was the venue of the Malmedy trial, in which more than a hundred former officers and men of the SS military formation were charged with (and the bulk of them found guilty of) the shooting of American soldiers they had taken prisoner in the Battle of the Bulge. In Dachau, too, the Mauthausen trial took place in which several of the guards and some of the inmates of the Mauthausen concentration camp in Austria were charged with brutality. One of the accused (he was also cited as a witness against other accused) was a German who himself had been sentenced to Mauthausen on suspicion of sabotage against the Third Reich. He was asked by the American prosecutor whether he had ever seen one of the guards strike a prisoner. "Tell the lieutenant," said the former inmate and still prisoner, that I never saw him [the guard] strike anybody, but it is possible that such a thing happened at some time or other. Sometimes such things were unavoidable if any form of order was to be maintained. . . . At the end of the war we had only one loaf of bread a day to feed eighteen men with. Do you know what that means? Under such circumstances, the impulse to deliver a blow could not be overcome when one of the prisoners took it into his head to steal a loaf of bread that was so severely rationed. Whenever we saw such a thing were any of us really minded to restrain ourselves? Not that we be-grudged the thief the loaf of bread but simply because this one man by so doing made any number of other people suffer. I'm here for the same reason! Hundreds of prisoners from all sorts of countries came to Mauthausen toward the end of the war. Every day there was less food to be had. In the kitchen where I worked we had the food we had prepared in buckets. Some of the prisoners would sneak up with ladles under their arms and try to steal the food out of the buckets. When I caught anybody trying to do this I admit that I struck him and I will never attempt to deny it. Why should I? What would have happened to the lot of us if we hadn't kept at least a little discipline?

It was this witness's misfortune that although an inmate in Mauthausen himself, he had been denounced by fellow inmates (perhaps by food thieves but who could blame them?).

The National Socialist regime did not manage to create a totalitarian society but it sometimes came close to it. Totalitarianism was one of the conflicting goals of National Socialism, and a totalitarian society—that is to say a police state—turns on denunciation. The semise-cret order known as the SS was in this sense the center and tentacular extention of power in the Third Reich. Apart from the "death-factory" aspect (which was not the original function of the concentration camps), the similarity between the Nazi camps and the DP camps is uncanny: both concentration and DP camp inmates were uprooted and removed from their "native or habitual environment," both languished in a Kaf-kaesque limbo of suspended animation and maimed existence, and al-though the DP did not have the distinct prospect of physical torture and extinction looming over him, his future—for the first few years anyway —was almost as uncertain as that of the concentration camp inmate.

Above all, the atmosphere of the DP camp was strangely similar to that of its ominous predecessor. In 1950 I came across a Polish refugee who, with his wife and four children, had spent almost four years in a DP camp in southern Germany. The man was slowly going mad with the frustration of his attempts to emigrate to a Western country—meaning, as always, North America. When I met him he had just been rejected by the security section of the Canadian Immigration Service. He had, he said, tried everything—even Eleanor Roosevelt had interceded in his behalf with the American Immigration Service.

As a last resort he had come to one of the voluntary agencies, the International Rescue Committee (IRC), the local office of which was headed by a Lithuanian. The Lithuanian was himself a DP but only technically. For the only way to "displace" Walter Banaitis would be to shanghai him to the moon: he was one of the few authentic citizens of the world in the Goethean sense of the term "Weltbürger." He was a man at home with humanity at large. To my astonishment Banaitis assured the hapless Pole in the most binding terms that he and his family would be in Canada within the month. "How can you say such a thing?" said the Pole. "After all these terrible years you must not toy with us—I won't be able to stand it." I, too, remonstrated with Banaitis. He interrupted me: "I have discovered that the reason preventing this family's immigration is an anonymous letter denouncing the father as a Communist. Tonight I shall sit down and write an anonymous letter denouncing the father as a Nazi. The two charges will cancel each other out. Mark my words." He spoke true: within a month the family was in Canada.

It is so much easier to dispose of a dead body than a living one. The problems involved in simply getting rid of a living body are tremendous: understandably nobody—no other body—wants to take the living body off your hands. There is inherent in the acceptance of responsibility for a living body the claim of that body on the acceptor. Quite apart from the very considerable clerical chores and the logistics involved (a living body has to be regularly fed, completely clothed, and somehow sheltered), the claim of the ward on the guardian is psychologically absolute. In the mind of the ward and in the back of the mind of the guardian it never disappears. It does not "bend with the remover to remove." Once in a wardship the living body says—not "in effect" but straight out— "Now that you have helped me you must always help me! Now I am yours forever! And if I am yours—you are mine!"

It is this that makes the resettlement of human beings so difficult. Local and national authorities are generally so severe and unapproachable on the score of the acceptance of living bodies because they know from experience what they are—or would be—letting themselves in for. The guardian-ward relationship is one to be avoided, I should think, at almost all costs because it is crippling to both parties. But it can only be avoided rather far in advance. The initials "DP," it was sometimes said, also stood for "dislocated personality." Being uprooted and thrown hundreds or thousands of miles to one side is a traumatic shock. But the worst of it is that it almost inevitably makes an object of the subject, forcing him into the ward-guardian relationship which maims him psychically. In one year in the camps I met only a handful of men among the Poles, Russians, Balts, and assorted Slavic inmates who had entirely withstood the seduction of wardship. It takes a man with an exceptionally strong sense of identity (that is a knowledge of and belief in his own importance) to do this.

The ward-guardian relationship is established in any form of incarceration. Camp life, any sort of camp life à la longue, is in itself wardship. It paralyzes and stultifies the personality. It is spiritual atrophy. I have often heard from friends who were political prisoners that imprisonment beyond a three-month period is likely to produce lasting effects. Seeing the Germans in reversed roles—as in Dachau and Buchenwald, particularly in reversed roles vis-à-vis the Jews who were often their keepers and overseers in camps run by the Americans and British—or in both roles, wards and guardians, in the camps for German refugees, brought home to me the underlying significance of guardian and ward in the German–Jewish relationship.

While visiting Dachau I passed by a display of the identifying insignia worn on the uniforms of the former inmates. I was stopped in my tracks by the realization that there was an umbilical connection between the Star of David on the uniform of concentration camp inmates and the national emblem of the State of Israel then emerging in the blood of battle in Palestine. The Germans and particularly the Nazis, although not entirely responsible for the phenomenon of Zionism, played a far greater role in the creation of the State of Israel than is generally appreciated. After the Nazis came to power they set about getting rid of the Jews in the Reich. It is important to see this enterprise against the background of the century-old ward-guardian relationship between the two peoples. This relationship explains much in the subsequent conduct of both.

As the ideological elite of the movement and the organization responsible for the security of the Reich, the SS was assigned the task of ridding Germany of the Jews. "The Jew," ran the lecture delivered to all SS units in 1936, "is a parasite. Wherever he flourishes, peoples die. From the most remote prehistoric times to this day the Jew has quite literally decimated and destroyed all those peoples who have played host to him when it lay in his power to do so. If we separate the Jew from our body ethnic (Volkskörper), it is an act of self-defense."

But this sentiment did not solve the problem of how to go about ridding the "body ethnic" of the Jews. As the executive organ for the "Final Solution," the section in charge of Jews did its best to discipline and channel the incoherent anti-Semitism of the Nazi party to a practical purpose. The SS strongly disapproved of the public harassment and persecution of Jews. As the official newspaper of the SS, *Das Schwarze Korps* (The Black Corps), put it in 1935: "The National Socialist movement and its state strongly oppose these criminal machinations. The party will not tolerate having its struggle for the most sacred values of the nation debased to the level of streetfights and damage to property." It is a matter of documentable fact that most of the SS leaders (as distinct from the party leaders proper) were not especially anti-Semitic. To the contrary, they considered anti-Semitism primitive, exceedingly harmful (especially to Germany's international prestige), and "counterproductive."

Indeed, some of the gruppenführer (heads of departments) and their chief assistants in the SS were in genuine sympathy with the Zionist movement. One of them, at least, Edler von Mildenstein, head of the "Jewish Section" of the SS Sicherheitsdienst (SD—security service), was the personal friend of several Zionist leaders. Von Mildenstein's attendance at Zionist congresses made it obvious to him that Zionism was the ideal solution for the problem of how to rid Germany of Jews. It was merely a matter of the competent sections of the SS cooperating to the full with Zionist organizations. Theoretically, the mass deportation of Jews from Germany could be made to blend with their immigration to Palestine. Such cooperation—and on no small scale—took place.

The biggest hitch proved to be the German Jews' extreme reluctance, and not infrequently their flat refusal, to leave Germany despite all the chicanery, harassment, and outright terrorizing on the part of the Nazis. The newspaper of the Central Association of German Citizens of Jewish Faith had expressed the resolve of the great bulk of German Jews when it wrote, "With dignity and with courage we will manage to bear the merciless measures of Germans against German Jews on the soil of our own homeland." Of the small number willing to leave Germany only a minority were willing to go to Palestine. In 1933 it was only nineteen percent of those emigrating; in 1934 the percentage reached the all-time high of thirty-eight; in 1935 it was thirty-six; in 1936, thirty-four; and in 1937 only sixteen.

There were of course other obstacles. In cooperating with the Haganah, the Jewish underground army in Palestine, the SD took the field against the British government, exercising the mandate in Palestine, and the Palestinian Arabs. Both of them were determined to reduce the Jewish immigration to Palestine to the minimum possible.

Nevertheless the Zionists regarded the SD's willingness to cooperate as a unique opportunity: "Zionism recognizes the existence of the Jewish question," wrote the *Jüdische Rundschau*, the official newspaper of the German Zionists, "and desires to solve it in a magnanimous and constructive manner. Zionism desires to gain the assistance of all peoples in this undertaking, the anti-Semitic as well as the philo-Semitic, because in the opinion of Zionism the Jewish question is not a matter of sentimentalities but rather a real problem in whose solution all peoples are interested." For the SD, cooperation with the Zionists in this enterprise meant above all fostering a Jewish nationalist feeling among German Jews—specifically the instilling and promotion of the tenets of Zionism. On May 15, 1935, *Das Schwarze Korps* editorialized in this vein: "The time should not be all that far distant when Palestine will again receive its sons who have wandered lost for over a thousand years. Our wishes, joined with the good will of the state, accompany them."

It was Von Mildenstein who brought Adolf Eichmann, then a sergeant, into the "Jewish Section" of the SD. Like Von Mildenstein, Eichmann was no anti-Semite. He had Jewish relatives and a Jewish girlfriend. What recommended Eichmann was his unflagging zeal to do the best possible job, whatever the job assigned to him. In the section Eichmann was assigned the field "Zionist Organization." It was in this capacity that Eichmann came into personal contact with Feivel Polkes, a commander in the Haganah's intelligence organization. Polkes was invited by the SD to come from Palestine to Berlin to meet Eichmann; he reciprocated by inviting Eichmann and an assistant to Palestine (they were frustrated of their destination at the last minute by an Arab uprising: the three men eventually conferred in Cairo). All these negotiations were concerned with promoting and facilitating the emigration of German Jews to Palestine (and seeing to it that they went to Palestine and not elsewhere). Polkes agreed to keep the SD informed of items of interest in Palestine—particularly with regard to the British and the Arabs—for a monthly agent's wage of fifteen pounds sterling.

Meanwhile it had dawned on Eichmann that the policy of promoting German-Jewish immigration to Palestine might prove a boomerang. He wrote a paper on this subject warning against the eventuality of a strong anti-German Jewish Palestine. Eichmann's colleague, Hagen, in another paper put his finger on the specific danger: "It is self-evident that Germany cannot approve of the formation of such a monstrous body politic since otherwise possibly the day would come when all Germany's stateless Jews would take Palestinian citizenship and then demand representation as a so-called minority before the German government." This was foresight. And Hagen's warning had application beyond Germany. A development parallel to this took place thirty-five years later in the relations of the State of Israel with the Soviet Union.

Despite these misgivings, the pressures to deport the Jews to Palestine increased when the Third Reich acquired another 300,000 Jews with the annexation of Austria. At this point inducement gave way to coercion. As a rule Austrian Jews were a good deal poorer than German Jews. Eichmann allowed Austrian Jewish leaders to travel abroad for the purpose of collecting funds for the immigration of the Jews of the Reich to Palestine. They managed to collect upwards of $100,000 in less than three months from the American Joint Distribution Committee. By this means Eichmann managed to engineer the immigration of 150,000 Jews in eighteen months.

But in promoting the specific Jewishness of the German and Austrian Jews, the SD ran afoul of the great bulk of the National Socialist party. Eichman's success particularly infuriated the official anti-Semite of the party, Julius Streicher, and the editorial staff of Streicher's newspaper, *Der Stürmer*. It was too much: the elite organ of the Nazi party, as a matter of concerted policy, was reconverting German Jews to Jewry! "To a religion," wrote *Der Stürmer*, "which recognizes the teachings of the Talmud as the highest law! Of the Talmud which permits every crime against non-Jews."

In the end, however, the policy and plans of the SD to solve the Jewish question by emigration were foiled not by Streicher but by the man who revealed himself in 1938 as the arch-anti-Semite of the Nazi movement: Joseph Goebbels. It was Goebbels who incited and organized the Kristallnacht in November 1938 in retaliation for the assassination of the German diplomat Von Rath by the German Jew Herschel Grünspan. The controversy that subsequently raged within the German government over Goebbel's anti-Semitic agitation revealed one of the major splits within the National Socialist party. Understandably, those Nazi leaders who were in any way charged with the maintenance of public order and tranquility were incensed. Reinhard Heydrich, the high chief of the SD, drew up a list showing the extent of the damage to life and property during the one night of November 9: thirty-six Jews were murdered and thirty-six seriously injured; 815 shops were destroyed, twenty-nine warehouses demolished, 171 private houses destroyed, seventy-six synagogues destroyed and 191 set fire to, 174 people were arrested for looting.

The issue had nothing to do with whether one liked or disliked Jews. This contrived explosion of hooliganism took place after five years of government by the Nazi party. No matter how interpreted, it was a direct and very serious reflection on the government: "government by hooliganism" is a contradiction in terms. "Germany," said SS General Wolff to the Indian politician Hafiz Khan, "has lost a moral battle." The president of police in Berlin, Von Eberstein, described the entire operation at the Nuremberg Trials as "pronouncedly indecent." It was more than that: it was the unmistakable sign of a government divided against itself. It was also the harbinger of the Final Solution.

Despite the drafting and promulgation of the Nuremberg Laws, the Nazis had never taken the trouble to think out and formulate a practical policy vis-à-vis the Jews. There were, of course, reasons for this neglect. The Jew had a key function in Nazi ideology: he was *the* enemy, the basic cause of *all* Germany's misery; the Jew was the butt, the scapegoat, the explanation, the very cause of the movement itself. Because of this key function and the emotional issue it had become, a practical solution to the Jewish question was a pressing necessity.

Because of the strange nature of the Nazi party a formulation of practical policy could only be worked out by factional struggle. In several respects the Nazi domination of Germany—the Third Reich—was not a government, as least not properly speaking, at all. It was, among other things, a highly heterogeneous party, quasi-revolutionary, quasi-archconservative, working in a vacuum left by the Weimar government. In a proper government Goebbel's deliberate goading of the mob to do violence to life, limb, and property of German citizens (for such they were, however déclassé) could not have been tolerated. As it was, several of the Nazi leaders demanded Goebbel's resignation: Göring, still head (nominally) of the Prussian police, and Himmler, as the first policeman of the Reich, both made strong representations to Hitler and intrigued to the best of their ability to remove Goebbels. It could not be done; Goebbels carried the day. He carried the day again with Hitler in 1940 when he persuaded the führer that the six million Jews whom the Reich had by that time acquired through conquest would have to be physically exterminated.

Because the SS was the implement of the Final Solution, it was assumed for the first two decades after the war that Himmler and Heydrich were responsible for the actual precipitation of the order of the Final Solution. There is no evidence to support this assumption; there is a good deal of evidence and there are the dictates of common sense (based on experience) to the contrary. In a memorandum of May 1940 entitled "The Treatment of Foreign Peoples in the East," Heinrich Himmler is on record as having rejected "the bolshevist method of physical extirpation of people from inner conviction as un-Germanic and impossible." Moreover it is always the police who have to do the dirty work: it was only natural that the SS as the implementer of the program to get rid of the Jews would favor the least unpleasant method; contrary to wide report the SS was only human. According to Felix Kersten, Himmler's personal physician, the SS chief complained that he himself had never wanted to exterminate the Jews. Until the spring of 1940 the Jews had been allowed to leave Germany without hindrance. The idea of destroying the Jews physically, said Himmler, was on the conscience of Goebbels; it was he who had convinced the führer "that the Jewish question could only be solved by the total destruction of all Jews. As long as one Jew was left alive he would always be an enemy of National Socialist Germany. Therefore every form of mercy and humanity was out of place." In the end the religious fanaticism which informed Nazi ideology prevailed. For the Final Solution was, as Himmler said, "impossible" as a political—that is, a *practical*—program. (At a later date Himmler confessed to an assembly of gauleiter [district leaders] that the Final Solution had become "for me the heaviest question of my life.")

It was for good reason that the first extermination task forces were set to work in the eastern territories—occupied Poland, the Baltic states, and Russia—and immediately behind the front line troops. In fact, in the beginning and for some time afterward the mass execution of Jews was carried out under the guise of antipartisan activity. Whenever a village or town in Russia was captured, the SS task forces would move in and clear the area of security risks of all sorts. Specifically, the order for the Final Solution was attached as a rider to the Commissar Order. I was reminded of Jodl's directive notation on the Commissar Order: "it is therefore best to handle it as a reprisal." The order for the physical extermination of the Jews was included in the Commissar Order and both were handled as reprisals, the concept of the reprisal having been extended to the broader concept of security measures against partisans in the rear areas. It was a comparatively simple matter to execute summarily almost anybody—except small childeren—on charges of sabotage, espionage, or general resistance in the rear area adjacent to the main battle line of an army in the field.

There were several reasons for handling the execution order in this way. Most important was the welcome pretext it afforded to the task-force executioners themselves. As sardonic as it sounds, the main psychic burden weighed on the unfortunates who were condemned to carry out the dirtiest of all the dirty work done by the Third Reich. These poor brutes and poorer minions who possessed some sensitivity did not give the order and they were not the intellectuals who thought out or il-luminated the theory that was behind the order.

The men who were the consulting intellectual architects of the ideology of anti-Semitism were too often "sensitive souls" like the physi-cian and lyric poet Gottfried Benn. It was he who pronounced that Christianity had not "penetrated the human gene," that it was only "a late facade" which did not "reach the core of the personality or the deeper levels of consciousness of peoples." Benn did not stop there. He went on to praise and proclaim the new biological type of man that was to come out of the Nazi alembic. According to Benn, whose salad days lasted too long and unfortunately coincided with the Nazi takeover, a whole new set of rules was in the making; the fabric of the conventional categories of perception had been rent: "One has had the experience," he wrote, ". . . one feels, indeed, that one is far less separated, far more intimately bound up with Being, than would seem possible from the antithesis of idea and reality that is at most two thousand years old." It is particularly dismaying to discover how much work in preparing the ground for the Nazi ideological foundations was done by Gottfried Benn and other "sensitive souls" and daring intellectual pioneers.

The guise of antipartisan and general security precautions was also an extremely useful and necessary disguise. For quite some time—weeks or months depending on the sector—the exterminators were by this means able to mask their work vis-à-vis the German army. But even after the true nature of the enterprise had become unmistakably clear to rank and file, the guise of imperative field security precautions continued to serve as a desperately needed (however "formal") justification, as at least something by way of a protective railing to cling to on the edge of the abyss. Of course, this aspect of the guise and disguise for the act of physical extermination of human beings was most important to the executioners. They had to believe that what they were doing was right and necessary.

I wondered and I still wonder whether Seyss-Inquart had any real inkling of what he was talking about when he testified in the dock at Nuremberg that he "had the impression, which will be confirmed everywhere, that the Jews, [as a matter] of course, had to be against National Socialist Germany. There was no discussion of the question of guilt as far as I was concerned. As head of an occupied territory I had only to deal with the fact. I had to realize that, particularly from Jewish circles, I had to reckon with resistance, defeatism, and so on." For Seyss-Inquart the Jews were guilty even before being formally charged. The charge had been made long ago and repeated incessantly. Seyss-Inquart's argument was exactly the same as that used by Goebbels to persuade Hitler that as many Jews as possible would have to be physically exterminated. And yet Seyss-Inquart, the devout Catholic, stoutly denied that he had even suspected that Jews under the control of the Reich would be, were being, or had been physically exterminated. The Third Reich was the traditional German battle royal among a large number of princes—in this case administrative princes—to protect old areas of competency and conquer new ones. Seyss-Inquart was not an aggressive prince: he was bent only on preserving his proper area of competency. Everything else he left to the genius and authority of the emperor of the Holy Roman Empire of the German Nation, "the greatest strategist of all time," in whom he believed implicitly.

Albert Speer, Hitler's architect and latterly his minister plenipotentiary for war production, has explained how it was that none of the Nazi leaders at Nuremberg knew of the atrocities against the Jews and other foreigners: the Nazi leaders were instinctively aware, as almost all Germans were, that there were goings-on in the Third Reich that were better left unknown. Knowledge of such things brought with it something that was to be avoided at all costs, namely the sense of moral responsibility —the complicity of conscience. It was this that the sensitive man could not bear.

Even the less sensitive knew enough to shun it and welcomed every pretext that would help them to do so. There were some clinical cases of sadism among executioners in the beginning, to be sure (there were more in the end) but they were few and they were soon unmanned by the surfeit of slaughter. I have seen pictures of blond Germans in uniform smiling as they hacked off the head of a Yugoslav partisan with a medieval executioner's axe. But I did not and do not believe my eyes. Bravado is the most common protective covering of a man in an eerie situation.

There is no need to belabor the point: the toughest of the extermination task-force members suffered nervous breakdowns, like the East Prussian strong boy and gruppenführer, Erich von dem Bach Zelewsky. Eugen Kogon cites the example of the soldier who, when forced at gun point to shoot a small Jewish girl, became a manic depressive and remained so for the rest of his life. One of the chief reasons for developing the gas chambers as a means of mass extermination was the incapacity of the members of firing squads to bear up under the horror of their work —and particularly the German members. For, as it was, the actual execution squads of the task forces were largely made up of Poles, Balts, Ukrainians—and Jews—whose own lives were forfeit if they did not carry out the work assigned.

Even after the adoption of the gas chamber as a more expedient means of mass execution (thereby also necessarily depriving the operation of the guise of a "legitimate" field security measure), Himmler found it necessary to continue—and increase—his "pep talks" to the troops. "Most of you will know," he said on one occasion cited at Nuremberg, "what it means when one hundred or five hundred or a thousand corpses lie alongside each other. To have been able to put up with that sort of thing and—apart from exceptions due to human frailty—to have remained decent, that has made us tough. This is a glorious page in our history that has never been written and never will be written." Kersten, Himmler's personal physician, presumably had no difficulty in perceiving the origin of his patient's chronic stomach cramps.

The point is often made that when Hitler, at the height of his military success in 1940, announced his intention to carry out a program of euthanasia for the elimination of congenital idiots, severe cases of mental retardation, and dangerous hereditary disease, he was forced by outraged public opinion to announce the postponement of the program "for the duration of the war." Understandably both confessions of the German church were in the forefront of the opposition to the euthanasia program. If anything like this opposition had been brought to bear against the Final Solution, it is pointed out, millions of lives would almost certainly have been saved.

The comparison here is seriously inaccurate: the Final Solution was never announced as a program or made public in any way. The executioners themselves and their accomplices did not "talk out of school" in the bosom of their families when on leave or anywhere else. Their work was not something to be boasted of or bruited about. On the contrary: there was every reason to keep the whole ghastly business under wraps

—especially if one was personally implicated. As I have tried to show, there is good reason to believe that the overwhelming majority of Germans knew nothing of the Final Solution—in a good many cases precisely because they were deeply concerned and determined not to learn anything.

The two processes are vastly different: the expression of outraged feelings along traditional religious lines, on the one hand, and the repression of guilt or of all curiousity for fear of moral involvement, on the other. The literal root meaning of the word "conscience" is "withknowing." In German "Mitwisser" ("with-knower") is the word for accessory. The entire dilemma and the rationale for the denial of the dilemma's existence was summed up by Pius XII in an interview with Eduardo Senatro, correspondent for the *Osservatore Romano* in Berlin. Senatro asked his holiness why he had not protested against the extermination of the Jews. Said Pius XII: "Dear friend, do not forget that millions of Catholics are serving in the German army. Should I bring them into conflict with their conscience?"

When Adolf Eichmann was captured and brought to trial in Israel, I toured West Germany with a television camera team interviewing old and young for their reactions to the then forthcoming Eichmann trial. To my astonishment, among the interviewees over forty years of age as often as not we heard the frankly stated opinion that the Jews had brought the Final Solution on themselves. How so? "Because they crucified our Lord Jesus Christ!" I had not been prepared for this: among other reasons because in 1957 when the play *The Diary of Anne Frank* was brought to Germany the reaction had been overwhelmingly positive. *The Diary of Anne Frank* broke all records; it ran for years: at one period there were eleven *Anne Frank* productions running simultaneously in West Germany. The youth of West Germany formed "Anne Frank Clubs" whose members numbered in the millions. In Austria, however, *Anne Frank* had a starkly different reception. In Linz (Hitler's home town) the production had to be discontinued during the second night (it was almost broken off during the first night at one point when the audience rushed the stage). In Vienna the play ran for slightly more than one week, having been greeted by devastating reviews. In the main the Viennese critics objected to the dramatization of the theme: "After all," wrote one, "for what happened to the Jews, the Jews have only themselves to blame."

The contrast between the German and Austrian receptions of *Anne Frank* did not surprise me; *after* World War II Austria (particularly

Salzburg and the Tyrol) was notorious as a hotbed of unreconstructed Nazism. Vienna was and still is notoriously the most anti-Semitic town in Europe. As one of my wife's Austrian relatives (himself one-quarter Jewish) explained to me: "A Catholic country *must* be anti-Semitic."

THE FIRST WORDS IN GREEK A STUDENT LEARNS TO read are likely to be these: "In the beginning was the word, and the word was with God, and the word was God." This was the establishment of the authority of the word. And the word was:

And the priests and elders persuaded the crowd to plead for Barabbas but to destroy Jesus. In answer the leader said to them: "Which of these two do you wish me to release to you?" And they answered: "Barabbas." Pilate said to them: "What then shall I do with Jesus called Christ?" They all said: "Crucify him." But he said: "For what evil did he do?" But they clamored exceedingly, saying: "Crucify him." Seeing that nothing would come of it but more noise, Pilate took some water and washed his hands, then turned to the crowd, saying: "I am free from the blood of this man: you are witnesses!" And answering, the whole people said: "His blood [be] upon us and upon our children." (Matt. 27: 20–25.)

"... The *whole* people said: 'His blood [be] upon us and upon our children.' " Nietzsche, the classical philologist, quipped that it was extraordinary that God should write such bad Greek. The study of a foreign language requires close attention to a given text. In return it gives the student a sense of the immediacy of the original: I have always been impressed by the force and finality of the language of the Bible. The fact of the crucifixion and the self-condemnation of "the whole people" of Israel compose the central issue of the struggle between Christians and Jews. It is a struggle in which there can be no quarter: one must either accept or reject Christ unconditionally.

The history of the Jews as a persecuted minority began with the conversion to Christianity of Emperor Constantine. For with the conversion of Constantine not only did the Christian Church become the state church; the empire became a church-state. Constantine's court bishop-chaplain lost no time in formally excluding the Jews from the doctrine of salvation. From then on the Jews were cited by the established church as the classic examples and objects of God's wrath. From then on began the discrimination and persecution. Under Constantine Jews could not keep Christian slaves; on pain of death no Jew could marry a woman employed in the imperial factories. The Jews were branded by the church as a dirty sect, as morally and sexually vicious. Theodosius the Great passed a law equating marriage between a Christian and a Jew with adultery. In the same decade synagogues in Italy, Rome, Africa, and Asia Minor were destroyed. Ambrosius warned his congregation that conversations with Jews were defiling in the extreme. The Emperor Justinian confiscated all synagogues in Africa and turned them over to the Christian church. He also enacted legislation depriving the Jews of all rights; he legalized the destruction of synagogues and largely succeeded in excluding the Jews from most of the normal walks of life, restricting them to a few carefully selected professions. This was the beginning of Jewish ghetto existence. "Ghetto" is an Italian word, presumably the tail of "borghetto," the diminutive of "borgo" (borough).

In retaliation, as in Caesarea in the sixth century, under Justinian II, the Jews revolted in league with the Samaritans and destroyed Christian churches. But such outbursts were fitful and few. The older chroniclers took it for granted that the Jews were "directly or indirectly" responsible for the persecution of early Christians. Far more important were the measures taken by the Jews in the third century—after the suppression of the armed resistance of the Jews by the Romans. They began shoring up their defenses inwardly. In addition to the Old Testament the Jews by the middle of the fourth century produced the Palestinian Talmud, the codification of Jewish law and commentary, the citadel of the spiritual, moral, and ethical substance of Judaism. Virtually within the same century, on the eve of the Middle Ages, the two institutions— Christian church and Jewish synagogue—are consolidated and established.

Ever since the establishment of church and synagogue there has been an interaction between the two communities of faith. The relationship has vacillated between attraction and repulsion but rests for the most part in mutual repulsion between the old faith and the new, between those who believe that the Messiah is coming and those who believe that the Messiah has come—and will come again. Remarkable throughout the history of the Christian-Jewish confrontation is the influence and effect of converts from either religion on the other. There was for that matter a tendency among Jews to regard Christianity as a revolutionary youth movement within Judaism. Many of the most fanatic persecutors of the Jews among the Catholic hierarchy, beginning with Epiphanius and culminating but not ending with Torquemada, were themselves Jewish converts. In the early Middle Ages such converts from Judaism to Christianity enjoyed great prestige because Christian theologians were no match for their Jewish colleagues in scholarship generally, the Jews meanwhile having become the mediators between antiquity and the Middle Ages, between the dominant cultures (Greek, Roman, and Arabic), and between linguistic areas. In the interconnections between nations, castes, and classes, they became the lubricant (thus exposing themselves to the charge of lubricity). Of course the great Jewish scholastic specialty was the Old Testament.

The Jews were the first hermeneuts (from Hermes, the messenger of the gods), the archpractitioners of the science of hermeneutics, the interpreting of scripture. The Jews were the first "people of the book" and they never let the Christians forget it. But once they had defected, their knowledge of enemy terrain made them excellent field generals in the service of the Cross. In this way they were rather like forerunners of Communist men of letters who defect to become crusading anticommunist men of letters. The first book burning in the Middle Ages was instigated by the Dominican Nikolaus Donin, a converted Jew from La Rochelle. Twenty-four wagonloads of copies of the Talmud were burnt in a public square in Paris. Donin had "denounced" the Talmud to Gregory IX as the most dangerous of written works.

It was natural then that Judaism should have been branded by the church as *the* false faith, as *the* superstition. The German word for false faith is Afterglaube, literally "anus-faith." In the Middle Ages folklore associated the devil with the anus as the wrong end, the end opposite the face, the source of filth, stink, and evil. The German word for superstition is even more important: "Aberglaube," literally "other-belief." In medieval history—and German history is medieval history par excellence—the "other-belief," superstition, is fully as important as *the* belief, Christianity. Indeed, the "other-belief" is the dark side of the definition of *the* belief.

"Other-belief" is a blanket term, of course: the absorptive capacity of the blanket is astonishing. Judaism has the distinction of being the first "other-belief" to have been (and remained) singled out for special censure by the Church, as in the formula "the damnable perfidy of the Hebrews" (ebreorum execranda perfidia). In the ninth century the words "concerning the perfidious Jews" (de perfidis judaeis) were included in

[162]

the liturgy. The Fourth Lateran Council of 1215 put the Jews in the same category as heretics, created the Inquisition, and decreed that all Jews must wear special badges or insignia for identification. Innocent III declared that the Jews are condemned by God to eternal slavery as punishment for the death of Christ. Thomas Aquinas incorporated the slave status of the Jews in his theological jurisprudence. In accordance with these tenets the Church, kings, and princes have the same right to dispose over the property of the Jews as over their own property. Similarly, the Church was responsible for directing the Jew into the function of usurer and branding him as such. (Ironically, the Christian ban against usury is based squarely on the rabbinical bans against usury for the Jews and the railings against money-lending for interest in the Old Testament.) In their status as slaves the Jews were bound over—as personal property—to the kings of the countries in which they were resident. As St. Thomas Aquinas put it, they were "assigned in eternal bondage to the princes as the desserts of their guilt." Thus the Jews transacted the financial business of the princes—which expanded enormously when it became necessary to finance the crusades—and became rich in the process. They also became the more hated and inviting of persecution as the stereotype of the gouging creditor. Henry III confiscated the great synagogue in London, and in 1282 the Archbishop of Canterbury closed all Jewish places of prayer in London. In 1290 Edward II signed a decree giving all Jews less than six months to leave England. The Jews left England for France where in 1288 Jews were burnt at the stake by the Inquisition on charges of ritual murder.

The most vicious and one of the longest-lived Christian calumnies of the Jews is the myth of ritual murder, according to which Jews kidnap and sacrifice gentile children in the wildest blood-orgies to placate their vengeful Jehovah. I made my first acquaintance with the myth while reading Chaucer. In "The Prioress's Tale" the "father of English literature" tells the story of little Hugh of Lincoln who was taken and murdered by envious Jews as he passed by the ghetto on his way home from school, singing a song in honor of the Virgin Mary. When the little corpse is recovered, the mouth opens and little Hugh bursts into his favorite song. At Oxford I was shocked at Lewis's unfeeling attitude to Shylock—after all that had happened in World War II—but I myself failed entirely to recognize "The Prioress's Tale" as part and parcel of the church-inspired and -sponsored myth of Jewish ritual murder. Seemingly I did this because the tale was part of a literary masterpiece (a sanction that covers many sins) and lay too far back in time—in itself an oddly inappropriate impression: I read or reread "The Prioress's Tale" some eight hundred years after Chaucer described the event with so much feeling (and animosity); presumably "The Prioress's Tale" will be read as long as the English language is read. The same point is to be made with added emphasis with regard to the passion plays. These reach a wider, more impressionable audience and traduce the Jews unmercifully (in recent years there have been efforts to remove the offending passages from the passion plays).

The Christian Church should have known from its own experience that persecution transforms a misdemeanant into a martyr. For their part the Jews canonized—by declaring them kadosh (holy)—Jewish victims of the Inquisition. Christian persecution prompted the reinforcement of the Jewish from within, just as Roman imperial persecution had done for the Christian faith. As always, the interaction of animosity made each side increasingly intolerant of the other or of any liberal deviation within its own camp. Each side provided the other with the hoped-for provocation.

Of course there was no real contest because Constantine's conversion to Christianity had tipped the scales of justice in the kingdoms of Western Europe for the next thousand years and more. The Jews were driven out of England (1290), France (1306), and Spain (1492). By far the bloodiest expulsion took place in Spain where—and because—the fusing of the Spanish, Moorish, and Jewish strains had taken place. This remarkable integration had produced a cultural efflorescence unique in that country's history and probably unsurpassed in the history of humankind: this was the Spain of the Three Rings. The expulsion of the Jews from Spain brought upon that country the same cultural sterility that the expulsion and extermination of the Jews in the Third Reich has brought upon Germany and Austria. The Spanish kings of the time, beginning with Ferdinand III, called themselves "kings of the three religions." The proudest of the "proud Spaniards" of the period were the Spanish Jews who formed the high officialdom in finance, administration, and the diplomatic service. The Spanish Jews had wealth, erudition, and refinement. They regarded themselves, and they still do—almost five hundred years after their expulsion—as "the oldest aristocracy in the world." They are the elite of the elite: they are the Sephardim.

There was the rub. The Christians in Spain were clearly outclassed by the Jews and they knew it. Most alarming was the attraction exerted on the Christian laity by the rabbis in the synagogues: they were far more learned, far more eloquent than their Christian counterparts. When

Christians began to convert to Judaism in considerable numbers, it was too much. The church authorities countered by forcing Jews en masse to convert to Christianity. The fact that forcibly converted Jews professed the imposed faith publicly while clinging to their old faith privately of course confirmed church authorities in their condemnation of the "perfidious Jews." Also, since conversion enhanced eligibility for office, it made the Jew a still greater threat within the state. Priests were soon predicting from the pulpit that the Jews would take over the state and reduce all Christians to the status of slaves—the threat of turnabout as unfair play. On June 6, 1391, the Judería, the ghetto of Seville, was sacked and upwards of four thousand Jews murdered. A great many others were sold as slaves to the Arabs. In Cordova two thousand Jews —men, women, and children—were slaughtered. In Castile at least seventy Jewish communities were laid waste. It is worth repeating that the massacres of the Jews in Spain were not merely tolerated, but instigated and exhorted by the church. This sudden flood wave of terror caused still more Jews to convert to Christianity. The vicious circle was complete. The effect was fatal to both sides: the Christians became more distrustful of Jews in general and converts in particular; the Jews turned inward and became increasingly conservative and intolerant within their own faith in the narrowest Talmudic sense. The Inquisition was introduced in Castile in 1478 by papal bull. The Inquisition first separated the conversos from the hard-core Jews, then invited the unreconstructed to denounce themselves (they were granted a thirty-day period of grace in which to do so). Then came the directive to the conversos to inform on themselves and the groundwork for a totalitarian organization was laid. In 1492 Ferdinand and Isabella signed the edict for the expulsion of all Jews from Spain. The reason given for the expulsion was the Jews' seduction of "newly converted Christians" to Judaism.

The first Jews to come to Germany were part of the Roman colonies west of the Rhine—at Cologne (Colonia) and Trier—and south of the Danube, the furthest point of progression being Regensburg. There is no record or evidence of persecution of Jews in Germany until the First Crusade (1096). There are rather signs to the contrary such as the carved and sculpted figures on public buildings of Jews bearing arms—proof in itself that they did not have the status of slaves but that of protectors of the realm. With the mounting of the First Crusade, however, the situation changed overnight. Jews had to be included among those categories of the population (priests, women, and peasants) requiring protection as announced in the public Peace of Mainz in 1103. The Fourth Lateran

[165]

Council in 1215 prohibited all intercourse between Christians and Jews. It was Germany's first nonfraternization order. Part of the same order was the prescription of special costumes and badges for the Jews so as to render them readily identifiable. (In the Allied nonfraternization order it was the Allies who were readily identifiable by virtue of their uniforms.)

The three most popular lies about Jews in the Middle Ages were then propagated with great energy: the defilement of the host, the poisoning of wells, and ritual murder. (The Germans believed that the Jews needed the blood of Christians for use as medicine to cure strange and terrible diseases which afflicted only Jews. Christian blood was also believed to be used in the preparation of unleavened bread for the Passover feast.) In 1298 roving bands of religious fanatics—most of them peasants—under the leadership of a self-styled aristocrat named Rindfleisch (beef) laid waste to 146 Jewish communities in Franconia, Swabia, Bavaria, and Austria. According to a Christian source some one hundred thousand Jews were slaughtered during this "crusade." In the course of the fifteenth century the Jews were driven out of virtually every city in Germany. As a result the Jews in Germany were forced to form new self-supporting communities outside the towns. This called for a tightly drawn, highly disciplined way of life and rendered the German Jews the most Talmud-bound and resentful of their brethren in Europe. But in Germany the Jews shared the fate of the Germans in one all-important respect: they were confronted, as all Germans were, with a fateful phenomenon that is fortunately without precedent or parallel in history; the tragedies of both peoples, Jews and Germans, can be traced to the same central source—the Reich. Or, to use the full title of the Reich's most durable manifestation: The Holy Roman Empire of the German Nation.

The arrival of the most German of all Germans on the scene did not alleviate the religious persecution of the Jews but enhanced it. Martin Luther took an extremely charitable view of the Jews while he was formulating his revolt against the mother church. In his pamphlet of 1523 Luther wrote: "The fools, popes, bishops, sophists, and monks, the crude donkey-heads, carry on with the Jews in such a way that any good Christian would rather have become a Jew." (Friedrich Heer, my source for most of this history, comments here that pity for the Jews' suffering under the Christians was the motivation for a good many conversions from Christianity to Judaism.) "They treated the Jews like dogs, beat them, and cheated them out of their property. . . . And yet they are the blood relatives, cousins, brothers of our Saviour—no people has been so distinguished by God as the Jews, he entrusted the Holy Writ to their hands." But once Luther's course was set and the true religion in its pristine purity uncorrupted by the distortions of fifty generations of churchmen stood revealed in the original word of God—then woe betide anyone who did not accept the truth. When the Jews refused to embrace the true old faith newly revealed, Luther condemned them out of hand as parties of the devil.

As he grew older and the Jews continued unrepentant, Luther became extreme in his abuse. His last sermon, preached four days before his death in his birthplace, Eisleben, he devoted entirely to the Jews: he demanded that they be expelled from all German lands. He had already advocated the burning of all synagogues and the confiscation of all books written in Hebrew. He even went so far as to demand that Jews be prohibited from praying. Luther proved to be a fountain of anti-Semitic propaganda. His pronouncements against the Jews are ingenious, over-powering, thunderous, final. Luther was of course chiefly responsible for the headlong pitch of religious conviction in Prussia particularly and in the German lands generally.

It is not in the least surprising that Luther should have been so horribly disappointed by the failure of the Jews to respond to his apoca-lyptic feat, the discovery of the meaning of grace; Luther regarded himself as a sort of second Saint Paul, whose crucial contribution was to be the conversion of the Jews. When the conversion of the Jews was not forthcoming, he took fright lest the Jews manage to infiltrate the Reformation, a fear he expresses in his first pamphlet against the Jews, *Letter Against the Sabbatians.* The renewal of religious conviction brought about by Luther made the renewal of the Jewish refusal to accept the Saviour all the more painful and all the more conspicuous. Luther was also prominent in his denunciation of the Jews as traitors, capable of any deceit, involved in the practice of black magic and every sort of witchcraft. He even accused them of being in league with the Turks who were then at the gates of Vienna. (It was not the Jews but the French who were in league with the Turks at the time: France had a treaty with the Sultan.) The same general charge was echoed three and a half centuries later in the February 5, 1898, edition of the Rome newspaper *La Civiltà Cattolica:* "The Jew has been created by God to serve as a spy anywhere where a betrayal is in the making." This particu-lar charge, as one example among many, was directed against what the newspaper called the "Jewish-German-republican-Freemason conspir-acy in France" that came to a head in the Dreyfus affair. For his part,

Luther did not scruple to exhort his readers to exterminate (ausrotten) the Jews. His language became so extreme that the Swiss reformer Heinrich Bullinger commented at the time in a letter to a colleague that Luther's anti-Semitic outbursts seemed to have been written by a swineherd rather than a shepherd of souls. The course of evangelical anti-Semitism in Germany is easily traceable from Luther's pamphlets to Streicher's *Der Stürmer*. *The Enemy of the Jews* was published in Giessen in 1570; *The Scourge of the Jews* appeared in 1604, as did *A Short Excerpt of the Frightening Jewish Blasphemies.*

After the Thirty Years War the Jews in Germany were pressed into the service of the princes as merchants, money changers, and diplomats. They were especially qualified for such functions since they were a floating population (with a network of family connections from ghetto to ghetto covering the whole of Europe) unencumbered with any of the restrictions of caste or guild: they had no status other than their positions as "court stewards" under the protection of the local sovereign and they had never been admitted to any of the guilds. The extraordinariness of their situation incurred the hatred of the petty nobility, the city dwellers, and the peasants. This was inevitable since the princes used the Jews to assert themselves and their interests at the expense of both the castes and the guilds. At the same time, however, the Jews gained something like equality with some of the professions, the bureaucracy, and certain sections of the developing intelligentsia. Until 1678, when the first Jew was admitted to a German university (in Frankfurt an der Oder), German Jews were obliged to go to Italy to attend a university. Other Protestant universities such as Heidelberg, Halle, and Königsberg followed, but it was not until more than a century later that a Catholic university (Vienna in 1787) admitted a Jew.

Toward the end of the eighteenth century the influence of the Enlightenment made itself felt through the crumbling spiritual walls of the ghettoes. The rationalist conception of religion loosened the strictures of traditional religious dogma. It was here that Luther's breakthrough proved most important. For Luther liberated the conscience of man from both the great traditional institutional monopolies—the ecclesiastical and the synagogal. When Luther declared that "the place in which we must learn to live together with God as man and wife is the conscience," he made the conscience—and the consciousness—of man the center of the universe. He also brought about a direct relationship, an intimacy and a confrontation, between God and the individual being that declares an equality in the relationship between the human and the divine. With

[168]

his reversion to Holy Writ, to the Word, as the sole authority in all matters of faith Luther took the implement of exegesis (by means of which the church could interpret and reinterpret Holy Writ to suit its hierarchic purposes) out of the hands of the hierarchy and placed it in the hands of the individual. It was a feat that almost belittles the term "Promethean." Each man interprets the Bible according to the dictates of his conscience; that is, the sole arbiter in all religious controversy was the common sense of the individual. Luther thus drew the problems of conscience into the province of reason. This was a complete turnabout from the traditional Thomist ecclesiastical use of subordinating reason to faith. It was a revolution without parallel in history. The influence of Luther's feat on the course of history can hardly be exaggerated. It was a very German thing to do. And it was altogether characteristic that the only German revolution should be a religious revolution.

The German revolution—the Reformation—was preceded by another very German phenomenon, without which the Reformation quite possibly might never have taken place. On the plinth of the Gutenberg Monument in Mainz these words are chiseled:

> Artem, quae Graecos latuit latuitque Latinos
> Germani sollers extudit ingenium.
> Nunc, quidquid veteres sapiunt sapiuntque recentes,
> Non, sibi, sed populis omnibus id sapiunt.

> [The ingenious art which remained hidden from the Greeks and
> from the Romans as well
> Was cleverly invented by the Germans.
> Now, whatever the ancients knew, the moderns also know,
> Not for themselves but for all peoples do they know it.]

Gutenberg's invention of the movable printing press, Luther's reformation of the Christian religion and his translation of the Bible from Hebrew and Greek (for which he necessarily and almost incidentally created the German language—fully as great a feat in itself as Dante's creation of the Italian language): this combination of achievements made the Germans "the people of the book," the Germans' modern claim—in their eyes at least—being as great as the Jews' ancient claim to the title. But which book?

Moses received the Tables; Luther turned them. The corollary of Luther's making conscience a part of reason was the reduction of religion to a province of philosophy rather than philosophy's remaining the handmaiden of theology. Without Luther, Kant would not have come upon his major theses. The very title *Critique of Pure Reason* is an advertisement of the basic result of Luther's revolution. Luther cut the connection between man and management, between the individual and the organization god of the ecclesiastical and synagogal systems—cut the connection and cast the individual adrift in a world that was "not only drenched and impregnated with God but is identical with God." Heinrich Heine went on to say that Germany was the most fruitful soil of pantheism, which is the religion of Germany's greatest thinkers and her best artists.

The Germans, thanks to Luther and Kant and company, have outgrown deism. "We are free and don't want any thundering tyrant. We are come of age and need no fatherly provision. Neither are we the concoctions of some great mechanic. Deism is a religion for slaves, for children, for Genevans, for clockmakers." But it is, says Heine, a mistaken opinion that pantheism leads to indifference. On the contrary, the awareness of his godliness (of his having been put on an equal footing with the divine) will inspire man to tell it to the world: now more than ever will the truly great deeds of a true heroism glorify the earth. Not that the German pantheist will struggle against or resist the materialism of the French Revolution and the Enlightenment. To the contrary, materialism will find only supporters among the German pantheists, supporters who draw their conviction from a far deeper source, from a religious synthesis. In Heine's eyes Luther unchained the Prometheus of the individual ego, gave carte blanche to the human will to make whatever it liked of life and the world. Heine foresaw the fatal combination of the natural philosopher tinkering with the cosmic forces latent in the natural sciences. When the natural philosopher comes into contact with the primordial powers of nature, when he discovers that he can conjure up the mighty spirits of the old German past, then there will awake in him the old German battle lust, the lust that springs not from the desire to destroy or to conquer, the lust that feeds on itself: the desire to do battle for the sheer joy of fighting.

For Heine, Christianity was the great mollifying factor in German life, it tamed though it could not break the brutal fighting spirit of the Germans. But once the Cross breaks, then the wildness of the old warriors, the senseless, berserk wrath, will rush to the surface again. Strange the appropriateness of symbols: the swastika is a broken cross. For the Cross, writes Heine—and he is writing in 1852—is fragile and the day will come when it breaks miserably apart.

Then shall the old stone gods arise again out of the vanished debris and rub the dust of a thousand years from their eyes, and Thor with his giant hammer will finally leap upward and destroy the Gothic cathedrals. Then when you hear the rumbling and the clanking, be careful, you neighbors' children, you French, and don't interfere in the business that we are transacting at home in Germany. It might ill become you. . . . Don't smile at my warning, the advice of a dreamer who warns you against Kantians, Fichteans, and natural philosophers. Don't smile at the fantastico who expects the same revolution in the realm of the physical as that which has taken place in the realm of the spirit. The thought precedes the deed as the lightning does the thunder. German thunder is of course very German and is not very flexible and comes rolling on rather slowly; but it will come, and when you hear it crash like nothing that ever crashed in world history before, then you will know that the German thunder has reached its goal. At this sound the eagles will fall dead out of the sky and the lions in the most remote savannahs will put their tails between their legs and cringe in their lairs. They will put on a show in Germany that will make the French Revolution look like a harmless pageant. . . . As though standing on the steps of an amphitheater the peoples of the earth will gather around Germany to watch the great war games.

In 1783 Moses Mendelssohn, "the Jewish Luther," published his translation of the five books of Moses and the Psalms, an achievement that scandalized the rabbis of Germany. Had he not profaned Holy Writ by taking it out of the protection of the Holy Language? Mendelssohn's German Bible was burned by rabbis in various cities (all of them, significantly, in Eastern Europe). But the parallel "secularization" of Christians and Jews in Germany continued relentlessly. The liberation of the Jews en masse from the ghettoes and from the restrictive legislation that made the ghettoes came with the Enlightenment. The Enlightenment came with the conqueror Napoleon, whom Hegel called "der Weltgeist zu Pferd," the world-spirit on horseback. The most revealing translation of Hegel's coinage is the French. Napoleon was "la raison à cheval"—reason on horseback. Historians generally hold that German national resistance to the Napoleonic invasion unfortunately evolved into German nationalist rejection of the Enlightenment. It was as if the whole ethical corpus of the Enlightenment had stumbled into the line of fire and suffered mortal wounds. The Prussians—and indeed the majority of Germans awakened into some sort of national consciousness by the French invasion—threw out the Enlightenment with the invader and persisted in rejecting most of what the Enlightenment involved because it was French and therefore anti-German. Goethe, who was German but anti–German-nationalist, welcomed Napoleon wholeheartedly and to his dying day castigated German resistance to Napoleon. Much of the emancipatory legislation introduced in Germany, especially concerning the Jews, in the wake of Napoleon was reversed. But by no means all of it.

In Prussia particularly the position of the Jews remained radically improved, despite some cutbacks, and continued to develop. Karl Marx was a product of the Prussian educational system. He was also the most German and the most Jewish of German Jews. He had the incisive, analytical genius of the Jews and the German passion for mechanistic abstraction. On the basis of the rapidly increasing population of industrial workers in Germany and Western Europe, Marx discovered the several points of resemblance between race and class, particularly between the positions of the new repressed international industrial working class and the old repressed international religious community of the Jewish race. Marx's feat was half discovery and half invention. He projected and transformed the concept of the homeless Jewish race into the concept of the international proletariat. Race can be made to equate with class. An ethnic group is assembled and held together by common usages, habits, and interests. An idea, a belief, and finally a faith molds a homogeneous mass of men and holds them together. The root of the Greek word for nation, ἔθνος, is ἔθω, "to be accustomed." Basically a nation is "a number of people accustomed to live together."

Whether in the wake of universal humanitarian considerations or through subconsciously striving to find a safe haven for his oppressed people, Marx created a new home for the oppressed of all nations. He did so by exchanging cultural and religious categories for social, economic categories, by substituting class for race. In conversation with Maxime Ducamp who defended nationalism, Marx replied angrily: "How can you expect us to be partriotic—we who have had no homeland since Titus?" With the creation of the concept of the proletariat and the battle cry "Proletarians of all countries, unite!" Marx brought the old world down around the ears of the captains and the kings. He ushered in, as his friend Heine clearly foresaw, "the world revolution." This, too, was a Promethean feat: it had, and still is having, worldshaking, titanic consequences. For one thing, it wrought new conceptual combinations, wedding the philosophy of materialism with the victims of oppression on the one hand and wealth with the practitioners of oppression on the other: it divided the world anew between exploiters and exploited. For another thing, it laid the Jews open to the charge of having created and

[172]

fostered communism. In opposition to this class movement that cut across all national boundaries, the Germans—including the majority of German Jews—rallied around classic, geographically defined folkism: tradition, blood, soil, roots, unbroken continuity of tenure. Salvation was sought in the racial collective, in the old German pagan tribal consciousness.

Here again the parallel between the egalitarian labor ethic of communism and the communal unity of the tribe is evident. Both posit collectives with the basic function of submerging the individual in the mass, but they are polar opposites in their sources and directions: the one submerging race considerations in the class, the other submerging class considerations in the race. Communism attempts to instill its "nationalism" (international solidarity based on the community of interests of all workers) through socialism, while fascism attempts to achieve some form of socialism—or substitute for socialism—through extreme nationalism. Communism is international fascism; fascism is national communism. Not for nothing was the German rallying to the tribal community called National Socialism. The early Nazi leaders, particualrly Otto and Gregor Strasser, were fully aware of the convertibility of the concepts communism and fascism. According to Marx, the community of material (economic) interests forms the basis of society while culture is the superstructure resting thereon. The general view of the traditionalists (not only "fascists" but capitalists at large) is that culture with its various components and determinants, such as religion and art, forms the basis while economics and the material aspects of life form the superstructure. These two positions, capitalism and communism, are interrelated and interactive in industrial society: there could not be one without the other. The question of which of the two systems provides the more durable solution is too broad to admit of anything but a contingent answer. Communism has not solved the nationalities problem (despite or perhaps because of Stalin's great theoretical work on nationalities); capitalism has not solved the class problem. Communism was not only unable to protect Europe's Jews: it was largely responsible for bringing destruction down on their heads. In this sense it is a fascinating fact that the Jews were the initiators of exemplary models of the two movements: Marxism for international socialism and Zionism for National Socialism. Theodor Herzl and Martin Buber clearly foresaw that in the interplay of opposing forces the reacquisition of traditional Jewish home ground and the defense of it along classic national lines offered the best chance of protecting the race from extinction.

All these factors account in good part for the astonishing similarities between Zionism and National Socialism. They also account for the often hidden but sometimes outspoken sympathy of Nazi leaders for Zionism. More to the contemporary point, they explain the almost tumultuous acclaim of both Germans and Austrians for the spectacular series of Israeli military victories culminating in the Six-Day War. Finally, they contribute to an understanding of the inevitability of the confrontation between Israel and the Soviet Union. For it could not have been otherwise: the Jews are their own international—the only racial international in the world. As such they have a claim on the Soviet Union for the release of some three million Russian Jews whose racial identity Soviet communism failed to submerge in the myth of egalitarian economics. By the same token, the Russians are in possession of three million Jewish hostages.

The great majority of German Jews became neither Marxists nor Zionists but gradually and with growing enthusiasm accepted assimilation as Germans. (Is there a tribute or a remonstrance due here?) Indeed, with the foundation of the German Reich, in which the Jews received full and equal rights according to civil statute, the majority of the Jews in Germany became German nationalists: the first German officer—a lieutenant—to be killed in action in World War I was a Jewish volunteer. All the children of Toni Ullstein, my wife's grandmother, were baptized as Protestants. My wife would never have been born if another Jewish volunteer, officer candidate Karl Ullstein, had not brought his commanding officer, First Lieutenant Fritz Ross, home to meet his sister. Karl Ullstein's favorite uncle, Rudolf (U-4), was a captain in World War I and adjutant to General Gallwitz. Another Jewish uncle of my wife, Heinz Pinner, was an infantry lieutenant in World War I and was awarded the Iron Cross first class. On a per capita basis the Jews received the highest number of awards for gallantry in action of all national groups in the Austro-Hungarian monarchy during World War I. In the eastern marches of the Reich and beyond—in Poland and the Baltic countries, in Hungary (witness George Lukács) and Romania—Jewish intellectuals were the great purveyors of German culture, language, literature, philosophy, and the natural sciences. The Jews distinguished themselves in German life, particularly in intellectual and professional pursuits, to a fault. At the end of the nineteenth century German institutions of higher learning were suddenly swarming with Jews. Within a few decades the Jews outnumbered the non-Jews in law schools and schools of medicine. At Nuremberg, Seyss-Inquart testified that eighty-five percent of the lawyers in prewar Vienna were Jews. They became the dominant element in many of the sciences and in the arts and crafts, even in music and particularly in the new industrial and applied arts.

This was the case in the German Empire. The situation in the Austro-Hungarian monarchy is described by the German-Jewish novelist Jakob Wassermann, who moved to Vienna from Berlin at the turn of the century and lived there for some twenty years.

> One circumstance nonplussed me even after only a short stay in Vienna. For while outside [in Germany] I had cultivated almost no contact whatever with Jews, and had met with one or two here and there who were neither advertised nor advertised themselves as Jews, it developed that here almost everyone with whom I came into any sort of intellectual or personal contact was a Jew. Moreover, the fact that they were Jews was emphasized by everyone including the Jews themselves. I soon discovered that all public life was dominated by the Jews. The banks, the press, the theater, literature, social events and occasions—all were in the hands of the Jews. It was not necessary to search very long for an explanation of this. The [Austrian] aristocracy was completely apathetic . . . the few patrician bourgeois families copied the aristocrats; there was no longer an autochthonous middle class, and the gap made by its absence was filled with officials, officers, and professors; after that came the solid block of the lower middle class. . . . The court royal, the lower middle class, and the Jews gave the city its character. It is in no way surprising that the Jews, as the most active group, kept everyone else moving incessantly. . . . My relationship to them, both personal and formal, was from the very beginning highly ambivalent. To be forthright about it, I must confess that at times I could not avoid the impression of having been forced into exile among them. With the German Jews I was more accustomed to bourgeois polish and social unobtrusiveness. But with these people I could never rid myself of a certain shame. I was ashamed of their manners, I was ashamed of their behavior. . . . At times this shame increased to the point of desperation and disgust. There were both trivial and significant occasions for such extreme feeling: their way of speaking, their premature familiarity, the misgiving that betrayed their recent ghetto environment, infallible opinionatedness, idle rumination about simple things, hair-splitting casuistry in the place of quiet attentiveness, subservience where pride was indicated, pompous self-assertion where modesty was called for, lack of dignity, lack of restraint, lack of any metaphysical ability. . . . There was a strain of rationalism that ran through all these Jews and beclouded their every innermost attitude. Among the lowly this expressed itself in adoration of success and wealth, in a lusting after advantage, profit, and power, and in social opportunism; among the high and mighty

it was the incapacity for ideas and intuition. . . . There was in them a general will and determination to divest the world of all its secrets, and they were so audacious in this that in many cases—for me at least—it was impossible to distinguish between shamelessness and progress.

For an Austrian, the German Jews, and especially the Berlin Jews, were just as objectionable—though perhaps not for the same reasons— as Wassermann found the Viennese Jews. But whether under a Habsburg or Hohenzollern emperor, the Germans were equally as bumptious as the Jews. Moreover, the combination of Enlightenment and industrialization created a middle class out of the mass of peasants and small artisans and brought it into public life. This was a process that paralleled the emergence of the Jews from the ghettoes. The result was a confrontation and competition for pride of place between German and German-Jewish bumpkins. The conspicuous success of the Jews in virtually all the professions and the arts excited the envy of the Germans who inevitably felt themselves crowded out of their rightful opportunities on their home ground by an alien people. The discomfited and déclassé individual instinctively takes refuge in the clan. With Germans this instinct has the strength of a primordial urge. The Jews were an elite who lived according to their own strict rules of conduct and mental discipline under the Law. The Jewish community was regarded as a closed shop: "Jews always stick together" runs the old saw. And for various reasons, most of them good but some of them bad, this was true. The discountenanced Germans set out to emulate the Jews: the folk movement in Germany was born of this conception; "the master race" theory of the Germans was the ultimate response to the Jewish dogma of the "chosen people." Both these claims, the ancient Jewish dogma as well as the newfangled German theory, are based on religious precepts. Both the traditional function of capitalist (usurious moneylender) imposed by the Christians on the Jews and the abolition of private property undertaken by Marx merely served to emphasize the materialism interconnecting the two extremes: "The Jew is Mammon." The church identified the Jews with both capitalism and communism.

The charge of money-grubbing leveled against the Jews by the church is age-old. The charge was politicized by the Christian socialist movement in Catholic Austria. In his speech in the Imperial Council in 1890, Karl Lueger, the most notable of the mayors of Vienna, yet who promoted "the anti-Semitism of the common man," stressed "the incredibly fanatic hatred, the unquenchable thirst for revenge" of the Jews.

"What are wolves, lions, panthers, leopards, tigers, or men," asked Lueger, "compared with these beasts of prey in human form?" The identification of the Jews with communism took a much sharper political form in the wake of the October Revolution in Russia. The prelate Ignatz Seipel, leader of the Christian-socialist "People's party" and chancellor of Austria from 1927 to 1932, summed up the charge in 1927 by quoting a passage from the party platform on the struggle against "the predominance of the undermining influence of the Jews." Seipel added: "The fact that the leaders and propagandists of Russian bolshevism, of German and Austrian communism (which is associated with bolshevism), and also the very radical . . . Austrian socialism are for the most part Jews is surely sufficient explanation of the anti-Semitic attitude of the people." Conservative Jewish politicians were comparatively rare in the German Empire and unheard-of in the Austro-Hungarian Empire. They were excluded from the right wing of the political scale by reason of both race and religion. In the folk reaction to everything the Jews were supposed to represent, namely industrialization, urbanization, modernity, rootlessness, godlessness (had they not crucified our Lord?), lawlessness, radicalism, socialism, bolshevism, revolution, and debauchery, there was a fateful convergence of German racism and the Christian religion. There was, moreover, a general convergence of movements in and around what had been the German and Austro-Hungarian empires after World War I. Parallel with the religicizing of political life manifested in the folk movement there was the sudden politicizing of German and Austrian church life. The German Catholic weekly newspaper *Allgemeine Rundschau* in its New Year's edition in 1920 demanded "an awakening of world Catholicism" in protest against the "crime" of the Treaty of Versailles. "Just as Christians were once thrown to the lions in the Circus Maximus in pagan Rome," ran the appeal, "so now are we—as it seems to us—being thrown to the greedy financial hyenas of the Freemasonic-Jewish world plutocracy."

As Friedrich Heer perfunctorily points out, this is the language of Hitler. The Catholic church in Germany and Austria, as elsewhere, was not a democratic institution. No more was the pagan German tribe. The devotees of both longed for a strong, guiding patriarchal hand; they blamed all the ills and abuses they saw in the changing world on the lack of maintenance of authority. The Catholic hierarchy in the twenties and thirties simply could not conceive of a nonpatriarchal society. As a result there were strong movements inspired and supported by the church in the direction of authoritarian government—as manifested in the regimes of Italy, Germany, Spain, Portugal, Hungary, Poland, Slovakia, and Croatia. This is not to say that the Catholic or the Protestant church deliberately supported fascist and "radical fascist" (Nazi) movements. The process that ensued was not nearly so simple as that. Almost as often as not, the church even tried to forestall fascism by preempting or "taking over" fascist theories, as in the plea for a "Christian anti-Semitism" as distinct from a mere political, opportunistic, or pseudoscientific anti-Semitism. Robert Körber, to cite but one of many Austrian writers and churchmen, announced (in the book he coauthored on anti-Semitism in the Reich after 1932) that ecclesiastical anti-Semitism was "almost as old as the Church of Christ itself." For some (and in any case too many) of the Austrian Catholic clerical authors, Christ himself was not a Jew at all but a "Galilean"—the first great "Aryan"—because the very meaning of his work was the rejection of Judaism for the *true* religion he was proclaiming and bearing witness for with his martyrdom on the cross.

Forced out of religion by Christ, the Jews retaliated by turning to the materialist world (following the Prince of the World) with a vengeance. "With the banishment of the Palestinian Jews into all the provinces of the World Empire," wrote the Viennese history professor Theodor Pugel, "the seed of a coming Jewish world revolution was broadcast, a revolution that even in the twentieth century has not yet entirely been averted." To my intense interest Pugel cites the prophet Akiba ben Josef as the prototype of the "Jewish world revolutionary" in the rebellion against the Emperor Trajan in the year A.D. 131 when "the demonic forces of the whole of world Jewry were engaged in the gigantic undertaking of establishing a Jewish world empire." An Austrian in Munich who had recently decided to become a politician took the same line. In his book Conversations at Table, published in the early twenties, Dietrich Eckart describes a scene:

"That's just it," he shouted, "we are on the wrong track! [Adolf Hitler is alluding to the hidden, secret power that maneuvers everything into a certain direction.] But that power is there. Ever since the beginning of history that power has been there. You know its name: the Jew." He reached for the Old Testament, leafed through it briefly, and "Here," he shouted, "take a look at the recipe the Jews have always used for the cooking of their hellish brew! We anti-Semites are great guys. We ferret out everything except the most important thing." And he read aloud, emphasizing every word, in a hard tone of voice. As follows. "And I will set the Egyptians upon one another so that brother will fight against brother, friend against friend, city against city, empire against empire. . . . "

Further on in Conversations at Table Eckart reminds Hitler of Martin Luther's demand that all synagogues and Jewish schools be put to the torch. "Putting schools and synagogues to the torch," says Hitler, "wouldn't help us much. That is just it: even if no single synagogue, no single Jewish school, no Old Testament, and no Talmud had ever existed, the Jewish spirit would still be there and would do its work. From the very beginnning it has been here; and there is not a single solitary Jew who does not personify it. This is most clearly the case with the so-called enlightened Jews. . . . " In a conversation in the Reich chancellery in 1938 with his then minister of justice, Hans Frank, Hitler quoted from the New Testament: "In the Gospel, when Pilate refuses to crucify Jesus, the Jews call out to him: 'His blood be upon us and upon our children's children.' Perhaps I shall have to put this curse into effect."

The interaction between politics and religion in Germany and Austria grew steadily. At the sixty-second General Assembly of German Catholics in Munich in 1922, which was opened by Cardinal Pacelli (later Pope Pius XII), an unbroken procession of Catholic leaders, including Konrad Adenauer, spoke out strongly against the "dictated peace of Versailles." Most vehement was the speaker from the Saar (which had been cut away from Germany pending a plebiscite) and the representative of the Danzig Catholics. "We will remain with you in spiritual union," said the latter, "until the hour of unification strikes again. Nothing so unnatural as the dismemberment of the German East can long endure." The speaker for the Sudeten Germans in Bohemia was equally emphatic: "We have come here to bind together more closely the community of faith and folk . . . we, too, feel ourselves to be true folk comrades. May the self-laceration in Germany one day cease—then will come the day of the German people—and also for us who languish under a foreign yoke." The president of the Catholic Assembly, Konrad Adenauer, in speaking against the "dictated peace of Versailles" appealed to French Catholics, "in community with the Germans, to find a way to help both our countries." Cardinal Faulhaber spoke of the force for peace which the church constituted and made violent attacks against France and the League of Nations. "As the League of Nations is constituted today," said the Cardinal, "it is a cord to strangle the economy of a people with. It is not a support for world peace but rather the tinder for new world wars, the gambling den of big money." Cardinal Faulhaber went further. He attacked the constitution of the Weimar Republic and its supporters. "The revolution," he said (alluding to the movement that forced the abdication of Kaiser Wilhelm and set up the Weimar

Republic), "was perjury and high treason: historically it has a hereditary disease and bears the mark of Cain."

But the confluence of the two broad movements, the politicized church militant and the religicized folk politics, was reached in the autumn of 1933 in the official publication of the Catholic youth movement in Germany, *Die Schildgenossen* (Comrades of the Shield): "When the Church defined papal infallibility in the year 1870," ran the statement, "it anticipated on a higher level the historical decision which is being taken today on a political level: for authority and against discussion, for the pope and against the sovereignty of the council, for the führer and against parliament." This statement could not have been made without the precedence of the Concordat. The Concordat between the Vatican and the Third Reich is perhaps the most controversial document of our time. It was signed on July 20, 1933 (a fateful date in modern German history); it represented thirteen years of untiring effort by Cardinal Pacelli: it was his achievement, just as it was his conviction that the church needed Germany fully as much as Germany needed the church. Pius XI accepted the Concordat for the same reason: he saw the Third Reich as the God-given bulwark against bolshevism specifically and against the gradual but relentless disintegration of authority in general. A great many Germans saw the Third Reich in the same way. Not a few Germans (and not only Germans) saw striking similarities between the church militant and the militarist German state, between the Christian mission, the monastery, monasticism, and the SS and the SA, between the Cross and the swastika (or the Hakenkreuz—"hooked cross"—as the Germans call it). This attitude was formalized in the Concordat, according to which newly appointed bishops were required to take the oath of allegiance to the National Socialist state (Article Twenty-six) and a prayer for the government and the German people was to be offered at the completion of every church service (Article Thirty). Most important, the Concordat broke the back of Catholic resistance to Hitler and National Socialism. The inevitable culmination of this attitude was represented by Hubert Lanzinger in his oil portrait of Hitler as a knight in shining armor on horseback bearing the swastika banner. He was Richard, he was Raymond, he was Godfrey at the Gate! He was Saint George killing the dragon of bolshevism.

Heer points out that the Catholic Adolf Hitler was never excommunicated, that Hitler's books were never placed on the Index. One wonders at which point in his career Hitler might have been excommunicated. In Bavaria before the abortive beer hall putsch in 1923? But the Bavarians

—government and people—were overwhelmingly on the side of the motley of nationalists who put down the absurd, june-bug "Soviet government" of Munich in blood. Despite its patent absurdity the "Soviet government" of Munich scared the wits out of the Bavarians. It also made a lasting, traumatic impression on the papal nuncio Pacelli, who happened to be in Munich at the time. For Pacelli it was a lifetime lesson in what was to be avoided at all costs. Pacelli was representative of the Catholic reaction to "the first Soviet Republic on German soil," which as luck would have it, seized power in Catholic Bavaria and numbered among its leaders two men who were not only foreigners but Russians to boot and Jews on top of it all. Who would have moved Hitler's excommunication in the Vatican—Pacelli? Hitler's success cannot be comprehended without attention to the protection afforded him by a state that has maintained its separate identity and autonomy within the shifting German context for a thousand years and does so today with undiminished vigor—Bavaria. It was by no means happenstance that Bavaria became the home of the National Socialist movement. Hitler's imprisonment in Landsberg was an enforced sojourn in a sanatorium with most of the amenities and almost unlimited visiting privileges. Moreover, Bavaria remained a safe haven for Hitler until he was ready to move to Berlin and make his bid for power.

But the larger significance of Hitler's not having been excommunicated or even threatened with excommunication (apart from the fact that he was in no sense a practicing Catholic) is this: Hitler—as Hitler—was always part and parcel of the National Socialist movement. Indeed, Hitler was (or better, he became) National Socialism. But National Socialism was not Hitler. Without the movement there could have been no Hitler. Without Hitler there would certainly have been a National Socialist movement of some sort and probably an equally successful one —quite possibly a more successful one. To excommunicate Hitler would have been meaningless. Hitler did not invent the führer principle; he merely filled the bill, or, rather, the billing. Hitler did indeed simply happen: he "just growed" like Topsy in the circumstances. But what circumstances! He was created by forces inside Germany and by their interaction with other forces bearing in upon Germany from the outside. What Hitler made of National Socialism was not nearly so important as what National Socialism made (and did not make) of Hitler.

MY JOB AS A DEPARTMENT OF THE ARMY CIVILIAN GS (General Service) Grade 9 brought me four or five thousand dollars a year and a four-room flat at 116 Hansa-Allee in Frankfurt am Main, just behind the I. G. Farben building, which served as the headquarters of the American High Commissioner for Germany—HICOG. In fact, we were living in the same row of flats I had occupied five years before as an Army liaison officer when the I. G. Farben building accommodated SHAEF. (At this writing the I. G. Farben building is still an American army headquarters.) In short we were in the Golden Ghetto and everybody knew it. There was an endless procession of peddlers, beggars, and petitioners of every sort who made the round of the HICOG housing area in those years. The doorbell would ring fifty times a day. This was two years after the currency reform, an act that saved the nation economically and split it politically; but the Germans were still destitute. Most of the callers were door-to-door salesmen who offered original paintings or sketches or homemade gewgaws. But they were all—the lot of them—pitiable.

One day the doorbell rang and I opened to find a small, scrawny, and rather scruffy middle-aged man, bareheaded but with the inevitable briefcase (Germans of all classes and walks of life are born with briefcases as natural appendages). For some reason I was more than ordinarily short with him: "Thank you very much," I said, "but whatever it is, we're not having any," and closed the door. The doorbell rang again immediately. I opened angrily but before I could expostulate, the scrawny little man raised his left hand in admonition: "I am your uncle Leopold," he said. "I don't have any uncle Leopold," I answered. "You do *now*," he said and walked past me into the flat. It was my mother-in-law's younger brother, Leopold Ullstein, or U-1-4 (that is, the fourth child of the first child of the original Leopold Ullstein). Leopold had not come out of German destitution but English austerity: he numbered among those members of the Ullstein family who had taken refuge in

England. These, in addition to Leopold, were the only survivors of the five brothers, "the collective genius of Ullstein"—Rudolf (U-4), Friedrich (U-5-1), known as "Sir Frederick" and not only because of his impeccable Oxonian English, and Tante Martha, the widow of the most prestigious of the five brothers, Louis (U-2), and owner of twenty-six percent of the stock in the family firm. All this—among various other family memorabilia—I learned within the first four minutes of Leopold's visit.

As we say in the American West, Leopold could talk the hind leg off a mule. We often had the flat full of the family, as it were, for Frankfurt was not only a traditional clearinghouse of Europe but also a most convenient stopover coming and going between Berlin and Vienna or Berlin and London. Those, like my father-in-law, who tried to escape the onrush of Leopold's rhetoric (if that is what it was) by taking refuge in the bathroom, only found themselves captive audiences by their own hand. Leopold would stand outside the bathroom door and continue his harangue undaunted through the door. When Leopold was a student at Heidelberg before World War II, he had been the roommate of Robert Oppenheimer. The Oppenheimer-Ullstein coresidence ended abruptly when Oppenheimer, according to the family version of the incident, "tried to kill Leopold by beating him over the head with a chair." The incident itself was not questioned: apparently Oppenheimer had indeed made at Leopold with a chair and the two of them had been suspended as a result. The incident was adduced by some members of the family as evidence that Oppenheimer was unstable, by others as merely another instance of a sensitive soul's being moved to desperation after suffering for months under the unrelenting pressure of Leopold's torrential palaver.

There was another reason for Frankfurt's prominence: it was the seat of the Allied court of restitution. The Hotel Frankfurter Hof, where most of the emigrés stayed while their cases were being considered by the court, was popularly known as "Restitution Hall." The bulk of the Ullstein family's holdings—or former holdings—was, of course, in Berlin. But they also had a restitution case, and no small one, in the courts in Vienna. This was the Waldheim-Eberle printing plant and publishing complex. The family had also had holdings in Budapest and Madrid. They had published books, magazines, and newspapers. Most of the best-known journalists and editors had worked for Ullstein. Most of Germany's successful authors had published their books under the imprimatur of the owl (the mascot-symbol of the family: the "Ull" in

Ullstein originally stood for "Eule"—owl). The chief claim to fame of my father-in-law was that he had accepted the manuscript (after twelve other publishers had rejected it) of *All Quiet on the Western Front* and published it for Ullstein. Erich Maria Remarque's first novel proved to be an all-time best seller; it went through countless editions and was translated into twenty-seven foreign languages, including Chinese. My father-in-law had all twenty-seven foreign-language editions in his library.

The various restitution proceedings had already been going on for years by the time I entered upon the scene. It took another two years or so before restitution was finally effected or, as in the case of Waldheim-Eberle (where the Austrian government had confiscated the property and was running the plant), compensation was granted. After a year and more of assorted relatives and their lawyers pacing the floors of all the rooms of our home (this pacing was known in the parlance of the family as "tigering") while shouting at each other and gesticulating like philharmonic conductors, I began to understand my wife's extreme and unwavering reluctance to speak of family matters. It was typical. Every member of the family was so fed up with the family that he or she never discussed the subject out of doors. Indoors it was "the House, the House, the House"—always "the House." Hermann, the youngest of the "genial" brothers Ullstein (U-5), had written and published a book in England during the war entitled *The Rise and Fall of the House of Ullstein.*

True, there was something to shout about. The property itself was worth many millions of marks. But what was far more important than the financial value of the property was the guaranteed quasi monopoly that went with it. This was not merely because the Ullstein printing plant, by far the largest in Germany (the family had employed some 12,000 people in Berlin), and the Ullstein archives (photographs and texts), without doubt among the best in Europe, had both been secured from destruction by custodians loyal to the family. Nor was it because of the much heralded "good will" of the House. It was preeminently because restitution would necessarily bring with it (since otherwise restitution would be meaningless) the licensing of most if not all of the former Ullstein publications, newspapers, and magazines.

Under the Allied military government in Germany, Germans were prohibited from publishing unless they were in possession of a license to do so. These licenses were issued by the Press Section of the military government in each of the three zones and were difficult to come by. Before a license was granted the applicant had to be cleared after a lengthy investigation into his past—especially his activities and political attitude during the Nazi period. The criteria of acceptability began with an exclusion principle: no one actively engaged in journalism during the Nazi period was eligible for a license as a publisher or for employment by a licensee. Only those applicants with a "clean vest" stood a chance of receiving a license and even then the chance was slim: there was a severe paper shortage in Germany for several years after the war so that even licensed newspapers were restricted to four pages in weekly editions. Moreover, much of the country's plant and equipment had been destroyed. Anyone who managed to come by a license in the immediate postwar period had a pole position and an enormous head start in the competition that was to come. Thus the main Ullstein printing plant and publishing center, which happened to be located in the American sector of Berlin, inevitably became the service printer for most of West Berlin's newspapers. The Ullstein property itself had been confiscated by the American military government in July 1945 as a matter of course.

At the time, the family was powerless to press its claim for restitution, having been scattered to the four corners of the earth: I have mentioned the English group; in the United States was Karl (U-1-3), the eldest son of the eldest son; Kurt (U-3-1) was in Brazil. Only one of the family, Heinz (U-2-1), had remained in Germany, hidden and cared for by his gentile wife. None of them—abroad or at home—had any money. One of the many ironies involved was that Heinz, the only German citizen remaining in the family, was helpless before the Allies for that very reason: his uncle and his cousins, who had meanwhile become British and American citizens, were in a far better position to press the family claim. Proceedings were further and greatly complicated by the extraordinary situation of Berlin. The fact that Germany's capital was effectively cut off from its hinterland had been brought home to the Western Allies during the blockade. Even before the blockade, the Western Allies had treated Berlin as a special case. The restitution laws in the Western zones of Germany did not apply to the Western sectors of Berlin until July 1949. A state of siege had been proclaimed in Berlin and confirmed: the viability of the city was the first priority and remained so. The result—as in all such cases—was a continuing state of emergency in which every established private interest becomes the common cause by virtue of the fact that it constitutes a part of the viability of the whole. The Western Allies were extremely reluctant to do anything even potentially prejudicial to the welfare of the small newspapers that made up West Berlin's gallant and beleaguered press.

Because of such formidable and various obstacles the Ullstein restitution case—in my mind anyway—began to assume the dimensions of the lawsuit in *Bleak House*. I recalled ominous lines from Dickens' novel to the effect that whole families had inherited legendary hatreds with the suit, that articled clerks were in the habit of fleshing their legal wits about it, and that no man's nature had been made better by it. In *Bleak House*, the estate which is the object of the interminable lawsuit is finally eaten up by lawyers' fees. In the bleak House of Ullstein there was no danger of this: the value of the property was increasing with every day that passed. By 1950 the printing plant in Tempelhof was employing 3,500 people. The trouble was that official reluctance to make restitution increased with the value of the property, especially since it represented a crucial investment in a unique and highly explosive international political situation. Rudolf (U-4) had returned to Berlin in mid-1949 to press for restitution. But he was seventy-six years old and had the wrong citizenship for the job since all the Ullstein properties were in the American sector.

The family finally decided in 1951 to send the one and only American Ullstein to Berlin to help Rudolf. This was Karl Ullstein (U-1-3), the eldest son of the eldest son, the chief of the Stamm Hans (the Hans Ullstein branch of the family). Karl arrived in Berlin in July 1951. I had preceded Karl to Berlin by two months, having meanwhile taken the job of liaison officer with the American provost marshal in Berlin. (After a break of five years I was back in Russian liaison.) In fact, we had set up housekeeping in Berlin just in time to play host to Karl, a thing we most gladly did for he was quite possibly the most charming man I have ever met. Moreover, he was my father-in-law's best friend, the "Kriegsfreiwilliger [volunteer soldier] Ullstein" who had brought his commanding officer home for the express purpose of loosing his sister on him; and he was the favorite uncle of the children of that union. Since Berlin was the focal point of the Ullstein suit and Ullsteins were continually arriving from all over for councils of war, with Karl's ensconcement as our permanent guest, our house in Berlin-Zehlendorf ("the green borough of Berlin") became the headquarters of the movement.

As a result there opened up a world to me that was new in every way and complete in itself. It was the world of the Ullstein family in Berlin; it was far more than their "circle" or the various "circles" of the members of the family. It was also everybody they knew and dealt with: publishers, editors, lawyers, doctors, printers, politicians, financiers, chauffeurs, gardeners, butlers, maids, cooks, carpenters, and writers. (By the same token, although this came some time later with residence there,

there opened up to me the world of the Ross-Ullsteins in Vienna.) I have deliberately omitted journalists from the catalog of Ullstein acquaintances. In my experience the Ullsteins had nothing to do socially with journalists except at the annual Press Ball in Berlin. Editors yes, journalists no. To include editors as journalists is stretching the point both ways. It was Leopold Ullstein (U), the founder of the firm, who said that if you wanted a good journalist you either had to cut him down from the gallows or get a Hungarian. In fact, the Ullsteins did not like writers either. As I discovered in time there was reason for this. As a class of professionals, writers are likely to be socially insufferable. If they are fiction writers they tend to be preoccupied with themselves and their characters; if they are nonfiction writers they tend to be Pooh-Bahs, pontificating on all points and still more self-centered.

The favorite professionals of the Ullsteins were painters. Here again my own experience bears them out and not only because it was ancillary to theirs. There is obviously something peculiarly satisfying and relaxing in painting. Professional painters (I can think of no exception in the round of my acquaintance) are the most contagiously happy of all artisans and artists. Indeed, the charmed circle of Berlin centered around a painter, one of the oldest friends of the Ullsteins, Professor Heinrich Heuser—"Heini."

Heini had an atelier in the Sybel-Strasse in Berlin-Charlottenburg, a sort of penthouse on top of a seven-story building. This consisted of one huge room, the entire ceiling of which was replaced by a very high skylight. A hot plate and a sink were half partitioned off to serve as a snack kitchen and there was a small bathroom at the back. There was a couch that doubled as Heini's bed or a bed that doubled as a couch, a straight-backed sofa, a table, and several nondescript chairs. The rest of the room was taken up with the various props and appurtenances of the painter's occupation. Heini was almost always there. And so was everybody else. Most of Heini's friends were performing or creative artists: painters, like Hans Scholz (Scholzi-Polzi), who was an indifferent painter but later became a best-selling novelist; sculptors—Fritz Reuter was a regular guest; actors like Walter Gross (then the best of the Berlin cabaret artists), Wolfgang Lukschy, Ernst Deutsch, Paul Hubschmid; and actresses galore—preeminent among the younger group was Romy Schneider. But there were also politicians (Felix von Eckardt, who became the first spokesman for the West German government, was one of Heini's oldest friends), businessmen, boxers, dancers, stage designers (the beautiful Viktoria von Schack, then the wife of Wolfgang Lukschy), and publishers. But what distinguished Heini's circle was the plethora of "Wiesenpieper" (literally, meadow-chirpers), the little floozies in flower-print dresses. They were the decoration in Heini's atelier.

For the rest, wit—or at least a lively appreciation of wit—was the only ticket of admission. The premium was on the art of the raconteur, an art in which Heini himself excelled above all others. Heini's stories were famous throughout Berlin and beyond. His turns of phrase have been handed down from generation to generation: "There was this old fool of a retired colonel. When war broke out he was recalled to active service despite his age. And then somebody pressed a battalion into his hand . . . ." Heini's nightly parties never broke up until some while after dawn (long after in the summer, when dawn breaks apple-green at two in the morning). There were serious political discussions from time to time. I remember Scholzi-Polzi railing against Brecht who lived only two miles away on the other side of the Brandenburg Gate and was then still accessible but even then in a different world. "What Brecht preaches is death: the death of art and the death of artists." There were also some lively philosophical discussions: "The idea of democracy is the travel ticket!" (Fritz Reuter). But the theme of all these evenings was invariably laughter. It was a time of hilarity, of great unconscious joy. Surely the best kind. And the great exhilarating influence was Berlin.

At that time, in the early fifties, Berlin was the most fascinating place in the world. For one thing it was dangerous (there were 247 kidnappings, all political, from 1945 to 1960)—but not very. Then, too, the Berliners were riding on the wave of the great moral victory of the West in breaking the Soviet blockade of the Western sectors of the city. But above all it was because Berlin was still the capital of Germany. Germany is and always was an abstract concept, but the abstract concept had an extract, quintessential reality: Berlin. Perhaps that is what made Berlin so fascinating. It was the quintessence of an abstraction. It was the focal point of the confrontation between East and West, just as it had been the focal point between the various confrontations in Bismarck's Reich, Weimar's Republic, and Hitler's phantasmagorium. It was where the twain could and did meet—and mix. A mother from Frankfurt an der Oder could meet and visit with her son from Frankfurt am Main in Berlin. Berlin was then still the clearinghouse of East and West Germany.

I have often wondered how to go about describing Berlin. The city has no distinct face: it can be seen and recognized only through the bracing effluvium of the collective personality of its inhabitants. Berlin is what London would be if all Londoners were Cockneys and plunked into the middle of the North German plain. There is a certain impishness that is alight in the eyes of every Berliner. Fritz Kortner, the actor and director, told a story about himself. He returned to Germany from exile in 1953 nursing a monumental resentment against the Germans. He flew into Berlin and landed at Tempelhof Airport in no mood to take anything from anybody. As Kortner settled into a taxicab outside the airport the driver turned to him and asked: "Where would you like to go, Mr. Kortner?" "What," exclaimed Kortner, in some astonishment, "you know who I am?" "Why, of course, Mr. Kortner," replied the cabbie, "in the old days I used to drive you to the theater every night." Kortner sank back in the seat somewhat mollified. When the cab pulled up before a traffic light the driver turned to Kortner again and said, "Tell me, Mr. Kortner, when did you leave Germany?" "In 1933," answered Kortner, "when Hitler came to power." The cabbie drove on in silence until the next red light before addressing himself to Kortner again. "And you've only just now come back?" he asked. "That's right," said Kortner. When they had finally reached Kortner's hotel the cabbie turned to Kortner again and said: "You know, Mr. Kortner—you didn't miss much."

There is another aspect of Berlin that must be mentioned. Not long after leaving the city in the mid-1950s for the first time, we received a letter from Karl Ullstein. "Fräulein von Reizenstein," he wrote, "recently opened the gas valve on herself. Not long ago she had married a man twenty years her senior. Now the widower walks the poodle alone." Fraülein von Reizenstein had lived directly across the street from us in Berlin. She looked to be in her mid-twenties. She was very blonde and pretty and always bright and cheery. We usually saw her in the mornings when she walked her poodle before going off to work. I suppose it was the early hour of these meetings coupled with her brightness that prompted us to call her "Rise and Shine" instead of Reizenstein. Fraülein Rise and Shine was the youngest suicide we had known—but only one of very many. Within a period of two years in Berlin seventeen women of our acquaintance committed suicide. Ever since World War II, West Berlin has had the highest suicide rate of the cities of the world. With 39.5 suicides per 100,000 persons Berlin's rate is almost twice that of West Germany. In 1971 the total of West Berlin suicides was 927, of whom 390 were women. In recent years the number of women suicides has declined both absolutely and in relationship to men suicides. Even so, in 1971 twice as many women as men threatened to commit suicide to the answering service of the Berlin Suicide Prevention Center.

There are a number of fairly obvious reasons for this sad distinction. First among them perhaps is the terrible battering the city had taken during the war. Then, too, the psychological effect of the ruins year after year as symbols of deprivation and bereavement depressed everyone. There was the disorientation of the Germans as a people: the explosion of the great vegetative mass provided by fascism into its component atoms—into so many isolated, individual consciousnesses. The pariah-dom of the Germans internationally had to be borne individually. There was no united moral force left—not even an identity—to bear the burden of imposed guilt and shame collectively. The decimation of German men during the war was a double bereavement—present and future—for the women. (There are more than three million Germans still missing from World War II. German post offices constantly display photographs and particulars in an attempt to establish the identities of young people who were found as waifs during the last months of the war.) For some twenty years after the war there were three times as many women of marriagea-ble age as men. It was this fact alone that made Berlin the greatest "man's town" in the world. I have never met the man who did not like Berlin: I have met very few women who did. There was the ludicrous situation of Berlin politically: the epic pratfall of the Grand Alliance in carrying out Four Power control of Berlin and Germany; the division of the city into sectors and then halves, the Western half an "island of freedom" in the "red sea" of the Soviet Zone. This context gave rise to a great many bizarre goings-on. One woman seduced her retarded son—ostensibly and proclaimedly—to "make a man of him"; she committed suicide not long thereafter. The macabre quality that is the hallmark in this century of Berlin has antecedent causes; and as a logical extension they led to the chaotic developments during and after both world wars. Berlin has been a garish island in Germany ever since the 1870s when the "bleak garrison capital" of Prussia became the capital of the Reich and was swollen with the influx of uprooted, poverty-stricken provincials from all over Germany.

The suicide rate for West Germany at 21 per 100,000 persons is lower than that of Sweden (22 per 100,000) and far lower than that of Hungary (35 per 100,000: the Hungarian rate has risen steadily since the Hungarian revolution; it was 21.4 in 1957). Even so, I would contend that the German has, by conditioning over the centuries, developed a special relationship to death. Perhaps the very German "thirst for death"

(Todessüchtigkeit) is overemphasized. But I am convinced that the Germans, like the Scandinavians, do not fear death the way other European peoples (especially the Latins) do. Suicide for the German constitutes a reasonable recourse in time of need. How else does one explain the rash of suicides that took place in Bonn during the six months from October 1968 through March 1969? An admiral, a major general, a doorman in the cultural section of the Foreign Office, an air force major, a secretary-stenographer in the Foreign Office, and assorted senior civil servants—fourteen all told—shot, poisoned, and hanged themselves in the federal capital. At the time, it caused quite a stir, chiefly because it was naturally suspected that most, if not all, of the suicides had been involved in an espionage ring. The majority of these suicides, however, were ascribed to fits of depression caused by strictly private woes.

By way of an example of the German matter-of-fact attitude to suicide, a district court in Hamburg in 1969 ruled in favor of a woman who had suffered temporary disability as a result of a suicide attempt. The court directed that her employer pay her expenses for six weeks' hospitalization and medical care, finding that suicides could not be judged by normal standards (the employing firm had argued that the employee was not eligible for sick pay because she herself had been the cause of her disability). The court apparently considered that the disability was an accident since it was patently not the intent of the suicide to disable herself. To avoid such accidents a Swedish philosopher last year made a plea for "suicide clinics," where candidates would receive instruction (of course only after every effort had been made to bring them from their purpose) in the art of committing suicide effectively and, above all, hygienically. For this purpose the philosopher (otherwise unidentified) even proposed putting an installation at the disposal of the practitioners of the art—gas chamber, stereo set (so that self-victim could die to his favorite music), kitchen complete with staff (to provide self-victim with favorite dish at final meal), etc. The Swedish philosopher had obviously read an earlier German philosopher. Friedrich Nietzsche insisted on the right of the individual to die a noble death when it was no longer possible to live a noble life. "Death freely chosen," wrote Nietzsche,

> death at the right time, with clarity and joy, [death] accomplished amidst one's children and witnesses, when he who takes his leave *is still there* to make a real evaluation of what he has achieved and desired, a summing up of his life—how all this contrasts with the miserable and terrible comedy which Christianity has made of the

hour of death. One should never forget that Christianity has misused the weakness of the dying man for the rape of his conscience, has misused the manner of death itself to make value judgments of the man and his past! Here it behooves us, despite all cowardly prejudice, to create the correct, that is, the physiological appreciation of the so-called natural death, which is finally also only an "unnatural death," a suicide. One never goes to destruction by someone else's hand, but only by one's own hand. Only it is then death under the most despicable circumstances, an unfree death, a death at the wrong time, a coward's death. Out of love for life one should desire death in another way, free, conscious, not by coincidence or accident. . . .

Of course, Nietzsche is talking about a sort of self-induced euthanasia with fitting ceremony attached (the ceremonial effect is peculiarly German). The Swedish philosopher was quickly assured by a number of psychiatrists that a suicide clinic would attract suicides, would incease the suicide rate untellably, amounting to a "suicide can be fun" propaganda campaign. Nietzsche, in fixing on the will to self-destruction, overlooks the instinct for self-preservation. The idea of the deathday party is unsalvageably grotesque: "You are cordially invited to celebrate the deathday of Wolfgang Maximilian Schulz . . . " Suppose the resolve of the celebrant should fail midway through or at the very end of the festivities—to be postponed to a more suitable occasion. In such a case there might be far more (abortive) deathday parties than birthday parties.

But to return to the brighter side: a young man met a beautiful young woman at the Olympic swimming pool in Berlin on a hot day in August 1950. For the young man it was love at first sight. He invited the young lady for a cup of coffee on the Kurfürstendamm. On the way to the café the young lady fell in love with a pair of shoes in a shop window. Since she was from East Berlin and forced to live in deprivation of the good things in life, the young man gallantly offered to buy her the pair of shoes. To his dismay the young lady accepted: the young man had exactly five marks in his pocket. Great was his relief, then, when they discovered that the shoes were slightly too large and would have to be adjusted, an operation that gave him some five hours' grace. The young man was a journalist and took counsel in his profession. He telephoned an international news agency in Frankfurt and informed them that he had a sensational scoop: a confidential, highly placed source had just put him in possession of the Stalin Plan for Germany. He was asked as a matter of course how many articles the plan included. Without hesitation the young man replied, "Eighty-five," not thinking that he would have to write all eighty-five of the articles. Here it was his unthinking extravagance that probably saved his hoax from detection: who would go to the trouble of producing eighty-five paragraphs of Sovietese just for a lark? He was also shrewd enough to know that the one thing he must not do was ask for money. That would have been the sure giveaway. It took the enterprising journalist three hours to produce the eighty-five articles, that is, to "translate them" from the nonexistent Russian original. His task was facilitated by his long, arduous apprenticeship in reading the gobbledygook of the official organ of the Socialist Unity Party (Communist) of East Germany. And so the Stalin Plan for Germany was born: when the Soviet Embassy in East Berlin issued a démenti it only served to contribute to the apparent authenticity of the story. After other members of the press corps had filed their stories of the story, they took up a collection for our journalist's source to the amount of eighty-five East marks (in those days of unimpeded thoroughfare within the whole of Great Berlin one carried both West and East German currencies), which they naturally entrusted to the young man for delivery. He was obliged to travel part of the way into East Berlin because his colleagues insisted on accompanying him triumphantly to the S-Bahn station (it was, after all, an epoch-making scoop). Once into East Berlin he doubled back to Kurfürstendamm, changed the East marks into West marks at the official rate of something more than four to one, and turned up just in time and with just enough money to pay for the shoes. The love affair itself scarcely outlasted the summer but it left a monument in the form of the front page of the August 15, 1950, issue of *Die Welt*, "the independent daily newspaper for Germany," which headlined the Stalin Plan for Germany and set forth all eighty-five of the plan's articles.

There is no point in mentioning names but it is a fact that some of Germany's best and most successful editors (the two adjectives do not necessarily belong together) served their apprenticeship, were convicted, and did time as intelligence fabricators. The fabrication of intelligence involves allowing oneself to be recruited by an intelligence organization and accepting assignments to provide information on certain people, areas, and installations for a fee. The intelligence fabricator pretends to carry out these fact-finding missions while in reality he stays home and dreams up the required information. Of course he must be both well informed and adroit in his phrasing in order to escape immediate detection. Intelligence operatives are not out-and-out fools. While I was a liaison officer in Berlin, an elderly White Russian gentleman, a long-standing member of Berlin's Russian colony, presented himself to me as a trusty informant. His object being payment for services rendered, he insisted on providing me with confidential reports on prominent members of the colony. I read only the first of these: it was an explosive exposé of flagrant homosexual practices on the part of the composer Peter Tchaikovsky. The czar, wrote my informant, was deeply disturbed by persistent rumors of his favorite composer's unnatural inclinations and had ordered him—on pain of imperial displeasure—to cease and desist. If my "informant" had been a good bit more imaginative and had updated and downgraded his product, if he had made his subject, say, the conductor of the Red Army Chorus or the commandant of East Berlin, and had chosen an appropriate displeased superior, it might have passed as a good piece of intelligence fabrication somewhere in the intelligence community and earned him ten or twenty marks (West) and, once his story was proved false, six months in jail (this was the statutory sentence for conviction on the charge of intelligence fabrication).

A good journalist could make a decent wage fabricating intelligence and, with any sense of timing, could fit in the inevitable prison sentence to cover the winter months. In the first few years after the war jails were among the few places that were well heated, and prison food was as good and as plentiful as anywhere else in the German economy. Also, it was good training (for the fabricators—not for the intelligence operatives). I know one German editor—he is one of the best in Germany and a very fine human being—who served two six-month terms as a fabricator before becoming the editor in chief of what was then one of Germany's largest newspapers. He still counts the experience as invaluable: the demands made on his talents by his employers grew more and more exacting to keep pace with their suspicions that they were being had. Too, there was a lot of leeway. Upon his release from prison a fabricator could always go to another organization within the intelligence community. There was of course a blacklist of convicted and suspected fabricators that was circulated throughout the community. But intelligence organizations are jealous, envious, and generally suspicious of one another. They are very often not prepared to take the word of a competing organization even within their own national community. There is also the fact that professional fabrications are not so easily detectable as one might think: journalists as a breed are uncommonly good at putting commonplace things in a portentous way. As Karl Kraus said, "Journalists write because they have nothing to say and they have something to say only because they write." Moreover, there was no moral stigma whatever attached to fabrication as such: life was a matter of gaining livelihood as best one could. For the same reason there was no moral stigma attached to black-marketeering at that time, unless it was organized on a large scale as a profit-making enterprise.

My job as liaison officer for the provost marshal put me into an office in American Military Police Headquarters in West Berlin. The liaison was mostly with the German police since the work itself consists largely of trouble-shooting—handling incidents involving Russians and Americans in the American sector—and the German police were usually the first on the scene. For the rest I was in regular contact with Soviet Headquarters in Karlshorst (East Berlin), with the Soviet Military Mission in Potsdam and with Soviet Army Headquarters in Wunsdorf. On the American side I worked—as liaison always does—under the G-2 (intelligence) officer of the provost marshal and was thus part of the so-called American intelligence community. The "community" looked like the aftermath of a rousing sneeze into the alphabet soup: MI (Military Intelligence), CIC (Counter Intelligence Corps), CID (Criminal Investigation Division), CIA (Central Intelligence Agency), ONI (Office of Naval Intelligence), AFI (Air Force Intelligence), DIA (Defense Intelligence Agency), the Public Safety Office, etc.

No small percentage of the incidents I investigated involved the shooting (and almost always the shooting to death) by East German border guards of drunken GIs who had blundered into the no man's land separating West Berlin from East Germany. I was continually astonished to discover the trigger-happiness of the East German "People's" Police and soldiery. At the scene of an incident they would stand along the sidelines affecting a nonchalant slouch as the Russian and American parties parleyed, very young men in sloppy half-uniforms—almost uniforms à choix—with cigarettes drooping from the corners of their mouths. They were an exceedingly curious sight. Their deshabille expressed their ambiguous status: Russians, like Germans, have a pronounced respect for uniforms. The Russians employed, as we did, civilian liaison officers, but they were always carefully surrounded by men in uniform. In the early fifties East German officialdom of all kinds was a self-conscious, disreputable motley. As for the young bucks who made up the soldiery and the "uniformed" police, they made a practice of spitting cherry stones at Westerners during the summer and kicking snow at them in winter. They were in fact a kind of political demimonde. There was something about their situation that smacked of a private army. At that time the East German regime was by no means a full-fledged apparatus. It was purely and simply an ancillary of the Red Army in Germany and not an easily controllable one at that. The Russians were frequently embarrassed (for the record anyway) by the vehemence of their charges and sometimes, after a particularly nasty, gratuitous piece of savagery, would promise that the person or persons responsible for a fatal shooting would be brought to account.

On one occasion, I remember, even the Russian liaison people were angry: an American sergeant, obviously drunk, had driven off the road into the unmarked sector-zone boundary area where his car came to a halt in the uneven terrain. He had been shot in the groin while still seated in his car. The guard had fired from a distance of three feet, the hole in the car door showing the downward trajectory of the bullet, the quantity of blood on the seat and the floor of the car giving testimony of the location of the wound. He was five days dying in the Red Army hospital in Potsdam. The Russians brought a detailed report of his agony and a number of photographs of his corpse. The sergeant was—that is to say, he had been—a large young man twenty-eight years of age who was running to fat. The sergeant was—had been—a man who ate and drank too much but exercised enough to keep the added weight in contiguous form with the musculature of his body. According to the Russian report he had ranted and raved and struggled to get up during the last two days of his life. The bandages on his wound continually came off, the wound reopening again and again. In the end they had had to tie him down. "A tragedy," said the Russian officer, and then he added through his teeth, "the dirty son of a bitch!" He was not alluding to the dead sergeant. It was then, under the psychological pressure of the moment, that I looked at the East German irregular soldiery and saw them as animals—not beasts, but animals, fine-looking young animals, thoroughbred running dogs: I was specifically reminded of Doberman pinschers, magnificent specimens, well trained but still dangerous to everybody, including their masters.

I received this impression again, the impression of the animal predominating in man to the extent that it was downright uncanny (almost as if an animal were masquerading as a man), when I was called in to interrogate two members of an East German Communist assassination team or goon squad. The leader of the goon squad had defected rather than carry out his mission of assassinating an East German politician who had defected to the West years before. The leader had then cooperated in rounding up his two assistants. These had readily confessed their participation in the mission, had been willing to demonstrate the use of the sophisticated instruments of murder they carried, and had divulged some of their personal history. But they were adamant in their refusal to give any further information whatever. To my surprise they refused not because of political conviction but simply and admittedly (and how voluble they were in their admission!) because they were afraid. They had what seemed to me an exaggerated respect for the universal Communist capacity to wreak vengeance on stool pigeons. These were action agents, practiced political killers; their credentials as fighters for the cause of the proletariat were impeccable: both were veterans of the Spanish Civil War, both—as we later discovered—had been entrusted with and had carried out several such missions. But neither of them had enough political savvy, let alone ideological conviction, to furnish a schoolboy with the theme for an essay. Instead, they were a pair of well-kept, well-trained dogs, like loyal cocker spaniels rather than beasts of prey. The larger and physically more powerful and more afraid of the two had soft brown eyes expressive of infinite manipulativeness. But these men had been properly and cunningly burned (as I read somewhere that trained dogs in a vaudeville act had their paws burned to insure obedience). Nothing we could do or say served to dispel their fear. They had already gone more than far enough to bring the full wrath of the apparatus down on their heads. Worst of all, their own careers were the most convincing testimony to what action their former comrades would take against them and how effective it was likely to be. I do not know whether the two met their nemesis. In any case they were provided with the protective cushion of a long prison sentence.

During my three years and more at the provost marshal's office I received a letter by way of Magdalen College stationery from Von Kalb whom I had met on the single occasion in Oxford. Von Kalb had settled in Karlsruhe and made the acquaintance (at least that) of an East Prussian countess whose husband had unfortunately been caught and sentenced to hard labor by the Poles. Von Kalb earnestly asked my assistance in delivering the count from durance vile and restoring him to his wife. What Von Kalb had in mind, whether he assumed that I disposed over a network of agents or the requisite diplomatic influence, I never bothered to inquire. But his request seemed to me to reflect the chronic German assumption of the existence of private power bases. Ordinarily such a request would have smelled of provocation. If it had come, say, from a Soviet official in East Berlin or elsewhere and concerned a count- ess instead of a count—or if the pitch had been tailored to the projected defection of a highly placed Soviet or satellite official contingent upon the deliverance of a loved one—it would have made some sense as a provoca- tion. As it was, Von Kalb's entreaty seemed to have a taproot in the Vehme, the tradition of private armies, private police forces, and private secret courts.

It seemed significant to me that Von Kalb's letter should have come when I was occupied and preoccupied with East German militiamen and action agents, both of which parties smacked strongly of the Vehme. The so-called People's police of East Germany reminded me hauntingly dur- ing those years of the French militia in Nazi-occupied France. The French militia gradually became an elongated arm of the Gestapo as the German situation in France grew desperate. In the last months of the war, in response to German pressure, a French "law" was passed creat- ing courts-martial. These were secret tribunals, each composed of three nonmagistrate "judges" whose identities were kept secret (there was no prosecution and no defense); only those whose death sentences were foregone conclusions met their "judges" face to face. The sessions of these courts-martial were invariably held inside the prison and sentences carried out then and there; the grave swallowed up the successive revela- tions of the judges' identities to all prisoners who appeared before them. As Jacques Delarue, whose account I refer to here, sums it up in his book *The Gestapo*, "I deeply regret having to write that most of the judges of these courts-martial could never be identified after the liberation." Privacy equates with secrecy and organized secrecy equates with con- spiracy.

One can characterize National Socialism and International Social- ism alike as conspiracies (it is not merely by chance that Germany is the birthplace of both): any one-party state is a conspiracy of one part against the whole. In those years, throughout the fifties and beyond, in Germany there were organizations—preeminently "Die Kampfgruppe gegen die Unmenschlichkeit" (the battle group against inhumanity) and the "Free Jurists"—established and maintained to keep book on East Germans who lent themselves to the dirty work of totalitarian socialism; their crimes were formally noted and registered for prosecution at a future date (that is, upon reunification). But these groups and the various organizations that with them made up the Allied and West German presence understood neither their own situation nor the situation of the East Germans under Russian occupation. The East German members of the People's police had certainly no more choice than the French militia-men under the Nazis. Conspiracy (unless it is official) against one's own people is treason. But in Germany treason is a congenitally ambiguous concept. In Germany there have always been too many private power bases, too many Vehmen, to allow for a hard-and-fast concept of treason. So runs the old saw (composed by Sir John Harington):

> Treason doth never prosper: what's the reason?
> For if it prosper, none dare call it treason.

In Germany there was always too good a chance that the upstart, tin-pot conspirator would prosper, particularly if there were foreign powers interested in supporting him for their own ends. And somewhere on Germany's periphery there was always an interested party or combination of parties. The Western Allies ignored the fact that Germany was divided. More strangely, their new ally, West Germany, also lost sight of the fact. Germans have always had great difficulty resolving basic concepts of government. The reason for this difficulty is the eternal subdivision of Germany among provincial rulers, whose behavior reflected a principle set down in the Treaty of Augsburg, "cuius regio, eius religio" (the ruler determines the religion of his subjects). Whoever ruled also determined under the same mandate the way of life of his subjects and the meanings assigned to words: "cuius regio, eius definitio" (whose rule, his definition [of everything]). To define is "to determine the boundary or limits of," territorially as well as conceptually. The commitment, the allegiance to Germany has always been general (in keeping with the indefiniteness of the idea of Germany). For this reason the fixing of limits has always been a continuing process. In Germany the act of definition is dynamic. It is part and parcel of the power struggle proceeding from a multiplicity of provincial power bases, the struggle to impose one's own definition over and beyond one's own (provisional) borders. "Everyone knows that we lack any relationship whatever to treason," commented the German soldier's newspaper when *Der Spiegel*'s editorial staff was formally charged with treason. How true! It either makes all the sense in the world to talk of treason or it makes no sense at all. In Germany it makes no sense at all because there is no generally valid definition. Treason in one part of Germany is by definition heroism in the other— and it pretty much always has been. By whose definition? By the definition of whoever happens to be ruling in the part and trying for the whole. The People's police and the People's courts in East Germany were outlawed by the Western Allies (and their German allies), whose defini-

GEORGE BAILEY

tion was purely negative because they did not have the power to impose their definition on the area in which the People's police and the People's courts functioned.

In those days we all thought we were doing something—we, the New Germans with our new allies, the Old Germans. And indeed we were doing something. But not what we thought we were doing. Friedrich Heer, the Austrian historian, traces the "satellite ideology" of the West, the regarding of East European countries as mere satellites of the Soviet Union, back to Calvin, who called Erasmus "the satellite of the devil." It was Calvin's political theology, absorbed and reexported to Europe by American Presbyterians, says Heer, that emerged variously as the policy of containment and liberation from, and rollback of, communism. This, contends Heer, did untellable harm, and not only in the case of Hungary where our damning of Hungarian Communists as satellites of Satan (Stalin) blinded us to the momentous developments that led to the Hungarian Revolution. I do not think that any other Western approach to the problem of communism, however enlightened, would have averted Soviet suppression of the Hungarian Revolution. But Heer has a point insofar as the black-and-white pigeonholing of political phenomena deprived the West of imagination and initiative in coping with communism.

There is perhaps a deeper point than the irony of a German invention, the Reformation, coming up from behind to plague the new would-be reformers of Germany. If it is not indeed a Holy Land, then Germany is the land of abiding religious obsession. Christianity, as Houston Stewart Chamberlain was at pains to point out, gave every single individual human being a totally undreamed of, immeasurable value—"All the hairs of his head have been counted by God" (Matt. 10:30). This was the investiture of the human animal with dignity. But it is that very dignity, counters Nietzsche, which forces a large class of men to insist on the loftiest of principles as moral cover when purely material interests dictate their submission to a party or a sect or a prince. These must be principles of an unconditional obligation—an obligation to which one can submit and about which one can parade one's submission before all and sundry. But Nietzsche was never above writing for effect. Here he is deliberately putting it too crudely. Christian dignity forces men, prepares and conditions them, to work with the loftiest of principles as a matter of course. They cheat even when they know it not—indeed, then most effectively. "A German," said Theodor Adorno, "is a man who never tells a lie unless he believes it." The superimposition of the lofty principle leads to

[200]

mistaking the part for the whole—the part the West held for the whole that was once there—as we did in the fifties in Germany. It is also taking the part for the whole on faith, as the Germans on either side or any side did and still do, as Seyss-Inquart did, mistaking his "Germany," which was really only German Austria, for all Germany.

THE ULLSTEIN FAMILY WAS RESTITUTED IN BERLIN IN January 1952. It began republishing one of its traditional newspapers, the *Berliner Morgenpost,* once the largest daily in Germany with a circulation of over one million, on September 26, 1952. In November 1953 the *BZ (Berliner Zeitung)* reappeared as a tabloid. In the same year the Ullstein weekly fashion magazine, *Brigitte,* the monthly construction magazine, *Bauwelt,* and the Ullstein books reappeared. The resurrection of the House of Ullstein was a momentous and thrilling event, especially because it had been so long in coming.

I was of course invited to all the gala openings and enjoyed the run of the huge office building and plant at the Tempelhofer-Damm near the airport almost in the middle of the city. I was as spellbound as a school-boy at the sound and sight of the great rotary presses in action. I particularly enjoyed the festive occasions when hundreds of printers would stand on the stage and in the pit of a rented theater in Neu-Köln, a workers' quarter, and sing "God save the art, the black art!" ("Gott schütz' die Kunst, die schwarze Kunst!") and "Heil Gutenberg!" Within two years the *BZ* had reached a circulation of more than a quarter of a million and the *Morgenpost* almost two hundred thousand. The other publications and the books also did well. Compared with the House of Ullstein's past status, however, these were but token successes. Ullstein suffered from the isolation of Berlin. All sorts of schemes were hatched to overcome this handicap, such as flying the *BZ* out to key cities in West Germany as the Ullsteins had done before Hitler's takeover. But the cost was prohibitive (the Ullsteins had no capital except their Berlin property) and Berlin was no longer the capital of Germany. The only hope was reunification or the acquisition of properties in West Germany. The family did open an affiliate in Frankfurt am Main, which published books, especially pocket books.

The pocket book indicated the reduced magnitude of the effort and its cause, Ullstein's chronic lack of liquid capital. In early 1954, however,

[202]

a unique opportunity presented itself: the British occupation authorities' newspaper for the German population in the British zone, *Die Welt* (The World), published in Hamburg, was released for sale to a German firm. This was Ullstein's big chance, since *Die Welt* was one of the three most highly regarded newspapers in West Germany. Moreover, the British office in charge of the sale made it clear that it would regard an Ullstein bid preferentially. But there was one condition—that the Ullstein family alone be the purchaser (the British were determined to prevent Ruhr industrialists from gaining an interest in the newspaper). The Ullstein House could not raise the money within the family and was forced to take out a loan—in fact, two loans. The larger of these was to be arranged with Robert Pferdmenges, the Cologne banker who was perhaps the most prominent banker in Germany because of his close personal friendship with Konrad Adenauer. The second loan was from Gerd Bucerius, the Hamburg publisher-owner of *Die Zeit* (Time) and *Der Stern* (The Star), and was to be repaid by according Bucerius a ten percent participation in the ownership of *Die Welt*. This arrangement was the result of the close business association between Bucerius and Fritz Ross, my father-in-law, who had set up the Austrian edition of *Der Stern,* even then Germany's largest illustrated magazine with a circulation of over one million.

The Bucerius participation was clearly at variance with the condition of sale imposed by the British. In any case, the condition was nonsensical: Ullstein could not have been bound by any terms of "ownership" not to resell to whomever the family pleased. However, Bucerius was hardly a Ruhr industrialist and ten percent is far from a blocking share of stock. Nevertheless, the secret of the Bucerius participation rankled Karl Ullstein who, as U-1-3, the oldest son of the oldest son, with restitution had become chairman of the board of directors of the family firm. On the other hand Karl had accepted the Bucerius participation, however reluctantly, in arranging the transaction with his brother-in-law and member of the board of directors, Fritz Ross. On a fine spring day Fritz had left Berlin for Vienna on the strict understanding that Karl would conclude the formalities of the purchase of *Die Welt* that same day. Early in the afternoon, in my presence, Karl telephoned Robert Pferdmenges in Cologne for last-minute assurance that the loan would be forthcoming. In answer to the question on the loan Pferdmenges said, "Zuversichtlichst" ("most confidently"). This was not good enough for Karl. He called the British negotiator and informed him that Ullstein would not be able to purchase *Die Welt*. Fritz Ross, Karl's brother-in-law and my father-in-law, never foregave him. For Karl the whole issue turned on the one word "zuversichtlichst." Did "most confidently" mean yes or no? Since—for Karl—it did not mean "yes," it meant no. For Fritz, "most confidently" coming from Robert Pferdmenges in answer to a question about a loan, any loan, meant "yes." And yet the real reason for Karl's decision not to buy *Die Welt*, which he as much as confessed to me before and after that fateful "zuversichtlichst," was that he was afraid of it. "Where would we get the editorial staff to run a newspaper that big and that important? We've got all we can handle as it is."

The fact of the matter was that Karl was not an Unternehmer (enterpriser); none of the third generation Ullsteins was. Indeed the only Unternehmer in the House was Fritz Ross. But Fritz's position was strange: he was not a Namensträger (name-bearer) but he was the husband of the oldest child of the oldest son (U-1-1). Moreover, he was only occasionally if frequently in Berlin, being the general director of Ullstein, Vienna, a book publishing firm which he himself founded after the war. The result was that he spent about half his time in one or the other city and the rest of it en route between them. Neither Berlin nor Vienna received his full attention or his concerted effort. He spent the entire postwar history of the House of Ullstein—some ten years—shuttling between the two cities. It was almost as if he were repeating German history in microcosm, not being able to decide between the two cities as capitals of the greater Reich—the small or the great German solution. Still the dilemma, for him, was real. It was unthinkable that he bow out of the Ullstein enterprise proper in Berlin: as his wife's executor he represented too large a package of the stock for that. On the other hand, leaving Vienna and his book publishing firm would have involved his relinquishing his office as president of the Austrian Publishers' Association. This was equally unthinkable: his presidency brought him concourse with the presidents of other national associations. Sir Stanley Unwin, Ernst Rowohlt, old George Brett of Macmillan, and Charles Scribner were among his favorites. Most important, the presidency of the World Publishers' Association makes the round of the national presidents year by year, each successive officeholder playing host to his colleagues at an annual congress. The office and the role of host fell to Fritz in 1958. Congress in Vienna, a favorite idea in the "congress city": the grand ball took place in the Hofburg, in the ballroom of the royal palace. It was the crowning event of Fritz's life.

The failure to buy *Die Welt* was the turning point in the story of the second "Rise and Fall of the House of Ullstein." For as soon as Karl Ullstein had decided not to buy, the newspaper was purchased by a young—forty-year-old—German who was already the undisputed press lord of West Germany: Axel Caesar Springer. Even then the catalog of Springer's publications and their circulation figures was unprecedented in German history. There was the *Bild Zeitung* (Picture Post), a tabloid with a circulation of over three million—"the largest newspaper on the European continent"; there was *Hör Zu* (Listen), a weekly illustrated radio magazine (television was then just beginning in Germany), circulation almost three million—it was and still is "the most successful magazine in the German language"; there was *Kristall* (Crystal), a biweekly illustrated "information" magazine, circulation 450,000; the *Hamburger Abendblatt* (Hamburg Evening Sheet), "the largest regular German daily newspaper" (that is, nontabloid), circulation 300,000 (Sundays, 460,000); *Das Neue Blatt* (The New Sheet), a weekly feature newspaper, circulation 500,000; and a one-third interest in the largest German fashion magazine, *Constanze*, circulation 530,000. The combined circulation of Springer's publications amounted to more than one-third of the total circulation of the West German press, including West Berlin.

Historically, Springer's towering preeminence in postwar Germany is ironic. With the memory of the Hugenberg press empire fresh in mind, the first thing the Allied military governors in Germany were determined to prevent was the reestablishment of any sort of monopoly of the press. But the very preventive restrictions imposed by the Allies were largely responsible for the emergence of Springer's empire, of *Der Spiegel*'s news magazine monopoly, and the toploftiness of *Der Stern* among the illustrated picture magazines. "Springer—mammoth publisher," as he used to sign himself in letters to his friends when he was no such thing, did not profit accidentally from the system of licensing introduced when the Allies occupied Germany in 1945. Having foreseen the defeat of Nazi Germany, he also foresaw the period of strict tutelage under the Allies that was to follow. The son of a small but prosperous publisher and printer in Altona, a suburb of Hamburg, Springer had the good fortune to be declared unfit for military service on a technicality. When the House of Springer—like all nonconformist publishing firms—was gradually throttled by Nazi censorship and forced to sell, young Springer set aside the proceeds of the sale—some three hundred thousand marks— as operating capital and waited his chance.

It came in 1944 when the Nazis were confronted with the drastic need of entertainment literature for the soldiery at the front and the air-raid-sheltered civilians at home. The opportunity was tailored to Springer's needs because it allowed the publisher to pursue his trade without compromising himself by publishing propaganda literature. Springer received a government contract and published hundreds of light novels, many of them by Jewish authors, for guaranteed sale. By the end of the war Springer had a clean bill of political health, something to show by way of publishing experience, and ready money, a combination of advantages then enjoyed by very few Germans. He had comparatively little trouble in obtaining licenses at a time when the West German public was starved for the printed word.

In both respects, censorship (licensing) and unsatisfied public demand, the immediate postwar period in Germany was an extension of the late Nazi period. The licensees by the same token were in the position of state-sponsored firms. Strict observance of Allied directives was assured by Allied control of the scant paper supplies and imports. There was some bootlegging but there was no point in bootlegging to anyone but a licensee whose circulation was outrunning his paper ration. Too, the Hamburg location was an enormous advantage. The first licenses were exclusive privileges to publish throughout the British zone. The British zone included both the Rhineland and the Ruhr, the two most heavily populated and richest areas of Germany. In exercising their privileges the early licensees were enabled and obliged to build up their own distribution organizations—the arteries and smaller blood vessels, the circulatory system, of a publishing enterprise.

There was yet another advantage. Many of the British information officers in Hamburg were newspapermen, in themselves Springer's connection with Fleet Street. But his most important connection was Hugh Cudlipp, coeditor of the *Daily Mirror*, then the largest newspaper in the Western world with a circulation of over four million. Springer went to London, took instruction from Cudlipp, and produced the *Bild Zeitung* on the *Mirror* model. But Springer added something: his own formula for the postwar German readership. The strange device on the banner Springer flew was not "Excelsior" or even "Amplius," but "Be Nice to One Another." "Be Nice to One Another" appeared in white letters on green cardboard plaques advertising Springer publications throughout West Germany. It was the substance of Springer's frequent direct appeals to the public. Indeed, it was Springer's message. When not explicit, it was imbedded in the affable fatuity of the editorial tone of most of his publications. In the case of the *Bild Zeitung* this was standard tabloid practice.

The *Daily Mirror*'s Wilfried says " 'Goo-goo' to his little friends." The *Bild Zeitung*'s dachshund mascot, Rübezahl, like a good German, was constrained to put his sentiments into verse:

> I wish for all whom here I greet
> A clear, cool head and toast-warm feet,
> A heart as soft as your money's hard,
> And all the best from your little pard.

Springer's editorial policy seemed to consist of firing broadsides of powdered sugar at the public. This was deplored by the rest of the German press as a "belittling to the point of harmlessness" of the serious problems confronting the German nation. But Springer's editorial policy was based on his own analysis of the postwar German situation. He had concluded—with considerable insight—that the German public would have to be regarded as convalescent patients. "After thirty years of war, inflation, dictatorship, and again war," wrote the *Hamburger Abendblatt* in the mid-fifties, "all people in Germany are basically suffering from exhaustion and in need of care. They want rest. Dispute and dissension actually cause them physical pain." On the basis of this diagnosis Springer prescribed a cure: a bland-sweet diet of entertainment, kind words, intimate concern with the rights and wrongs of the individual and the little things in life—"a confidential dialogue between the writer and the reader." He borrowed and contrived an enormous collection of tender traps and used them unstintingly: human interest stories and fetching photographs of destitute old ladies, children, puppies, birds, flowers, pretty young women, struggling young men, etc. He played the Germans' intense love of animals for all it was worth. "Mecki," *Hör Zu*'s bedraggled, good-natured hedgehog mascot, all but replaced the German black eagle as national emblem. Political events, however, were assiduously avoided or played down: "From the human point of view . . . the *Hamburger Abendblatt* does not put much stock in programs and ideologies. Not so long as there are heaps of rubble along the streets. Not as long as refugees still lead a miserable existence."

Something else that was new was added. In those years Springer was a superlative funster. He very often managed to achieve a combination of public amusement and civic betterment in the various games and prize contests constantly featured in his publications. (Springer's short history of his firm was entitled *Newspapers—Fun and Utility.*) In conjunction with the government-sponsored Traffic Instruction Week, for example, Springer launched "Operation Zebra," so called because of the white stripes marking paths for pedestrians on the pavement. The inevitable animal mascot was there to personify the operation: "Max, the zebra, wags his tail whenever drivers are especially considerate. For the pacification of animal lovers the zebra is, of course, not genuine. Beneath its striped hide two Swedish entertainers are to be found." Each week three thousand "cavaliers of the steering wheel" were chosen and cited in an "honor list" on the front page of the *Hamburger Abendblatt.* The cavaliers were then invited by letter to a meeting place in Hamburg where they were regaled with coffee and presented with *Hamburger Abendblatt* windshield stickers bearing the sublegend "especially considerate driver." Also prizes donated by "noted firms," that is, firms advertising in the *Hamburger Abendblatt,* were liberally apportioned. Finally, and the most memorable of all Springer's public games, was the series of contests whose winners became "mayor for a day."

The accuracy of Springer's diagnosis was attested by the popularity of his prescription, as revealed in the biblical increase of circulation figures. But the mammoth looked more like a diplodocus, a bland, good-natured, even friendly monster whose only really alarming characteristics were its size and its weight. It was not that Springer was wrong-minded politically but rather that he was not politically minded at all. For this reason all politicians were hard on him. "Just one slight turn of the screw," said a member of Parliament, "and Springer's machine could become an infernal machine." (Here spoke the hagriding fear that Springer's nonpartisan stance would turn into an antipartisan, antipolitical party movement: the Germans had had enough of movements for a while.) Even the "Old Man," Adenauer himself, tried to persuade Springer to abandon apolitical journalism. Axel would have none of it. His diagnosis had proved itself. In those years just after the war German publishers faced a public exhausted, disillusioned, and blasé to an extent unparalleled in the country's history. Politics were anathema—especially party politics (to have been a Nazi party member was made a statutory crime by the Allies). Moreover, the German press had totally discredited itself during the Nazi era. And equally spectacular had been the failure of the Weimar Republic's political press as an instrument reflecting and molding public opinion. In Berlin in 1932, for example, the newspapers representing the bourgeois leftist State party had a circulation of 450,000. The party itself drew only 13,251 votes. The German National party newspapers also had a circulation of 450,000, but the party polled only 76,163 votes. By contrast, the Nazis, whose Berlin press had a piddling circulation of 20,000, received 281,531 votes. When I dug out these statistics, I was reminded of the remark of Georg Bernhard, the famed editor of Ullstein's patrician *Vossische Zeitung* before World War I. Bernhard was once told that his newspaper's circulation had substantially increased. "Good God!" he said. "There must be something wrong with my editorial policy." The inverse relationship between editorial excellence and circulation seems a constant.

There seemed to be only one thing that Axel Springer believed in: reunification. And it was this device, written still larger on his banner than "Be Nice to One Another," that spelled doom for the Ullsteins. For the moment that Karl Ullstein failed to secure a foothold for the family in West Germany by buying *Die Welt,* Axel Springer moved into Berlin. He did so by starting a local Berlin edition of *Bild Zeitung,* a logical enough step since there were already local editions of *Bild* in Munich, Frankfurt, Essen, and Hamburg. Nevertheless, Springer's breaching the citadel of West Berlin was a sensation because of the limited market the "island city" provided. Springer's entry was certain to signal a Berlin firm's exit. But there was no way to stop Springer: all protection had disappeared with the system of licensing in 1954. Even so there was great wailing and gnashing of teeth among Berlin newspaper publishers. The West German mammoth was about to crush the local pygmies. The East German exile publishers even petitioned the federal government to protect their interests once the country was reunified. Their fear was hypothetical. Their hypothesis—and Springer's—was the reunification of Germany. His bridgehead in Berlin was supposed to provide Springer with a springboard into East Germany come "X Day" when Berlin would again become the capital. Springer's preparations for "X Day" were his reasons for the move to Berlin. These apprehensions seem grotesque now. But then the division of Germany was still fresh, the wound was still open and bleeding freely. Above all, there was still freedom of movement within Berlin.

But the greatest obstacle facing Springer was the scarcity of good journalists. Many had been killed during the war, more had been compromised by cooperation with Goebbels. For at least the first two decades after the war the best German-language newspapers were not German but Swiss. Switzerland's best, the *Neue Zürcher Zeitung,* has long specialized in clear, detailed, and impartial evaluations of international events and pays special attention to the German scene. During the Adenauer era the *Neue Zürcher Zeitung*'s Bonn correspondent, Fred Luchsinger, now the newspaper's editor in chief, was at times something very much like the West German foreign minister. At the time Springer

[209]

pointed out that the comparision was unfair, saying that the Swiss, in their detached neutrality, could afford to wait and see before rendering an opinion while the Germans were forced to grapple with a welter of changing events which directly concerned them. This was not a new situation. The extent of Germany's dependence on international developments has always presented the German press with the strong temptation to exaggerate the importance of the news—especially foreign news. Specifically, it has always been the tendency of German newspapers to speculate on the "possible" ultimate significance of news items. In contrast Springer's newspapers were wont to debase the intrinsic value of factual information by adding irrelevant expressions of pathos and good will. Between the two tendencies was the difference in primary emphasis that distinguishes a haymaker from a pat on the back. Humanity prefers to be patted on the back. Especially because humanity basically is made up of many individuals. In keeping with its traditional fragmentation into many hundreds of "sovereign states" (most of them no bigger than an American farmer's back forty acres), Germany is a country of many small newspapers (seventy percent have a circulation of under ten thousand, twenty-five percent under fifty thousand). Germany has always been divided into a thousand and more parts: the "divide" already given, the "conquer" quickly follows. Moreover, in a country so empire-conscious, anything at all sizable is immediately hailed or decried as an empire. The mammoth was obliged to move discreetly. Any considerable and conspicuous new acquisition by Springer could, conceivably, beget an organized "Stop Springer" campaign on the part of a group or groups of smaller publishers. (It did—although it was ten years and more before the campaign materialized.) The acquisition was Ullstein.

George Orwell once advised that the best way to become a writer was to marry a publisher's daughter. This I had done. Simultaneously I had married a publisher's niece, a publisher's cousin, a publisher's granddaughter, and a publisher's great-granddaughter. Also, living with the Ullsteins inexorably drew me into the toils—and toils they were— of the family business. Family firms are family firms. There is no great point in accusing them of nepotism. Both my wife's mother and sister were translators, and good ones, for the house. For my part, I was asked often enough to read books or manuscripts in one or another of the Slavic languages or in Hungarian and write reports on their eligibility for the German market. In answer to the foreseeable objection that I, the American—at best a métèque—had no basis for judging the proclivities of

German readers, it could justifiably be said that nobody knew what the German readers wanted except possibly Axel Springer.

By way of added attraction there was Karl Ullstein. Over a decade we lived with him or he with us or we were next-door neighbors. He was the head of the family, titular and tutelary. Most important, the persona of the man was overwhelmingly attractive. He beamed. He was a solar source of good will, optimism, and glee. As a young man in World War I, he had spent five years as a prisoner of the French, and had not returned home until 1920. Imprisonment is a shortening of life. The experience had left him, as it so often does, with something like a compulsion to make up for the fun lost. His favorite story related the introduction to French prison camp of a group of Imperial Prussian officers, including the shavetail Ullstein. When the old French commandant entered the hall where the Prussian officers were seated, they all jumped up and stood at attention. "Messieurs," he said, "restez assis: la France est généreuse!" ("Gentlemen, remain seated: France is generous!") I have never met the Prussian who didn't think this story funny. I have never met the Frenchman who found it in the least amusing. ("France *is* generous," said a French friend of mine apropos.) Karl had two favorite sayings: "Rich people are very silly" and "Nothing is sillier than a dead millionaire." His oldest sister described him as "the laziest child" she had ever seen, his favorite game being "dead warrior": he would lie spread-eagle on the floor while his two sisters wept and wailed over him. But Karl was anything but lazy in the twelve years of our acquaintance: he spent an average of four hours a day writing letters (almost all of them to members of the family). Karl was incorrigibly boyish and unrestrainably confiding. He was forever soliciting advice from all family members, friends, enemies, young editors who were virtual strangers, copyboys—anybody. "My mother is ill: do you think I should go see her?" I thought he should. (I sometimes wondered that Karl ever managed to come to a decision about anything. His irresoluteness explains, I think, the voluminosity of his correspondence: he was engaged in setting forth wide varieties of alternatives with the objections that attached to each and every one of them.)

I also thought that if there was ever a time for a would-be writer to leave government service and take the plunge it was at this conjunction of favorable personal and national circumstances. I did so and shopped my qualifications around the editorial offices of New York. I had the good fortune to meet Philip Horton, executive editor of the *Reporter* magazine, with the result that I received the assignment—on

speculation—to write an article on the German press with special attention, inevitably, to Axel Springer. Accordingly I set about examining the
Springer legend.

In his salad days Springer earned the reputation of playboy. Despite
the passage of two decades it had stuck. The legend also had Springer
a dandy who postured in mortal dread of a sartorial solecism, a showman
much given to living in the grand style while carefully screening the fact
from the public. It was rumored, for instance, that Springer owned four
Ford Thunderbirds, all painted red to disguise their plurality. In fact he
owned one Thunderbird—painted black. But the rumor was more significant than the truth. In Germany, as in most places in the Western world,
great wealth has become embarrassing. F. Scott Fitzgerald was convinced that rich people are essentially different from poor people, that
they are not bound by the same codes of conduct or subject to the same
civil statutes. This may be because wealth—in the Western world—has
become the only differentiating factor in society. Isolated as such, it
looms larger than ever before and seems a throwback to the feudal past
—the private yacht, the private island, the private police force, the
private army. In Germany when the "economic miracle" was still young,
great wealth sorted ill with the role of champion and chief confidant of
the little man. The *Bild Zeitung* provided the Pecksniffian undertone:
"This is indeed the paradox of our merciless times: while many do not
know what to do with their money, others must eke out a miserable
existence from day to day." As my investigations proceeded, I found that
Springer's circle of acquaintances was divided between those who swore
by him and those who swore at him. Out of modesty many of Springer's
old friends had withdrawn their countenances and given him up as a
genius. Not that they had forgotten Springer or he them. One of his
former cronies, in attempting to describe Springer's effortless charm in
dealing with his staffs, made the lapidary statement: "His presence glad-
dens; his look askance saddens." ("Seine Gegenwart beglückt; sein
schräger Blick betrübt.") After that I didn't know what to expect.

Meeting Springer personally was a pleasant surprise. "I'll tell you
everything," he said when I stepped into his office in Hamburg. Exuberance is always engaging. He was still a young man then—hardly eight
years older than I. He was a patent medicine man. His only politics was
peace: "Be Nice to One Another." He called war "international civil
war" and "war among brothers" (Brüderkrieg). I wrote then that
Springer gave the impression of a man cheerfully engrossed in the con-
trivance of miracles. More, this engrossment instilled the expectation of

[212]

miracles in others. To be sure, they were very minor miracles such as the contest that made the winner "mayor for a day." But they were exhilarating and the promise was there. No minor miracle and still very much in abeyance was reunification, Springer's great article of faith. He believed in it, he said, "with every fiber of his being." It was to be achieved by the creation of good will on all sides. As for the embarrassment of wealth in Western society, Springer laughed it off. "Envy," he said, "is a major German trait. What I have and what I do with it would cause no stir at all in America. The Germans have not yet learned to be unenvious." In Springer's system of values there was no room for envy. Exuberance precludes envy. Springer was bursting with projects and always busy implementing them. He had set up a continuing fund from the earnings of the *Die Welt* complex to finance fifty provincial apprentice journalists for one year's study and work abroad. (The recipients of these stipends were obliged to pledge to return to their provincial newspapers for a certain period upon completion of their tours abroad.) He had two hundred young men enrolled in special preparatory courses for executive positions in his own enterprises.

At one point I asked Springer, for he was so very much a newspaper publisher rather than a book publisher, what books he read. "Must I tell you?" he replied. "Well, then, religious books. I read books about religion." I did not pursue the point and I did not mention it in my article. This was a crucial omission because religion is the key to Springer's character.

In the end it was a matter of no consequence because the article never appeared. I had just finished the final draft when Karl informed me that Tante Martha had just sold her twenty-six percent of Ullstein stock to Axel Springer. For several months, indeed, ever since restitution, various members of the family—naturally only those who were not employed by the family firm (but these were in the vast majority and living abroad)—had been trying or threatening to sell their shares. First and foremost of these was Tante Martha, who could see no point whatever in holding on to her huge bloc of shares for a piddling stock dividend (in the first few years most of the firm's earnings had of course to be ploughed back into expansion and maintenance). But the sale did not help the Ullstein company. To the contrary: it brought the most dynamic force in German publishing into the firm and left those Ullsteins still in the firm as strapped for operating capital as ever. A few rather frantic attempts were made to find a buyer (who was not a publisher) for a composite bloc of shares. One, a young Bavarian millionaire, eliminated himself by suffering a heart attack while driving his Mercedes 300 SL at 130 miles an hour.

In 1959, after much twisting and turning, the family decided to sell outright to Springer. In addition to their lack of capital, there was another reason for the decision. All the family members of the firm, excepting Frederick alone, were approaching or past seventy. Those members of the next generation who showed any promise as publishers had all married into the family (and hence were not name-bearers) and, to further complicate matters, had all married into the same branch, the Stamm Hans (U-1). The non–Stamm Hans members had effectively blocked every attempt to bring in younger members who had already proved their ability. A pity, for the candidates—two in particular—were outstanding: Doctor Heinrich Treichl, now the general director of the Credit Anstalt, Austria's national bank, and Robert Layton, then a vice-president of Ford Motor Company, now a member of the board of directors of the Friedrich Flick concern. It was not hard to see the sellout coming. Ullstein had a series of books popularizing the arts and sciences. They were known as the "You and . . ." series (Du und . . .) because the two words figured in every title: *You and Music, You and Electricity, You and Painting*. The last book in the series, I said, would be *You and Axel Springer*.

HERE WAS ONE GREAT, CONTINUING ARGUMENT IN the family. Who was right: those who stayed in Germany during the twelve years of the Thousand-Year Reich, stood their ground as it were, and took the consequences, or those who left the country, emigrated to the Western democracies and, in some cases, even bore arms against the fatherland? The family never stopped wrangling over the point—and it was the sorest possible point. For they were all still Germans, despite British, American, Brazilian, and Canadian citizenship, and it was a question of honor and loyalty as Germans. Which, under the circumstances, was the more patriotic thing to do—go or stay? Rebel or conform? Stick with the tyrant because he happened to represent the fatherland or desert to the other side to take up arms against him and bring about his downfall? The issue was never resolved, nor could it be. Nor can it be. Nor was it an issue in which the German-Jewish side of the family stood in a clean confrontation against the German side. In those cases where the German-Jewish members of the family stayed they were protected or if necessary hidden by the German side.

In this endless debate the family was representative of a great many German families. I know a good many families that were split down the middle by the question of membership in the Nazi party, like that of a young lady whose mother was a Jewess and whose father was an SS officer. Heinz Ullstein (U-2-1) remained in Berlin throughout, protected and hidden by his Aryan wife; Hilde Ross (U-1-1), my mother-in-law, remained in annexed Austria, protected by her Aryan husband. Two of their half-Jewish children, including my wife, found refuge in an exclusive girl's school in Hesse, where they were sponsored by their uncle, Colin Ross, who knew Hitler personally and was an outspoken Nazi sympathizer. (My wife was prevented from studying medicine by the Nuremberg Laws—but she was privileged to sit in the royal loge in the Vienna Opera House because of her uncle's friendship with the gauleiter of Vienna, Baldur von Schirach.) In the girl's school a classmate of my wife's was the daughter of the horselike hereditary prince, zu Waldeck-Pyrmont, whom I had met in Rosenhof in 1945. In the school the daughter had the reputation of a Nazi; small wonder with a father who was an SS general. But my wife remembers the daughter's telling how furious her grandfather was with his son for throwing in with the Nazis: they had not been on speaking terms for years.

Colin Ross's family had been wiped out except for his daughter. He had entered a suicide pact with his wife and shot her and himself shortly before American troops overran the residential area near Munich where they lived. Their son Ralph had been killed in a freak accident on the Eastern front in 1942. He was sunning himself on a raft in the middle of a Russian lake with two comrades. A solitary cloud was in the sky, directly overhead. The cloud discharged a bolt of lightning that killed Ralph on the spot and left his comrades untouched. So went the family legend.

The position of the Colin Rosses within the family reminiscence was draped in myth. Everything about it was strange. At the Thorhof, the country place of the Ross family in the valley of the Traisen, there are seven tall pillars of granite standing like sentinels in formation on a knoll overlooking the bend in the river. They are all that is left of the block-house father Ross had built for Colin as a wedding present in 1911. The house burned down in 1932 when Colin's younger sister hung her washing over the stove. A piece of clothing fell onto the stove and caught fire. Everything about Colin Ross—excepting the one daughter—seemed to have ended in disaster. There was also the family's reticence in talking about Colin. This was not pronounced but it was persistent. But the most important deterrent to finding out anything about Colin was my own disinclination to do so. For I could not explain the man to myself or anyone else. At that time I attributed the conduct of the Germans in general to their extraordinary provincialism. But Colin Ross had known the world at large as few people in our time. He was by profession a foreign correspondent and perhaps the best in Germany. He had written some twenty books, all but one of them about foreign countries. (Two of them went through more than twenty editions.) He had not only traveled all over the world but lived abroad for lengthy periods. He spent four years in South America in the early twenties, some eight years in Asia, and four or five years in the United States. How could just such a man have chosen to make common cause with the Nazis? I still believed half consciously in the conspiracy theory propagated at Nuremberg.

How could the literate, cultivated professional traveler, foreign resident, and observer have fallen in with a clique of country bumpkin high school dropouts, vengeance-ridden noncoms, and caricature career officers? I was hardly mollified when I discovered years later in some account of the Nazi period that Colin Ross had warned Hitler to his face that the United States was certain to enter the war on the side of England and that this fact alone would spell disaster for Germany.

In the course of my reading as the years went by I encountered the figure of Colin Ross again and again. In Hans Grimm's curious book *Whence and How—But Where To?*, Colin is mentioned as an indoctrination officer in the German army in World War I, who ranged far and wide in German-occupied territory, apparently on secret missions. His was a complicated role in a confused situation: in family albums I had found a good many photographs of Colin in which he appeared to be a member of the soldiers' councils. This the family dismissed casually with remarks like "Oh yes, always the madcap," "Colin was a real go-getter," and "He was a man who acted on his convictions." Toward the end of World War I Colin Ross's specific mission was to gather information on the morale of the German troops on the western front. He was a cross between an intelligence officer and a public relations officer. Grimm, who worked directly under Colin, was thoroughly shocked at what he heard among the German foot-sloggers: expressions of defeatism were rampant during the fourth year of the war. He was shocked, again, at Colin's reaction when he reported his findings. "Yes—they too want the war to end," said Colin, "at least, as it is being conducted now. Does it surprise you that they say such things among themselves?" Grimm reports that he slowly realized that this very brave man was opposed to the kaiser and convinced that Wilhelm II, as "supreme warlord," was responsible for everything that had gone wrong. Grimm also notes that Colin carried a number of books by Walter Rathenau in his luggage and constantly read them. These included (as Grimm also notes) Rathenau's *The Kaiser* with its "god-forsaken" comment: "If the Kaiser should ride through the Brandenburg Gate on a white charger as victor, then world history would no longer make any sense."

As one of the leaders of the soldiers' councils it is a matter of record that Colin personally prevented a good deal of bloodshed during those weeks in 1918–1919 when two pathetic revolutionary innocents, Karl Liebknecht and Rosa Luxemburg, tried to make and control a revolution. According to his daughter, Colin never talked within his own family of his role in the soldiers' councils except to say, in later years, that he thought he had been mistaken in exercising so much restraint then, that it would have been better for Germany in the long run if they had had a genuine, blood-running-in-the-gutters revolution. I think his attitude is easily understandable. The most exercised proverb in the German language is "Wenn schon, denn schon" (if it is to be done at all, then do it properly). In the German-speaking world this is an admonition, not an assertion. The Spartacus revolt of 1918–1919 was such a piddling affair, such a timorous petticoat pratfall, with sailors playing soldier and soldiers playing policeman, with a manly little woman trying to guide a womanly little man. Dear Rosa, poor Karl! Dear Rosa, the brave little Polish-Jewish bel esprit, a woman of great culture who bought German citizenship by paying a German burgher to marry her, who studied revolution by the book, mushing through a set passage of the *Critique of Pure Reason* every morning, rubbing herself down with a sponge and brush to keep in shape, trying to put together a conspiratorial technique with poor Karl, whose nervous system was so volatile that he was frequently carried away during his own speeches. And the two of them unably seconded (but who could have ably seconded such a pair?) by another Polish Jew, the agent of Moscow and just possibly the most despicable character—certainly the most tragic figure —in the world history of revolution: Karl Radek. Poor Rosa and dear Karl! Hunted down and shot by half-crazed Prussian officers and dumped in the Landwehr Canal in Berlin. (Radek, the Soviet citizen, was thrown into prison where he remained for almost a year.) I have never been able to make up my mind whether I feel sorrier for dear Rosa and poor Karl, the absurd but noble pair, noble but absurd, or Germany. But dear Rosa and poor Karl were what Nietzsche called "free spirits," with apologies to nobody. And Rosa saw through Lenin long before he became the ruler of Russia.

In 1919 Colin quit Germany abruptly with his family and emigrated to Bolivia. It was certainly prudent to leave Germany but his choice of South America as a haven may have been dictated by the ease of admission. He spoke not a word of Spanish. In the next three years he devoted himself entirely to writing a book on South America while his wife kept the family alive by working as an English teacher in a school in La Paz. The family returned to Germany in 1922. In 1923 the family was enriched by the addition of a son, Ralph, and the completed manuscript, entitled *Süd Amerika, die aufsteigende Welt* (South America, the Rising World). The book was a substantial success; it established Colin over-

night as a writer of travel books. It was Colin's third book and the first
to be published by Brockhaus. He began writing articles for the Ullsteins,
where his brother Fritz had long since been employed in a junior executive position. Colin remained an Ullstein contributor until the firm was
"bought out" by the Nazis.

Fritz Ross returned home from the western front in November 1918
and entered the Ullstein firm in the trade division. His account (in his
unpublished memoirs) of Colin's and his own activities during the immediate postwar period is interesting. "During the following weeks in
Berlin," he writes,

> we had a lively time of it; the battle for political power was raging.
> As had already happened in Kiel, workers' and soldiers' soviets had
> been set up: my brother played a leading role in the supreme soviet.
> At first the influence of the returning soldiers was paramount. They
> held mass meetings in the Reichstag and in the Circus Busch. My
> brother was installed in the office of a minister in the Herrenhaus.
> It was here that I visited him shortly after my return. He asked me
> if I would not like to join them. I declined. I have never been a
> revolutionary. Even so he provided me with a laissez-passer issued
> by the supreme soviet of the workers and soldiers. Shortly thereafter
> my brother set up his headquarters in the Schiffbauerdamm near the
> Reichstag. There one could meet the most remarkable people—for
> example, a Bismarck and, above all, Curt Hahn, who made a special
> impression on me. These young people were the driving force be-
> hind a number of ministers in the government of Prince Max von
> Baden. My brother, for his part, was behind the Würtemberger
> minister Hausmann. Hahn, on the other hand, unquestionably had
> considerable influence on Prince Max. He wrote probably the great-
> est part of the Prince's memoirs. He came from an industrialist
> family—the Hahn Pipe Works—and was an especially good-look-
> ing man, of great knowledge and with a highly developed political
> sense. He soon withdrew from politics and founded a modern school
> in Salem Castle in Baden which became famous. When Hitler came
> to power Hahn left Germany because of his [Jewish] extraction and
> founded a second Salem school in Scotland, which the duke of
> Edinburgh later attended. My brother, who had always been much
> interested in things military, tried to organize the soldiers in the
> Berlin barracks into a force loyal to the government. For Friedrich
> Ebert (who, as first chancellor of the Weimar Republic, had suc-
> ceeded Prince Max) had no effective command over the military.
> This attempt excited the suspicion of the left, that is to say, of the
> Independent Social Democrats under Liebknecht, and above all of
> the Spartacists, who were nothing else than Bolsheviks. These tried
> to undermine his dominating position as a former officer, but he was

very popular among the troops. After the bloody Spartacist upris-
ings in January 1919, in which he took part in the assault against
the *Vorwärts* [Forward] headquarters building, he was arrested by
the Spartacists and held a few days. This and the constant struggle
over per diem expenses exasperated my brother to such an extent
that he withdrew from politics. My thoughts in these days of revolution were devoted less to the "rising of the masses" than to my own
bourgeois future because I didn't want to loaf around.

In the foreword to his book *Süd Amerika, die aufsteigende Welt,*
Colin Ross gives something of an explanation of his "withdrawal" to
South America after his revolutionary activity in Berlin.

The wish to perform pioneer service, to discover new territory, to
help open up possibilities for life and livelihood for the thousands
who were deprived of them by war and revolution, was the main-
spring that moved me to make this trip. Perhaps also a little fatigue
and disappointment that after terrible physical and psychic exertion
during four years of war, the revolution in its turn nipped almost
all the budding hopes which pure enthusiasm had engendered after
its outbreak.

Fritz, the brother whose thoughts were devoted to his own "bourgeois future," found himself on the other side of the barricades for that
very reason. His father-in-law gave him a job in the family firm, in the
trade book department. Every morning he and his father-in-law (U-1)
would travel together to the Ullstein House in Kochstrasse from the villa
in Grunewald either by streetcar or subway. On the morning of January
6, 1919, the two of them arrived in Kochstrasse to find the Ullstein
House cordoned off and guarded by Spartacist militiamen. The Spartacists refused entry to any and all, opening fire on anyone who stepped
on the sidewalk on the building side of the street. During the night the
Spartacists had occupied all the buildings on Kochstrasse, the Fleet
Street of Berlin. "We trembled because of the [printing] machines,"
wrote Fritz. "One hand grenade was enough to wreck any one of them.
At this point Louis Ullstein [U-2] walked up to one of the Spartacist
sentries (he took his life in his hands when he did so) and said that he
wished to go up to his office and get his cigars. Impressed by this display
of pluck, the representative of the proletariat allowed the exploiter-
capitalist to enter the building. Sure enough, Louis reappeared some time
later with his cigars."

The Spartacists held the newspaper quarter of Berlin for a few days.
They withdrew when a volunteer troop of soldiers loyal to the govern-

ment stormed the headquarters building of *Vorwärts,* the official organ
of the Social Democratic party. When the Ullsteins found themselves in
undisputed possession of their property again, they were obliged—as
were all others—to organize their own military force for its protection.
The new government still had no regular troops at its disposal. Ex-
servicemen from among the employees were formed into a house militia.
One of the publishing house directors, a reserve captain, was appointed
commandant, with Fritz as his deputy. The premises were fully guarded
with sentinels posted every night. This went on until the formation of the
Guards Cavalry Division was completed and it paraded through the city
with the tall, powerful figure of Gustav Noske, the minister of the
interior in Ebert's government, at its head. Order was restored in Berlin,
but not for long. As Fritz wrote in his memoirs:

> After the pendulum had swung so far to the left, it was only a
> question of time until it would swing to the right. This followed then
> in the event in 1920 with the so-called Kapp putsch. . . . This time
> we were occupied by real soldiers. The plant was shut down because
> we were a democratic publishing house, which made us something
> not very different from Communist publishers in the eyes of the
> Kapp people. We were able to come to an arrangement with the
> commander of the troops occupying the House so that one of the
> owners was allowed to remain in the building. At first this was
> Rudolf Ullstein [U-4] who was spelled by Dr. Franz Ullstein [U-3]
> after two days and nights. I myself remained in the building during
> the entire occupation of the Ullstein House. In Rudolf's large office
> two field beds were set up. The telephone switchboard was forced
> to work under military supervision; however, one of the telephone
> operators had surreptitiously managed to plug the board so that we
> could monitor all calls in Rudolf's office. No calls were allowed to
> be switched to us; we were actually cut off from the outside world.
> Or should have been. The soldiers did not know that Rudolf Ullstein
> had a phone in his office with a direct connection to his villa. So we
> were able to get news out. I tried to reach my wife over this tele-
> phone by having the receiver of the phone in Rudolf's villa put next
> to the speaker of his regular telephone. But we were just barely able
> to understand each other.
>
> The Kapp putsch did not work the way its initiators had ex-
> pected. The government managed to flee Berlin and find safe haven,
> where it took the necessary measures to put down the revolt. In-
> deed, even in Berlin only the center of the city was in the hands of
> the putschists. As a result, in the suburbs the appeals and proclama-
> tions of the legitimate government were posted and distributed in
> the Ullstein branch offices—a development not very favorable to the
> representatives of the firm held prisoner in the Ullstein House. The

situation became unpleasant. We were able to gather from overheard telephone conversations that the putschists were planning to
arrest the five Ullstein brothers and the editor in chief Georg Bernhard and threaten them with execution if the Ullstein Publishing
Company did not desist from making attacks (through its branch
offices) against the Kapp government. It did not come to this,
however: the Kapp putsch came to a pathetic end. The soldiers
evacuated the premises without damage to the buildings or the
printing machines.

The Kapp putsch was better organized but hardly more effective
than the Spartacus revolt. In February 1920, Karl Ullstein (U-1-3) returned after spending five years as a French prisoner of war. It took him
more than a year to find his way back to the routine of bourgeois living.
The more so since, as Fritz reports, his political philosophy had taken
a sharp turn to the left during his imprisonment. In time the bend was
straightened out.

In 1920 Fritz noted a new and most colorful aspect of Berlin: the
presence of several thousand Russian émigrés. All of a sudden there were
several excellent Russian restaurants in the city and even a Russian
cabaret. Also the émigrés enjoyed entrée in Berlin society: "After all it
was only the Russian elite that fled from bolshevism." The Russian
émigré colony of Berlin differed from that of Paris in one respect only:
the Berlin Russians had money—or, at least, a good many of them did.
And, like Russian émigrés everywhere, they were politically and culturally engaged. As a matter of course, therefore, a group of them approached the Ullstein House with a proposition for the joint
establishment of a Russian-language newspaper and a Russian book
publishing company. Ullstein rejected the idea of the joint newspaper
venture "because we did not want to assume responsibility for the politics of an émigré group." They did, however, agree to print the newspaper, which was given the name *Rul* (Steering Wheel), and handle the
advertising. The émigré group that published *Rul* belonged in large part
to the Cadets, a left-of-center bourgeois party in Czarist Russia. One of
the members of its board of advisers was Mikhail Nabokov, a nobleman,
son of a minister of the czar and himself a minister in the government
of Prince Lvov. Nabokov, who had the posthumous distinction of having
sired the well-known American novelist, Vladimir, made a tremendous
impression on Fritz:

Nabokov was a grand seigneur such as I never met again, and I have
met many an aristocrat of higher rank and older title. I can still

recall exactly how he entered the house of my parents-in-law for the first time. It was as if a star suddenly began to gleam in the room. But it was not the external nobility of appearance of this very tall man but his inner culture that made him the complete grand seigneur. In addition to his native language he spoke German, French, English, and Italian fluently. Moreover, he was astonishingly well versed in the cultures of these five language areas. He had married a wealthy woman and had owned a palais in the best quarter of Petersburg where he kept seventeen servants.

Mikhail Nabokov died a tragic death. During a lecture by the former Russian foreign minister Milyukov, Nabokov was shot dead by a White Russian officer who had drawn aim on Milyukov. Nabokov, who had just effected a reconciliation with his party colleague after years of feuding, threw himself into the line of fire and thus saved his newly rewon friend. The incident was a tremendous sensation. Both Fritz and Karl, among other Ullsteins, were present in the Berlin Philharmonic Hall when the shooting took place.

The Russian book publishing company, called Slovo (The Word), was founded in Danzig as a joint enterprise between the Russian émigré group and Ullstein. Fritz Ross was appointed the Ullstein representative. Danzig was chosen as the site because it was thought it might serve as the gateway to the Soviet Union. Apart from this idea—the siphoning of bourgeois or other anti-Bolshevik literature into the Soviet Union— a Russian book publishing company made a great deal of sense. Several hundreds of thousands of Russians had fled the October Revolution. Of these the great majority had gone West, settling in and around Berlin and Paris, taking little more with them than the clothes on their backs. There was the great and obvious need for inexpensive Russian books, beginning with editions of the classics. This need Ullstein was able to fulfill by using the rotary presses that had done service in turning out the millions of one-mark books, forerunners of the pocket book editions. The Russian classics published by Slovo were bound in a half-cloth cover and sold for two marks. Slovo also established and developed the "Archives of the Russian Revolution," a repository of the memoirs and accounts of distinguished Russian contemporaries who had either taken part in the Revolution or observed it at first hand. It could not fail to be and will remain an important source for historians of the Revolution. In addition, Slovo published, as often as not in first editions, the works of Alexander Blok, Fedor Sologub, Ivan Bunin, Mark Aldanov, and the first novel of Vladimir Nabokov.

[223]

When one of Russia's foremost physicists arrived in Berlin as a refugee, the Russian director of Slovo suggested that he was qualified to undertake the translation of a work which had just caused a sensation in the scientific world. It was in this connection that Fritz met and negotiated with the Berlin professor who had written the material being translated—Albert Einstein. The Russian edition of *The Theory of Relativity* was one of the first translations of the work. The stream of Russian refugees to and through Berlin continued into 1921 and beyond. It contributed greatly to making Berlin the center of Europe culturally, politically, and socially. It helped transform the bleak garrison capital of the seventeenth and eighteenth centuries into the most colorful and stimulating city in the world throughout the twenties. Among the many forces unleashed in postwar Europe—especially in the early twenties when most of the countries east of the Rhine were in a state of flux or continuing upheaval—it is not surprising that the old idealistic role of the Reich as clearinghouse and center of mediation between conflicting systems and interests took on a new luster. In this spirit in mid-1921 Walter Rathenau signed a trade agreement with the Soviet Union. This was the pilot operation of the Treaty of Rapallo which followed in April of the next year.

It was in this context of events and attitudes that Fritz Ross conceived the preposterous idea of leasing printing presses and paper factories in the Soviet Union preparatory to setting up a Slovo publishing enterprise. Fritz protests that this project was not nearly so harebrained then as it looks in hindsight. Being an adventurous spirit (of the purely commercial type: there wasn't a political bone in Fritz's body), he even considered moving to Moscow to take up residence there as codirector of the firm. Despite the understandably emphatic warnings of his émigré Russian colleagues (he was, they said, sure to be arrested), Fritz determined to make an exploratory trip to the Soviet Union. Once there, he was indeed arrested, but only at the end of his stay. Before that, shortly after his arrival, he was admitted to the Kremlin where he was received by none other than Karl Radek. (Fritz carried with him a letter of introduction from Georg Bernhard, senior editor at Ullstein, who had been friendly with Radek before the war during the latter's incarnation as a journalist.)

It was really not very long before the door was torn open [aufgerissen] and a small, bearded man plunged into the room. In fluent German he excused himself because of the delay and conducted me into his office. What astonished me in the very first moment in this

[224]

room was a gigantic map of Germany which hung on the wall behind his desk. And indeed he ran straight to this map, pointed with his finger at the areas in which battles with the Communists were then raging, and said in an antagonistic tone of voice: "What do you say to this? Now it has started in Germany again! But this time we shall win!" I was rather taken aback by this manner of beginning our discussion and I took some time to get used to it. Then, too, I didn't know how matters really stood with regard to the fighting in Germany. I had not read a German newspaper for days. As for *Pravda* and *Izvestia,* their battle reports from Germany were all favorable to the Communists.

"Without doubt, Herr Radek, the fighting going on at present is more violent than ever before. Nevertheless I am convinced that you will not win. In Germany you do not have any leaders, in contrast to your situation here in Russia where you have a large cadre of leaders at your disposal."

"You are perhaps not entirely wrong in that contention," said Radek, "but do the others have any leaders? Is for example that ox Ludendorff a leader?"

"No, certainly not, but then General Seeckt."

"Yes, Seeckt is a man to reckon with; but nevertheless I am sure that this time we shall win."

And so the skirmishing went for some time. Radek was surely not very edified by my stubborn persistence in my point of view. Then he inquired after Georg Bernhard, who he said had once been a Social Democrat but had unfortunately become bourgeois.

Fritz Ross notes that one of the reasons Radek was sure the Communists would win in Germany was the inflation that was enveloping the country. My favorite minor German poet, Ringelnatz, who lived and died a pauper, once (in 1923) earned one and a half million marks for some poems. At that time it was enough to buy eight pounds of beef.

Reading the memoirs-cum-diary of someone actively engaged (however unpolitically) in Berlin public life between World War I and World War II, one is struck far more forcefully than when reading a historical account of the period by the rapid and unremitting succession of blows that followed. "Never before," so Fritz begins his memoirs, "has a generation experienced so revolutionary a change of epoch as mine did." Rosa Luxemburg, Karl Liebknecht, Kurt Eisner, the first and last minister-president of the Bavarian Republic, the Independent Socialists Haase and Gareis, and the former minister of finance Matthias Erzberger had already been cut down by assassins' bullets. Fritz returned to Berlin from Russia in time to take the impact of the murder of Foreign Minister Walter Rathenau by a trio of Free Corps hirelings. Then inflation in

Germany assumed grotesque proportions. The German mark was finally stabilized in November 1923 through the devices of the president of the National Bank, Hjalmar Schacht. But in the same month, on November 8, Hitler and his cronies marched on the Feldherrnhalle in Munich in an abortive attempt to take the Bavarian government by putsch. In 1925 Friedrich Ebert died in his mid-fifties. He was overworked and embittered to the point of distraction by the relentless attacks on his honor both as a public official and a private person. He made the mistake Germans so often make, becoming involved in tortuous lawsuits with his detractors. Ebert was succeeded, most ominously, by Field Marshal Paul von Hindenburg, "the victor of Tannenberg," the hero of the eastern front in World War I. The significance—if not the importance—of Von Hindenburg in interbellum Germany can hardly be overrated. He was the guarantor of victory over the Russians, he was Brest-Litovsk, he was the living proof that Germany had not lost the war, but only half a war, while winning the other half. The election of Von Hindenburg as president of the Weimar Republic was a substitute for the restoration of the Wilhelmian Reich. One of the officers seconded to the honor guard at the foundation ceremony of the German Empire in 1871 in the Hall of Mirrors at Versailles was the twenty-three-year-old second lieutenant Paul von Beneckendorff und von Hindenburg. The field marshal was seventy years old when he was obliged to help engineer Wilhelm II's flight from the Reich and then watch the Reich itself go to ruin. He never reconciled himself to the disappearance of the Reich and the succession of the Republic. It was not mere coincidence that on March 21, 1933—on "Potsdam Day," and after a ceremony at the grave of Frederick the Great—Paul von Hindenburg, the regent of the Second Reich, gave his hand to Adolf Hitler, the prophet and master builder of the Third Reich.

"Before his departure to the United States in the spring of 1933," writes Fritz,

Colin had a very long interview with Hitler. I was actually the one who set the machinery in motion for the interview since I was of the opinion that Colin could not go abroad for an extended period before getting a firsthand impression of the powers that were now ruling Germany. And so it was that Professor Karl Haushofer, Albrecht's father, arranged the meeting with Hitler. Colin had just returned from Switzerland where he had spent several months with his family. Until that time his attitude toward National Socialism was one of the greatest reserve.

[226]

But this conversation with Hitler brought about an absolute transformation. It so happened that Colin was my guest in Grunewald at the time so that I was able to talk with him immediately after his meeting with Hitler. Colin, who in the course of his restless career had met and consorted with a whole procession of world-famous personalities, was so deeply impressed by his meeting with the then master of Germany that I was roundly shocked, for I had from the beginning a strong antipathy against this man.

The conference with Hitler, originally scheduled for half an hour's duration, lasted for more than two hours. As Colin emerged from Hitler's office, all the Nazi cabinet ministers were waiting in the anteroom, Göring at their head. All wondered for whom it was that the "führer" had sacrificed so much of his time. And yet, unfortunately, I never discovered what the topics of this discussion were. My brother refused to give me any further information. He did make the remark that he would not even tell Lisel, his wife, anything more—Hitler had been that frank and outspoken with him. When I asked about what he had been so frank and outspoken, Colin only said: "About everything."

"But perhaps you will answer me this one question even so, Colin, because I am so skeptical about this fellow: is he really such a great man?"

"Yes!" my brother answered with great emphasis. "Fritz, he is really a great man!"

One thing is in any case certain: Hitler, who was endowed with great hypnotic powers, had completely captivated my brother, who was as sensitive as an antenna. I was not very happy about this, but after all Hitler was able to make a strong impression on a great number of men who were not in the least Nazis.

In February 1935 Fritz and Hilde Ross sailed to America on the *Bremen* at the invitation of Colin who had meanwhile set up housekeeping in Chicago. (Colin and family spent four years in the United States on this occasion. His daughter Renate took her Ph.D. in zoology at the University of Chicago during this time. It was then, too, that Colin's son Ralph, began gathering material for his first and only book, *From Chicago to Chunking*—with the subtitle *The World Discloses Itself to a Young German.* The book appeared shortly after Ralph's curious death by lightning in the Ukraine on the eighteenth day of the German invasion of the Soviet Union.) As Fritz puts it, his brother had invited him to tour America for his distraction after the fall from the "Ullstein heaven." As the only certifiable "Aryan" in the family Fritz himself had tried to negotiate with Rudolf Hess to avert the forced sale of the Ullstein enterprises. Hess was as adamant, though presumably not so aggressive, as

Goebbels or Hitler would have been. Colin also had the idea that Fritz might want to look the new world over as a prospective home for himself and his family. Colin was more conscious than most of what furious complications a Jewish wife and four half-Jewish children could bring. (In 1936 Colin's daughter, Renate, reminded Commander Georg von Trapp of his similar dilemma during a cruise of the Adriatic. The commander's late first wife had been a zebra, the daughter of Robert Whitehead, the inventor of the torpedo. Robert Whitehead had joined the Austrian Lloyd company at Trieste in 1848–1849 where he subsequently built several Austrian warships and developed his torpedo. It was here, as a young Austrian naval officer, that Von Trapp met Whitehead's daughter, one consequence of the union being that Trapp was allowed to fire the first torpedo in a naval engagement. Another consequence was that Trapp's first seven children were one-quarter Jewish. Trapp was astounded at the reminder. A man whose entire life had been taken up and remained taken up with naval affairs, he had never given a thought to the possible consequences of a Nazi takeover—domestic or German Reich—to his family because of his deceased Jewish wife. Trapp finally bundled his family off to the United States in 1938, after the annexation of Austria to Germany.) As for Fritz, he and Hilde spent four months touring the American West and Southwest (Professor Haushofer had glowingly recommended the Grand Canyon) in Colin's car. He returned to Germany in the summer of 1935 and then withdrew with his family to his native Austria in the same year. He had purchased an estate on the banks of the Danube some thirty-five miles upriver from Vienna. This was Weinwartshof where his children grew up and their children played their childhood away. In 1938, after the Anschluss, his two older daughters went horseback riding with German Wehrmacht officers who were stationed nearby. One year later, when it was clear that the war was coming, he sent his oldest daughter, Jutta, to Canada. She returned— for her first visit—in 1953.

As for Colin, his only son Ralph entered the German army in 1940 at the age of seventeen, joining his father's and his grandfather's regiment, the Twenty-seventh Bavarian Artillery. Here is Ralph's last letter, written to his sister a few weeks before his death:

Dear Renate,
    Today is Whitmonday. This Whitsuntide in Poland is perhaps the finest and most peaceful in my life. The trees are putting forth their leaves and the young green almost completely covers the thatched roofs of the peasant cottages. The people pass by the graves

of soldiers on the road leading from the village to the church.

But I have come out in the opposite direction over the level fields to a hill which strangely attracted me. I am standing now on this lonely height and before me stretches the land of the pathless forests. The view from the hill here ranges far, far into enemy territory on the other side of the river. There it will undoubtedly come to a second battle before the wounds of the first have healed. There must have been a good deal of action around this hill also two years ago. Here the Poles almost certainly set up an observation post. The earthworks and billets are still visible—and between them deep bomb craters.

In one of these bomb craters I have been sitting for the last hour: after all, today is Whitmonday and I have time. I have time, for once, to write to you what I can write only to you. For today is Whitmonday and I have time, only I don't know how much longer.

Everything can come to an end overnight. This uncertainty endows our lives with a certain solemnity [Weihe]. We know that it will soon begin again and since we have been assigned to the first wave we also know what this can mean for us. A gas war awaits us. Perhaps the enemy has also prepared other surprises for us. But we are convinced that no surprise can really surprise us. In our inner selves neither friend nor foe can touch us. I, too, am braced and ready for everything. And you, dear Renate, you must be too.

If death should find me in battle, do not harbor resentment against your God. Everything depends on you. Apart from Mamma and Papa you are probably the only other person in the world I mean anything to. And so the idea of death is not so bad for me as for my comrades, all of whom have friends, wives, and children. Their deaths will leave a gap while mine will hardly make a scratch. They all have a profession, I had a calling, but I did not live up to it. They have done something for their fellowmen; I wanted to do something by creating a decent state and country, but I have failed. I saw the war and all the rest of it coming and said nothing. That makes me an accessory to all the injustice and misfortune.

If my life was of no service to my religion and to the Reich then perhaps my death will be. I was always too cowardly to speak my opinion. But now I can send my pamphlets out with equanimity: they can't kill me twice. This feeling makes me happy. Finally freed from my greatest failing, ambition, by danger, I can for once be honest. Now, when nothing more can happen to me I can finally speak freely and find out whether there are still decent people with any feeling for Christian and social principles. If such there be then I shall not have spoken out in vain and, if fate so decrees, neither shall I have died in vain. If not, then it is only fitting that a being such as I with views as antiquated as those of an archaeopteryx, mastodon, or ichthyosaurus should disappear from the earth.

[229]

I do not write these lines for the purpose of conjuring up death. Suicide is cowardice before God and worse than cowardice in the face of the enemy. I shall not seek death, but if death should seek me then I shall not fear for my life for I know that I have nothing to lose. I am not sure whether I want to die, must die, or should die. But if I do desire death then it is because they have taken away from me what it is that makes life worth living. If I must die then it will be in order to clear the way for a time, an epoch that I cannot understand because in such an epoch there will be subhumans [Untermenschen] instead of men and supermen instead of gods. If I *should* die then my death should be a symbol of that fate which Germany still in the eleventh hour must be spared. I have traveled the road of temptation and made inquiries about the destination only after it had already become difficult to turn back. I then went on and on against my better judgment because I hoped to the very last moment for a happy end. Because I wanted to be brave in the eyes of men I was a coward before God. I see now that I did not distinguish sharply enough between good and not good. We must learn to do this as a people, too. It won't do that as a community we honor and apostrophize as realpolitik those things which we despise as individuals. This realization may cost us much in treasure and territory, but it is better so. One cannot fight against God with Stukas.

I have often talked with you about these things; now I can prove that I meant every word I said. Now I must act and stop writing. From this hill I can see that a storm is gathering in the east. The lead-gray mass of decision lies and weighs heavily over the land. In the west the sun is setting, it will soon be night. But in the sun we have a beautiful symbol for the resurrection—let us believe in that.

We shall rise again!
We shall meet again!
Much love,

Your Ralph

Ralph was killed quite literally by a bolt from the blue on July 9, 1941, six days after his eighteenth birthday. The pamphlets he mentioned were the products of his connection with an anti-Nazi resistance group of high school students in Munich. It was quite possibly the "White Rose" group that came to light two years later when Hans and Sophie Scholl and some of their friends were executed for "high treason"—for distributing anti-Nazi leaflets and painting slogans such as "Down with Hitler" on walls. Colin never recovered from the shock of Ralph's death and the discovery that Ralph had felt strongly opposed to the Nazis for at least two years before his death. As I have previously mentioned, Colin killed his wife and himself shortly before American troops entered Munich. His last letter is dated Easter 1945.

. . . It was my tragedy to have clearly foreseen the general collapse in the First World War. I did what I could to draw the attention of the responsible authorities to the revolution that threatened. It was in vain. I then tried to intercept the revolution so as to prevent the worst from happening. I made the leap from the Army High Command to the Executive Council (of the soldiers' councils). I probably foiled the bolshevization of Germany, but I expected and hoped for something entirely different from that which then happened. And so I suffered a shock then from which I perhaps never entirely recovered. In any case I saw for myself no possibility of starting anew then, so I emigrated in the autumn of 1919 with my wife and my daughter to South America.

Under these circumstances it is understandable that I took a skeptical, wait-and-see attitude toward National Socialism, and this especially since I could not share their views on the Jewish question. However, and even though we lived abroad, at the beginning of 1933 my wife and I could no longer see any possibility of remaining neutral. Confronted with the question "for or against," we decided in favor of "for" because after all the fate of Germany was at stake. At the same time we were fully aware that in all probability the National Socialist movement would end in catastrophe. We were nevertheless determined to remain true to the flag to which we had pledged allegiance, whatever happened, and to go down with it if need be. We keep this faith now.

We could of course not blindly subscribe to the party program if only because of our general background and on the basis of our experience abroad. On the other hand, we recognized that National Socialism is *the* secular idea. It was a matter of releasing this idea from the narrow, folklore entanglement of a single people and allowing it a worldwide, international development. Only by this means, in my view, could the conflict that threatened to break out between a National Socialist Germany and the rest of the world be avoided. It was here that I saw my twofold mission: to transform National Socialism into a worldwide idea and thereby prevent war. I have worked to fulfill this mission until today when I must admit that I have failed and that I was doomed to fail. I had the good fortune to be in personal contact with Adolf Hitler and leading personalities of the movement. I had the larger misfortune of not being able to convince them of the rightness of my views. I have just now reread the long, seemingly endless series of memoranda and letters which, beginning in the spring of 1934, I addressed to Hitler, Rudolf Hess, and Ribbentrop. In these I warned first of the war, then of the entry of America into the war, and finally of the oncoming catastrophe.

[231]

Far be it from me to ascertain with a certain bitter satisfaction that I was right and that things would have been different if they had listened to me. I know that it could not have been otherwise. Even the führer could not have done otherwise than he did in order to carry out the will of fate. In my tête-à-tête meetings with him I recognized his genius and his demonic nature. The one is not to be separated from the other.

This much by way of comment: when Colin wrote that he and his wife recognized National Socialism as *the* secular idea he was referring to the general quest for a secular idea to replace the religious idea which, as the basic moral force and ordering factor in German society, was visibly on the wane.

WHAT IS MORE DECEPTIVE THAN THE PICTURE of events achieved from the vantage point of hindsight? Nobody knew after World War I what was going on in the Soviet Union. Nobody knew what the Soviet Union was or what it wanted to be; nobody knew what Germany was or wanted to be; nobody knew much of anything. It was the year zero—a new beginning with a clean slate open to all possibilities—or so it seemed. This explains, in part anyway, why it was such a silly time. There was also the question of identity, always present in Germany but exacerbated by the absence of an effective central government. Who was who? And who was to legitimize or authorize whom? The Bavarian "Soviet Republic" was denounced by the Reich (that is, the Berlin "government"), by the Bavarian Communists, and by the Social Democrats. The commissar of foreign affairs of the Bavarian soviet sent a telgram to Moscow protesting the sequestration of the keys to his ministry toilet. He then announced to his colleagues that he had declared war on Württemberg and Switzerland because "these dogs" had not immediately loaned him sixty locomotives. At this point his fellow commissars forcibly removed him from office. But meanwhile the commissar for public instruction had publicly announced that attendance at the University of Munich was open to everyone and that the instruction of history, "the enemy of civilization," had been suppressed.

But by far the most utopian and mystical of such manifestations was the Council of Intellectual Workers whose strange device was "All power to the intellectuals!" The council demanded universal disarmament, the establishment of a league of nations, the abolition of capitalism in favor of worker-owned cooperatives, and educational reform in which international committees would supervise all education, teachers and students would be placed on an equal footing, and all history textbooks revised (no piddling enterprise this). The members of the council also demanded freedom of the press (but only *after* "degraders of the press" had been purged), the abolition of religious instruction in schools, and of capital punishment. Moreover, they proclaimed the right of the individual to use his body as he pleases and to commit suicide. The manifesto of the council issued at its first congress in November 1918 in Berlin called for the creation of an all-German socialist republic to be presided over, in effect, by the council. For the council was to select candidates for the presidency of the Republic to be elected by the Parliament. But the members of the council were to be neither elected nor appointed: the council was to "regenerate itself spontaneously." Perhaps the strangest aspect of these Alice-in-Wonderland doings was the presence in the council of writers like Robert Musil, Manfred George, Lou Andreas-Salomé, and Heinrich Mann (who was chairman of a separate Council of Intellectual Workers in Bavaria).

But as preposterous as these attempts at political innovation were, they were nonetheless sincere responses to an all too obvious need. There had indeed been a tremendous, unprecedented, epoch-making change. Or rather, World War I had revealed that such a change had already taken place some time before. Since 1890 at the latest, the Reich had been an industrial state growing increasingly uncomfortable in the antiquated agrarian uniform of the landed aristocracy. World War I, which was primarily an economic, technological struggle, burst the threadbare agrarian uniform at the seams and the industrial state emerged for all to see. The conduct of the war and the "war effort" quickly passed from the hands of the kaiser and German princes into the hands of the industrialists. It destroyed the make-believe of throne and crown, king and emperor. The kaiser and the German princes had in effect left the scene long before the kaiser abdicated. The abdication of Wilhelm II was the formal confirmation of the disappearance of an anachronism. But the disappearance of the anachronism also gave the signal for the start of the centrifugal "cut away from Berlin movement" of the various component states and territories of the Reich. Not only was the empire without an emperor; the princes who had ruled the constituent states of the empire had also been swept away. Prussia had unified the Reich and kept it unified. But it had been Prussia as a monarchy and the Reich as a conglomeration of kingdoms, grand duchies, duchies, and baronies. Now all these royal houses and their heads and members had suddenly disappeared. The players had left the stage; the stage was empty. Royal houses a thousand and more years old had abruptly been swept into the dustbin of history. It must have been a fantastic impression, particularly for peoples with immemorial traditions of homage and obedience to their hereditary rulers.

So if the Reich was to be a republic, what sort of republic was it to be—federal, confederal, or centralized? Theodor Heuss, then thirty-five years old, laid the problem on the line at a congress of the German Democratic party in Stuttgart in January 1919:

> If the future Germany is to possess any sort of inner balance, then Prussia will have to be dissolved—the provincial borders should not be held sacred, we should rather consider economic, confessional, and tribal-ethnic points of view. But there should be clarity on one point: The "predominance" of a Prussian free state would certainly be much more "oppressive" than that of the monarchy in which there were always dynastic considerations and counterpressures that made for restraint and tact. And then: one need only imagine the president of the German and the president of the Prussian republics standing side by side in order to realize the enormous amount of friction that would result—and in such friction the Prussian, against the background of the Prussian administrative machine, would be the stronger.

This is one of the most curious aspects of the German question: Prussia was the "state within the state," the federateur of Germany. This was as true of the Third Reich as it was of the Bismarckian Reich. "If Hitler had remained in Bavaria," said Seyss-Inquart in Nuremberg, "he would never have achieved very much. People would certainly have followed him with great fanaticism, but they would never have allowed themselves to be carried away to the point of committing excesses. In Prussia, on the other hand, there reigns the categorical imperative 'orders are orders!' The Nazi system combined the emotionally conditioned southern anti-Semitism with the blind obedience of the Prussians. That was just it." In this sense Prussia provided the psychological foundation as well as the administrative machinery for the Nazi takeover. The Prussian spirit of Kadavergehorsam (cadaver-obedience), at once so admired and so hated in Germany, was the product—because it was the prerequisite—of Prussia's rise to power. Prussia came to be a world power capable of uniting all the Germans through the prodigious feats of field captaincy and statesmanship of two men, Frederick the Great and Bismarck. Frederick transformed a tin-pot marshland kingdom of two million souls into a world power almost overnight—by deception (for who would have expected invasion and aggressive war from such a diminutive bel esprit, poetaster, playboy prince and author of the *Anti-Machiavel*?). The rape of Silesia "made" Prussia. But to take Silesia and —even more—to *keep* Silesia, Frederick had to incur the undying enmity of Europe, especially since he followed the invasion of Silesia with the invasion of the neutral kingdom of Saxony, thereby setting an ominous Prussian precedent. For his part Bismarck was obliged to hood-wink, lure, and entrap the various European powers one by one or in combination in order to unite (most of) the German tribes.

The point here is that Prussia was a dinky, "right little, tight little" second- or third-class European power that could hope to raise itself to the status of a first-class power—against enormous odds—only by dint of prodigious feats. These prodigious feats in turn could be performed only by breaking every rule in the book, by running roughshod over all the conventions. "Poor mortals that we are!" said Frederick. "The world judges our actions not by our reasons but by the success that crowns them. What remains then for us to do? We must have success." To make the fight at all the Prussians had to fight dirty; to justify their fighting dirty they had to be victorious. This was the foundation of the cult of "victory at all costs." Encircled and outnumbered by the system of alliances—as Frederick had been—the leaders of the Reich in World War I openly admitted the necessity of striking first and finishing quickly for reasons of self-preservation: "Our troops have occupied Luxembourg and perhaps already Belgian territory," announced Chancellor Beth-mann-Hollweg immediately after the outbreak of the war. "This contra-dicts the precepts of international law. The wrong that we herewith do we shall make good again as soon as our military objective has been reached. Whoever is threatened as much as we are can allow himself only to think how to win through." (In order to justify his invasion of the "neutral" kingdom of Saxony in 1756 Frederick had to produce the appropriate documents from the royal Saxon archives proving the com-plicity of Saxony with Austria and Russia against Prussia. In order to come by the documents Frederick was obliged to have them taken forci-bly from the queen of Saxony who died shortly thereafter, apparently as a result of the indignities and privations to which she had been subjected by the Prussian authorities. The scandal of the queen's death totally eclipsed the effect of Frederick's producing the incriminating documents —a prime example of the means adopted foiling the end thereby achieved.) At this point "all Germany [so writes a chronicler], blind Germany, arose against Frederick, sixty [German] princes declared his proceedings to be highway robbery, and it was solemnly resolved to wage war against him by decree of the Reich . . . ." It is unquestionably true that Germany's most popular leaders were at one and the same time Germany's most hated leaders. And this because they were both Prus-sians who personified the spirit of Prussia. In order to unite Germany Prussia had to wage war time and again against a variety of German states. It was unification by aggression. The result was that even—or especially—in Germany, Prussia was always respected, sometimes admired, seldom loved, and often hated.

The Rhinelanders by and large, and particularly the Catholic Center party, rejected the idea of continuing Prussian hegemony as carried over into a republican system of government. There were reasons for this rejection. Prussia proper was itself the Reich in small, a state made up of heterogeneous and scattered elements held together only by fealty to the House of Hohenzollern. Now that the Hohenzollerns were gone, so argued the Rhinelanders, Prussia had lost its justification for existence. But there was also a strong feeling of the need for an energetic defense against the "fruits of the revolution," against the new, Red Berlin from which the revolution was to be imposed upon the whole of the Prussian state. In this regard the sillinesses committed by the Spartacists, by "Poor Rosa" and "Dear Karl," the cap-and-bells politics of the revolutionary heroes and the Council of Intellectual Workers, had not gone unnoticed: "Even after the first transitory manifestations of the revolution have been overcome," wrote one of the Rhineland movement leaders, "we must continue to guard ourselves against Berlin. For again and again the same poisonous fumes will arise from this half-German, big-city witches' cauldron and threaten Germany's culture and freedom with death and destruction."

None of the Rhineland leaders—not even notorious "separatists" like Dr. Hans Dorten—pleaded for an autonomous Rhine republic separated from the Reich; whatever the form of state desired for the Rhineland it was always within the Reich. The separatism applied only to Prussia. "We have nothing against Berlin's remaining the capital of the Reich," wrote Klaus Kraemer, an early proponent of Rhenish independence, "although Berlin lacks much that is desirable—especially if it is also supposed to be the capital for South Germany including German Austria. But we have no inclination to annex ourselves to Berlin as the capital of Prussia. *We do not wish to be Prussians.*" Much of this ill will, of course, was out of the reservoir of resentment built up by Bismarck's Kulturkampf persecution of the Catholics. The Rhineland has always been predominantly Catholic. It is too easily forgotten that the Kulturkampf was necessarily concentrated against the Rhineland, German center that it was of ultramontanism, containing the three archbishoprics of Cologne, Trier, and Mainz.

Here was another age-old struggle that had never been resolved: the Catholic princes of the Reich, remembering their privileged position in the Holy Roman Empire, were especially loath and never reconciled to subordinating themselves and their subjects to a Protestant power. Bismarck's Kulturkampf added fuel to the already flaming resentment. When I first interviewed Konrad Adenauer, he prefaced all his remarks on Germans by pointing out that Bismarck had cruelly persecuted the Catholics and the Socialists and had kept both from entering the government. Had he not done so, there would have been a great Liberal party in the West and a great Conservative party in the East. And the Social Democratic party would never have become what it had become. "Every state," summed up Adenauer, "gets the socialist party it deserves."

The Rhenish aversion to the Prussians is not quite so strong as that of the Bavarians, whose favorite curse is Sau-Preuss (pig-Prussian), but since the Rhinelanders never enjoyed the traditional separate identity of the Bavarians, they were all the more chagrined at the mistaking of Prussian for German. The fact that Prussian and German had become interchangeable as terms and concepts was particularly infuriating to Hans Dorten. As far as he was concerned, it was not Germany who had waged war against France and then the world: it was Prussia masquerading as Germany. Indeed, as Dorten wrote in his book, *La Tragédie Rhénane* (The Rhenish Tragedy), published in Paris in 1945, Bismarck remained convinced that only by means of war could he consolidate Prussian hegemony over the Germans. The waging of war for the purpose of achieving or preserving stability in internal affairs (war as the continuation of domestic politics by other means) is a rule of thumb of political science. The reason usually given for the German Empire's entering World War II, however, is the Junkers' fear of German Social Democracy, not of German Catholicism. It was Bismarck's fear of Catholic Alsatia's combining with the Catholic Rhineland to oppose Protestant Prussia in the Reichstag, says Dorten, that moved him to oppose the annexation of Alsace-Lorraine. When this was done despite his opposition, he saw to it that Alsace was ruled from Berlin as a province and so deprived of representation in the Reichstag. According to Dorten, Bismarck later adopted two anti-Catholic measures in the Rhineland: he established and promoted the National Liberal party (which resulted in the creation of the Catholic Center party as a local countermeasure) and he chose as the site of Germany's titanic weapons smithy the Rhineland, specifically the valley of a Rhine tributary: the Ruhr. (Dorten neglects to mention that the presence of huge coal and ore deposits might have had something to do with the choice of the site.) The heavy industry of North Rhine–Westphalia was itself part of a larger complex including

[238]

Lorraine and Luxembourg that developed as "a unified economic organism" (during the period of German industry's establishment and
growth Lorraine was part of the Reich and Luxembourg an economic
appendage). The fact that after World War I Lorraine again became part
of France created a common economic interest between Germany and
France in the area North Rhine–Westphalia/Lorraine/Luxembourg. Indeed, the emergence of this industrial triangle during the fifty-year life
of the Second Reich changed a very great deal. In the summer of 1918
when it was already clear to most that Germany had lost the war on the
western front, Captain of Cavalry (Rittmeister) Dorten visited the Club
of Rhenish Industrialists, of which he was a member, in Düsseldorf. "We
are persuaded," he was told by his fellow members at the club,

> that a victorious France will annex the left bank of the Rhine, while
> the regions beyond the Rhine will become the booty of bolshevism.
> Thus, one part of us will be handed over to the French to do with
> as they please, the other part will be at the mercy of the Spartacists.
> In order to avoid this hornet's nest it is necessary to avoid at all costs
> the separation of the two banks of the Rhine. How can we do this?
> We can't invite France to annex the right bank of the Rhine as well;
> on the other hand, a defeated Germany, truncated and impover-
> ished, will no longer offer us sufficient markets. In addition—and
> still more disastrous—through Germany's defeat we shall have lost,
> for a long time to come, the necessary access to world markets. Only
> one possibility remains open to us: to adopt the idea of the creation
> of an independent Rhenish state which would include the near
> totality of the industrial regions on the two banks of the Rhine.
> Once established, such a state would permit us to deal directly with
> the victors and form the basis of a collaboration with France whose
> economic way of life corresponds better with our needs. Will you
> work with us in this?

This by his own admission, was the first time Dorten ever even heard of
the idea of a separate Rhenish state. "My state of mind was such,"
continues Dorten, "that I was prepared to participate in any attempt
whatever that would encompass our escape from Prussian domination;
a genuinely Rhenish enterprise sorted perfectly with every wish of my
heart." The best laid plans of mice and men and Ruhr industrialists. . . . In addition to being a devout industrialist Dorten was also a
devout Catholic. But even if he hadn't been, his involvement in so
political an undertaking as the creation of a state propelled him into
professional (and confessional) political circles, the largest and innermost of which was the Catholic Center party with its guaranteed abso-

lute majority in the regional parliament: at that time it had seventy-five percent of the seats.

The strong man of the Center party was the governing mayor of the stronghold of Catholicism in Germany, Cologne. From the moment the Rhenish movement was officially launched in December 1918 its fate was in the hands of one man: Konrad Adenauer. Adenauer's attitude toward a Rhenish free state changed as the circumstances changed, except in one respect: anti-Prussian though he was, he always insisted that the new state should remain within the Reich. There was a time when he expressed his opinion that the formation of an independent Rhenish state outside and totally independent of the Reich might well be the only alternative to outright annexation by the French. But this time quickly passed. The Western Allies were authorized by the Treaty of Versailles to occupy most of the areas of the Rhineland (the entire left bank, with "bridgeheads" on the right bank) over periods of five, ten, and fifteen years. More important, British, American, and Belgian zones of occupation in addition to the French were established in accordance with the treaty. To Dorten's dismay, the all-important "holy city" of Cologne was apportioned to the British zone of occupation. Also, while the very fact of the plurality of the occupying powers in the Rhineland enabled the Germans to play the Allies off against each other, it also ruled out the proclamation of a Rhineland republic without the concurrence of all four occupying powers. Thus, while Adenauer had at one time secured the concurrence of the British and the Belgians, French and American approval were still outstanding. When Dorten secured French approval for the South Rhineland (through General Mangin, the commander of the French army of the Rhine), the project was foiled by the American commander in Coblenz. (The republic could not be proclaimed in French-occupied territory because a separate Rhenish state was too obviously in the French national interest as a substitute for annexation; the French project for annexation had been vetoed by Wilson and Lloyd George.) When Dorten, in growing desperation, tried to arrange a solemn proclamation of the republic in Aachen, he arrived only to find that the Belgians had meanwhile withdrawn their concurrence—having been threatened to that effect by the Reich government in Berlin with a general strike in their zone.

Even so the occupation proved a useful weapon to the French. Their authorization included the right to defray their occupation expenses from the economic product of the area (in case of the Reich's defaulting in the payment of such costs) and the right to erect customs barriers between the Rhineland and the rest of the Reich. Mangin had the full backing of Marshal Foch and Clemenceau who shared his conviction that France's permanent protection against a German attack could only be achieved through French control of the left bank of the Rhine; that is, control of a good part of the great German weapons smithy and the industrial complex that went with it. They applied a wide variety of measures to force, cajole, and lure the Rhinelanders into forming a Rhineland republic. They commandeered factories, confiscated payrolls, exacted tolls, and arrested factory managers and political leaders. They flooded the Rhineland with French products while interrupting traffic of all kinds between the Rhineland and the rest of Germany. They bribed local hooligans to invade and occupy town and county government offices under the aegis of "the Rhineland Separatist Movement."

But the French were far from united in their efforts. Some, like Dorten's French administrateur supérieur, in Wiesbaden, regarded the project as a complot on the part of the German Catholic clerical infiltrators and hence a breach of the principle of the separation of church and state. Others, like Raymond Poincaré, while largely in favor of the project, were necessarily open to other influences, such as British and American pressures. The British withdrew their approval of the project when they realized that the southern Rhineland was to be included: this was too much of an aggrandizement for France, a masked annexation. (Adenauer was correct in his assumption that it was not in the British interest to allow France to increase its strength overmuch at the expense of Germany. It was the British, with American help, who insisted on the recall of General Mangin in the fall of 1919. Even so the Rhenish republic was finally proclaimed (for the first time) in the French zone: "I had placards put up of the proclamation of the Rhenish republic in the small hours of June 1, 1919, in Mainz, Wiesbaden, and certain other cities in Nassau and Hesse," writes Dorten.

> The small amount of time we had at our disposal did not permit us to do better, especially since it was necessary to submit the placards in advance so that they could be stamped by the local authorities. After I had been informed that the placards were affixed, I had telegrams of notification sent to the Peace Conference, to the president of the Reich, and "last but not least" to Herr Scheidemann, the president of the Council of Ministers of the Reich and of Prussia. But it was above all necessary to form a provisional government. In this regard I realized immediately that we had been placed in a special situation. Not knowing what the reaction of the French government would be, I could not yet expose men of prominence

[241]

but had to content myself with those who were courageous enough to accept the risks. Nevertheless, the composition of the provisional government was not bad: there were three jurists, one judge, one administrator, and one lawyer, two professors, one manual laborer, one farmer, and one functionary. Once constituted, we solemnly betook ourselves to the Nassau Statehouse in order to take possession of it symbolically and await the development of the situation . . . especially the reaction from Versailles.

There was none. Or rather, the French government reacted by sending a senator to order General Mangin to cease and desist from support of the Rhenish separatist movement. Dorten was not able to see Mangin on either June 1 or 2 but was ordered to appear before the anticlerical French administrateur supérieur in Wiesbaden. "Do not be surprised," said the same to Dorten,

that you have as yet received no sort of official communication on the part of the French government. You do not exist, as it were; you have installed yourselves in the Nassau Statehouse but you have undertaken no measures against the Prussian government, the local representative of which is here in Wiesbaden. To make it possible for people to take your proclamation seriously you will have to occupy the Prussian Government House. In this way you will be performing an act of independence vis-à-vis Prussia. Perhaps the Prussians will attempt to impede you but they have no weapons; here is a revolver which will enable you to force your way into the building and remain there.

The revolver was not in the scenario Dorten had discussed with General Mangin; still, the administrateur assured Dorten that in offering the weapon and the advice he was merely carrying out the order of General Mangin. When Dorten took the revolver and walked out of the office, he was intercepted by the administrateur's adjutant. "If I were you," whispered the adjutant in Dorten's ear, "I would not take that revolver; if you think it useful to follow the advice you have just received then be very careful and trust no one." Intrigued (but not intriguing), Dorten gave the revolver to the adjutant and went to consult with his colleagues. They decided to do what had been suggested since they had in fact not undertaken to make a gesture against a Prussian institution.

We quit the statehouse and made for the Prussian Government House where we entered without difficulty, those officials present submitting immediately to our authority just as did a Prussian commissioner of police who happened to be there. After having looked into the offices in search of the Prussian regional president whom I could not find anywhere, I seated myself in his office and awaited events, for I was quite sure that something would happen. Suddenly the center door was pushed open violently and the Prussian regional president, whom I had not been able to find, entered at the head of some twenty officials and ordered me to quit the premises immediately. My colleagues came running in and I raised my hand to calm everyone. At that moment, the regional president shouted: "He is going to shoot!" and left the room precipitously, followed by his acolytes. We remained in possession of the field, more than a little surprised at the headlong flight of the officials. But a few minutes later a band of hooligans armed with clubs and knives attacked us. We defended ourselves as well as we could and succeeded in barricading the doors and so remained in the two rooms which formed the office of the regional president. Some blood had been let on both sides. We had just called for one of our automobiles in order to transport one of our wounded to the hospital when the administrateur supérieur arrived in person. Whipping his boots with his riding crop, he apostrophized me literally as follows: "Get out; it's all over!" But my indignation was too great to allow me to keep silent; I sensed in a confused way that there was some sort of foul play in all this. I came right back at him with my reply: "I go, mon colonel, but I shall address myself to France!"

Dorten writes that he later discovered the advice offered him by the administrateur was a design to get rid of the provisional government and discredit General Mangin. The design succeeded on both counts: thereafter Adenauer characterized Dorten as a "ridiculous figure" and General Mangin was relieved of his command and recalled to Paris in October 1919. There were other proclamations of the Rhenish republic (in Aachen, Trier, and Düsseldorf among other places) in the crisis year 1923, when a good deal more blood was let. But the original farce-fiasco in Wiesbaden set the style as well as the precedent: after every attempt Dorten was left with nothing to do but address himself to France. Indeed, some of the proclamations (such as the Belgian-inspired one in Aachen in October 1923) were made without Dorten's knowledge. Far from being fully in charge, Dorten was never even fully aware of the scope and variety of the forces at work for (and against) Rhenish independence.

Dorten was the dupe of the French, but not the only one: the French had other irons in the Rhenish fire. The French "Committee of the Left Bank of the Rhine," whose raison d'être was the annexation of the left bank ("promised a thousand times by French statesmen and just as often abandoned," writes Dorten), were particularly interested in the projects of Joseph Smeets, a Rhinelander and member of the Independent Socialists, who had taken part in the November 9 "revolution" in Cologne. Smeets, an out-and-out separatist, had broken with the Marxists when they opted for a centralist (Prussian) Germany and had formed his own party, the Rhenish Republican Popular party (another pleonasm: pubpop). For his part, Dorten divided the Rhineland independence movement into three groups: the "legalists" (or "opportunists"—they would be quick to get on the bandwagon), headed by Konrad Adenauer and including the Center party; the "autonomists," including Dorten himself and his followers; the "separatists," including all those like Smeets and his "party" who desired an independent state separate from Germany and Prussia, that is, outside the Reich. Dorten and Smeets came to an understanding: Smeets agreed to let Dorten represent him in matters of diplomacy and their two organizations agreed to vote as a bloc if it came to a plebiscite, the Smeets group with the Dorten group if the plebiscite were so worded as to exclude a separation from the Reich, the Dorten group with the Smeets group if the plebiscite excluded the autonomous state within the Reich sought by Dorten. Apart from these arrangements they agreed to live and let live. Later, Smeets also entered into contact with the Belgian National Political Committee, an organization which Dorten characterizes as "expansionist" and interested in a North Rhineland state as a satellite of Belgian heavy industry.

The Treaty of Versailles satisfied no one. Harsh as it was, the annexation of the Rhineland by the French and Belgians was not among its terms. Harsh as it was, it obliged the French to deal with the central government of the Reich in Berlin and not with outlying provincial capitals—a fact that in itself should have given pause to Dorten and the other active separatists. Harsh as it was, it involved all the major Allies with the Germans in the furious and disastrous imbroglio of the reparations problem. The fixing of a sum upwards of eight billion marks in reparations made Germany a debtor to nations who were in turn debtors to the United States. "The original and fatal error," reflected Henry Stimson when he was secretary of state a decade later, ". . . was the notion that huge, interest-bearing loans made for emergency purposes could ever be repaid by one government to another. Debts incurred in a common struggle will never be repaid to a country which hates imports."

A struggle is as common to an enemy as it is to an ally. The reparations bill presented to Germany in the Treaty of Versailles was blank (the amount was bracketed by maximum and minimum "estimate demands" as late as a year after the treaty was signed). Just as the United States refused to accept the payment of war debts from her allies "in the only practical way they could be made—by the transfer of goods and services," so the Allies refused to accept reparations payments in the same way from Germany: France and Belgium were just as loath to import more than they exported as were Britain and the United States. The result was international financial ribaldry. Germany stated flatly that it was unable to pay the three billion gold marks annually for thirty-five years which was the original minimum set. The next, reduced amount that was finally established was 132 billion gold marks to be paid in annual installments of two billion plus twenty-six percent of Germany's annual exports. (I find it hard to believe these facts and figures but they are accurate.) When Germany defaulted (at least in good part because of the crippling effects of the occupation of the Rhineland), France and Belgium invaded and occupied the Ruhr, an act which rendered Germany still less able to make reparations payments. These were the way stations to the great German inflation, the blight that wiped out the accumulated savings of three generations of Germans and thereby destroyed the German middle class. There is no question but that it was the struggle over the Rhineland—culminated by the occupation of the Ruhr—that was primarily responsible for the ruinous pitch of the inflation. The real battle of the Rhineland was fought out in the field of economics and high finance. The most depressing thing about it is that it inevitably had to be fought out: there was no way to avoid it. In the forty or fifty years before the end of World War I, Germany, France, and Belgium had grown together, had become inextricably entwined with each other economically. There was no way to undo the knots that had been tied.

It was anything but happenstance that the conception of the Rhenish state, as the embryo of a West European economic community, originated with Rhineland industrialists. The practicalities of an already existing situation literally forced the idea upon them. Tragically and ironically the same war that had contributed so much to the economic growth of the binding ties (within the area overrun and held almost four years by the Germans) also made the idea of the community psychologically unacceptable. No one save a few farsighted politicians and personally interested businessmen was prepared for such an idea. As Hugo Stinnes, one of the Rhineland's greatest captains of industry (and the son of a French mother), expressed it in a letter to the journalist Maximilian Harden: "With the French we must see if we can't undertake some grand cultural mission or other . . . and at the same time I should like to do what I was certain of doing as the representative of a victorious Germany, namely prepare the ground for a customs union between France and Germany, if possible with the immediate accession of Holland, Belgium, and Switzerland. Only if this succeeds do I see the possibility of avoiding another war."

Perhaps the most extraordinary aspect of the time and place was the general conviction that another war was in the making and even imminent. "The next European war," said Adenauer in a speech in February 1919, "would come in the foreseeable future, just as soon as it will somehow be possible for Germany to wage war and just as surely as the sun rises. . . . A realization of French plans for the Rhine would lead naturally and necessarily to German vengeance." The establishment of an autonomous Rhenish state within the Reich but with special separate relations with France was the only possibility of avoiding war in the long run. But such a state could only be realized, as Adenauer immediately foresaw, with the approval of Berlin. Before the Treaty of Versailles was signed, it looked for a time as though such a state could be realized only with the approval and backing of Paris. This, of course, was Dorten's (mistaken) assumption throughout. Adenauer also foresaw that Britain, "following its traditional policy, would align itself with a weaker Germany over and against a stronger France." This in effect is what happened and it helped set the pattern of events leading to World War II. By the same token, Britain was instinctively against any sort of economic community between France and Germany, for such would have been the prelude to a united Western Europe, a development that did not in the least square with the traditional British policy of maintaining a European balance of powers. Thus Britain could be counted upon to oppose France on the German question and on the separation of the Rhineland—in whatever connection—as well. Gustav Stresemann, as German foreign minister, perceived this and built his policy on the perception.

After the signing of the Treaty of Versailles dashed all hope for an annexation of the Rhineland (either outright or in the form of a French buffer state), Dorten and his industrialist friends set to work on the economic union of the Rhineland and France. They created the Central Bureau of Suppliers to the Allies. Dorten points out that the main object of this organization was to constitute a mixed Franco-Rhenish bureau and, above all, a Franco-Rhenish bank. The bank was vital to the enterprise because, as Dorten says, left to themselves the industrialists would take recourse to the great German banks, all of which had their central offices in Berlin. This was what happened anyway. The only positive result of these homegrown Rhenish efforts was the conclusion of the Loucheur-Rathenau pact. Louis Loucheur, grand captain of French industry, preferred to go over the heads of the Rhinelanders and deal with the central government of the Reich in Berlin. As for Walter Rathenau, industrialist par excellence, he understood the economics of the Rhineland situation at least as well as the Rhinelanders themselves. It is clear, moreover, that Dorten was not associated with the biggest and best of the Rhineland industrialists and bankers. These, men like Hugo Stinnes, Louis Hagen, and Robert Pferdmenges, were friends of Konrad Adenauer. Adenauer tried to interest the French in a Rhenish state within a German federal republic. He did so on the basis of Hugo Stinnes's declared willingness to give up twenty-five percent of the shares of his holdings to the French in exchange for the same percentage of shares in a Lorraine group holding. But Adenauer and Stinnes were outbid (in the eyes of the French) by Arnold Rechberg (who overbid in the eyes of the Germans, even Stinnes forcefully dissenting). Rechberg, an internationally prominent sculptor and sometime resident of Paris and Florence as well as an industrialist, drafted an agreement with his friend Paul Reynaud (who was a relative of Schneider-Creusot, the French steel king). The Rechberg-Reynaud draft agreement foresaw the resolution of the reparations problem by what amounted to French acquisition of thirty percent of the shares of all German industry in exchange for nothing more than the evacuation of the Rhineland and the Ruhr. Apparently the only German who favored the Rechberg-Reynaud plan was the archbishop of Cologne, Cardinal Schulte.

In *La Tragédie Rhénane* Dorten quotes the text of an agreement allegedly presented to Walter Rathenau by David Lloyd George:

In France we have been warned that the machinery of government must be fed, for a certain period, by financial reparations from Germany; one is aware in England that France will be obliged to take recourse to English credits if the German payments are stopped; however, the British financial world does not desire to grant advances to France which will serve no other purpose than to establish the domination of France on the Continent at the cost of the British Commonwealth; the power of the latter will find itself singularly diminished if France is able to seize hegemony over Europe by virtue of an army financed by German reparations. The great banks of Britain are completely in accord with the British government on this subject. It is this reasoning which is the foundation of the following agreement between the Bank of England and the Reichsbank and confirmed by Mr. Lloyd George: the director of the Reichsbank will address to the director of the Bank of England a request for a loan to be accorded to Germany; to this demand London will reply with a refusal [par une fin de non recevoir] while declaring that Germany, impoverished by the reparations payments, is not worthy of credit. France will receive a copy of this letter which will at the same time be the best response to the request for credits addressed to London by French industry, for one will announce that by reason of the probable cessation of German payments, French industry will have to offer other collateral than the aleatory payments from Germany to France.

The British refusal to grant the loan was duly published in Berlin and used as the basis for the German declaration of inability to continue the reparations payments. Dorten contends that the entire phenomenon of German inflation was a Prussian plot to feign bankruptcy so as to sabotage reparations payments. However this may have been, it is true that before the end of 1922 what Dorten calls "the systematic devaluation of the German mark" had totally compromised the continuation of reparations payments in German money in any case. Loucheur appealed to his partner-in-the-pact Rathenau, who did what he could (precious little) to halt inflation. And then, in June 1922 in the Königsallee, Berlin—just a few blocks from where I write this—Rathenau was assassinated by youthful rightist thugs for his "policy of fulfillment" (of the Versailles Treaty).

It was Loucheur who moved the French government to invade and occupy the Ruhr as the only means of securing payment of reparations from the Germans. The result was an undeclared war between France and Germany on many fronts. Technically the area of operations was the Ruhr, actually it was the whole of the Rhineland. The French and Belgians imposed an economic blockade by erecting a customs barrier between occupied and unoccupied German territory from the Dutch to the Swiss borders. The Reich countered by ordering all citizens of the Ruhr to offer passive resistance to all Franco-Belgian attempts to man the mines and factories; it also imposed a ban on all reparations from the Ruhr to France and Belgium. By and large the orders to resist passively were followed, resulting in a general strike and leaving the French to "dig the coal with their bayonets." The French tried to combat passive resistance by introducing the franc de la Régie, that is, their own scrip, which, in contrast to the ever weakening German mark, would buy goods and above all food at French-controlled supply points. It was this move that made it imperative that the Reich continue to pay the rapidly increasing sums for the support of two million unemployed and part-time workers plus the wages of all civil servants (many of whom were prevented from discharging their duties by the French). The consequent increasing drain on the treasury over the months crippled the Reich.

On November 23, 1923, the German mark sank to its nadir on the Cologne exchange: one dollar was traded for twelve billion paper marks (on the Berlin exchange one dollar was worth only 4.2 billion marks). On the same day, after receiving a vote of no confidence, Stresemann resigned as chancellor. Both sides resorted to terror. When the French brought in 3,000 officials and railroadmen to run the trains, the Reich retaliated by sending in demolition teams to blow up tracks, bridges, and trains. French firing squads shot dozens of saboteurs and arrested and deported German workers and managers by the thousands. In the small hours of January 26, 1924, the editorial offices of Dorten's newspaper, *Rheinischer Herold,* were laid waste. Six weeks later the Gutenberg Press in Coblenz, which had done printing work for Dorten, was visited with the same retribution. In mid-March a number of Smeets's men were killed and Smeets himself mortally wounded by a "patriotic detachment" under the leadership of Leo Schlageter, a Nazi Free Corps veteran who was later captured and executed by the French. Schlageter's fate automatically placed him in the official Nazi gallery of martyr-heroes. At about this time Dorten was asked by the French to unfurl the green, white, and red Rhenish colors and again proclaim the republic in the Ruhr. According to his own testimony, he refused, pointing out that his Rhenish People's Union could not be placed in the position of appearing to approve French coercive measures. Dorten went to Paris in April 1924 to secure active French support (harping as always on the necessity of creating a sound Rhenish franc in order to put an end to the harrowing effects of the inflation in the Rhineland). Specifically Dorten went to Paris to plump for the reinstallation of his friend Mangin as commander of the French occupation forces in Germany. He achieved only a minimum of semiofficial French support (Poincaré refused to receive him, one of his reasons being that Dorten had been officially declared a traitor by the Reich and a warrant issued for his arrest).

When Dorten returned to the Rhineland, he found yet another Rhenish independence movement on the scene. This was called "Free Rhineland" and was led by one Matthes, a native Saxon late of Bavaria who for reasons long unknown had chosen the Rhineland as his political arena. Most of Matthes's immediate entourage were freebooters and he recruited his following chiefly among the ever growing number of unem-

ployed as well as local criminal elements. When Matthes's men took over
the city of Düren, both commissars appointed by him were exconvicts
who had been convicted of forty-three felonies between them. His appointed commissars in München-Gladbach were likewise exconvicts.
Then, too, the Communists had suddenly become active again, organiz-
ing strikes and demonstrations—perhaps in sympathy with Communist
attempts to create a Communist republic out of the three states of
Saxony, Thuringia, and Braunschweig. It seemed the entire country was
being overridden by the Four Horsemen of the Apocalypse. Dorten and
his French and Rhenish friends decided to call out the republic once
again in Coblenz. Six thousand supporters were on hand for the occasion.
A short while afterward Dorten was visited by Herr Von Metzen, a
former director of the Krupp concern who revealed himself as the em-
ployer-superintendent of Matthes and asked for Dorten's collaboration
in the forming of a common front for Rhenish independence. Dorten
agreed to act as leader of the union. It was further agreed to continue
staging "monster rallies," as Dorten calls them.

Among his papers that remained in Tante Hanna's villa I found
several newspaper clippings; one of them, from the October 30, 1923,
edition of the *Minneapolis Journal,* is a picture of "Handsome Adi," as
they dubbed him, at his dashing, dapper best, monocle, close-cropped
curly hair and all. "Separatist Leader in Rhine Republic Move" reads
the caption. And the subhead reads "The man of the hour in Germany
today is Dr. Hans A. Dorten, leader of the Rhineland republic movement. Two months ago he set into movement the separatist plans which
now have culminated in actual military and political secession in the
Rhineland." Dorten had his hour and that was all. But before then he
had already had his comeuppance, according to the book he published
twenty-two years later. The united separatist movements under Dorten's
leadership decided to celebrate a Rhenish Day in Düsseldorf. This was
to be the culmination of the separatist campaign. It was. September 30,
1923, was "bloody Sunday." Twenty thousand separatists converged on
Düsseldorf on this day to march, demonstrate, and listen to speeches.
Among them were Matthes's Rheinlandschutz, storm troopers for the
protection of separatist assemblies. Dorten insists that Nazi SA action
commandos had infiltrated the ranks of the Düsseldorf traffic police.
Indeed, in Dorten's account the fateful melee was started by Hitler's SA
disguised as Rheinlandschutz. One wonders what sort of disguise was
needed: both organizations were made up of the same elements—exconvicts and strongboys otherwise unemployed. It is a matter of record

that six regular German policemen were killed in Düsseldorf that day and perhaps a hundred assorted citizenry killed or wounded (Dorten says "hundreds"). Dorten paints a vivid scene and, in fact, there were at least six distinct groups involved: German police, French military, separatists, antiseparatists (both Reich-sponsored and not), Nazis, and Communists (a Communist might have been a separatist and a Nazi was certainly an antiseparatist, but the reverse in either case was by no means necessarily true). When the first shots were fired (machine guns were allegedly also used), the crowd panicked and, finding all exits from the city's central square blocked, they ran into the artificial lake where they were shot like so many ducks.

All this happened but a few steps away from the French quartier général and during this time, by all accounts, the French did nothing. They finally brought tanks into the center of the city to restore order. The prestige of the French on the Rhine, says Dorten, was ruined. As usual after a fiasco (Dorten calls it "carnage," "a massacre") Dorten addressed an "indignant protest" to Paris. As always he received no official reply. Unofficially he was told that Rhenish blood would have to flow in order to achieve the desired goal. "Whose goal?" writes Dorten. "Certainly not ours! I was certainly constrained to realize that we were chess pawns to be moved according to the needs of the game and in obedience to a design entirely different from that of Rhenish liberty. The victory that I imagined to be firmly in my hands turned into a defeat of all our dearest aspirations. We were dupes, sacrificed so that the hazardous enterprise of the French in the Ruhr might be brought to a successful conclusion."

I don't think Dorten ever knew or realized how far he had always been from becoming the chief of a French-sponsored state on the Rhine. The object of French policy in the Rhineland and Ruhr was to force the Reich government in Berlin to concede the independence of the Rhineland. Such independence could only be achieved with the concurrence (however achieved) of the Reich because the Anglo-Americans had made it clear that they would regard any separatist solution to the Rhineland problem as a breach nullifying the Treaty of Versailles and the French right to reparations with it. This is why the French were forced to turn to Adenauer in the end. For while Dorten considered Smeets a separatist and himself an autonomist, the French considered Dorten a separatist and Adenauer an autonomist. As it was, the French came within a hair-breadth of forcing the Reich to allow Adenauer to allow himself to be forced to head an autonomous Rhenish state (*within* the Reich). What it was that almost forced the Reich government to cede the Rhineland was the inflation. In the course of the struggle in which German money had poured into the Rhineland years on end and for no return, the mark had become all but worthless. It was primarily the near worthlessness of the mark that had wrought death, famine, and destruction in the Rhineland. By November 1923 the whole of the Reich was threatened with chaos because of the continuing payments to officials and unemployed in the Rhineland. On November 20 Hjalmar Horace Greeley Schacht introduced the rentenmark which was issued in only limited amounts and covered by a mortgage on the entire industrial and agricultural resources of the country. This was an innovation strikingly reminiscent of Mephisto's issuance of the king's currency in the Second Part of *Faust*. It was hailed ruefully by Dorten as a stupendous piece of financial wizardry. Even so the Reich government came to the unanimous but reluctant conclusion that all Reich subsidies and payments to the Rhineland would have to cease forthwith in order to save the rentenmark. The decision to cease all such payments was taken by the cabinet and confirmed by the president of the republic—and indeed the announcement of the decision was to be accompanied by a solemn declaration that the Rhinelanders were thereby left to their own devices to look after their interests and security as best they could. If it had been announced and acted upon it would have thrown the population of the Rhineland and the Ruhr into the arms of the French. For in order to survive, the Rhinelanders would have been forced to accept the franc de la Régie, the currency introduced by the French occupation forces and thus the de facto separation of the Rhineland from the Reich.

The decision was not announced and never put into effect because of the opposition of one man: Konrad Adenauer. Adenauer simply refused to allow the Reich government to discontinue the payments. Said Adenauer in one of the many emergency sessions of the Reich cabinet in November: "The Reich minister of finance always asserts that the Reich can no longer make certain payments to the occupied area. I deny that the Reich is in so serious a financial situation. Let even the rentenmark along with the paper mark be driven into the abyss because the Reich makes substantial payments to the occupied territory, the Rhineland must be worth more than one or two or even three new currencies." By taking this stand and persevering in it, Adenauer saved the Rhineland for the Reich: the Poincaré government in France had only two months to live; Poincaré's successor, Eduard Herriot, reversed the French Rhineland policy. But even before then the French had been constrained to acknowledge defeat in the Rhineland. Poincaré himself had to bow before British and American pressure because the Anglo-Americans held the purse strings: Poincaré, as the saying goes, "had neglected to secure his economic foundations" for such an undertaking as the acquisition of the Rhineland. The dashing Doctor Dorten was likewise forced to leave. The Reich had prevailed and he had been declared a traitor by the Reich. He was also charged with having diverted (by interception) Reich payments to the Rhineland. This he freely admitted since he had done so to finance the operations of his own "government." Moreover, he had been authorized—tacitly, as always—by the French to do so. In the night of January 1, 1925, Dorten quit the Rhine forever to make his way to Nice, which, as he writes, had been assigned to him as residence. It must have been a bleak New Year's Day.

Adenauer saved the Rhineland for the Reich, but by doing so he did indeed drive two German currencies into the abyss, with the result that the German middle class was irremediably ruined. The ruin of the German middle class was a major link in the causal chain that led to the Nazis' accession to political power. But not only the individual "stands on the land mine of coincidence." The far greater tragedy is that a nation, a whole continent, a whole world, may stand there, too. Konrad Adenauer was the unsung hero of the struggle for the Rhineland. It is an astonishing trick of history, making for an extraordinary career, that the same man who fought and won the struggle to keep West Germany within the Reich after World War I should have been called upon again in the struggle to keep East Germany within the "Reich" after World War II.

THAT PART OF THE OLD REICH WHICH IS NOW CALLED
Austria is the strangest place I have ever lived in. It is
not easy to say why this is so. The name Austria derives
from the Latin noun "auster," the south wind. Austria
then is the land of the south wind. But part of the
difficulty is that "Austria" is not so much the name of
a place as the name of a time, a time that ended abruptly in 1919. Even
more so, Vienna is the name of an epoch that began, say, in the middle
of the seventeenth century and trailed off into the thirties of this century.
Life in Vienna is not a pastime but a time past. It is the cult of the status
quo ante. A few years ago I stepped into a taxi in London and gave the
airport as my destination. "Which flight, sir?" asked the cabby.
"Vienna," I said. "Vienna!" he exclaimed, "what a wonderful word!"
Indeed. There is no more magical word in any language. But it is a word
that, like the place, is a memorial to the autochthonous past. My friend
Osgood Carruthers was standing on a streetcorner in central Vienna not
long ago when a tourist asked him for directions to the museum. "You're
in the middle of it right now," answered Carruthers; "this whole place
is a museum!"

When I arrived in Vienna for the first time in the late summer of
1949, I had a bottle of beer and a pair of frankfurters at a kiosk in front
of the West Bahnhof (railroad station) and floated down the Mariahilfer-
strasse into the center of town on the euphoria of the first belch. To my
delight I found corn on the cob in a restaurant directly behind the
Cathedral of Saint Stefan. The name of this restaurant was, significantly,
Das Deutsche Haus (The German House), and the service was good.
Many years later I noticed something far more significant: a small metal
medallion set into one side of the main doorcase. The inscription on the
medallion read: "This is the property of the German Order." The next
day I was in a party of five dining in another highly recommended
restaurant in Vienna's inner city. The food was superb, perhaps the best
I had ever had, although noticeably slow in coming. The sole waiter

might well have been eighty years old. After he had served the dessert, the old boy simply disappeared. We waited a full hour, called, shouted, and stomped on the floor. I ventured as far as the kitchen door and found it locked. After another fifteen minutes we made our way out of the restaurant, slowly, noisily, with much ado. Once we had emerged from the restaurant we expected to be overtaken at every step by some breathless busboy or an irate restaurant owner. Nothing happened. I did not know it then, but my friends and I were merely being introduced to the dream that is Austria, and encapsuled in the Austrian proverb: "Isn't is wonderful to live in a place where nothing happens when nothing happens!"

The next day I went by train with Fräulein Ross to her home, Weinwartshof (always alluded to within the Ross family by the initials WWH—Weh-Weh-[as in Oy vay!] Hah) some thirty miles upriver from Vienna on the edge of the Tullner Feld, a river flat on the other side of the Vienna Woods. Weinwartshof was an estate of 150 acres on the banks of the Danube just outside a village called Muckendorf (mosquito village) near the county seat of Tulln. The manor house was in the midst of perhaps four acres of park, a park embowered by great trees with a clearing one hundred by fifty yards in front that served as a garden. At the far end of the garden were two hothouses which formed the boundary between the park and the Wirtschaft or farm. This was a regular farm, a small village in itself, with farmer's house and quarters for the farm help, barns and stalls for horses and cows, and a sty for pigs. The bailiff who lived in the farmhouse was the salaried administrator of the estate. The farm help, whose number varied with the seasons, were sometimes Hungarians but more often Slovaks. (Vienna is only some twenty-five miles from Bratislava, the capital of Slovakia. Before World War II there was a streetcar line connecting the two cities.) The manor house was three stories high and contained twenty rooms, including maids' and cooks' quarters but not including baths and pantries. The kitchen was only slightly smaller than the kitchen of Magdalen College, Oxford.

Here the resemblance ended. The discrepancy in the quality of the products of the two kitchens was well nigh total. The cook at the manor house was a huge Viennese termagant who had lived twenty years in Transylvania and spoke good Hungarian. Käthe was quite possibly the best cook (as distinct from chef) whose culinary art it has been my good fortune to enjoy at length. Every meal Käthe prepared was an event that could be savored in anticipation. To be sure, she cooked only one meal a day—more would have been too much in the diurnal round. More would also have been in violation of the regimen established by the lord of the manor, my father-in-law, Fritz Ross, whose rule it was to eat like a king at breakfast, like a bourgeois at dinner, and like a beggar at supper. Breakfast at Weinwartshof was the duke's mixture of the English and Austrian traditions of breaking fast. There were eggs, fried or soft boiled, and salami or paprika bacon (a bar of the sheerest bacon fat covered with paprika on one long side against the rind; it was the same size and shape as a bar of gold bullion and worth as much in gustatory pleasure). Or one might pick at a cold roast pheasant. Instead of toast there were fresh Semmeln, the Austrian fine white-flour bun; and there was coffee, the most sublime cult of the culture, the drinking of which, at any time of day, is the axis on which life in Austria turns. In Austria there were traditionally two breakfasts: the early morning cup of coffee with a Semmel, butter, and jam (apricot or plum), and then, around eleven o'clock, the Gabelfrühstück (fork breakfast) consisting of a small steak or some goulash. The main meal was at one o'clock or one-thirty and began with a soup, usually a clear beef broth with chopped liver dumplings or large, toasted flat noodles called Fredatten. The main dish was either beef, boiled or roasted, or game, venison or wild boar, with dumplings, works of art made out of the Semmel, and two or more vegetables, including one of a variety of mushrooms. At times Käthe would produce a Hungarian goulash (or what is so called outside Hungary). On high holidays or other special occasions there would be duck—tame or wild —pheasant, or goose. Never a turkey (the Austrians, like most Europeans, consider turkey meat too dry). Supper was cold cuts, sometimes a paté of game. At dinner one chose wine or beer; at supper beer was drunk.

I do not hesitate to designate the Viennese cuisine the best inland cuisine in the world because it includes the cooking lore of the various components of the empire: Hungarian, Serbo-Croatian, Czech, and Italian (preeminently but not only). The specific Austrian or German element in this magnificent conglomeration is the game. Without the venison, the wild boar, the wild ducks, the pheasant it could be anybody else's cuisine but it could not be Austrian.

Indeed, game on the menu is even more distinctly Austrian than it is German. Austria is still largely forest land—far more so than Germany. Hence hunting plays a far greater role in the life of the average Austrian than among the Germans. In Germany the hunt is well on its way to becoming an affectation or at best the occasion for social functions: invitations are issued to an "armed promenade" (bewaffneter Spaziergang). In Austria the hunt characterizes life and not only to the extent of putting food on the table. On the other side of the park in Weinwartshof, diametrically opposite the farm, was the hunter's house and garden. Herr Pieringer was a small, rather stocky man with a dark gray beard more than a foot long. He was always in uniform, the dark green hunter's jacket and knickerbockers with gray flashes and gray knee-length heavy wool stockings ending in dark brown brogans. Pieringer always carried a rifle. Most of his hounds, to my surprise, were long-haired dachshunds (he had five or six of them). But he also had a German pointer, a lanky, brownish gray short-hair. Herr Pieringer was also the keeper of the family mascot, the Uhu (as in "oo-hoo"), a great horned owl with luminous, bright orange eyes bigger than silver dollars and eyelids that clicked audibly like the shutters of a box camera when he closed them. Directly across the river from the estate was the hunt. The area was called the "Au" (as in "ow"), the German word for "meadow," but it was a hunting forest with tall trees and very thick underbrush. It was, in fact, the forest primeval staring the manor in the face just across the river. One evening while we rowed back across the the river from the hunt, Fritz Ross said to me, "Now perhaps you can see why I could never bring myself to leave this place—even when the Nazis came. Where else in this world can you shoot a fourteenpoint buck and be at the opera forty-five minutes later? And at the Vienna opera!"

There were two or three cherry trees in Weinwartshof. They produced the most magnificent cherries I have ever seen or tasted. ("To know what cherries and berries taste like," wrote Goethe, "you must ask children and sparrows." But there was a worm in every single one of them, a result of the Rosses' refusal to spray the trees; they considered insecticides "unnatural." So they cheerfully ate the cherries while joking about the bonus of worm's meat that went with the delicious fruit.

Fritz Ross's children called themselves "children of the Danube" (Donaukinder) and they were. Strong swimmers all, they would jump into the river, swim into the main current and let themselves be carried half a mile or so downstream, then swim ashore and walk back. This is exhilarating sport because the Danube is an uncommonly swift and powerful river, far more so than the Rhine. One thing the Danube never was—not in Austria, anyway—was blue. When Johann Strauss saw the "Blue Danube," it was he who was "blue" (German idiom for "drunk"). The Danube is gray at best (as any river should be that flows from the Black Forest to the Black Sea), yellow at worst—"yellow by broken bridges in the flood," for it is often an angry river, overflowing its banks with baneful regularity. For his services to the community during the terrible flood of 1954 Fritz Ross was made an honorary citizen of Muckendorf. As the largest landowner in the area he was merely protecting his own and therefore more than his own. He was inordinately proud of the citation and the plaque that went with it. Indeed, his only enduring official position was that of vice-mayor of Muckendorf. "Bürgermeister" is a much more sonorous and meaningful title than "mayor"; vice-"burg master" (the English corruption) is still more sonorous.

There were five or six domestic servants employed in and around the manor house: the cook, the gardener, the chauffeur, and three maids. The maids were country girls and women, the daughters, nieces, or cousins of former servants. They all came from the vicinity of the Ross family homestead in the valley of the Traisen, a mountain river that flows into the Danube above Tulln from the south. It would not be quite accurate to say that the Weinwartshof maids were a part of the family; they were literally ancillary to it, more like friends of the family, permanent houseguests who were willing to put up with less spacious quarters and to do most of the chores. They were, it is fair to say, much loved. Perhaps more important in so subtle a relationship, they were respected and invariably treated with great tact by the family (the same could not be said for the family's treatment of most of its own members). I shall not forget my first visit to Weinwartshof when I gave Fräulein Ross my two and only spare shirts to be laundered. Within five minutes she came back to my room with the shirts. "I am sorry," she said, "but I cannot give these shirts to the maid." I asked why not. "They are much too dirty." I argued but it was hopeless. I had to wash the shirts myself to get them clean enough to present to the maid for washing. It was not that Fräulein Ross was scandalized by the condition of my shirts; it was her concern for the maid. There was nothing so crude as social distinction practiced between the family and the servants. The family (excepting of course the lord and lady of the manor) would visit the servants in their quarters and the servants would stop in the course of their rounds and chat for ten or fifteen minutes at a clip. Herr Pieringer could and did come in at any time (into the library, that is, which as befits a publisher was the living room of the house). His visits were naturally less frequent but he made much of them, talking at times for a half-hour in a dialect it took me two years to learn to understand.

What impressed me was the harmonious blend of the various relationships together and the attentiveness of the family to the servants. Sometimes, indeed, I asked myself who was serving whom. There was long-range concern for the various maids and their relatives, all of whom were long known to the family. Would Feferl or Annerl be happy doing this or that, or marrying this man or that man, and how about it anyway? If one maid married or left for some other reason, she was automatically replaced from the grand reservoir of cousins and nieces. There was thus no such thing as having an utter stranger introduced into the household. The children of former maids were introduced first as playmates for the family's children and grandchildren and then as apprentices. There was no conspicuous inequality in the apportionment of labor, because on a farm everybody works more or less anyway. As for serving at table, it was passed off as a game, with words of encouragement and jokes thrown in. "Doesn't she do it well!" "That must be very heavy!" "Thomas, help Hannerl." "Danke, gnädige Frau, es geht schon!" When the maids were grown up, they were almost invariably drawn into the table conversation whenever they appeared in the dining room with the food.

Even now, more than twenty years after my introduction to the Austrian dream, when so much has changed and so many dear faces have disappeared forever, the family maids and retainers are still there, some-where. During the summer of 1971 at the "hunter's lodge" in the Traisen valley: "This is Frau Krause. She is the wife of Annerl's brother. Do you remember Annerl?" How well I remember Annerl! I remember them all. Did I not grow up in kitchens? Am I not the great lover of all ancillaries? An ancillariolus? I might have married a maid as well as a daughter of the house. As an American I was outside all classes and could move freely among them. But no member of the family, as far as I know, ever ran foul or fair of a serving maid. Nor did I ever hear of such a thing on the part of any other family of that class in the round of the Rosses' acquaintance. Trouble with the maid was a phenomenon of the bourgeoi-sie, where neither servant nor master was sure of his place. There was "trouble with the maid"—in this case the cook, Maria Anna Schickel-gruber—in the Frankenberger household in Graz, Austria, in 1837. Only five years later did the cook marry the miller's apprentice Johann Georg Hiedler. The cook's illegitimate son, Alois, was forty years old before he changed his name from Schickelgruber to Hitler, a variation of his stepfather's name. The Frankenbergers were Jewish. Frankenberger sen-ior paid alimony for the care of the child for fourteen years, a fact adduced as proof that Frankenberger junior was the father of Alois. If so, then Alois's son Adolf Hitler was one-quarter Jewish.

Fritz Ross was a member of the untitled Austrian aristocracy even before he married into the Ullstein family and became Herr General

Direktor, and later Herr Präsident of the World Publishers' Union. His
father was called to Vienna from Cologne (where he had his own electri-
cal engineering firm) by the Karl Lueger administration to undertake the
electrification of Vienna. There is the weak but persistent rumor that he
refused to accept a title from the Emperor Franz Josef for his services.
As far as my father-in-law was concerned, the family's proudest title was
the Scottish clan name Ross. But the family moved almost exclusively
among the professional and commercial elites and the titled aristocracy
of Austria and Hungary. When the Ullstein connection came in, it did
not hurt. The Ullsteins belonged to the top flight of the new German
commercial aristocracy. Of most interest to me was the Austro-Hungarian titled aristocracy, all of it being, or having been, large landowners.
The best conversation stopper I ever heard or hope to hear was during
a Sunday dinner at Weinwartshof. One of the fourteen diners was a very
old friend of the family, Prince Lajos Windischgrätz. At one point "an
angel flew through the room" (German idiom for the silence that ensues
from a sudden break in the general conversation). Just then Windischgrätz made a calm, matter-of-fact statement: "King Zog is my nephew."
(This was King Zog of Albania.) And as if they had prearranged to recite
alternate lines in the Twenty-third Psalm, my brother-in-law added: "I
shall not want." It was true, Windischgrätz had become Zog's uncle
when the former's niece, the celebrated beauty, Countess Aponyi, married Zog. The connection was a good example of "tu, felix Austria nube
. . . ," the apostophizing of the House of Habsburg, the family that
founded an empire and made its greatest conquests by marrying off its
sons and daughters to foreign rulers. When the poet Hugo von Hofmannsthal visited Marrakesh in 1925, he recounted his meeting with the
French governor-general: "The old Marshal Lyautey received me with
great friendliness. He came toward me very quickly, indeed he ran
through the great hall to me, took my hand in his, and said, 'Monsieur,
you are at home here—you are in *your* house and here is why: I command here, and I am a Lorrainer, your emperors are my dukes, and I
regard the destruction of Austria as the most deplorable of crimes.'" One
of the Ross family doctors in Vienna is a specialist with the surname
Françoise: her French ancestor went to Vienna with Francis of Lorraine
as the duke's gardener.

Frau Doktor Françoise was the only direct result I ever saw of one
of the greatest catches the House of Habsburg made. "Austria" was a
world empire that included thirteen nations. At various times and for
long periods the ruling house owned what is now Belgium and a good

part of modern Holland; in some cases its rulers were also the rulers of Spain, and for almost four centuries its emperors were the emperors of the Holy Roman Empire of the German Nation. Vienna was for centuries the seat and center of the greatest political and ethical power on earth. How then the up-country lassitude, the rural tinker's way of life of the aristocracy? Die Frau Baronin (baroness), a frequent guest, was fat and ugly, and sloppy as a hillbilly. At three in the afternoon she would still have what looked like crumbs from breakfast in one corner of her mouth, but which (since Austrians eat all the time) would almost certainly have been from a Kipferl or some other fine pastry she had taken from a jacket pocket and eaten two minutes before appearing on the scene. Count Ségur (a great name in Austria) was the biggest slob I ever met: he looked as if he had just rolled out of a boxcar. The peasants and the servants adored him. He was the best-loved man in Lower Austria. In fact, he was widely known as "der Bauerngraf"—the peasant count. He, and he was typical of the lot, was a tramp with a title. He had no manners; but the point is he didn't need any. Austrian aristocrats are above manners. Instead, they have a manner to which they are born and bred. There is an essential bond, an umbilical cord between the aristocrats and the peasant. Indeed, an aristocrat is a peasant with a twofold title. One is to his land: this is why aristocrats have names that incorporate place names; "Von" and "De" mean *from* such and such a place. Hohenstauffen is a hill in Swabia, so is Hohenzollern; the Habsburg was a fortified location in Switzerland. The second part of the title; the rank among men, derives from the first, since the possessor of the title could not have rendered himself worthy of the bestowal of rank from his liege lord without geographical power base, the German term for which is "Hausmacht": only a "house-power" can become a powerhouse. There is such a thing as provincial globalism (as demonstrated by the English in their world empire, "that talent for far dying"), and also a global provincialism, which is the Austrian version of imperial style. ("Asia begins on the Landstrasser-Hauptstrasse," a main street leading from downtown Vienna to the East.) The Austrian aristocrat is totally unassuming. It is his distinction to be so. (It was this same almost severe simplicity of style that impressed Friedrich Wilhelm II, the father of Frederick the Great, when he visited the Emperor Josef in Bohemia.) He possesses the perfect self-assurance which is achieved in American society perhaps only by the tramp. He (the aristocrat or the tramp) is not concerned with the impression he makes or whether others know who he is. *He* knows who he is; that is all that counts. This is true "class" (one of the most meaningful Americanisms). It was quite possibly the most carefully tempered, most harmonious type that society has ever produced. And it served its purpose for as long as the world was in joint. To say it was natural—which it was, too—is to oversimplify. It was the result of and dependent on a balance of ethical forces which were natural once upon a time but after a millennium or two gradually ceased to be so.

In Austria, as the saying goes, everybody but a dog has a title. Even the English word "mister" is a title: I was often addressed as "Herr Mister Bailey." On my honeymoon the staff of the Hotel Goldener Hirsch in Salzburg dubbed me "vice-consul" the moment I registered, and stuck to it for the length or our stay. Here is an article apropos from the *Berliner Morgenpost,* datelined Vienna, December 13, 1970:

> A breathtakingly bold, indeed downright revolutionary deed has just been done by the Vienna city fathers: they have abolished 640 of a total 761 official titles—certainly not their own, of course; they continue to style themselves magistrate-counselors, high-[ober] magistrate-counselors, and senate-counselors, but they have eliminated the titles of their most subordinate subordinates, the workers. This uprooting of the underbrush in the municipal title registry was urgent. It comprised thirteen pages of small print and was strongly reminiscent of the long-dead poet Herzmanovsky-Orlando [a good Austrian name] who forebodingly invented an "assistant fireman's deputy-candidate-substitute-helper." He who was employed by the Vienna city administration could be—until now—a soot-blower, an undertaker's first assistant, a paver-superintendent, a high-pressure-machine-helper, a ditchdigger or coffin-bearer first class—or likewise a frequency-counter or water-tank-caretaker, scoria-stripper or tar-manipulator. And with any luck at all he could be a siphon-caretaker, a closet-smeller [sic], or a naphthalene-preparer [etc., etc.].

There was of course a storm of protest against this merciless decimation of the Austrian's proudest possession. "Humanity," runs the Austrian proverb, "begins with the rank of baron." But for the great mass of subhumanity below the rank of baron, a title was all the more important. The protesters defended "this Austrian tradition stemming from the imperial past" and further pointed out that Austria had always made a practice of compensating poorly paid government officials with the bestowal of hierarchic honors as expressed in a resounding title and the respect thereto accorded. (The average annual wage of an Austrian government official is to this day something less than four thousand dollars.) It was in vain. With one blow the bearers of 640 highfalutin titles found themselves stripped to the loincloth designation "servants of the city of Vienna." Their only consolation was the continued existence of 121 "relatively normal-sounding" official titles.

In Austrian society when a man is introduced to another man or a woman to a woman, they immediately adopt the familiar form of address "du" instead of the formal "Sie." This is a use that has come down to the middle class from the aristocracy, either by emulation or by the intermarriage of destitute aristocratic and bourgeois (often Jewish) families. In Germany, however, even fairly close friends may remain on formal terms of address throughout their lives. The shift from formal to informal (unless it comes with the first kiss between lovers) is accomplished in a ceremony—like so many things in Germany—in which the "Duz-Freunde" lock drinking arms and toast Bruderschaft (brotherhood). ("What is your first name, my dear?" asked Countess Dürkheim in Berlin of the American woman to whom she was teaching German. "I find it too complicated to call you Mrs. Johnson." The American lady's given name was Romona, which the two quickly agreed to shorten to "Moni." "And now what shall I call you?" asked Moni. "Oh," came the answer, "you can just call me Countess Dürkheim.")

One of the reasons for the enormous confusion, both unconscious and intentional, in the concepts of race and class in modern German thinking is that the word "Geschlecht" means both species and family (as descent or lineage) and families tend to perpetuate themselves in their respective classes. Nietzsche makes the point that factory owners and industrialists generally lacked the sovereign style of the aristocrats (Nietzsche calls the aristocrats "the higher race"). If, continues Nietzsche, the industrialists and captains of commerce had had the refinement of style of the hereditary aristocracy (hereditary, hence "the higher race"), then perhaps there would have been no socialism of the masses. But the rise of the industrial masses gradually deprived the aristocrat of his milieu which was the peasantry. We watched this happen with dramatic effect in Weinwartshof—in two main directions: more and more of the hereditary maids went off to work in the factories and more and more of the factory hands came up the river to surround Weinwartshof on all sides, and worst of all on the other side of the river, with their slap-to weekend houses. To make up the loss, some Austrian families I know even brought in Italian maids beginning, to be sure, with South Tyroleans who are "booty Italians" (the South Tyrol was a largish tidbit thrown to the Italians in the Treaty of Saint Germain) but going on to employ Italian Italians.

Berlin is surrounded by Communists but Vienna is marooned, and marooned in time as well as space. Austria is basically still a feudal society. In this sense it is quintessentially German. But the feudal base is disappearing rapidly, even in Austria, as is attested by the inexorable progress of socialism in both countries. In Germany socialism came to political power as National Socialism in 1933; in Austria socialism was prevented from coming to power in 1934 only when the conservative clerical party put the movement down in blood and outlawed it. At this writing both countries have Social Democratic governments; in Austria the Socialists even have an absolute majority.

As distinct from the German Reich, Austria-Hungary unquestionably lost World War I and was destroyed as it stood. "For the Germans," writes Hans Weigel, "territorially little was changed in November 1918, a dynasty that was not hundreds of years old abdicated; the Germans lost a war in 1918, we lost a world. . . . We woke up one morning and our grandparents were all foreigners. . . . In the nineteenth century not only our emperors were lost to us, not only provinces or colonies, but a mission—the mission of maintaining an eminently constant, delicate balance between many nations by means of improvisations and tradition —a commonwealth united in snafu [Pallawatsch]." Austria is a nation of widows and widowers still in mourning for the monarchy. The past is so much with them because it is still indeed recent and because the empire no sooner died that it was transubstantiated into a cult, the most intensively cultivated of our time. All that is left of the Thousand-Year Empire of the Habsburgs is a wall decoration in a wine tavern. So that this should not be so, all of life in Austria is centered in the past. The only national pursuit is advance planning for the past. This is not strictly true, of course, but it is a fair way of expressing the immensity of that past, the brilliance of the glory that was Austria, and the lasting effect of that colossal shock when the House of Habsburg disappeared like a house of cards. (The face cards are still lying—face up—strewn about the country or near it.) It is also a fair way of expressing what desperate straits the Austrian ship of state must navigate on a voyage from an Atlantis that has sunk beneath the sea to some Pitcairn Island, the coordinates of which the ship's crew neither knows nor desires to know. Austria, the republic, has been rightly called "the state that nobody wanted." Those who wanted it least were its own inhabitants. Austria itself is frozen in a state of transition, becalmed between "no longer" and "not yet." Helmut Qualtinger, perhaps the greatest comedian in Europe, calls his country "the Disneyland of Europe"; Friedrich Torberg, a Jewish son of the old monarchy and the best polemicist in the German language, has described the difference between the old Austria and the new—that is, to come—as the difference between Hellas and modern Greece. But Austria's questions of cultural identity and territorial integrity are not nearly so simple as those of Greece, complicated as those were. A more accurate description of the dilemma is provided by Alfred Polgar, the Viennese theater critic, in his comment on Linz, Adolf Hitler's hometown: "Until March 1938 Linz lay in Upper Austria, then it lay in the Gau (Nazi-resurrected German archaism for "district") Upper Danube, now it lies in the American zone. Cities get around a lot these days."

A far more dismal fate had already befallen Vienna. The catastrophe of 1918—it cannot be said too often—transformed Vienna overnight from the capital of the world empire into a living monument to its former self. The Austrians never got over the shock. Nor could they be expected to. The nation composed of nations was sentenced to death by the treaties of Saint-Germain and Trianon and put to the guillotine: Vienna is the decapitated head of the empire. For Vienna, the city of dreams and fairy tales, was geographically, politically, culturally, and mystically at the center of the empire. It stood at the edge of the foothills of the Alps, at the edge of the Great Hungarian Plain. It was almost as much Hungarian, Czech, and Slovakian as it was a German city. It is the only non-Hungarian city that has a Hungarian name: Bécs (border). Its citizenry was largely of Czech and Slovakian extraction and still is: the Vienna telephone book reads like the Prague telephone book. To a far greater extent than Paris, Vienna was in every way "la capitale des peuples." When the blade of the guillotine fell, it cut Vienna off from more than three-quarters of its component parts, severed it from the Hungarian Plain, and left the Viennese a group of forlorn flatlanders teetering on the edge of a mountaineer's country. It left an enormous state apparatus with nothing to do, a huge fist of cunning with nowhere to strike, a wealth of lore, a great reservoir of wisdom with no point of application. One of my wife's relatives explained his decision to leave Austria for Germany in this way: "The amount of intrigue in Vienna is still tailored to the proportions of the empire. It is totally disproportionate to little Austria. This makes for an intolerable situation: they keep shooting at sparrows with heavy mortars." This is one of many ways to describe the process of provincialization. "Vienna," wrote Anton Kuh, the wittiest of the café literati, "that was once a noble asylum for eccentrics, where every barefoot boy of the spirit and body . . . enjoyed special attention and love; Vienna no longer protects its fools and jesters but is hauling them into court. . . . Is it any wonder under such circumstances that the author of this book left the country? That he preferred to live in Berlin among the Viennese rather then in Vienna among Kremser?" (Krems is a small town on the Danube above Tulln.)

Austria received the death sentence, but the Austrians received worse than the death sentence. They were condemned to live forever with the truncated corpse of their country, always reminded (and reminding) of what they had been and no longer were, doomed to eternal frustration. It is small wonder that the Viennese are in general the most introspective, involuted, ill-tempered people in Europe, and a great wonder that some Austrians are an exception to the rule. Vienna is the world capital of nostalgia, full of magnificent vistas that lead nowhere.

The irritability of the Austrians in good part at least is a corruption of that much treasured sensitivity of spirit that was and, in spite of everything, still is an Austrian cachet. But the irritability was also inherent in the ethnographic situation left by succeeding tides of migration. When the flood of Islam had finally receded, the resulting residue of displaced people formed an intricate mosaic throughout the area east of Vienna's outskirts, the high-water mark of the Turkish invasion in Europe. On the Linke Wien-Zeile, the street running along the left bank of the dinky river Wien that transects Vienna and gave the city its name (Wien), at the corner of Moritzgasse, halfway between the center of town and the Palace of Schönbrunn, there is a Turkish cannonball stuck in the edge of an old building, preserved and fixed in its place as part of the monument-city. In the comparative linguistics course at Columbia College, a set problem was the drawing of equitable national borders through the ethnic Thousand Islands of Greater Hungary—linguistic islands within linguistic islands within linguistic islands—by way of an alternative to the ethnographic butchery of the Treaty of Trianon. There was no "school solution" to the problem. And small wonder: it was and is impossible to reduce the dispersion to a system of interconnected areas, however sinuous the configurations. The only solution was the monarchy itself—the solution in which the various colloidal bodies found themselves suspended. Vienna was the head and heart of all the ethnic bodies large and small—or should have been. But there were other "heart and head" cities: Prague for the Czechs, Budapest for the Hungarians, Bratislava for the Slovaks, Agram-Zagreb for the Croats. Before the guillotine blade fell, each central city sent out lifelines to its own isolated ethnic bodies intermingled with all the others. There were not only German strips and globules in the area at large. Hungary lost more than one-third of its ethnic Magyar population to Czechoslovakia, to Romania (more than two and a half million alone), and to Yugoslavia. Indeed, the supreme irony of Trianon and Saint-Germain was that each of the so-called successor nation-states to the Austro-Hungarian Empire was as multinational in microcosm as the empire had been. On the other side of the Sudeten question was a jerry-built multinational simulacrum state in which a Czech majority proved no more capable (if indeed as capable) of handling its minorities than the Habsburg monarchy had been. The Sudeten Germans insisted on national representation and autonomy within the Czecho-Slovakian republic just as the Czechs had done in the Austro-Hungarian monarchy—and with the same right and with the same results. This was why they enjoyed British backing: the British understood this.

One of these Sudeten Germans was Arthur von Seyss-Inquart. Seyss-Inquart was born in the village of Stannern, which was part of a German language island in a Slavic sea in Moravia. Today the village is called Stonarov and lies in Czechoslovakia. The center of this German island was Iglau, a town midway and almost exactly on a line between Prague and Vienna. Iglau made a name for itself as a Sudeten German bulwark, a refuge for Sudeten Germans in the republic of Eduard Beneš and an incubator of great German chauvinists. It is noteworthy that the Seyss-Inquart family was split down the middle in its attitude toward their Moravian neighbors. The father, Emil, a German Gymnasium director, was tolerant and urged his children to learn Czech. His oldest son, Richard, did so gladly and was impartial between Czechs and Germans in his choice of friends. It is recorded that Richard by no means always took the German side in the Czech-German interracial clashes that were common at the turn of the century. Not so at all with Arthur von Seyss-Inquart and his younger sister Irene. Both refused steadfastly to learn a word of Czech. Both were fervent advocates of German national unity and looked to Bismarck's German Reich as model and spiritual home. At the same time another German schoolboy in another area threatened by Czech migrants and encroaching Czech nationalism reacted in the same way. The schoolboy in Linz, less than twenty miles from the present Czech border, became obsessed with the history of the Franco-German war. But then came the question

... whether and what sort of difference there was then between these Germans who fought battles and the others? Why had not Austria also fought in this war, why not my father and all the others too?

Are we not then the same as even all other Germans?

Do we not then all belong together? For the first time this problem began to gnaw at my young mind [Hitler wrote "my little brain"]. With inner envy I was obliged to take for answer to my cautious questions that not every German had the good fortune to belong to Bismarck's Reich.

I could not comprehend this.

Years later in Vienna this extreme nationalism provided the seedbed for his anti-Semitism. And yet it was not the Austrians who took Hitler seriously. The saving grace of the Austrians, administered largely by the Viennese, is their humor. Even in the worst of times. The Austrian Eduard Heinl, a member of the National Council, went to London to negotiate a loan in the thirties. The loan was refused and Heinl had this statement to make to the press: "We Austrians have one failing: we always kiss the wrong ass."

I RETURNED TO VIENNA FROM BERLIN IN MID-OCTOBER 1956. Lori, the former regular Hungarian army officer and regular weekend guest at Weinwartshof, took me aside. "This situation in Hungary is going to explode any day now," he said. I said I had heard that prediction often enough before. "Have you ever heard it from me before?" he asked. Three days later I was driving my Volkswagen overland across the Hungarian border (the Hungarian border guards had cleared paths through the minefields "so that the world can come and see what is happening in Hungary"). The world saw in some small part through my eyes: the massacre in Moson-magyarovar, the establishment of the revolutionary councils throughout Hungary (I witnessed the first proclamations of the council in Györ). Everybody in Hungary in the streets, everybody with the red, white, and green ribbons over the heart, everybody talking at once and tirelessly except the quiet men, the revolutionaries who said nothing or very little, who did not drink, who did not dance, but made their rounds singly and saw to it that order was kept. I ranged western and northern Hungary in a dreamlike atmosphere of exhilaration and disbelief. They had won! It was the dawn of creation. It was lovely. On the fourth day in Hungary I came down with violent stomach pains. I could not account for them until I remembered that I had not eaten in four days. I thought the atmosphere of the French Revolution must have been something like that. When I went back into Hungary from Vienna for the second (and last) time with two hundred oranges in the car, I disregarded the preference in Ezra Pound's lyric:

> And I would rather have my sweet,
> Though rose-leaves die of grieving,
>
> Than do high deeds in Hungary
> To pass all men's believing.

My high deeds in Hungary consisted of distributing oranges to children and chauffeuring various desperate people (usually distraught

[269]

women) from one point to another. I was in Györ when the Russians returned. They were dirty and gray, as gray as their tanks, and their faces were gray as their uniforms. They looked like the golem, mudmen. They were silent and dispirited. But they came. The effect of their return was simply devastating. It was the end of the world. Worst of all was the Luciferian plunge from the pinnacle of exhilaration to the most profound despair.

I dwell on the Hungarian Revolution because it was a watershed, a turning point in history and not only in German and European history. It happened just before the American presidential elections, and if Adlai Stevenson ever had a chance before the Hungarian Revolution (which he almost surely did not), then he most certainly never had a chance after it was suppressed. Similarly, the following year, the year of the Hungarian refugees, was also the year of the West German national elections. In Germany the Hungarian Revolution and its suppression doomed the Social Democrats just as surely as it had doomed Adlai Stevenson: Konrad Adenauer's Christian Democratic Union was returned to parliament with an absolute majority. It was the first absolute majority in German history. But the revolution also did something else in Germany. The only time I saw a foreign journalist step out of line in Hungary was when a Hungarian army unit was trying to set up a field gun behind a curve in the road to Sopron to knock out the lead tank or tanks in an approaching Soviet column. Suddenly a German magazine correspondent ran up and began haranguing the Hungarian artillerymen: "This is the worst possible place for the gun, bring it forward to that rise there and train it low." He obviously knew the gun, twirling the wheels to lower its muzzle while explaining that he had been captain of artillery in the Wehrmacht. He took charge of the detail. Whether he remained to await the arrival of the Soviets I do not know.

But the most violent reaction to the crushing of the Hungarian Revolution was in West Berlin. On November 5 one hundred thousand West Berliners marched in protest up the Avenue of the 17th of June to the Brandenburg Gate and were on the very point of continuing their march through the Gate and into East Berlin when they were distracted and then dissuaded from their purpose by the newly elected mayor of West Berlin: Willy Brandt.

Since this was the incident that catapulted Willy Brandt into international prominence, I can do no better than tell the story in Brandt's words, as he told it to me when I interviewed him not so very long after the event:

[270]

On the 5th of November, just after Hungary was crushed, a mass protest meeting was held here before the Rathaus. The crowd was already seething. I was *not* one of the speakers. Unfortunately the speakers talked right past the crowd. [Actually one of the speakers, a senior SPD functionary, was hooted and whistled down.] All of a sudden someone shouted, "To the Brandenburg Gate!" and the crowd quickly began to form into columns and move out of the square in the direction of the Brandenburg Gate. At that point the microphone on the speakers' stand went dead so I rushed back into the Rathaus and used the public address system there. First I called "You don't know whom you are following!" Then I thought of a divisive maneuver and cried, "March with me to the monument of the victims of Stalinism on the Steinplatz." [On the way to, but a longish way from, the Brandenburg Gate.] I went to the Steinplatz, made a speech, and then jumped into a police car and drove to the Avenue of the 17th of June [which leads into the Brandenburg Gate] where a police cordon blocked the path of the demonstrators. There was a real tussle—a dozen policemen had been struck down. I went through the police cordon to the police car which had already been pretty well wrecked—its windows were broken and so forth—and got hold of the microphone of the loudspeaker which was still working. I introduced myself and then said "You are providing the Communists with an edifying spectacle—bloodying each other in their sight!" Then I bethought myself of singing—what's the best way to distract a German?—get him to sing. So I said, "Let's sing the song of the good comrade and our national anthem." It worked, and as if by magic police and demonstrators stood side by side at attention and sang. A "Sprechchor" [a term for a group chanting slogans] was spontaneously organized and set up a chant, "Shakos off, Shakos off!" These were youngsters unaware that the police should keep their helmets on at all times—even while singing the national anthem. But I was very thankful for this added diversion. By this time, however, another part of the crowd had gone directly —through the Tiergarten Park—to the Brandenburg Gate. They were running up to the Gate and throwing lighted torches into the East sector at the People's police [Volkspolizei]. I must say that the Vopos really showed remarkable restraint. Among those present in the crowd—à la mode of the demonstration leader in a leather coat —was the police president of West Berlin. He said to me, "You must promise them that the Soviet monument will be removed!" Well, Reuter once promised that—but here? Anyway, all that is told is not always gold. At this point the British Military Police arrived; it was their sector, and they inadvertently provided the greatest diversion of the day. With the cry of "Suez Schweine" [Suez pigs] the crowd turned on the British MPs. (It was clear to well-nigh everyone the moment the Anglo-French forces invaded Egypt in late October 1956 that this sealed the fate of the Hungarians in their struggle

[271]

against the Soviet occupation force.) They were really pretty badly
beaten up. I invited them to the Rathaus a couple of days later to
make amends: they were very good about it. All three city commandants thanked me.

Here I insert a translation of "I Had a Comrade," the song of the
good comrade to which Brandt referred, because it is the most important
song in the German language. It is usually sung at funerals and on other
solemn occasions:

> I had a comrade;
>   You won't find a better one;
> The drum called us to battle,
> He walked by my side,
>   Keeping pace and step,
>   Keeping pace and step.
>
> A bullet came a-flying:
>   Is it for me or is it for you?
> Him it tore away;
> At my feet he lies
>   As if he were a piece of me,
>   As if he were a piece of me.
>
> Wants to shake my hand once more,
>   Just as I am reloading
> I can't give you my hand;
> May eternal life be yours,
>   My good comrade,
>   My good comrade.

This was the first time I had met Brandt. I was surprised by his
appearance and manner. He gave the impression of massiveness and
strength, an impression he did not give in his public utterances and
appearances. When excited—as he was when he told this story (he
relished the telling)—he swung his arms in a scissoring motion like a
boxer waiting for the bell. I made the mistake, as immediately evident,
of asking Brandt if he were of Norwegian extraction. The question was
doubly indiscreet. First, because Brandt was the illegitimate child of an
unknown father; second, because Brandt's "Norwegian connection" was
a political issue of the first magnitude. Brandt had fled to Norway after
the Nazis came to power and had become a Norwegian citizen after the
Nazis had officially deprived him of his German citizenship. Jingoist
German circles accused Brandt of having borne arms against the German people (that is, the Third Reich) as a member of the Norwegian

[272]

army. Brandt denied this, maintaining that he had merely donned a Norwegian soldier's uniform to escape detection and death when the Nazis invaded Norway.

Brandt prevented the West Berliners from marching through the Brandenburg Gate into East Berlin, but he could not (and would not) stop the masses of East Germans who were coming through the Brandenburg Gate into West Berlin to be airlifted to West Germany. In July 1958, Otto Grothewohl, then prime minister of East Germany, cited the tremendous losses in manpower through refugees, and admitted that the "continuing flight from the Republic is problem number one." The same summer Walter Ulbricht, first secretary of the SED, or Socialist Unity party (Communist) of East Germany, put the situation to Nikita Khrushchev in still more forceful terms: "If the Soviet Union can't get the Allies out of Berlin, I can't hold East Germany." Ulbricht was assuming that the only way to close the open city—and shut the escape hatch—was to force or inveigle the Allies to leave the city. Khrushchev responded by formally telling the Allies to get out of town within six months. This was the Berlin ultimatum of November 1958 and one of the silliest things Khrushchev ever did—a sweeping statement. One result he did achieve with the ultimatum was my return to Berlin. I returned just in time to attend the grand opening of the Berlin Hilton. This consisted of three banquets-cum-grand-balls on consecutive nights. (A Berlin milkman made a delivery to the hotel kitchen at the beginning and disappeared for three days.) On each occasion Conrad Hilton (whose exit from the elevator into the main lobby was announced by fanfare: six trumpeters and a herald) proposed the same seven-word toast: "Ladies and gentlemen, I give you freedom!" While Conrad Hilton was giving it, Nikita Khrushchev was trying to take it away. But Khrushchev's ultimatum was poorly timed: it immediately preceded the quadrennial West Berlin elections which, in keeping with Western tradition of free elections, were the only elections in Germany open to all parties, the Socialist Unity party (Communist) being represented by its West Berlin branch—the Communist party of West Germany had been banned as unconstitutional. Inevitably, therefore, attention was centered on the kind of showing the Socialist Unity party would make in the new atmosphere created by Khrushchev's ultimatum. After all, the Socialist Unity party was the party of the people, according to the Communists. Also according to the Communists, the imperialist oppressors—that is, the Western Allies—had rigged previous elections in West Berlin (in 1954 the Communists had polled 2.7 percent of the vote). The Allies had now been put on notice by the Khrushchev ultimatum. But the ultimatum also made the Berliners angry. Most important—this was the major tactical blunder—coming when it did, the ultimatum turned the elections into a plebiscite for or against the Soviet proposal on West Berlin. Looking back, it is clear that the Communists realized much too late how much was at stake in the elections.

Even so they launched a full-scale attempt to make a decent showing. The party held four mass meetings in West Berlin during the campaign and enjoyed the full and expert protection of the West Berlin police. There was plenty of money; the party was unstinting in its use of posters, leaflets, and brochures exhorting Berliners to accept "the normal solution to the Berlin problem." For about two weeks before the elections young Communist students from Humboldt University in East Berlin were sent to the Free University in West Berlin. About twenty agitators came over each day. Working in groups of three and four, they stationed themselves at vantage points of the Free University campus and drew West Berlin students into political discussions during free periods. One discussion I overheard ran like this:

> EAST: It is undemocratic to have a five percent clause [whereby any party polling less than five percent of the popular vote does not receive a seat in the Senate]. Almost three percent of West Berliners belong to the Socialist Unity party. They have a right to representation.
> WEST: What is the population of Hungary?
> EAST: What? Oh, about nine million.
> WEST: How many Hungarians would you say took part in the Hungarian uprising?
> EAST: Less than a million—about nine hundred thousand, not more.
> WEST: But that is ten percent of the Hungarian population.

End of discussion. That was pretty much the way it went throughout. There was nothing the Communists could say, nothing they could do. Elections provide poor ground for Communist activity—especially when the electorate has a Communist country with its model of "elections" staring it in the face. As Djilas, the great Yugoslav renegade Communist put it, a Communist election is a horse race with one horse. It is interesting how often the Communists generally do violence to definitions. Their "elections" are not elections because it is not possible to elect where there is no choice. In a Communist state the Communist party is not a party because it is the whole. A People's Democracy is a tautology—"a people's people's rule"; a democratic republic, as in the German Democratic Republic, is merely a Greek and Latin repetition: "demo" and "public" both mean the same thing.

On Sunday, December 7, the Communists polled 1.9 percent of the vote. This was a loss of ten thousand votes or one-third of the total they had polled four years before. In effect, the elections turned an attempted Communist advance into a complete rout. But above all, the elections were the personal triumph of Willy Brandt. It was then, too, that the first faint lines of fissure between Bonn and Berlin became noticeable. Three days before, Konrad Adenauer had come to Berlin to plump for his Christian Democratic party candidate (for Adenauer, too, the juxtaposition of the ultimatum and the elections was unfortunate). The chancellor had been ill-advised enough to set aside only half an hour to confer with Brandt on the Berlin situation. Brandt countered that this was hardly time enough to have a worthwhile discussion of so crucially important an issue. The meeting did not take place. The Berlin public was quick to sense the anomaly and immediately sided with Brandt. Here, too, it was almost inevitable that the chancellor of West Germany and the mayor of Berlin should be leaders of opposing political parties; the Social Democratic majority in Berlin was almost as traditional as the Catholic conservative majority in the Rhineland. When we journalists went to the Schöneberger Rathaus that evening to see Brandt in his moment of triumph, we found him trembling with anger. He had also had something to drink—not enough to make him drunk or even tipsy, but enough to be noticeable and enough to steel his determination to take up the gauntlet. This victory was not only a stinging rebuke to the East German Communists and their Soviet masters. "This is also Berlin's answer," said Brandt, "to certain people who believed that they could come here and slight Berlin's lord mayor and other leading figures." Everyone present knew whom Brandt meant.

I interviewed Brandt again in September 1960, after the Berlin crisis had blown over, the four foreign ministers having met and haggled in Geneva the previous summer to no avail other than Khrushchev's trip to the United States and the "Spirit of Camp David." The interview was meant to serve as a sort of postmortem of the Berlin crisis. I began it by citing Mayor Brandt's book, *From Bonn to Berlin,* which had appeared in 1957 and strongly urged moving the capital of the Federal Republic from Bonn to Berlin. Said Brandt: "Bringing the capital of West Germany to Berlin would have been possible in 1957 or 1958 because the British and Americans would most probably have been ready then to agree to such a move. Only the French had reservations. At that time, too, the Allies were in a much stronger position than they are today internationally and in general. Today it is no longer possible—it is impractical and would bring no advantages." I said that it seemed there were two schools of thought on how to handle the Berlin problem. One held that the political identification of West Berlin with West Germany should be further developed and promoted. The other school held that the political connection between West Berlin and West Germany should be played down to the point of disappearance and the West's stand in Berlin should be made exclusively on the basis of the Four-Power Statute. Brandt replied:

I do not see any conflict between the two courses of action. They are complementary, not mutually exclusive. The two concepts should coincide, not conflict. That is what happens in the Federal Republic and I do not see why it should not happen here. Let's take an example: the Saar was integrated into the Federal Republic some time ago. This integration of the Saar could have taken place without any trouble even if the Saar had been occupied by Allied troops and it had been decreed that Allied occupation was to continue. As far as Berlin is concerned, I do not believe that one should do any more in the direction of further political identification of West Berlin with West Germany, but I do not believe that one should do any less than has been done in the past—no more, but also no less. We cannot allow others, outsiders, enemies, to determine by threat or protest what is to happen or not happen here with us in West Berlin. Berlin is legally the capital of Germany. West Berlin is a state of the Federal Republic according to the Basic Law [Grundgesetz, Article 23]. That article was accepted by the Western Allies when the Basic Law was drafted. . . .
     I cannot say anything for publication about the possibility of holding the West German parliamentary session here in Berlin. But I'll tell you quite frankly that I am for holding such a session for the reasons I have just given you. Let me tell you a story in this regard. Last year when the presidential electoral assembly was in the offing we announced our intention of holding it here in Berlin. The Communists reacted very sharply, cried "provocation," and threatened countermeasures. Gerstenmaier, the president of the West German Parliament, was originally all for holding the electoral assembly in Berlin. But when I stopped in to see Gerstenmaier on my way to Geneva, I found him a bit hesitant. He had a pile of secret intelligence documents a foot high on his desk, all of them indicating very strongly that there would be hell to pay if the electoral assembly were held in West Berlin. These documents were extremely detailed. They gave the exact number, identification, and

strength of the Soviet Air Force (and the name, rank, and serial number of its commanding general) and asserted that it would go into action immediately to block the air corridors if the electoral assembly were held in Berlin. Gerstenmaier said that the situation was obviously very critical and that the Western Allies were against holding the electoral assembly in Berlin under the circumstances.

When I arrived in Geneva two days later, I had lunch with Mr. Herter, M. Couve de Murville, Mr. Selwyn Lloyd, and Herr Heinrich von Brentano. After lunch we sat around coffee and talked. All of a sudden Selwyn Lloyd put down his cup and said, "I want to make a statement in the presence of the mayor of Berlin." Then, turning to Von Brentano, he said, "Heinrich, when the three of us, Mr. Herter, M. Couve de Murville, and I, told you a couple of weeks ago that we had no objection to holding the electoral assembly in Berlin, you told us that the West German government had grave doubts about holding such a session at this time. . . . Since then the Western press, and particularly the German press, have complained bitterly about the fainthearted English whose trepidations are blocking the holding of the electoral assembly in West Berlin. That is all I want to say—I have no further comment to make." That is a good indication of the way things go. . . . Since then, of course, the British have modified their position somewhat. But the point is that the two areas of authority—that of the Western Allies and that of the Germans—interconnect. In practice during the last several years the Western Allies have left the decision of what should happen in Germany to the discretion of the federal government and the Berlin Senate. As a matter of fact the complementary responsibility of the Western Allies and the West Germans is documented specifically in the Deutschland Vertrag of 1955 [known in the West as the Paris Treaty, its German name, significantly, is "Germany Treaty"]. The main body of that contract specifies those areas of responsibility in Germany which the Western Allies reserve to themselves. But there is a codicil to the contract in which the Federal Republic accepts responsibility for the financial status of West Berlin—primarily the monetary system—and also for the economic development of West Berlin. The Germany Treaty of 1955 is a solemn, formal agreement which is legally binding for all signatories. Neither the Federal Republic nor anybody else can deny the responsibilities set forth in that document. Incidentally, the document is very little known.

As far as Berlin is concerned, what can we do? Sebastian Haffner, Berlin correspondent for the British weekly, *The Observer,* whom I regard highly, has proposed that the Allies march into East Berlin to act as proxies for the Soviets in controlling East Berlin until the Soviets see fit to reassume their responsibilities in their sector. Such a move would be completely legal and entirely defensible within the framework of the Four-Power Statute. But it would be impractical because the Allies were not able to intervene during the uprising of 1953. They were also unable to intervene when the Communists declared East German sovereignty over East Berlin in 1955. If anything they are less able to intervene now. Perhaps I am getting old. Earlier I might have come out strongly for such a move but no longer. It would be a very bold move but it probably wouldn't bring any long-term advantages. In connection with the compatibility of the Four-Power Statute and the political presence of the Federal Republic in West Berlin, the Allies can do whatever they like so long as it is politically practical, legal, and in conformity with their own security considerations. These are the three measuring sticks to be applied. Practically, over the years, the situation in Berlin has come down to this: a three-power Statute of the Western Allies exists in West Berlin, and a one-power statute of the Soviets exists in East Berlin. There are, of course, still some connecting links between the three and the one, and they are not confined to occasional cocktail parties. However, in the main and in terms of all positive action, we do not interfere with them in their sector and they do not interfere with us in ours.

I told Brandt that in my experience the West's only hope of reunification hinged on the belief that the East German economy would collapse one fine day as a result of the continuing loss of manpower through the refugee flow to the West. "That sort of talk is illusory," said Brandt.

The economic situation in the Soviet zone—at least in terms of priority production—has become progressively better. The progress is not great, but at least the situation is considerably better than it was a few years ago. I agree with you that the Soviets and the East German Communists must stop the flow of refugees. But that is already happening. In all probability the refugee flow will be substantially stopped by the end of this year. That is the reason for the latest control measures along the sector boundary dividing East Berlin from West Berlin. I do not expect an economic collapse or anything similar in East Germany. However, I can very well imagine a disturbance or even a rebellion taking place in the Soviet zone for other reasons—for spiritual or moral reasons. For that matter we—Bonn and Berlin—could broadcast an appeal to the East Germans to revolt and they could do so. But what good would that do? We know what comes of that sort thing from two fairly recent examples, East Germany on June 17, 1953, and Hungary in 1956. However, if the Soviets or the East Germans ever tried to take Berlin by force, we—Bonn and Berlin—would broadcast an appeal to the East German people to revolt. If one must go down, then it is better to go down with the flag flying.

I had an additional question, one pertaining to the peculiar double nature of the Federal Republic—West Germany was allegedly neither flesh nor fowl nor good red herring but rather the mongrel offspring of the "economic miracle" and the cold war, half or three-quarters German state and half or one-quarter Western Allied province. Brandt said that he saw the Federal Republic as an economic society. It was, he said, an administrative structure, the leadership of which had succeeded admirably in harmonizing a very wide variety of often conflicting impulses from a large number of economic and social interest groups. It was a fascinating sociological study.

Turning to my list of subheadings Brandt pointed to the federal army. "This," he said,

> is what I am afraid of. There are forces within the Federal Republic which might begin to assert themselves if the situation were to change and they would do so through the federal army. When I mention such forces I do not mean the chancellor or even the leadership of the federal army. The overwhelming majority of the higher officers are surprisingly decent, able, and right-thinking men. But it would be a very great mistake to give the federal army atomic weapons. This would cause a great deal of ill-feeling not only in the West, but also in the East and even in Germany itself. We have the heritage of Nazism on our backs and we shall have it on our backs for at least another generation. I say this not because I am morally against atomic armament or that I find some things so dirty that only our friends should soil their hands with them. But we simply cannot afford to arm atomically. There is a way, of course, to get round this obstacle rather elegantly. We can arm the federal army with antiaircraft, even antitank and antimissile rockets so long as the federal army is an integral part of the NATO forces and the possibility is ruled out that it would charge off in any direction on its own initiative and without proper authority. As long as the federal army is integrated into the NATO forces, this danger will not exist. But if not, then there is the strong possibility—although there are no indications of this at the moment—that certain "distortions" will take place in the Federal Republic. This is why I disapprove of General de Gaulle's most recent press conference so much. If de Gaulle insists on full sovereignty for France and France's dissociation from NATO, he will force us to take the same direction.

De Gaulle did just that, less than four years later.

I first met and interviewed Konrad Adenauer in December 1960, in the lull before the storm. A few months before he had publicly decried the lack of national feeling among Germans. I asked what sort of national feeling the chancellor had found lacking—for the Federal Republic as such or for Germany as it existed in 1937, or what? He answered by expounding the catalog of German catastrophe. The trouble began, he said, with Bismarck, whose fault it was that there had been no healthy inner political development in Germany. He then cited the inflation after 1919. It had all but destroyed the middle class, which was the main pillar of the state. This was followed by National Socialism, which caused the greatest confusion politically and in the very thought processes of the people—not only among ardent Nazis, he emphasized, but also among fellow travelers and those who passively tolerated the system. (In short, as I thought to myself, the overwhelming majority of the German people.) Then came war, the collapse of the Third Reich, and occupation. Many of the nation's teachers had been compromised during the Nazi period and preferred to keep silent. Likewise a great many parents were unwilling to speak of the period, so that the new generation did not stand on solid national-historical ground. The chancellor made it clear that for him national feeling was love for one's people, not allegiance to some ruling house or set of national boundaries. As far as the theory of "collective shame" was concerned, he said it was both true and not true. Of course, one was ashamed of the period and ashamed that such a thing had happened in Germany. But he added that Germany was not the only country with a shameful past. And there were a great many things in Germany's past that one could be proud of. There were, for that matter, people who had been in the Nazi party and had remained decent and harmless throughout but who were deeply ashamed after it was all over. Such people, too, were loath to speak to their children about German history. And yet it was necessary to inform the youth of the country about the period—fully and openly. "German youth," he summed up, "must learn German history in continuity."

He rejected out of hand the suggestion that young Germans should be forced to acquaint themselves with the Nazi chronicle of horrors merely because they were German and in order to prevent a sort of atavistic relapse. But he said that because the Germans were somewhat unstable as a result of the last sixty years of their history—the empire, the Weimar Republic, National Socialism, the occupation and all its accompanying turmoil—because they were afflicted to a certain extent and rendered rather susceptible by developments extending over decades, it was essential to enlighten German youth on the full significance and value of freedom.

The Old Man, "der Alte" as he was called, looked at me steadily while I rattled off my questions. The only thing that was old about der Alte was his eyes. They were bright and twinkling—but tiny. They were the eyes of an elephant. They looked as if they had been fixed in the side of his head. They made his full face look as if it had been put together by taking his right and left profiles and juxtaposing them in the flat. They made it seem that the Old Man was looking at me, with a slight wry smile, across the span of time he was discussing—sixty years. "Do you think," I asked, "that the Germans have finally surmounted the shock of World War II and the moral and psychological effects of the whole period?" His answer was no and again no—not yet. It was also, he added gratuitously, a mistake to regard the Germans as a wealthy nation. It was simply not true. In this regard Germans overestimated themselves and were overestimated by others. All this talk about an "economic miracle" —nonsense. "That's what I dislike so much about the Germans," he burst out suddenly, "they are such a bunch of big mouths—they can't ever keep their traps shut!" Adenauer had the reputation of being anti-German. He was not. He was merely being, as in this outburst I have cited, very German. Germans are much given to running themselves down (there is a curious parallel here with the phenomenon of Jewish self-contempt). I have noticed that when a German criticizes his fellow countrymen he always refers to "*the* Germans," never to "*we* Germans." The German critic of Germans instinctively dissociates himself.

Adenauer went on to say that the Germans were in fact on a very thin economic foundation. It was only the great difference between then and ten years before that tended to dazzle. But just let an economic reverse come along, he warned. A key to the chancellor's agitation was the fact that prosperity had become the panacea for German spiritual ills and the cornerstone of German political structure. The only real guarantee of continued German political health was (and is) continuing prosperity. Similarly, the postwar reconstruction period, which, as Adenauer pointed out, was (and is) still not closed, is regarded by West German leaders as something very like a nationwide state-subsidized program of occupational therapy. The profits of the program have been ploughed back in for maintenance and expansion: directly in the form of government subsidies or tax write-offs for investment in German industry, and indirectly by steadily increasing wages to enhance the buying power of the worker. The result is the highest standard of living in German history and a mass consumer society based on the American model— and inflation. For Adenauer the most important internal political aspect of prosperity was that it brought about not only the creation of a majority

[281]

middle class but also, in effect, the bourgeoisization of the proletariat and hence destruction of the economic tenets of socialism. During our talk the chancellor mentioned that a recent poll conducted by the Allenbach Institute of Demoscopy had ascertained that exactly half the members of the Social Democratic party interviewed were still against any form of West German army.

After the war Adenauer had been entrusted by the Western Allies to build a state out of the ruins and apathy unprecedented in history. To do so he realized his conceptual masterpiece, the Christian Democratic Union, a political organization derived from the old Catholic Center party but expanded to cover the broadest possible base—a catchall for the adherents of the cultural heritage of the Christian West. It was a grandiose conception. As Kurt Schumacher, Adenauer's Social Democratic rival, put it: "The first CDU man was Charlemagne." The assault led by Adenauer on Germany's multitude of political and psychological problems, the insistence on due process of law coupled with the refusal to engage in a blanket persecution of ex-Nazis so as not to split the nation by creating a mass of second-class citizens was a costly and laborious process (particularly since the mass of potential second-class citizens were fully enfranchised and could vote out of office any government that did not make allowances for them). Above all, it was an exercise in rehabilitation, the establishment of the Germans' bona fides—"certificates of good conduct" as the Germans called them—as well-behaved "solid citizens" eminently worthy of acceptance as equal partners in a grand alliance with the traditional democracies. It also meant dealing singly with dinosaurs as they emerged or were dug up out of the mud of the Nazi past.

But the cure cost the Germans more than patience and money. In the headlong drive for increased industrial capacity and production, they were forced to resort to irregular practices. Most common of these was the investing of money from short-term loans on a long-term basis. At the expiration of the term, say three months, renewal was requested and continued to be requested at each expiration until the creditor's patience was exhausted. The long-standing short-term loan was finally paid off with money from a second short-term loan, and so on. Another practice was pledging the same security for various loans concurrently. The most serious and widespread of all was the bribing of local and federal government officials, usually by contractors. Fusion of government and private interests in economic fields often made it difficult if not impossible to discern infringements of legality (the West German Parliament was

[282]

frequently referred to as the "Federal Economic Council"). This had resulted in a series of corruption scandals (a series that proved to be but the first in a larger series), the latest of which then was the "courts-of-justice" crisis in Berlin, where the district attorney and other high officials of city and state were accused of systematically quashing bribery charges. At that time in West Berlin alone there were 767 charges of bribery being prepared by the public prosecutor and pending. This was the seamy side of the apparently sound but also glaringly materialistic new German society. Still, it was small wonder that Adenauer was money-conscious. There was a chronic shortage of liquid assets because the Germans were constantly investing their own and foreign capital in expanded and modernized plant. The Germans were by that time among the most heavily taxed people in Europe. Twenty-four percent of the per capita annual income was siphoned off into federal and state treasuries. The largest block of the federal budget—almost forty percent—came under the heading of social security and included care and maintenance of war victims, returnees, and the never-ending stream of refugees from East Germany. Another standard budgetary item was reparations to victims of Nazism, including states as well as individuals. The largest single item went to Israel—more than 400 million marks per annum for an ultimate total of three and a half billion marks. More than a billion marks per annum went (and still goes) to finance the economy of West Berlin.

But what weighed most heavily on the West Germans was the dilemma imposed by the necessity—and the deep-felt need—of demonstrating good conduct to the world: how to shine as exemplary peaceful citizens and at the same time agitate for the reunification of the country? In order to pursue reunification actively but inconspicuously, the Germans clothed their claim to German unity in the articles and official trappings of statehood. The Federal Republic *was* the West German reunification policy. The preamble of the Basic Law (or constitution) explicitly sets forth the territorial claims of the German state. Moreover, these claims were "enshrined" in the corpus of international agreements. Every major diplomatic instrument signed by the Federal Republic stipulates that the Republic is the only legitimate German state, the only German state legally entitled to represent Germany as a whole. This was the basis of the so-called Hallstein Doctrine, according to which the Federal Republic rewarded those nations accepting its exclusive claim— by extending credit or making outright grants, for example—and penalizing those refusing to accept its claim—by withholding diplomatic relations or breaking them off, as it did when Yugoslavia recognized East Germany in 1957. (The only country where an exception was made to the Hallstein Doctrine [until 1968 when West Germany established diplomatic relations with Romania] was the Soviet Union; it forced the establishment of diplomatic relations by making them a condition for the release of 100,000 German prisoners of war.) Every member of the Bundestag must take a solemn oath to uphold the Basic Law and hence pursue the goal of reunification. The Federal Republic does not rest on a territory but on a legal definition: the definition is a territorial claim. "According to the word and spirit of the Basic Law," wrote Willy Brandt in 1957, "the Federal Republic is nothing other than the manifestation of our state political life (Staatsleben) in those parts of Germany in which external power relations have made it possible to inaugurate the reorganization of state political life as a whole." The Western Allies signed various instruments binding the Federal Republic to the Western democracies and, most important, securing a German defense contribution in exchange for the solemn Western Allied undertaking to help the Germans by all peaceful means to achieve the reunification of the country.

But at the time I first interviewed Adenauer, the Old Man was waiting for the young man. John F. Kennedy had been elected president of the United States the month before. There was already talk about the new administration's having a new German policy, of its being determined to come up with a new answer to a very old problem. At that time Adenauer was mainly interested in Kennedy's choice for secretary of state and in the new American foreign policy in Europe. In his opinion, the chancellor said, the great prerequisite for dealing with the Russians was Western unity. "And where," he asked impassionedly, "where is Western unity now? Where is it?"

VER SINCE I WAS OLD ENOUGH TO HAVE ONE, MY abiding preoccupation has been with refugees. I grew up among immigrants: and immigrants are political or economic refugees. My real introduction to refugees in this broader sense was the railroad and the railroad led me to Chicago. Chicago was then the world capital of immigrancy—"the second largest Polish city in the world, the second largest Hungarian city in the world," etc. New York was the first port of call for world refugeedom in the direct sense. In my stint with the American army during and after World War II or with IPW (Interrogation of Prisoners of War) or Order of Battle teams, refugees—in this case defectors—were the sources of most of the information we managed to gather. They were the raw material we processed ("process" is the term used in the trade of intelligence gathering). Similarly, my liaison with the Red (later the Soviet) Army largely involved me with Soviet defectors, just as did my work in trying to resettle them. The story of postwar Europe is the story of refugees—again and again in spectacular manifestation when they flee from Hungary or Czechoslovakia; constantly, implacably when they flee from East Germany despite walls, minefields, and armed patrols. It was natural, then, that I should have become sensitive and perhaps oversensitive—if that is possible—to the phenomenon of refugees. I saw them where most observers would not see them. Indeed, Europe's titled aristocrats (I specify "titled" because there are other kinds of aristocrats) are refugees who have fled from a bygone age into the present, for the most part having salvaged only their names.

The Hungarian Revolution, like the Berlin Wall five years later, like the Prague Spring twelve years later, and the Polish riots fourteen years later, came as the result of economic stagnation. In the case of those Eastern European countries opening directly on the West (Yugoslavia excepted) the barbed wire, minefields, and armed guards are there to protect the country's borders from its own citizens, cordons sanitaires not against infiltration from without (as they of course are claimed to be) but against exfiltration from within. The refugee flow from such countries (all of them suffering from chronic manpower shortages in the best of times—Yugoslavia again excepted) constitutes the only direct threat to their internal stability. In a sense the threat is caused by the neighboring country and the countries beyond insofar as they constitute attractive havens for the refugees. To do so, the foreign countries need meet only two requirements: they must be relatively prosperous and they must steadfastly refuse extradition. The postwar political history of Germany has been determined by the refugee flow, by the largely desultory efforts of the West to promote it and by the constant, often frantic, and sometimes desperate efforts of the East to prevent it. Preeminently these three factors have determined the postwar history of Berlin. Until August 13, 1961, Berlin was the escape hatch of East Germany. By 1961 more than four million East Germans had fled the Soviet zone for West Germany (it was not officially revealed until much later but more than ninety percent of these came out through Berlin). This was more than a fourth of the population of East Germany. It is the greatest voluntary mass migration in recorded European history. More significantly, the refugee flow from East to West Germany continued for seventeen years undiminished. The average annual total since the end of World War II was about a quarter of a million. The most striking aspect of the refugee flow was its uniformity. Fifty percent of the annual total of refugees were always under twenty-five years of age, seventy-four percent under forty-five, and over ninety percent under sixty-five. The effect of this drain on the population structure was staggering. The East German statistical yearbook for 1960 showed a loss over a nine-year period of almost a million (or thirty-two percent) in the six-to-fifteen age group, and a loss of more than a millon and a quarter (twenty percent) in the age group from twenty-five to fifty. Conversely, the over-fifty population has increased by well over half a million (ten percent), while people over sixty-five have gained more than 400,000 members—an increase of eighteen percent. The mass of the East German population had either already retired or was rapidly approaching retirement age.

For the Russians it was a question of gaining time to do anything possible to stop the refugee flow. They actually succeeded in diminishing the total for 1959 by better than one-quarter of the 1958 total. During this period an increased trickle of returnees from West to East Germany produced some semblance of a "refugee" flow in reverse. But the causes were not what the Communists assumed they were. Whenever negotiations on Berlin were in course or an atmosphere conducive to negotiations existed, the East Germans took to watching and waiting and the refugee flow slackened accordingly. When Khrushchev torpedoed the summit conference in the spring of 1960 in Paris, the refugee flow increased abruptly and continued strong until the Kennedy–Khrushchev summit in Vienna in the spring of the following year, after which the flow became a torrent.

On the phenomenon of the East German refugee flow to West Germany I wrote an article in early 1961 which appeared in *The Reporter* magazine under the title "The Disappearing Satellite." Using the available statistics I pointed out that the Germans were reuniting—in West Germany. Moreover, I emphasized that East Germany's loss was West Germany's gain. The refugee flow was a transfusion that was draining East Germany of its lifeblood while strengthening the already flourishing West Germany. "There are some indications," I wrote,

> that the Soviet Union and its East German minions have finally drawn the ultimate conclusion that the only way to stop the refugees is to seal off both East Berlin and the Soviet zone by total physical security measures. The regime has already alerted specialized Communist formations to man the East Berlin sector boundary sometime this spring. . . . They are transferring tough and experienced customs officers from zonal border duty to checkpoints in the city. Berliners are reckoning with the distinct possibility that Khrushchev will make good his threat of a separate peace treaty and ring down the Iron Curtain in front of East Berlin—with searchlight and machine gun towers, barbed wire, and police dog patrols. Technically this is feasible. But the very feasibility of the measure poses two questions: Why was it not taken long ago? Can it be taken now?

I said that there were many reasons for not sealing off East Berlin and that they would hold good for the foreseeable future. The "foreseeable future" proved to be slightly less than six months long. "Such an action would mean cancellation without notice of the interzonal trade agreement." It did not but it should have. ". . . And would precipitate an international crisis of the first magnitude." It did that. "There would be major domestic disturbances in the East zone and particularly in East Berlin." There were not. There were several incidents of barn burning in the Soviet zone and there were several spectacular individual and group escapes and escape attempts into West Berlin. These have continued. But by and large East German resistance to the closing of the hatch was passive. Nothing remotely resembling a mass uprising occurred. Indeed, one gradually came by the impression that the majority of East Germans were experiencing something curiously like a sense of relief at the restoration of order, and the removal of the last possibility for unsettling decision and disruptive action.

But at the time I wrote the article it was clear to me that the policy of the Western Allies—insofar as they had one—in regard to East Germany was based on the expectation that the East German Communist regime would not be able to stabilize itself. The only reason the regime could not stabilize itself was the refugee flow. Thus Allied policy was ultimately based on the assumption that the refugee flow would continue virtually undiminished until such time as the Russians saw themselves forced to come to terms. Throughout the fifties and after, the West German government made frequent pious appeals to East Germans to stay put. But whenever the refugee flow diminished there was an undercurrent of alarm in the official expression of satisfaction, and whenever the refugee flow increased there was an undercurrent of satisfaction in the official expression of alarm. Khrushchev's Berlin ultimatum of 1958 was the first Soviet response to an East German situation that was rapidly becoming untenable. The Soviet's giving the Western Allies six months to clear out of Berlin was in reality a defensive reaction carefully disguised as a political power threat. It was, in fact, a desperate bluff. The bluff produced the ten-week mummery of the Foreign Ministers' Confernece at Geneva in 1959, during which the Russians mimed insistence on their phony maximum demands, and the equally phony Spirit of Camp David.

It was as a result of the double defeat in 1959—in negotiations as well as refugee stoppage—that the Russians realized the definite failure of Soviet policy in East Germany. At about the same time, the Allies were bound to realize that the initiative in the German question—by virtue of sheer accumulation of refugees (weighing East Germany's loss against West Germany's gain)—had passed into their hands. There was evidence that Allied leaders had become increasingly aware of their advantage. In striking contrast to Allied reluctance even to mention the subject of refugees at the Foreign Ministers' Conference in 1959 for fear of "provoking the Soviets," Harold Macmillan, the British prime minister, speaking at the United Nations in 1960, calmly recited the numbers of the East Germans who had gone West and added that "there is some lesson to be learned from these dry statistics." Less than a month later the British foreign minister, Lord Home, was quoted as saying that the Allies had no Berlin problem. "If the Soviets have a problem," he added, "then we are prepared to sit down and discuss it with them." The implication of this statement, I wrote then, is as clear as the truth it involves: West Berlin is not a holding action; East Germany is a holding action—and the Bear's grip is slipping. It is the Soviets and not the West who have a Berlin problem, within the context of their much larger East German problem. This is why the Soviet "free city" plan for West Berlin has never been spelled out: in the face of the realities of the German situation it is clear that no such plan would work. The West's main problem is to provide some way out for the Soviets with as little loss of face and as many guarantees of security as possible.

"The Disappearing Satellite" attracted a good deal of attention. The president of the United States read it and had the statistics and claims in it checked. But I did not know that or even suspect it until several years later (despite *The Reporter*'s claim that its most avid and careful readers were on Capitol Hill and in the White House). On the other hand, I was soon informed that the article—or rather its thesis—had made a great impression on Axel Springer. I was invited to have lunch with Springer and a group of his editors (among them my old friend Karl-Heinz Hagen) at Springer's estate on the Falkensteiner Ufer near Hamburg. The estate made a great impression on me—some forty acres of rolling, lawn-covered hillocks, now and then a grove of beech or elm trees, four white manor houses set spaciously apart from each other. One of these belonged to Springer's financial director, Karl Voss, the other three to Springer's two former wives (whom my editor-escort described as "queen mothers") and his then wife, Rosemarie, née Lorenz, a noted equestrienne and the daughter of SS Obergruppenführer Werner Lorenz. Springer's house was set on the forwardmost knoll commanding a superb panoramic view of the Elbe. When I entered the house, I was drawn to the enormous picture window—a glass wall overlooking an almost precipitous falling away of the lawn to the river—and I stood there transfixed by the grandiose sweep of the great river. Suddenly Axel Springer stood at my side and, gesturing at the view, said, "Don't be taken in, my dear George Bailey—this whole thing—everything you see here is a deception!" I looked at him inquiringly. "I mean," he said, "that life is not at all like this view here would make it seem. Life is ugly and dirty and vicious. This view is a complete deception!" This was said rapidly, impulsively, like a good many things Axel Springer says. It struck me as whimsical; I did not know what to make of it. But I was immediately asked to expound my theory of "the disappearing satellite" by Hagen, who had already ballyhooed it as "revolutionary" (umwerfend). By the time I had finished my recitation we were in the middle of lunch. There was no need in that company to belabor the question the thesis posed: what to do to exploit the initiative in the German question that now lay with the West as a result of the continuing refugee flow? Something had to be done and done quickly. It was clear to all present that the situation—precisely because it had continued unchanged for so long—could not possibly continue unchanged for very much longer. In the ensuing discussion of what sort of press campaign would best serve to bring home the urgency of the situation to Allied governments, we very soon came to grips with the question of whether the press was really able to exert any appreciable influence on government policy. The editors finally agreed that the press was indeed able to exert such influence but only at enormous financial expense. At this point Axel Springer put his hands to his head and exclaimed, "My God! If only I were a multi-*billionaire!*" When the laughter at last died down, I pondered what a change was here—from the apolitical journalistic gamester to the single-minded crusader who strove to bring his influence to bear on government policy. And this in less than four years.

But the evidences I so hopefully cited of Allied leaders' fixing the blame in the German problem where it belonged—with the Soviet leaders—quickly proved to be straws in the wind. Instead of the Allies' making something of the initiative that had come to them with the refugees, the Soviets correctly assessed Allied reluctance to run any substantial risk of war over Germany and acted on their assessment. Khrushchev read the riot act to a president only four months in office and presented him with an aide-mémoire renewing the threat of a separate peace treaty which would nullify all Allied rights in Berlin, automatically seal the borders, and stop the refugee flow. The Soviets published their aide-mémoire on June 10, 1961. There was a corresponding increase in the number of refugees. Beginning July 1 the flow became a flood, suddenly doubling and tripling. By the middle of July, East Germany was losing an average of a thousand people a day. It was an utterly grotesque situation. For years the East German regime had accused West Germany of carrying on a mass recruitment campaign among East German workers for the munitions industries of the Federal Republic. This claim was nothing more than a sop devised by East German leaders for themselves. Not even the party propagandists expected anyone to take the slogans about "slave traders" and "headhunters" seriously. Party boss Ulbricht explained away the refugee flow by stating publicly that a certain percentage of the population was made up of unreconstructed Nazis. The regime tried desperately to stop the flow by every means short of sealing off the mid-city sector boundary. Travel controls on the periphery of Greater Berlin were increased drastically. Administrative devices such as special stamps in identity documents permitting and restricting travel were employed. Dozens of show trials were held, including televised interrogations of "confessed" West German recruiting agents. As the refugee flood continued to mount, an emergency session of the People's Chamber in East Berlin was called. After an address by Deputy Premier Willy Stoph, who accused West German slave traders of kidnapping a four-month-old baby and demanding that the parents follow west by way of ransom, the Parliament gave the National Council carte blanche for whatever measures it considered necessary to counter "the recruitment program." But the most harried and harassed people in Germany in that fateful summer were the officials and personnel of West Berlin's sixteen refugee camps, all but one of them set up on an emergency basis to accommodate the victims of the panic flight from the "Democratic Republic." The appeal for doctors, nurses, and kitchen help issued by the Berlin Senate in early August was generously answered but the need continued as the refugee flow continued to increase. Ernst Lemmer, Adenauer's minister for all-German affairs, an elephantine, pathetically sincere politician (he was himself a refugee from the "Democratic Republic") was tireless in his efforts to make life easier in the camps. His appeals to the West Germans went unanswered: the long, deep digestive sleep of prosperity in the Rhineland, in the Pfalz, and in Bavaria continued undisturbed. As far as Axel Springer was concerned, he had the *Bild Zeitung,* Berlin's largest newspaper, issue a headline warning to the Communist police: "Do not forget," it ran, "that one day all Germans will be reunited—therefore conduct yourselves today so that you will be able to look your fellow countrymen in the face with a good conscience in the future."

At three-thirty in the morning of Sunday, August 13, I was awakened by a telephone call from my friend John Daly, who happened to be visiting Berlin. His message was short: "They have closed the sector boundary." I arrived at the sector boundary at four. It was already light and the morning was clear. Members of the People's police and East German troops had already strung barbed wire across Leipziger Strasse where it enters Potsdamer Platz from the east. To the left soldiers were sinking concrete pilings and stringing more barbed wire across them. Beyond, where the sector boundary runs through Ebert-Strasse to the Brandenburg Gate, People's police and firemen were ripping up a strip six feet wide in the middle of the street. A police captain in a plum-colored dress uniform was applying a pneumatic hammer to the pavement. With a cigarette in the corner of his mouth, he smiled as he worked. The rest of the city was still asleep and apparently serene. On the Western side, confronting the Communist military, a small knot of civilians, late revelers and early risers—four or five cameramen, as many journalists, one West Berlin policeman, a few gray-haired charwomen, two bar girls—stood watching in silence. Some of the women were crying. Some young people, dressed for a night on the town, walked or rode up in taxis to the Brandenburg Gate. A few hesitated and turned back, but others walked between the huge yellow columns into East Berlin, turning, before they disappeared, to wave back at us. "We shall never see them again," said a woman next to me.

By seven, the first phase of the sealing-off was completed. The twenty-five-mile sector boundary running north and south through the city was either barricaded, wired off, or manned by police and army troops. At ten o'clock two battalions of the East Berlin factory militia marched up Unter den Linden to the armory in Klara-Zetkin-Strasse, where they were issued rifles and machine guns. The middle-aged militiamen in sloppy brown overall uniforms with cloth-visored caps were immediately deployed to reinforce the Communist troops along the boundary line. By noon it was practically impossible for East Berliners to get within two blocks of the Gate. They were turned back by militiamen or police as soon as they identified themselves—but often not before a fairly lengthy argument. I wondered at the restraint of the East Berliners and the patient politeness of the East German police. West Berliners, West Germans, and foreigners were allowed to pass freely. By this time the decree of the East German government had been posted throughout East Berlin at the entrances of all the subway and surface train stations. The proclamation, which stated that thenceforth no East Berliner or East German would be allowed to enter West Berlin or West Germany (to protect them against West German "slave traders and recruiters"), was posted alongside a proclamation signed by the Warsaw Pact countries asking East Germany to take the necessary measures to secure its border in Berlin against the West.

The first dramatic reaction to the Communist coup came from Willy Brandt. Flying in from Nuremberg, where he had been electioneering for the chancellorship, Brandt arrived in Berlin at eleven in the morning and immediately went into conference with the three Western Allied commandants and the Berlin Senate. The mass of Berliners came alive to the situation in the early afternoon. By four o'clock half a million people crowded along the sector boundary. The main body of the crowd was on the west side of the Brandenburg Gate and extended back a good half mile, choking the gate's western approaches to all traffic. At first, strangely, it was a typical holiday crowd, diverted from Berlin's outlying lakes by the news that the sector boundary had suddenly become a curiosity. The result was the worst traffic jam in Berlin's history.

The first threats of violence came from the other side of the line. Some 500 East Berlin workers faced two platoons of the People's police before the Gate's north boundary at eleven o'clock and angrily demanded the right to pass. The officer in command finally threatened to open fire if they did not disperse. Later about 300 young West Berliners rushed the barbed wire fence just south of the Gate and trampled a thirty-yard section of it down before they ran up against a line of Communist soldiers with bayonets fixed and presented. This was the most serious incident of the day. Here, too, order was soon restored by intervention of the West Berlin police. In sharp contrast to the systematic, carefully timed measures of the Communists, Western reaction in the next few days was fitful, disjointed, and glaringly inadequate. On Monday the Brandenburg Gate was closed, and 53,000 Grenzgänger (border-crossers), who lived in East Berlin and worked in West Berlin, failed to appear for work. By noon the Communists had cut all telecommunications between East Germany, including East Berlin, and West Germany, including West Berlin. That evening, in a campaign speech in Regensburg, Konrad Adenauer made possibly the greatest blunder of his career. He attacked his opponent for the chancellorship both bitterly and personally, apparently forgetting that Brandt was also the embattled mayor of West Berlin. Public reaction in both West Berlin and West Germany was furious. On Tuesday the Communists began building the Wall, a cement block structure five to six feet high and two feet thick, all along the sector boundary. The building of the Wall seemed to have been prompted by the spectacular defection of an East German soldier in full uniform and equipment. In view of a dozen Western cameramen, the soldier sprinted across the line, hurdling the barbed wire entanglement. It was the picture of the year. Half an hour later, a group of East German workers with a mobile crane began putting the concrete blocks into place, walling off the street. Of course the blocks had been ready and waiting for some time.

Late Tuesday the Western Allied commandants of Berlin finally delivered a protest note to the Soviet garrison commander of East Berlin. The stilted, dry language of the note only produced dismay in West Berlin. On Wednesday morning Axel Springer's *Bild Zeitung* exploded in headlines three inches high: EAST ACTS, WEST DOES NOTHING. PRESIDENT KENNEDY KEEPS SILENT, MACMILLAN GOES HUNTING, AND ADENAUER INSULTS BRANDT. In the accompanying front-page editorial the chancellor was taken to task for putting the West German elections before the fate of his country. That afternoon Willy Brandt spoke before a mass demonstration of half a million Berliners. A large placard read: "Have we been betrayed by the West?" Brandt announced that he had written a personal letter to President Kennedy informing him, "Berlin expects not merely words but political action." Brandt ended his speech by saying that he had put all personal political animosities behind him and would wholeheartedly welcome the chancellor in Berlin as soon as possible. This was a reminder that Adenauer had still not come to Berlin or even announced his intention of coming. Instead the chancellor met with Soviet Ambassador Smirnov on Wednesday evening. The result of the meeting was an unfortunate communique containing Adenauer's assurance to Smirnov that "the Federal Republic is undertaking no steps to aggravate its relations with the Soviet Union." On Thursday, August 17, the Western Allies went through the formality of sending identical notes of protest to the Soviet Union. By this time the number of defectors fron the Communist troops guarding the sector boundary totaled more than fifty. On Friday the West German Parliament met in emergency session, but the three largest parties were unable to agree on a joint declaration of protest (a commentary that is the sadder for its being so typical). To Berliners, West Germany seemed farther away than ever. Late in the afternoon came the announcement that Vice-President Lyndon Johnson would arrive in Berlin on Saturday and that a 1,500-man battle group would be sent to reinforce the American garrison in Berlin. That evening Walter Ulbricht, the dictator of East Germany, celebrated his triumph in a television address. Grinning slyly, he informed the Germans that the sealing-off of East Berlin "had demonstrated to the world the actual power relationship in Germany." The entire action, he said, had caused less damage than a rock-'n'-roll session in a West Berlin dance hall. Then Ulbricht turned the knife in the wound: the Brandenburg Gate, he gloated, had become the symbol of Communist hegemony in Germany.

More than a million Berliners thronged the streets in a sporadic rainstorm to greet Lyndon Johnson on Saturday, August 19. His message—"To the survival and to the creative future of this city we Americans have pledged in effect what our ancestors pledged in forming the United States of America: 'Our lives, our fortunes and our sacred honor' "—deeply moved all who heard it. But somehow, the very pitch of the enthusiasm for Johnson's visit brought the realization that something was wrong. After long silence, this sudden, spectacular American demonstration of solidarity was surely welcomed. But West Berliners were not protesting and demanding action because they themselves feared being left in the lurch by their Allied protectors. The immediate and main reason for the West Berliners' protest was the sealing-off of East Berlin, the construction of the Wall running through the center of the city and cutting off East Berlin and East Germany from West Berlin. They were demanding for themselves and as proxies for the East Berliners the restoration of the integrity of their city. The American demonstration of solidarity was pointedly restricted to the West Berliners and conceded in effect that the East Berliners were "off limits." It degraded an insistence on principle to the status of an animal urge. As one Berliner put it, "We were fighting for self-determination, not self-preservation." It was true: the Four-Power Statute of Berlin was a guarantee that the German problem had not yet been decided; the abrogation of the Four-Power Statute, accomplished by sealing off East Berlin, was the signal that the Communists had decided the German problem unilaterally.

When I went to see Axel Springer, I found him in a towering rage. "I have just about all the evidence," he said; "I still lack only one element of it—that the sealing-off of East Berlin was a put-up job, that the Western Allies were in cahoots with the Russians to allow the building of this damned wall." Axel never found the missing link because it did not exist. There had been no "deal," not actually. But there had been the evolutionary development of an unspoken understanding between the Russians and the Western Allies via the way stations of the Soviet suppressions of the East German uprising in 1953 and the Hungarian Revolution in 1956 and the Western acceptance of same. The understanding was that the West would allow the Russians to put their house —their "legitimate sphere of interest"—in order as best they could; that is to say, in whichever way they saw fit. Not that this refinement of the "deal" helped matters any: the end result was the same. When Max Ascoli arrived in Berlin at the end of August, I took him to see Axel. "My son is in the army," Axel told him. "He frequently brings some of his NATO buddies home with him. The Englishman says he is an English soldier. The Frenchman says he is a French soldier. My son says he is a NATO soldier. Now, I suppose, for the sake of this alliance in which we have believed, we shall be asked to betray our sixteen million fellow Germans in the East—to condemn them to an existence without hope behind barbed wire. Could you blame Germans if they came to feel that they have been betrayed by the Allies?" There was a psychic extension of the Wall, separating far more than East Germans from West Germans, that became discernible only with the passing of the years. But when the Communists struck on August 13, Konrad Adenauer reacted like the chancellor of West Germany and returned to Bonn, the provisional whole capital of the halved country. His opponent in the then current West German election campaign reacted like the governing mayor he was and returned to Berlin, the halved traditional capital of the whole country. In this process, given the imposed scheme of things, Brandt gained and Adenauer lost. Because he returned immediately to Berlin and fought desperately for the residual German unity that was symbolized by Berlin, Brandt was on his way to becoming something like "Mr. Germany." In returning to Bonn, "a small town in Germany" that most Germans still associate with Beethoven, Adenauer found himself, in the eyes of many Germans, and for the first time in several decades, in the company of an old familiar ghost: Doctor Hans Dorten. People dredged up the almost forgotten epithet "Rhenish separatist."

The Wall in Berlin did not stop the refugee flow but it did progressively reduce it. From August 1961 to the end of 1964, more than 23,000 East Germans escaped to the West across all borders; nearly 3,500, including 433 uniformed guards, by way of the Berlin Wall. As escape became increasingly difficult and dangerous, escape attempts became more ingenious. The number of Sperrbrecher (barricade-breakers), as they came to be called—those who came over the Wall or ran the obstacle course of minefields and barbed wire dividing West and East Germany—slowly declined. In 1963 the total number of barricade-breakers was 3,692; in 1964 it was 3,155; in 1965 it was 2,943. By 1971 the annual total had been reduced to 847. But in the same year almost 6,000 East Germans fled to the West while vacationing or traveling on business in Eastern European countries. The propaganda value accruing to the West through increasingly spectacular escapes was nullified by the tawdriness and corruption that crept into the engineering of them. In general, the most spectacular and elaborate means of escape was the tunnel. Increasing security measures by the East necessitated longer and more costly tunnels; the cost of a tunnel one hundred meters or more long was likely to be at least $20,000. The tunnel diggers were therefore forced to abandon their amateur standing and turn to public sources, particularly the press, for money. This was in line with another main consideration, the publicizing of such operations as a means of bringing the plight of Berlin to world attention. The NBC tunnel, so called because the diggers sold the exclusive rights to the story to the National Broadcasting Company, which won the Emmy Award for 1962–1963 with its documentary of the escape, brought the diggers the necessary funds but also a good deal of scandal: there were charges and counter-charges among the various members of the tunnel team over apportion-ment of the money paid by the network. In the first two years after the Wall the diggers were widely hailed as "pumpernickel Pimpernels," humanitarians undergoing the ordeal of tunnel work and risking life and freedom to help their brothers in the Soviet zone. This favorable atmos-phere then radically changed.

A case history that demonstrates the development of the change in relations between escape helpers, officialdom, and the public was pro-vided by Wolfgang Fuchs, the best-known and most controversial tun-nel-team leader and exfiltration expert in West Berlin. Fuchs, then twenty-six, escaped with his wife and child to West Berlin in 1962 and stayed on to help his relatives and friends make their escape. Persistence in aiding escapees inevitably led to political involvement. To complicate matters Fuchs was an idealist. When Willy Brandt and the West Berlin Senate decided to commemorate the third anniversary of the Wall with an hour of silence (in order to minimize the danger of violent demonstra-tions), a great many Berliners took exception to the idea. Fuchs and his friends protested the Senate's decision by painting slogans on the west side of the Wall such as "Silence? Not Even for an Hour!" and "One Hour of All-German Sleep!" When they returned to the locations later the same day they witnessed a highly significant spectacle: West Berlin police were scrubbing the Wall clean. In a letter to Brandt, Fuchs pro-tested "the protection of the Wall from the West," citing several occa-sions when he and his friends had been prevented by West Berlin police from approaching the Wall and even from cutting an escape hole in the barbed wire, on the grounds that it would constitute "the willful destruc-tion of property, even if it was the property of the German Democratic Republic." Fuchs asked whether the West Berlin police had the legal right to hinder persons approaching the Wall with the intent to carry out propaganda actions or to render assistance to refugees.

In December 1961, less than four months after the Wall went up, and again in December 1962 the East German Communist regime of-fered the West Berlin Senate an arrangement that would provide West Berliners with passes to visit their relatives in East Berlin over Christ-mas. These offers were severally rejected by the West German government, the Allied commandants in Berlin, and the West Berlin Senate. On both occasions the West Berlin Senate rejected the establishment of East Berlin pass offices on West Berlin territory and refused to negotiate with the government of the German Democratic Republic (the Senate was in the habit of negotiating, when necessary, with the East Berlin magistrate). In 1963, however, the Senate accepted both conditions and the Christmas pass agreement was signed and carried out. The Berlin Christmas pass agreement was the turning point in German postwar history. The preparation of the public for this new departure had been started five months before. On July 15 in Tützing, West Germany, Egon Bahr made a speech. Its title, "Change Through Closer Relations," soon became a byword in Germany. It represented Bahr's and Willy Brandt's adaptation to the German problem of their conception of John F. Kennedy's New Frontier strategy of peace. The Tützing speech was the direct result of President Kennedy's speech at the American University the preceding month. Bahr defined the American strategy "by the formula that Communist rule should not be removed but reformed." Later Bahr added: "If it is correct, as Kennedy said, that the interests of the other side, too, have to be recognized and taken into consideration, then it is certainly impossible for the Soviet Union to have the zone (East Germany) snatched away for the purpose of strengthening the Western potential. The zone, with the consent of the Soviet Union, has to be transformed. If we could get that far, we would have advanced a great step toward reunification." Of course Bahr had to guard against the charge that this policy would involve the recognition of the East German regime. He did so in an interesting and revealing way: "The minister of the interior of the German Democratic Republic, on August 13, 1961, forbade the Allies stationed in Berlin to make further use of their right of entering the Eastern sector . . . by all means of access, and confined them to the one crossing point at today's Checkpoint Charlie. When the Allies heeded this instruction, no one contended that this was a recognition of the German Democratic Republic." For good measure Bahr mentioned one of the sorest points in the Berliners' attitude towards the Allies. "If today a refugee swims across the Spree (which forms part of the border between West Berlin and the zone) and is being shot at, or if a bus is caught in the slalom system and the people are being shot at, then crimes are being committed—or aren't they? But our police must not shoot back or do anything to prevent these crimes. And no one has dared say until now that this is the most brutal form of recognition." This bitter statement was not strictly true, but it was true enough. The West Berlin police guarding the borders were (and still are at this writing) under orders to provide covering fire for escaping refugees only if East German fire should strike West Berlin territory and endanger life there. Before the necessary conditions could be determined it was too often too late.

Thus Willy Brandt was confronted with the choice of siding with the commandants against the Berliners or siding with the Berliners against the commandants. The change in Brandt's attitude took place gradually over a two-year period. It derived from his steadily increasing stature as a politician of world repute as well as from his growing disillusionment with the Allies in Berlin. While he was the president's special representative in Berlin, Lucius Clay pointed out to me the anomaly of having a governing mayor of Berlin who was likewise a candidate for chancellor and a leader of a major political party, a man who toured the world and was received by heads of state everywhere only to return to Berlin to sit at the foot of a conference table and be called to account by three major generals. Before the Wall was a year old, Brandt and the Senate began to take matters more and more into their own hands. They sharply reduced consultation between the Senate and the Allied commandants and, for that matter, between the Senate and the West German representative in Berlin. Or they postponed consultation until issues became public and the onus of an eventual veto could be publicly fixed. As Egon Bahr put it, "Of course we consult with the Allies on all matters—whenever we consider that matters are ready for discussion." As a result, neither the commandants nor the West German government knew in advance what Brandt would do in the final stage of the negotiations of the Christmas pass agreement. In effect, Brandt presented the Allies—and the West German government—with a fait accompli. The initiative in the German problem had passed into the hands of the Social Democrats in Berlin.

Meanwhile, back in the tunnel, Fuchs was visited by a Senate official and told to postpone completion of the tunnel until January 5 so as not to prejudice the pass negotiations then in progress. Fuchs claimed later that he was threatened with expulsion from Berlin and with closure of the tunnel if he refused to comply. Moreover, he claimed that the Senate's intervention a few days before the final breakthrough all but ruined the operation. The tunnel was being built to issue into a coal yard in East Berlin. The main consideration was that the coal yard would remain vacant and unattended over the Christmas and New Year's holidays, which ended January 2. To delay until January 5 was to risk immediate detection. Fuchs was forced to delay. Only three of the sixty East Germans alerted and waiting managed to escape through the tunnel before it was detected. In his protest Fuchs contended that Senate intervention in this case was tantamount to the denial of the right of asylum. To be sure, free movement within Greater Berlin is guaranteed by the Four-Power Statute as well as the city's constitution; but in signing the pass agreement the Senate made itself a party to an instrument predicating the abrogation of the Four-Power Statute and the right of freedom of movement. Then, too, for the East German regime the pass agreement was the first step toward its goal of establishing the Wall as a legally recognized state border.

More important than the juridical implications of the original and subsequent pass agreements was the psychological effect, particularly among the youth of the city, of setting an example and standard of general conduct in the Berlin situation. By 1965 the authorities had become alarmed over the development of leftist and outright Communist influences in the student organizations of the Free University of Berlin. This development was fostered by the dearth of East German students since the Wall—a decrease from forty percent to eight percent in four years—and by a strong increase in West German students who came (and still come) to Berlin to avoid being drafted into the West German army (West Berliners are exempt from the draft). But it was basically determined by the pass agreement itself, the spirit of which was largely if not wholly incompatible with the spirit of rebellion against totalitarianism in which the Free University was founded. When the mayor and the Senate reached an official program of accommodaion with the Communists—the policy of small steps—public officials and organizations could do little but follow suit. So ran the argument. The result was a society that was no longer geared or conditioned to support a resistance movement.

The Senate's new policy of increasingly close control of escape efforts received strong impetus from the public outcry that followed the completion of Fuchs's "Tunnel 57." The breakthrough of Tunnel 57 into East Berlin occurred early in October 1964, just before the fifteenth anniversary of the East German regime. Fifty-seven refugees were brought out through the tunnel before it was discovered by East German police, one of whom was shot dead in the ensuing gunfight with the diggers guarding the tunnel's eastern end. The sergeant had to be given a state funeral, and a hate campaign was mounted against the West Berlin "gangsters and murderers." The regime's scheduled anniversary celebrations were ruined. The Tunnel 57 incident was also prejudiced by the scope and nature of the financial transactions surrounding it. Three enterprising German journalists obligingly relieved the diggers of the time-consuming burden of public relations. Germany's largest illustrated magazine, *Der Stern*, contracted to pay $5,000 for the exclusive rights to the story. Three-quarters of this sum was paid by way of advances and options; the fourth quarter was never paid because *Der Stern*'s editors recoiled from the adverse publicity attendant on the policeman's death. *Paris Match* paid $2,000 for the French rights, and *Life* $4,000 for the American rights. The *London Daily Mail* bought the British rights for $1,400, and the Associated Press and the United Press International paid $370 apiece for several pictures of refugees crawling through the tunnel. Finally the digger who fired the shots at the mouth of the tunnel sold his story (over the protests of Fuchs and the tunnel team) to the German illustrated magazine *Quick*, the chief competitor of *Der Stern*, under the title "I Killed the Vopo." There followed a sordid squabble over alleged breaches of contract for coverage rights among various journalists involved in the transactions.

All this drew public charges of flagrant venality, not against the journalists, some of whom profited heavily as middlemen, but against the tunnel diggers in particular and all "commercial escape helpers" in general. Indeed, there was a striking similarity in the treatment of "the dirty business" of escape assistance by the East German Communist press and an important segment of the West German–West Berlin press. A preliminary investigation on the charge of manslaughter was initiated against "Unknown" by the West Berlin attorney general's office. A good deal of sympathy was generated for the dead East German policeman, while the tunnel diggers were characterized as armed thugs by two West German publications, *Die Zeitung* of Stuttgart and *Die Zeit* of Hamburg. These and like charges led to widespread public discussion of the legal nature of the Wall itself. Such discussions usually ended with agreement that the Wall was, in effect, a no-man's land, a strip outside the law separating two essentially opposite and opposing political and juridical systems. The contradictions are nowhere more striking than in the case of the refugees, who under East German law are not refugees but fugitives. When the East Germans made "flight from the Republic" a serious offense in 1957, attempted escape was raised from a misdemeanor for which the culprit was often released with a warning, to a felony for which the maximum penalty is three years' imprisonment, first offenders usually receiving an eighteen-month sentence. At the same time, escape assistance was also made illegal and punishable by a maximum sentence of ten years' imprisonment. The Communists frequently attempt to reinforce this concept by trying to show that individual refugees are guilty of common crimes and are fugitives from justice. There are no refugees from West to East because, among other things, there is no federal law prohibiting change of residence from West to East Germany. There is a federal law against "deprivation of freedom," which covers preventing a refugee from carrying out his intention to flee.

The essential conflict of East and West German laws governing escapes is frequently illustrated. In October 1965 a young East German woman who had stowed away on an East German barge jumped into the canal while the barge traversed West Berlin. Before she managed to do so the barge captain and his wife and the tug captain had tried to detain her forcibly. The West Berlin police boarded the craft and took all three East Germans into custody on the charge of "deprivation of freedom." They were soon released, the West Berlin authorities recognizing that had the East Germans not tried to stop the woman they would have been liable to prosecution under East German law for aiding and abetting "flight from the Republic." It is not easy to imagine a more perfect dilemma. In October 1971 an East German passenger on an East German ship that had put in at Hamburg escaped by jumping overboard onto the pier. When the ship's captain refused to allow the escapee's wife and child to follow him, he went to the harbor police, who boarded the East German ship and brought the refugee's wife and child ashore, the East German crew wisely offering no resistance. In these and many other instances an act of heroism in West Germany is a crime in East Germany and vice versa.

But discussions of the Wall usually ended with a condemnation of violence in the service of any cause. This conclusion generally militated against the escape helpers, who actively (and literally) undermined the status quo, using force if necessary, rather than against the East German border police who were charged with protecting the status quo, by force if necessary. The judicial investigation of the charge of manslaughter in the Tunnel 57 case was blocked for lack of evidence: the East German authorities refused to provide the West Berlin Justice Department with the results of the autopsy on the slain policeman, a departure from established practice that suggested that the sergeant might have been accidentally killed by East German machine gun fire rather than by the five pistol shots fired by the tunnel digger.

The most persistent charge leveled against the tunnel diggers was that they exacted exorbitant advance fees from the refugees, allegedly as much as $1,500 to $2,000 a head. *Die Zeitung* claimed that the diggers had received at least $80,000 from the refugees of Tunnel 57. These and like charges were vehemently denied by Fuchs and his colleagues, who obtained affidavits from all the refugees of Tunnel 57 to the effect that no payment whatever had been asked or made. Fuchs brought libel suits against both *Die Zeitung* and *Die Zeit* and won a half retraction from the latter. In the end, Fuchs was persuaded by his lawyer to drop his suit for lack of funds and public interest. *Die Zeitung*, a fly-by-night publication only recently started, folded shortly thereafter. After the Tunnel 57 incident the West Berlin police watched Fuchs closely and generally frustrated his attempts to mount operations, often alleging Allied disapproval. Even so Fuchs managed to engineer the escape of a young man from an East German graveyard abutting the Wall. The would-be refugee, who had managed by forged documents to obtain permission to visit the grave of an ostensible relative, was to be hoisted over the Wall by a mobile construction crane Fuchs had hired for the purpose. However, the West Berlin police ordered the owner to remove the crane, saying that its presence near the Wall was in violation of a traffic ordinance. Fuchs finally brought out the refugee by substituting a truck and ladder and using the Wall itself as a fulcrum—not for nothing is his name Fuchs (fox). The entire operation lasted ten seconds and was photographed and published in *Der Stern*. It was also covered by a TV newsreel team. In three years Fuchs brought out about 150 refugees, built tunnels, three of which were successful, and mounted a wide variety of small operations involving one or two refugees at a time.

But Fuchs was a throwback, a Social Democrat of the Ernst Reuter school, who believed, as the late mayor of West Berlin had, that Berlin was a Western asset, "a harpoon in the Communist whale." An engraver by trade and agitator by nature, he became obsessed by the idea of making the Wall the overriding issue in German political life. In breaching the Wall he displayed considerable brilliance as a tactician with a gift for improvisation. His answer to the cement-lined retaining ditch, ten feet deep and fifteen feet wide, which the Communists began building around West Berlin in 1965 and completed in 1970, was that the project was as stupid as the Maginot Line. "The more complicated the Wall becomes," said Fuchs, "the more opportunities for escape it will offer." This was a political pronouncement, not a tactical assessment. It presupposed both the expansion and intensification of escape assistance and hence, ultimately, the reactivation of Reuter's anti-Communist crusade. Fuchs's career as an escape helper was finished long before the completion of the Communists' retaining ditch. He is now a pharmacy owner in one of the boroughs of West Berlin. Still, he had his moments of glory. One month after the completion of Tunnel 57, Fuchs and his wife were invited by the German-Italian Friendship Society to make a three-week lecture tour of Italy where he was feted as a hero. The next year he repeated the tour, all expenses being paid by the Federal Press Office in Bonn, that is, with the approval of the Christian Democratic government. It was significant that the great bulk of general support for Fuchs and his group came from conservative elements in Berlin: two-thirds of the funds needed to build Tunnel 57 came from the Berlin headquarters of the opposition Christian Democratic Union; the ruling Social Democratic party's contribution was two shovels. Fuchs insisted passionately that Germans must not passively accept Communist tyranny as they once accepted fascist tyranny: "We would be making the same mistake our fathers made—despite the warning of their example." But the left's interpretation was exactly opposite. Peter Fechter, a young East German would-be refugee who was shot by Communist guards and bled to death in the no-man's land along the Wall in 1962 and whose death sparked the first anti-American riot in West Berlin, was characterized in a West Berlin cabaret as a neo-Nazi martyr because his death, allegedly, was seized upon "as a nationalist fetish."

The Wall put the East German regime (and behind it the Soviet Union) into a position to blackmail the Berlin Senate and with it, by logical progression, the West Germany government. The effectiveness of the blackmail was increased by the fact that the division of a city, the most highly developed sociological organism of which civilization is capable, is a much more brutal thing than the division of a country. Germany suffers both. The Wall forced the pass agreement. The pass agreement lent the Wall a quasi legitimacy and thus rendered it doubly provocative, an incitement at once to acceptance and rebellion, splitting the West Berlin–West German body politic and public, and driving the two halves toward opposite extremes. On the one hand, in response to increasing security measures along the Wall, exfiltration attempts necessarily took on the nature of paramilitary operations; on the other, local official response was to cordon off the Wall from the West in compliance with the Senate's policy of negotiated and controlled transit. The East German regime (and the Soviet Union) sought to play off the two extremes of Western response against each other. In so doing, it displayed a venality peculiar to itself, ransoming captured escape agents (among other political prisoners) for political, economic, and even diplomatic gains—as when it released two Swiss nationals in return for entry permits for East German delegates to attend the Geneva conference on nonproliferation of nuclear weapons in 1965.

The history of the ransoming of political prisoners by the East German regime began in 1958 when the Ministry of All-German Affairs in Bonn agreed to prorate economic contributions at an average of $10,000 in luxury goods (coffee, chocolate, tobacco, etc.) per head. The volume of exchange increased sharply after the construction of the Wall. The regime repeatedly stipulated and was often promised, primarily by the then vice-chancellor and minister of all-German affairs, Erich Mende, who broke precedent by meeting with the East German negotiator personally, that the transaction would be kept secret. However, the Berlin newspaper *Tagesspiegel* broke the story in October 1964 when the East Germans tried to make a particularly large exchange within the scope of the much-publicized amnesty of 10,000 prisoners, who incidentally were desperately needed for the labor force. The story had, of course, long since been known to journalists through returnees from the East, even though all of these had been thoroughly indoctrinated by both East and West German officials that divulgence would seal the fate of those political prisoners still in Eastern custody. Perhaps as much as seventy-five million dollars has been paid out by the Bonn government to the East German regime for this purpose. There is no telling how much has been paid by nongovernmental organizations and private individuals.

The rationale of both parties to the transaction is a study in itself. The East German regime acts for economic reasons, for immediate political gain, to relieve congestion in its prisons and to increase the range of its official contacts with the Federal Republic. The Federal Republic indulges in the practice for obvious humanitarian reasons, out of a nouveau riche sense of guilt ("We have so much money—to what better use could we put it?"), and in the calculation that the release of prisoners on a straight commercial basis will discredit the regime in the eyes of its followers. A more abstract consideration is what is widely referred to as "the national concern," the conviction that in the face of Allied noninvolvement, an increased range of official contacts for a humanitarian purpose is the best possible substitution for reunification.

The transactions are initiated by means of lists, one containing the names of those whose release the West is especially interested in obtaining, the other containing the names of those the East is most willing to release. A composite list is then negotiated. The results of this method have of course never been wholly satisfactory. The East has never fully complied with the agreed list. It has nevertheless made a number of mistakes in its selection of "releasable" prisoners, one of whom gave his story to *Die Zeit*. A former official in the East German Ministry of Justice, he had gone to the prison in Bautzen to investigate charges that prisoners had been sentenced without due process of law. When he discovered that the charges were true and said so, he himself was sentenced (without due process) and had spent fourteen years in Bautzen at the time of his release. Individuals seeking the release of relatives or friends are blackmailed into silence with the usual threat of heavier sentences for other hostages. On the other hand, there is no doubt that harsh sentences are deliberately imposed in order to increase the amount of the ransom money. Both private and official payers of ransom money play their parts with clenched teeth. But they continue to pay. The effect of these transactions on East German prisoners who are released on the understanding that they will remain in East Germany is interesting. Out of resignation, many of them and their relatives and friends come to accept the regime on its own terms. Their release by purchase then often awakens them to the realization that the regime is not even consistent within its own terms. In most such cases resistance is then reborn with a vengeance. This is a main element in the formula for defection. There are other elements. Why does an ideological regime stoop to the sale of political prisoners? The answer: because of the ideology, one of the premises of which is that capitalistic societies and their governments are by nature rotten to the core with corruption. Since capitalists' money stinks anyway, the Communists have no compunction in taking it from them. Besides the Communists need the money.

The one fairly sure method of escape that remains involves either stealing or obtaining by ruse the passports of visitors to East Germany, leaving the hapless victims to report their plight to the East German authorities and take the consequences. The East Germans are in a genuine dilemma here since it is often difficult to distinguish between mere victimization and active participation in an escape scheme. In 1965 there were 155 Germans and foreign nationals (most of them university students) from West Berlin under sentence or awaiting trial as escape helpers in East Germany. Easily the most elaborate case of entrapment to date was that of a young refugee from East Germany who settled in Hamburg, courted a young lady, and, after their engagement had been announced, persuaded her to accompany him on a visit to East Berlin. Once there he took her passport on some pretext and disappeared. He then brought out his East German wife with his "fiancée's" passport. He had spent two months in selecting a candidate who fitted his wife's description so as to pass muster at the exit control point. Indeed, in the ensuing trial in Hamburg, it developed that the victim was his second, more careful choice. Several months earlier he had entered East Berlin with another candidate only to discover at the last moment that her eyes were the wrong color. Rather than risk discovery, he returned with his "fiancée" to Hamburg, broke with her, and started again.

T HE STATE DEPARTMENT OF THE UNITED STATES coined a phrase some twenty years ago and has been minting it ever since: "We can't be more German than the Germans." The truth is we, the guardians, have to be, we can't help but be, we couldn't possibly be any less German than the Germans because the "Germans" aren't Germans. We have had to take their place. In 1961 I was at work on a book about Germany when the Wall went up. I never finished the book: the Wall ruined my concept. But I wrote a memorable (to me) beginning of the first chapter:

> The great complicating factor of the German Problem is the nonexistence of Germany. There is no Germany. There is no "Germany." There are no "Germanies." There is a German Federal Republic consisting of the combined American, British, and French zones of occupation, a Soviet zone of occupation called by Communists the "German Democratic Republic," a city of Greater Berlin (a creation of the still not entirely defunct Four-Power Statute), a city of West Berlin, and a city of East Berlin.
>
> The Third German Reich ceased to exist with the capitulation of the Doenitz government on May 11, 1945. Since then there has been no German government. These are simple statements of fact. But the nonexistence of Germany for the last sixteen years has had ramifying consequences that are largely unknown or unnoticed. The remembrance of the Third Reich, or rather the remembrance of what the Third Reich was popularly thought to be, carried over and applied to the myth of the continuing existence of Germany, has generated a complex of misapprehensions, exaggerations, and other distortions that has obscured the reality of the vacuum.

At the time I wrote this I did not realize that there had never been a Germany—if one excepts (as one should in justice to everybody, including Adolf) the phantasmagoria of the Third Reich.

The Germans have been wandering around in an inner diaspora for centuries, condemned to a spiritual exile imposed by the absence of political (and cultural) unity. Their "national" dispossession, like that of the children of Israel, made the dream stronger than reality. "The highest form of religion," wrote Ernst Arndt, is to love the fatherland more passionately than law and prince, father and mother, wife and child." This outburst has been compared, with good reason, to the implacability of an Old Testament prophet. The poet Novalis hailed German nationality as "genuinely Roman"—a comparison that John F. Kennedy repeated in 1963 in Berlin. "The instinctive policy and tendency of universalism of the Romans also inheres in the German people," wrote Novalis. But the more telling comparison is with the people of Israel, the chosen people whose history, according to the Scriptures of the Old Testament, God has furthered, caused, and governed toward their salvation as a model for all peoples. The divine election of the Jews has seldom been dismissed as mere romanticism. In the same vein it is frivolous so to brand the solemnly assumed obligation of the Roman-German emperors to bring order to the Western world as the viceroys of Christ. The explanation usually offered by historians, namely that the German emperors crowned in Rome never dreamed that their sacred mission could be turned to a power-political purpose, is surely unhistorical. The most significant of the titles—itself an obligation—of the Holy Roman Emperor was Mehrer des Reichs (Augmenter of the Reich). That this pledge to augment the wealth of the Reich was understood to apply to spiritual values rather than earthly goods is implausible. The Roman-German emperors tried hard to multiply the material wealth of the Reich on a largely if not exclusively power-political basis. It was when they had unmistakably failed that romanticism came in (I do not say "German romanticism" because romanticism is not a German patent). "Germany," continues Novalis, "is making a slow but sure progress in advance of the other European peoples. While the others are occupied with wars, speculation, and partisan spirit, the German is educating himself with all possible industry to be the contemporary of a higher epoch of culture and this progress will certainly give him a great predominance over the others in the course of time." As with the Israelis, the spiritual claim of the Germans (the claim to spiritual superiority) grew out of the failure to make good the material, political claim. "The sacred air-cities of hope" replaced "the mean clay hamlets of reality." The greater the discrepancy grew, the more fervently did the Germans cling to the "impossible dream" of the sacrum imperium, the Reich. It was this (now as then) ineradicable discrepancy which guaranteed the continuity of the illusion. It was not just the inherent hopelessness of trying to nationalize a supranational entity. The German tribes were never really united among themselves and never really wanted to be. Along with the passion for petty regionalism (in German "local patriotism") goes the messianic drive (Drang) for universality, for cosmopolitanism. "His thoughts," wrote Nietzsche of Wagner, "like those of every good and great German, are more than German [überdeutsch], and the language of his art speaks not to peoples but to humanity." But being more than German it is more than ever German.

Napoleon had no very clear idea of what he was doing when he destroyed the Holy Roman Empire of the German Nation. For it was only then that the European dimensions of the German problem began to emerge. The sacrum imperium had held Europe together for almost a thousand years. When Napoleon divided Germany between the Rhine bound to the west and Prussia and Austria to the east, he opened the way for the North-South division sixty years later between Prussia and Austria. (Just as the division of the Reich between Protestant North and Catholic South as a result of the Thirty Years War opened the way for the French invasion and annexation of one hundred miles of the west bank of the Rhine. France could always turn the flank of one German power by leagueing with the other.) Worse still, the destruction of the Reich exposed and drew attention to what was in it: the Germans. When the Allied powers began to pick up the pieces at the Congress of Vienna, they were immediately confounded by Arndt's question—"What is the German's fatherland?" Metternich was willing to concede that Italy was a geographical concept. But the "German people" (let alone "Germany"), he said, was an abstract concept. He insisted that not unity but plurality was the characteristic feature of the Germans, with which they had been endowed by nature and confirmed by history. "The patriotism of the Germans has various purposes," he wrote. "There are in the common fatherland, since its emergence, separate ethnic voices. Provincial patriotism is closest to the heart of the German citizen; he seizes it with his infant hands when he leaves the cradle, and thirty generations have given him no reason not to honor it as the most natural and most fitting trait, for the Brandenburger like the Austrian, the Bavarian like the Hessian are at the same time Germans." Metternich added that no Bavarian desired to be an Austrian, no Austrian desired to be a Prussian, no Prussian a Bavarian, no Bavarian a Württemberger and no one in all the German marches desired to be a Prussian if he didn't already happen to be one.

In 1789, the year of the French Revolution, the beginning of the end of the Holy Roman Empire of the German Nation, the Reich consisted of 1,789 separate political and administrative units, all of them "reichs-unmittelbar," that is, subject to the emperor alone and hence independent. The Reich, like the German Federation that followed it, was a crazy quilt of unequal and disconnected geographical patches. It consisted of the Austrian Empire, the great kingdom of Prussia, the smaller kingdoms of Bavaria, Saxony, Hannover and Württemberg, the electoral principality of Hesse, the grand duchies of Baden, Hesse-Darmstadt, Luxembourg, Mecklenburg-Schwerin, Mecklenburg-Strelitz, Sachsen-Weimar-Eisenach (where Goethe was privy councillor), and Oldenburg, the duchies of Holstein-Lauenburg, Braunschweig, Nassau, Sachsen-Gotha-Altenburg, Sachsen-Coburg-Saalfeld, Sachsen-Meiningen, Sachsen-Hildburghausen, Anhalt-Dessau, Anhalt-Bernburg, and Anhalt-Köthen, the principalities of Schwarzburg-Sondershausen, Schwarzburg-Rudolstadt, Hohenzollern-Hechingen, Hohenzollern-Sigmaringen, Liechtenstein, Waldeck, Reuss-Greiz, Reuss-Schleiz, Reuss-Ebersdorf, Reuss-Lobenstein, Lippe, and Schaumburg-Lippe, the landgraviate Homburg, and the city-states of Hamburg, Bremen, Lübeck, and Frankfurt. The Holy Roman Empire of the German Nation was, without being understood as such, the centerpiece, the linchpin of the European comity of nations. It was not merely after the disintegration of the Reich that Germany's neighbors intervened in German affairs to protect their own interests by securing a sort of right of codetermination. As Heinrich von Treitschke put it, all the powerful princes of the hemisphere belonged to the German Reich either as members of the Imperial Diet (Reichstag) or as guarantors of the Emperor's Peace. So it was in large part and for some time with the German Federation. Until 1837 the king of England was also the king of Hannover; until 1864 the king of Denmark was the duke of Holstein and Lauenburg; until 1866 the king of the Netherlands was the grand duke of Luxembourg. Germany has always been the reflection of her neighbor nations and their policies.

Centuries before the destruction of the Reich and its partial replacement by Napoleon's Rhine Federation, most of the dinky duchies and petty principalities that made up the larger part of the Reich (not only those along the Rhine) with their miniature replicas of Versailles, were suborned and subsidized as a matter of policy by the French. Most of the German "princes" were in French pay and had been for generations. Notoriously destitute, they could not have survived without the French subsidies—not in the fashion to which they had become accustomed by means of the French subsidies. It was in the interests of all of Germany's neighbors to foster the particularism that preserved Germany as a cloud-cuckoo-land abstraction, an Arabia felix in the middle of Europe, a composite reality made up of 1,789 carefully cultivated and jealously defended illusions. Within the Reich even the most diminutive princeling was equal to the most powerful king in his direct relationship to the emperor, to whom alone all "sovereigns" owed allegiance. The Reich was a mosaic of "sovereign" fragments held fast in the magnetic field of the ecumenical idea. Within this immobile system the magnitude of the feat of the great elector of Brandenburg becomes clear: defying the magnetic field, he managed to transform his princely coronet into a king's crown, by expanding the principality of Brandenburg into the kingdom of Prussia. The forcible aggrandizement of Frederick the Great inspired the rulers of rump realms to emulation. Within the confines of a few hundred acres, benevolent despotism took on an antic air, character became caricature, and what had been silly became ludicrous or worse. In attempting to apply modern tax reforms and a variety of philanthropic schemes, many a shortsighted absolute monarch of all he surveyed made life miserable for his subjects. In Oettingen-Oettingen the directory (government) was required to provide detailed reports (accompanied by notarized expert opinions) on the "name, breed, use and external appearance" of every dog in the principality.

Naturally, the particularist princes preferred to kiss the shoe of a foreigner rather than willingly subordinate themselves to a German commonalty. Their fierce independence was the corollary of their weakness. Very few of the princes had anything in the most general nature of an army, standing or otherwise disposed. Goethe describes the men-at-arms of Duke Karl August of Sachsen-Weimar-Eisenach (one of the larger grand duchies) as numbering fourteen hussars who were employed largely as couriers, aides-de-camp, hunting companions, and menials. Their number was restricted by the duke's perennial financial straits. Thus the great majority of German princes were obliged to seek support —or at least protection—wherever they could find it and still maintain the trappings of independence, that is, discretionary powers in internal affairs. It was this condition that dictated defiance at home and subservience abroad: a foreign prince was interested only in compliance with his foreign policy, leaving the princeling a free hand at home. Subordination to a German commonalty, on the other hand, would tie the princeling's hands at home, reduce his function to the ceremonial, and delimit his identity to his title. The German princelings, particularly those situated on the periphery of the Reich, were sitting ducks for Germany's powerful neighbors.

Treitschke is merely stating the obvious when he notes that Napoleon's German policy was only a grandiose development of the old French statecraft which had constantly striven for a protectorate over the small German states ever since Henry II. And yet there was and is an outwardness attending the tradition of foreign domination in Germany. In Düsseldorf even today, Napoleon's jackanapes youngest brother, Jerome, the sometime king of Westphalia, is held in a sort of indulgent reverence-cum-nostalgia. Toward the end of the last century, Hannoverians still clung to the memory of their British-German kings. Here is an outburst of Julia Schraade, an erotic Wilhelmian belle whose passionate nature did not work itself out entirely in her almost indiscriminate love affairs: she wrote "poetry," as so many Germans did and do, and she was a typical particularist patriot:

> May their god go up in smoke!
> Prussians are as bad as Russians!
> He who thrashed us stroke on stroke
> To make Prussia safe for Prussians,
>
> There he sits in peace and plenty:
> Prussia's Iron Chancellor
> Who, so far from penitent, he
> Smote poor Hannover the more.
>
> Bismarck! So they call this hellhound:
> What a fate has caught us here!
> Brought us bondage, kept us spellbound,
> Swallowed us—and belched for cheer!

The Hannoverian connection with England was of vast importance in German history, influencing the course of German affairs at various removes and in devious ways. Frederick the Great's disdain of the Reich and "Germany"—in contrast to his father's inborn and irreducible loyalty to the emperor—was largely conditioned by the fact that he was the grandson of the king of England: his mother was Sophie Dorothee of Hannover, daughter of George I of England. For some ten years Frederick was officially engaged to the Princess Royal, Amalia, of England, and his sister betrothed to the Prince of Wales in a double marriage contract. This ambitious project was finally thwarted by agents of the emperor (Grumkow, the Prussian king's first minister, and Seckendorf, Austrian ambassador to the Prussian court). The Austrians knew what they were about: had the double marriage project succeeded and proved fruitful, the next king of England would have been half-Prussian while the next king of Prussia would have been more than half-English. Moreover, the two great Protestant kingdoms in the world would have been united by ramifying blood ties. Frederick's genealogy and religious persuasion bode ill enough for the empire as it was.

Germany's radial geographic susceptibility was complemented by foreign political emphyteusis at all points of the compass. Nowhere is the multiracial emphyteusis that characterizes Germany more conspicuous than in Prussia. Here there has been an intermingling of racial strains, especially between Germans and Poles, but also between Wends (a small Slavic tribe that settled in an area some fifty miles southeast of Berlin in the ninth century) and more than ten thousand Huguenots who found refuge in Prussia after the revocation of the Edict of Nantes. A few years later (1728) several thousand Protestants from the Salzkammergut in Austria were allowed to emigrate to Prussia. In Farther Pomerania (bordering the Baltic Sea east of the Oder estuary) the landed nobility was largely made up of Flemish settlers brought in when the area was a duchy. There was a sequence of linguistic overlaps: before Prussia partitioned Poland, Poland partitioned Prussia—in 1632, when Prussia was little more than a geographic embryo. The blend was there to begin with and was reinforced steadily both ways, inward into Prussia and outward into Poland. As a result, until the Civil Code of the Empire was enacted in 1890, the Reich was a welter of foreign administrative and juridical systems. In the western provinces and in the western and southern states generally, the Code Napoléon still applied; the Austrian Code of 1811 applied to portions of Bavaria; Saxony had a code of its own; in Prussian Pomerania there were still relics of Swedish law. In addition many of the minor territories and the city republics had legal and judicial systems of their own.

I must admit that I am partial to the Prussians. The German-Celtic combination with the Polish admixture I find physically and psychically attractive: the Slavic cast is delightful mixed with a solid German base. Also the genius of the place—the plains that stretch from Berlin eastward through East Prussia and beyond the flatland lakes and the shimmering birch trees—has made its imprint on the character of the people. There is the bracing roughness and readiness and urgent humor of the pioneer and the breadth of view of the plainsman. "The farther east you go," said Count von Flemming, "the larger the schnapps glasses get and the smaller the washbasins. When you get so far that both are approximately the same size then you're right on—that's my home." East Prussians will seize any opportunity that presents itself to celebrate with food and drink. There were, as always in Germany but more so, a wealth of official holidays in addition to the many birthdays of large families. In East Prussia large families were the rule: ten and even twelve children were not uncommon. There were also the church holidays, meaningfully called "feast days" or days of celebration. On the first day of Christmas, close relatives were invited; on the second day of Christmas, friends; on the third day of Christmas, distant relatives. Too, the East Prussians make as much use of wakes for the dead and christenings for the newborn as the Irish do. However a man dies, so the saying goes, be he suicide, accident victim, or the prey of old age, he will be washed to the shores of the great beyond on waves of alcohol. They don't call themselves East Prussians "because nobody really knows what an East Prussian actually is." Instead they call themselves Masurians, Oberlanders, Königsbergers, and Samlanders. They could say the same thing about East Prussia: nobody knows what East Prussia is but all "East Prussians" remember where it was. The most important thing about East Prussians is that they are no longer where East Prussia was. East Prussia is a fading vision, it was the fata morgana followed by the Order of Teutonic Knights. These were the quintessential representatives of the Holy Roman Empire of the German Nation, the products of the perfect fusion of religious zeal and military valor, the black Maltese cross on the white tunic, the classic practitioners of the church militant—"Onward Christian Soldiers"— with the Holy Book in one hand and the long sword in the other.

This is the German Problem: what, where, and when is, was, or will be Germany? "Germany" was never more or less what it should have been; it was always less or more than it should have been. The "Germans" have always been more than a nation and therefore always less than one. They were, in fact, many nations and tribes, but the whole was always less than the sum of its parts. At the time of the völkerwanderung (the mass movement of Germanic and other peoples to the west and south of Europe in the fourth and fifth centuries) the various tribes did not even have a common name. And yet there was a kind of cloudy identity that attached to anyone who crossed the Rhine westward in the first centuries of the Christian era. But often enough these were Celts and others fleeing before the oncoming Germans. Until World War II German scholars were in the habit of designating any tribe or tribal leader defeated in battle by the Romans as "Celtic" and any who defeated the Romans as "Germanic."

Identity has always been the main aspect of the German Problem. The Germans have shown a remarkable lack of the sense of identity: they have fought each other in full enmity down the ages. They have banded together with foreigners against other German tribes as often as they have allied themselves against foreigners: Germans have always been more than willing to fight Germans. They have never been united in the sense that the classic nation-states of Europe were and remain united. Probably the greatest lie ever told by a German was Bismarck's statement at the foundation ceremony of the Wilhelmian Reich: "The German people, united in its tribes. . . ." Of the three original German tribes, the Franks, the Saxons, and the Bavarians, the Franks went too far too fast. Those who went too far west became French, those who went too far south became Italians (that is *northern* Italians), those who went too far southwest became Spaniards. A few centuries later some of the Saxons and their outlying cousins went northwest overseas and became English. Those who stayed in the heartland of Europe, between the Alps and the North Sea, but gradually moving beyond the Rhine and the Elbe westward or eastward, became the Germans—without anybody's ever having been able to figure out to the general satisfaction what a German is or even *where* precisely he should be. (There has seldom been a lack of suggestions as to where he should go.) The question has come ringing down the corridors of time with reverberations of such intensity that it was put into a song and became the unofficial national anthem: "Was ist des Deutschen Vaterland?"

> What is the fatherland of the German?
> Is it Prussia? Is it Swabia?
> Is it where the grape ripens near the Rhine?
> Or where the sea gull flies along the Belt?
> O no! No! No!
> His fatherland is larger still.

> What is the German's fatherland?
> Name me then that great land!
> As far as the German tongue is heard
> And God in Heaven is singing songs,
> So far shall it stretch!
> So much, brave German, call your own!

Trying to fix the German geographically is like trying to fix him chronologically: when was the German most German—at the outcome of World War II? An inquiry into World War II reveals that its causes are to be found in the experience and outcome of World War I. An inquiry into World War I . . . and so on. The inquirer soon finds himself in the German forests with Tacitus.

Enveloped in the great forests, the early Germans developed a radial susceptibility to their surroundings. They were naturally predisposed to pantheism. The majesty, the solemnity, the spectral atmosphere of the great forests was conducive to nature worship, to speculation on the mysteries and symbolic suggestiveness of the elements. In every element the German worshiped some supernatural being. They were the forest-worshipers par excellence. They still are. There is certainly no characteristic acknowledged to be more typically "German" than the adoration (breathless or bosom-heaving) of the great woods.

But the great, dense forests that covered the German lands were also proof against the insinuations of civilization. They had to be cleared by fire or hacked down with the polished stone ax. Historians estimate that the civilizations of the Nile and the Euphrates were more than two stages ahead of Germany, where the neolithic culture, blocked by the great forests, was slowly hacking its way up from the south.

Of course the Germans were not alone in their conviction that only God could make a tree. Tree worship was common to all Europeans in antiquity and later. But it was the Saxons who worshipped the great ash tree, Yggdrasill, as the universal pillar upholding all things. At Uppsala, the old religious capital of Sweden, as Sir James Frazer recounts in *The Golden Bough,* there was a sacred grove in which every tree was regarded as divine. But to show how serious the worship of trees was, Frazer cites "the ferocious penalty appointed by the old German laws for such as dared peel the bark off a standing tree. The culprit's navel was to be cut out and nailed to that part of the tree which he had peeled, and he was to be driven round and round the tree till all his guts were wound about its trunk. The intention of the punishment clearly was to replace the dead bark by a living substitute taken from the culprit; it was a life for a life, the life of a man for the life of a tree." In 723 near the town of Geismar in Hesse, the English missionary Saint Boniface cut down with his own hands the oak tree sacred to the German god Donar (thunder), the equivalent of the Norse god Thor. The conversion to Christianity of the Germans was a hideously bloody affair, particularly the conversion of the Saxons, who were the last heathen holdouts. Charlemagne's Saxon wars lasted almost thirty years. In one day at Verdun in 782 upwards of 4,500 Saxons were executed. Hundreds of thousands of the stubbornly pagan forest-dwellers were slain before the wars finally ended, which is why Charlemagne in Germany to this day has a controversial reputation: he is hailed as the first German emperor (he lies buried at Aachen) and the first Christian ruler, but he is also damned as "der Sachsenschlächter," the Saxon-slaughterer. The first missionaries in Germany, the men who Christianized the German tribes, were Scottish and Irish monks in Alemania, Franks in Bavaria, and sometimes Englishmen like the greatest of them, Saint Boniface, who worked the Rhineland, Thuringia, and Hesse and was finally martyred by the Frisians. (He became the patron saint of the Germans.) These missionaries did not simply dismiss the old tribal gods as nonexistent, the figments of overheated barbaric imagination, nor did they seek to incorporate them, as was often done, in Christian hagiography. The old gods were too diehard for that. They kept them on, confirmed their existence, but condemned the lot as devils. They thus accomplished the first partition of Germany, namely the partition of the German psyche into "Glaube" (faith) and "Aberglaube" (other-faith, or superstition). This was a common enough practice in the conversion of pagans to Christianity. The story is told in the word "anathema," literally an "up-putting," an offering, originally "a votive offering set up in a temple" (Sophocles). In the New Testament it became "anything devoted to evil, an accursed thing." The pagan German, as Heinrich Heine puts it, lived in a world "drenched with deity" (durchgöttert). When his multitude of gods was banished by the missionaries to the nether regions, his world became "drenched with deviltry" (durchteufelt). This for the Germans was The Fall, the banishment from Paradise to Purgatory, the change from one extreme to the other—from pantheon to pandemonium. They never recovered. The old German forest gods were a pretty grim bunch to begin with. But when consigned to devildom by the Church fathers they became demons, monsters, dragons, goblins, gargoyles, poltergeists, kobolds, elves, poisonous dwarfs, and, above and below all, witches. Worse still, the practice of propitiating their old gods was decreed by the Church to be black magic. The French historian Jules Garinet, writing at the beginning of the nineteenth century, stated that Charlemagne himself

> had several times given orders, that all necromancers, astrologers, and witches should be driven from his states; but as the number of criminals augmented daily, he found it necessary at last to resort to severer measures. In consequence, he published several edicts. . . . By these every sort of magic, enchantment, and witchcraft was forbidden, and the punishment of death decreed against those who in any way evoked the devil, compounded love philters, afflicted either man or woman with barrenness, troubled the atmosphere, excited tempests, destroyed the fruits of the earth, dried up the milk of cows, or tormented their fellow creatures with sores and diseases. All persons found guilty of exercising these execrable arts were to

be executed immediately upon conviction, that the earth must be rid of the burden and curse of their presence; and those even who consulted them might also be punished with death.

Thereafter, the great witch-hunt of the Middle Ages and after—long after—was on. Prosecutions for witchcraft are mentioned frequently by French historians, but the practice and the punishment of the black art were by far widest spread in Germany. German demons were easily the most frightful. Compared with the grisly crew arising out of the gloom and ground fog in the forests, nymphs like Melusine of French fairy tales or the river sprite Rusalka of Russian folklore are things of beauty. Morgan le Fay would have been frightened out of her wits, says Heine, if she ever met a German witch. These, all of them hideous hags, naked and smeared with foul-smelling salves, ride on broomsticks to the Brocken, a craggy mountain topped with huge boulders in Hesse, the traditional trysting place of Teutonic pandemonium. On the topmost peak sits Satan himself in the form of a black ram. The devil as Judas-ram has two faces, one fore and one aft. His aft face, with anus for mouth, is his true face, symbolic of the nether regions, exhaling odious gases and spitting excreta from his own and the earth's entrails. Each of the witches approaches him with a candle in her hand and kisses his true face. Thereafter the ladies dance around him furiously, singing "Donderemus, donderemus!" ("We are destroying the Lord!") while the black he-goat baas appreciation. If a witch lost a shoe during the dance, it was a sure sign that she would be burned at the stake within the year.

In fact the Brocken was hallowed ground sacred to the pagan Saxons. The Saxons preyed upon the superstitions of their Christian conquerors by prancing around the Brocken dressed as witches and riding broomsticks to protect the place as a pagan sanctuary. By the same token, Christians seized upon the charge of witchcraft as a pretext to accomplish mundane political ends. Imputations of witchcraft were used to bring the republican confederacies of the Middle Ages under the feudal yoke of local liege lords, as in the case of the Frieslanders who held their annual diet under a large oak tree at Aurich on one of the coastal islands of the North Sea. They managed their own affairs in a fairly democratic fashion and independent of the clergy and nobility. This was unforgivable. The archbishop of Bremen and Count Burckhardt of Oldenburg at the head of the local nobility leagued against a group of the Frieslanders called the Stedingers and finally subdued them. In 1204 the Stedingers revolted, refusing to pay taxes to the feudal lords or tithes to the clergy. They remained in revolt for twenty-eight years, at times utterly defeating their oppressors on the field of battle. Finally, the archbishop of Bremen appealed to Pope Gregory IX "for spiritual aid" against the Stedingers. The pope complied by pronouncing anathema against the Stedingers as heretics and witches and exhorting all true believers to assist in their extermination. This act placed a hunting license in the hands of thieves and fanatics who promptly swarmed into Stedinger territory, murdering, looting, and burning wherever they went, sparing no one. The Stedingers managed to drive them out, killing their leader Count Burckhardt and many of his henchmen. Pope Gregory was again appealed to. This time he preached a crusade against the insurgents. "The Stedingers," wrote His Holiness,

> seduced by the devil, have abjured all the laws of God and man, slandered the Church, insulted the Holy Sacraments, consulted witches to raise evil spirits, shed blood like water, taken the lives of priests, and concocted an infernal scheme to propagate the worship of the devil, whom they adore under the name of Asmodi. The devil appears to them in different shapes, sometimes as a goose or a duck, and at others in the figure of a pale black-eyed youth, with a melancholy aspect, whose embrace fills their hearts with eternal hatred against the Holy Church of Christ. This devil presides at their sabbaths, when they all kiss him and dance around him. He then envelopes them in total darkness, and they all, male and female, give themselves up to the grossest and most disgusting debauchery.

(The recurring charge of "disgusting debauchery" refers to the sexual act performed as a fertility rite in pagan worship. Its constant condemnation by the Christian Church attests its persistence.)

In response to this letter from the pope, Emperor Frederick II of Hohenstauffen pronounced the ban of the Holy Roman Empire of the German Nation against the Stedingers. The bishops of Ratzeburg, Lübeck, Osnabrück, Münster, and Minden leagued with the duke of Brabant, the counts of Holland, Cleves, the Mark, Oldenburg, Egmont, Diest, and many others, at the head of a force of 40,000 men, attacked the Stedingers, who numbered 11,000 men. Eight thousand of the Stedingers were killed in battle. Then the entire remaining population, women and children and old men, too, were put to the sword or burned at the stake.

In all ages there has been a close if hidden connection between the divinely plagued madman ("Whom the gods destroy, they first make mad") and the divinely inspired prophet or seer, between the village idiot and the white magician, between μαγία as inspired frenzy and μαγτεία, prophetic power. Both words come from the same Greek root. The dividing line—when there is one—can be extremely tenuous. Man has always striven to hold converse with superior beings, to achieve *vision,* especially into the future. The difference between true and false prophets is a contingent one. There have always been imposters who preyed upon the credulity of mankind. But the problem of true and false prophets involves vaster complexities than imposture or even the mechanism of political contingency which decides whether a revolt becomes a revolution or a potential revolution is quashed as a revolt. History decides both before and after—perhaps centuries after—the advent of a prophet whether (and by whom) he is to be regarded as true or false, bad or good. Leaders are those who, knowingly or unknowingly, are able to exploit the psychic makeup of the group, the clan, the people, the race, or the adherents of a creed. Whether they are right or wrong for the right or wrong reasons is usually only ascertainable in the aftermath, and then as often as not only by the standards of material success or failure. The psychological process, at work in peoples and races as well as in individuals, of accommodating the past to the present involves conscious or unconscious forgetting, and the historical importance of past events is itself always questionable in terms of absolute standards. To a greater or lesser extent, "Verdrängung" (suppression, repression) is falsification, If the process is unconscious it is all the more effective. There are issues, moral as well as other, in the lives of peoples and nations that are never solved. The present is more or less falsified because it rests on a past which has to be falsified in order to preserve sanity, that is, a workable psychological balance (or what appears to be one). In religious wars such as the never-ending series between Christian and pagan Europeans, and Christians and Jews—where the two sides are often enough at war within the same individual—each side struggles to maintain what it conceives to be a workable, lasting psychological balance in its own way for its own reasons. Knowingly or unknowingly the witches, goblins, dragons, demons, and spirits were more significant and "real" than is popularly realized now or was theologically admissible then. The witches and demons fulfilled and were conceived to fulfill genuine psychological needs. And the German needs were great. As psychic projections they were, and are, as "real" as anything else in the phenomenal world.

The members of hierarchy of the Christian Church were especially vigorous in their prosecution of the various forms of witchcraft because

[321]

they felt instinctively that the epidemic, as it was called, foreshadowed the coming of Antichrist. Florimond, in his work on Antichrist, summed up the situation:

> All who have afforded us some signs of the approach of Antichrist agree that the increase of sorcery and witchcraft is to distinguish the melancholy period of his advent; and was ever age so afflicted as ours? The seats destined for criminals in our courts of justice are blackened with persons accused of this guilt. There are not judges enough to try them. Our dungeons are gorged with them. No day passes that we do not render our tribunals bloody by the doom which we pronounce, or in which we do not return to our homes discountenanced and terrified at the horrible confessions which we have heard. And the devil is accounted so good a master that we cannot commit so great a number of his slaves to the flames, but what there shall arise from their ashes a sufficient number to supply their place.

In Germany it proved impossible to mark a dividing line between belief (Glaube) and "other-belief" or superstition (Aberglaube).

In this regard, the preface to the German *Encyclopedia of Superstition,* published in 1927, is significant. In it the editors explain the reasons for their decision to retain the word "superstition" (Aberglaube) rather than adopt the term "folk belief" (Volksglaube). "The advocates of the latter term," wrote the editors,

> pointed out emphatically that the word "superstition" pronounces a value judgment and is therefore unscientific. With the word "folk belief" the concept of folklore includes all manifestations of belief insofar as they belong to the realm of folklore. In the same way that we have folk songs, folk customs, and folklore, we should then find folk beliefs in all strata of the population, since folklore does not deal with the imaginative world of a certain socially defined stratum of society. Here, as with folklore in general, it is a matter of the thought processes of humanity at large and the formation of their imaginative world. Folklore would not have to determine in accordance with rationalistic or ethical points of view whether the belief of the folk be good or condemnable; that would be the job of theologians; there too the determinations would vary, depending on whether the judges were Catholic, Protestant, Christian or non-Christian, freethinkers or environmentalists. If, on the other hand, we should use the word "superstition," we should be pronouncing such judgments as are only relative and not scientifically ascertainable. There is yet another reason that would speak for the word "folk belief." In such an encyclopedia it would be impossible to avoid discussing manifestations of belief that belong in the sphere of

Christian dogma. The Church would take exception to our denominating as superstition expressions of belief which the Church approves and admits. And from its standpoint the Church would be entirely in the right to do so. We, however, would not be able to claim any right for ourselves, since the judgment of what can be called belief and what must be called superstition can only be relative. . . . The word "superstition" may indeed be ambiguous insofar as it involves a value judgment in itself. But still more awkward, it seems to us, is the term "folk belief," because under "folk belief" we are obliged to understand the entire range of religious activities and feelings of the folk, its conception and realization [Gestaltung] of Christianity at least to the same degree as the pre-Christian and non-Christian rudiments which it has maintained for itself.

What the folk movement gave the National Socialists was a blanket concept that covered a multitude of sins and attracted the widest possible variety of feelings, emotions, tendencies, attitudes, impulses—political, religious, cultural, and social. The imprimatur of the "folk" accommodated and sanctioned them all. It was the catchall that caught all and put it, at least in the beginning, at the disposal of the führer.

The German need to believe proved too great to be contained. Too much of a good thing is worse than not enough. Excessive zeal in belief and in disbelief (wrong belief) was equally suspect. The legend "convicta et combusta" (convicted and burned) after the names of men, women, and children of all ages in the criminal registers of virtually every large city in Germany attests to the intensity and corruption of official zeal. The punishment, particularly its severity, proliferated the crime, made it interesting, lent it meaning, and so sanctioned it. The devil became far more interesting and accessible to the popular imagination than the Trinity. Medieval witches—as distinct from those of antiquity—extended their powers beyond mere prophecy to that of working their wills on the lives, limbs, and possessions of mankind. This extension of discretionary powers could be acquired only by signing a pact in blood with the devil himself under renunciation of baptism and forfeiture of the immortal soul. The pact with the devil, of course, is the theme of Goethe's *Faust* and the leitmotiv of German history—to add "in a metaphorical sense" seems irrelevant. The Christianization of the Germans, overdone and underdone, was not the stabilizing factor that it has sometimes seemed to be. Scratch a German Christian and there is always a chance that under the veneer you will find either a pagan who avails himself of Church ritual to conform to society or a religious fanatic whose extremism deviates into anti-Christianity.

The history of German witches is particularly terrible. Take a ballad entitled "Die Druten Zeitung" (The Witches' Gazette), which enjoyed great popularity in Germany in the seventeenth century. The title page of a copy printed at Smalcald in 1627 describes it as "an account of the remarkable events which took place in Franconia, Bamberg, and Würzburg, with those wretches, who, from avarice or ambition, have sold themselves to the devil, and how they had their reward at last; set to music, and to be sung to the tune of 'Dorothea.' " The agonies of the witches at the stake are described in great detail and the poet pokes fun at the victims when they writhe with excruciating pain and rend the air with their screams. But the most significant feature of the ballad is the account of a trick that is used to beguile a confession out of a woman who had steadfastly refused to confess that she was in league with the devil. The commissioners proposed that the hangman disguise himself in a bear's skin, with horns and a tail, and enter the accused woman's cell in the dungeon. The woman, crazed with fear and superstition, in the gloom of her cell believed herself to be in the presence of the Prince of Darkness. The imposter told her to have courage and promised to release her from the power of the authorities. At this she fell on her knees before the "devil" and swore to dedicate herself thereafter, body and soul, to his service. The British historian Charles Mackay in his *Memoirs of Extraordinary Popular Delusions and the Madness of Crowds* (1841) adds that Germany was "perhaps the only country in Europe where the delusion was so great as to have made such detestable verses as these the favorites of the people." He might have added that even more distinctively German was the recourse to ruse, to deception, to make-believe, in order to extract a confession from the victim. We here encounter the all-important role of the delusion, deliberate or accidental, contrived or derived, in German life. Throughout this dreadful period, says Mackay (and the period lasted some two hundred years),

> the delusion of the criminals was as great as that of the judges. Depraved persons, who in ordinary times would have been thieves or murderers, added the desire of sorcery to their depravity, sometimes with the hope of securing impunity in this world by the protection of Satan. One of the persons executed at the first burning (in Würzburg in 1627), a prostitute, was heard repeating the exorcism which was supposed to have the power of raising the arch-enemy in the form of a goat.

The exorcism ran as follows:

Lalle, Bachery, Magotte, Baphia, Dajam,
Vagoth, Heneche Ammi Nagaz, Adomator,
Raphael, Immanuel, Christus, Tetragrammaton,
Agra Jod Loi. König! König!

The most popular exorcism, according to Horst in his *Zauberbibliothek,* was to be read backwards, except for the last two words:

Anion, Lalle, Sabolos, Sado, Pater, Aziel,
Adonoi Sado Vagoth Agra, Jod,
Baphra! Komm! Komm!

The inclusion of the Hebrew word "Adonoi" (God) in this mishmash is significant. "This nonsensical jargon" (we are with Mackay again)

> soon became known to all the idle and foolish boys of Germany. Many an unhappy urchin, who in a youthful frolic had repeated it, paid for his folly the penalty of his life. Three, whose ages varied from ten to fifteen, were burned alive at Würzburg for no other offense. Of course every other boy in the city became still more convinced of the power of the charm. One boy confessed that he would willingly have sold himself to the devil, if he could have raised him, for a good dinner and cakes every day of his life, and a pony to ride upon. This luxurious youngster, instead of being horsewhipped for his folly, was hanged and burned.

In 1962, according to an Associated Press dispatch, a number of swastikas (the swastika is an old Aryan magic sign) were found painted on a garage in Bad Godesberg (whose name commemorates the first appearance on the Rhine of the old German god, Wodan). Bad Godesberg is a small Rhenish town bordering on Bonn, the capital of West Germany. For this reason and because swastika-daubing in Germany always raises a hullaballoo abroad and therefore at home, a full-scale police investigation was launched. In time the culprits were discovered: three boys aged six, eight, and ten.

The most sinister figures in Germany as elsewhere during the witch mania were the professional witch-hunters. In the fifteenth century Jacob Sprenger, the most infamous of these, in his book *Malleus Maleficarum* (Witches' Hammer) codified the proceedings against witches and fixed a form of interrogation for the discovery of the guilty. The series of questions included whether the suspects had had midnight meetings with the devil, whether they had attended the witches' sabbath on the Brocken, whether they had their familiar spirits, and whether they had had sexual intercourse with Satan. According to Mackay's account, torture never failed to educe the answers required by the inquisitor. Numbers of people, whose imaginations were filled with these horrors, went further in the way of confession than even their tormentors anticipated, in the hope that they would thereby be saved from the rack, and put out of their misery at once. Some confessed that they had had children by the devil [cf. *Rosemary's Baby*], but no one who had ever been a mother gave utterance to such a frantic imagining, even in the extremity of her anguish. Only the childless confessed it, and were burned instanter as unworthy to live.

It is, of course, impossible to tabulate the number of witches burned in Germany during the mania. But it was agreed "on all hands" that Sprenger himself burned more than five hundred in one year. Successive popes appointed new witch-hunting commissions "for fear that the zeal of the enemies of Satan should cool." One was appointed by Alexander VI in 1494, another by Leo X in 1521, and a third by Adrian VI in 1522. They were all armed with the same powers "to search and destroy." The commissioners seldom stopped short at one victim. The confessions extorted at the rack in most cases implicated a dozen or more people. At Bamberg in Lower Bavaria from 1610 to 1640 executions occurred at the rate of about a hundred a year. Later, for many years, the district of Bamberg burned upwards of 400 witches annually. The city of Cologne at the same period achieved an annual total of more than 300. Within the lifetime of Doctor Nicolai Remigii, the "hanging judge" of the duke of Lorraine, 800 women were burned at the stake as witches. Women accused of witchcraft were subjected to a special form of trial: bound hand and foot they were thrown into the water; if they sank they were innocent, if they managed to float they were adjudged guilty and burned at the stake. Such, says Heine, was the logic of the times. (After completing an authoritative book entitled *Demonology*, Doctor Remigii came to believe that he himself was able to cast spells. Conscientious Teuton that he was, he did not fail to register himself as a master of witchcraft—a sort of infernal pimp —in court. He was burned at the stake.)

In his book *Anthropodemus*, Doctor Heinrich Prätorius describes a popular species of German demon:

> Our forebears were unable to imagine poltergeists as anything else than human beings in the form of small children dressed in a bright motley coat or small clothes. Some add that some of them had knives stuck into their backs while other were hideously misshapen in other ways, after having been murdered by one means or another.

For the superstitious believe that these were the ghosts of people murdered in the same house. And they tell all sorts of stories about kobolds who do various favors for maids and cooks in the household and become so well liked by them that the domestic help fervently desire to see them and pester them with requests that they make themselves visible. This the poltergeists would never willingly consent to, on the plea that humans could not behold them without being frightened out of their wits. However, when the curious housemaids could not forbear, the kobolds agreed to present themselves in the flesh at a prearranged place in the house, stipulating that the human being bring along a bucket of cold water. And so the kobold presented himself, lying on the floor on a pillow, stark naked with a huge carving knife stuck into its back. At this horrible sight many a maid took such fright that she fainted. Whereupon the kobold jumped up and poured water on her until she regained consciousness. After such an experience the house help lost interest in seeing their demon friends. Kobolds are all supposed to have special names but in general they are called "Khim." They are also supposed to do all the household and barnyard chores for maids, cooks, and handymen whom they take a liking to—feeding and currying the horses, cleaning out and washing the stables, as well as looking after the household proper. Indeed, they take such good care of the animals that these are supposed to thrive especially as a result. In return, the kobolds must be pampered by the hired help, who must take care never to neglect to feed them and never to make fun of them. For example, once a cook has accepted the services of a secret helper she must see to it that she bring him a plateful of good food at an appointed time and place and then go on her way. After this she can be as lazy as she likes and go early to bed; the next morning she will invariably find her housework done for her. But if she forgets her duty to the ghost, particularly if she neglects to provide him food, then she must do her work alone and suffer every form of accident: for she will either scald herself with boiling water or break the dishware or spill the food on the floor so that her mistress and master must take her to task. On such occasions the laughter or giggling of the kobold is supposed to be distinctly audible. Such kobolds are thought to remain always in their same households regardless of how often the domestic staff changes. Indeed, a departing housemaid recommended the local kobold to the care of her successor and strongly advised her to gain his good graces. When, however, the successor refused to do so, she was plagued by an unbroken sequence of misfortunes so that she was forced to give up her position shortly thereafter.

From the same source Heine cites some horror stories:

A maid had befriended an invisible house spirit over the years and had arranged a place for him near the hearth where they talked away the long winter evenings. Finally the maid asked Heinzchen, for so she called the spirit, to let himself be seen as nature had shaped him. But Heinzchen refused at first but then relented, saying that the maid should go down into the cellar where she would be able to see him. So the maid took a lamp and went down into the cellar and there, in an open barrel, she beheld a dead child swimming in its own blood. The maid had given birth many years before to an illegitimate child, had murdered it and thrust the corpse into a barrel.

One of the most popular of the kobolds was Hüdeken who provided the stuff for many a tale belowstairs in old Saxony. Here is an excerpt from an old chronicle:

About the year 1132 an evil spirit made himself visible to a great many people over a long period of time in the bishopric of Hildesheim. He appeared in the shape of a peasant with a hat on his head, which was why the peasants called him "Hüdeken" [Saxon dialect for "little hat"]. This spirit found pleasure in consorting with human beings, making himself visible and invisible to them, putting and answering questions. He never insulted anyone without reason. But whenever anybody ridiculed or berated him he returned payment for the injury received in full measure. When Count Burchard de Luka was killed by Count Hermann von Wiesenburg and the estates of the latter were in danger of becoming the booty of de Luka avengers, Hüdeken took it upon himself to wake the bishop, Bernhard von Hildesheim, in the middle of the night and addressed him as follows: "Get up, bald head—the county of Wiesenburg has been abandoned and forfeited by an act of murder and can therefore easily be occupied by you." The bishop quickly assembled his men at arms, invaded the lands of the guilty count, and united them, with the approval of the emperor, with his own. This spirit frequently warned the bishop of impending danger and made frequent appearances in the palace kitchen where he talked with the cooks and did them all sorts of favors. When Hüdeken had become familiar to one and all, one of the young scullions made bold to tease him whenever he appeared and even to pour slops on him. The spirit asked the chef to forbid the unruly youngster such liberties. Answered the chef: "You are a spirit and are afraid of a boy!" Whereupon Hüdeken replied threateningly. "Since you refuse to punish the boy, I will show you in a few days how much I am afraid of him." Shortly thereafter the boy was sleeping alone in the kitchen. The spirit seized him as he slept, strangled him, and tore him to pieces, putting these in pots of water on the stove to boil. When the chef discovered this fearful prank, he cursed the spirit roundly and so Hüdeken the

[328]

next day spoiled the roasts on the spit by pouring the poison and blood from toads over them. His revenge provoked the chef to another outburst of verbal abuse. The spirit finally retaliated by luring the chef to fall to his death in a deep gorge over which he had produced the illusion of a bridge. At the same time he haunted all the walls and towers of the town throughout the night, forcing the watchmen to remain constantly on the alert.

A man who had an unfaithful wife, as he was about to leave on a trip, once turned to Hüdeken in jest and said: "Good friend, I recommend my wife to you; guard her for me carefully." As soon as her husband had departed, the adulterous wife invited one lover after another. But Hüdeken permitted not one of them to touch her, but threw them all out of the bed onto the floor. When the husband returned from his trip, Hüdeken went out to meet him far beyond the limits of the town. "I rejoice at your return," he told the husband, "because it frees me from the heavy service you imposed upon me. I have by dint of taking indescribable pains protected your wife from actually committing an infidelity. But I implore you never to entrust her to me again. I had rather tend all the pigs in Saxonland than a woman who strives by ruse and subterfuge to gain the embrace of her lovers."

The customary dress, not to say the uniform, of the kobolds was gray with a red cap. At least this was the way they dressed in Denmark, where they seemed to prefer to congregate. Heine thought this preference derived from the kobolds' love of red currants which abound in Denmark. (However, Hans Christian Andersen told Heine when they met in Paris that the favorite food of the "Nisses," as the Danes call kobolds, is mush with butter.) Once the kobolds have made their place in a house, they are disinclined to leave it soon. On the other hand, they never come unheralded, and if they wish to move in somewhere they give notice to the landlord in the following way: at night they carry all sorts of wood shavings into the house and throw farm animal dung into the milk. If the landlord does not clean out all the shavings, or if he and his family drink of the dirty milk, then the kobolds will remain with them forever. A poor Jutlander at length became so irritated by the company of such a kobold that he wanted to give up his own house. He loaded his belongings onto a cart and drove to the next village in order to settle down there. On the way, though, when he happened to turn around he caught sight of the red cap and small face of the kobold, who was just peeking over the top of an empty barrel. The kobold gave him a friendly yell: "We're moving, too!" he said. (Throughout these passages I could hear the raucous laughter of Till Eulenspiegel, the rascally master prankster

[329]

of the fourteenth century who specialized in the filthy practical jokes, such as dumping a pile of dung by night on the doorstep of a pious, early-rising burgher.)

With such background and conditioning it is small wonder that the German has an inborn need to believe. There is perhaps no race or racial group that is so open to the reception of ideas and so prone to indigestion as a result of bolting their spiritual food. For the German's readiness to believe is coupled with a peculiar stubborn persistence in believing: "What is new is not true," runs the German proverb, and "what is true is not new."

The German need to believe is the desire for a great all-encompassing faith—a great, single answer to all problems. He is willing to believe anything that he can accommodate within the indistinct range of his faith. "In Germany," said Stendhal, "impassioned hearts are strangely divorced from logical heads. And so the honest Teuton is never slow to assume the existence of anything whose existence appears to be desirable." The German is a metaphysical hamster. His passion for order is ultimately his desire to subordinate all phenomena to the great central stalk of his innermost faith. William James noted that while the Latin races are apparently able to split up the pressure of evil into "ills and sins in the plural, removable in detail," the Germanic races tend to erect one "Sin in the singular, and with a capital S . . . ineradicably ingrained in our natural subjectivity, and never to be removed by any piecemeal operation."

Recently an attempt was made to erect one "sin in the singular"—with a capital E. A few years ago there appeared a book entitled *Envy* by the Austrian-born Helmut Schoeck, a professor at the University of Mainz. Schoeck's thesis is that envy is the primum mobile of behavior in human (and higher animal) society. Virtually everything in man's life with other men in a community, and particularly in primitive communities, turns on some form of envy or precautions and reactions against envy. Envy, says Schoeck, is a basic anthropological category. "It is a psychic process that necessarily has a social precondition: two or more individuals." As Schoeck puts it, man in groups and societies is associable and sociable "first and foremost thanks to his constant, often subliminal impulse to envy." A second major point Schoeck makes (and carefully documents) is that the more primitive the society, the more equal its members in their possession of goods and opportunities, then the greater the intensity and prevalence of envy. A chief characteristic of envy is that it cannot be satisfied—for the more ostensibly equal the lots

[330]

of individuals in society, the more suspicious the envious become, the more wide-ranging and imaginative in their quest for "hidden inequalities."For this reason it is disastrous to cater to envy: the donor does nothing but increase the resentment of the envious; his act of generosity categorizes him as superior and the recipient, just because he is the recipient, as inferior. Schoeck contends that mankind is especially prone to envy because of the inordinately long youth of the human animal (relatively longer than that of any other species) which exposes the young for too long a period to the school of envy, as it were, namely the envy among brothers and sisters in regard to parental favor. The taboo against incest, a taboo that exists in all societies, serves primarily to reduce envy within the family, the basic and most important unit of society.

Almost all cultures and all religions have condemned envy and the envious. Schoeck attributes the scarcity of literary and scientific works on envy to the deliberate suppression of the subject as "unmentionable" in society. This is primarily because envy pure and simple is entirely destructive, as the curious term "Schadenfreude" (damage-joy, literally) aptly expresses. Schadenfreude is defined as "malicious joy at another's misfortune" and described as closely related to envy by Schoeck. Another revealing German term is Neidbau (envy-construction), "a building that is erected not for one's own advantage but only to the disadvantage or irritation of a neighbor." There was also in early medieval times an "envy-pole" or stake (Neidstange) that often had the head of a newly slaughtered horse fixed to the top of it; it was set up both by the envious to ward off good spirits and by those afraid of the envious (the two great categories of humanity) to ward off bad spirits. In this connection, Schoeck emphasizes the central roles of envy and the fear of envy in the use or supposition of black magic and the prevalence of superstition. In primitive societies when crops fail or someone takes sick it is laid to black magic practiced by the envious. (The question, as in African tribal practice, is not what causes the disease but *who* causes the disease.) This is "envious sorcery." In Austria and Bavaria peasants mix "envy herbs" into the fodder so as to protect their livestock from "envious sorcery" ("Schadenzauber" in primitive societies, "Verneiden" in Germany). The actual source of the belief in witches and superstition at large, as Schoeck adduces a good deal of evidence to demonstrate, is the "envy dynamic" (envy and particularly the fear of being envied). A very ugly old woman is suspected of being a witch because she is ugly (and therefore envious of others) and because she is old (and so envied by others for her long life: she is suspected of having purchased longevity by shortening the lives of others). In primitive societies, and by no means only there, man lives in constant fear of envy, specifically fear of "the evil eye" fixed on the envied by the envious. Envy and the fear of envy are the basic ingredients in the creation of a god of fate and the escape-value concepts of good and bad luck.

Schoeck's theory of envy, how the uses, subtle and brutal, inform the whole of society, indeed how the checks and balances of the myriad forms of envy make up the very warp and woof of life in a community, sets the scene for the major thesis of his book: "The more highly developed, the more widespread the fear of envy is in a society, the easier that society can be persuaded by politicians to take refuge in the egalitarian welfare state." Moreover, "the belief in black magic prevalent in primitive peoples is only very little different from modern notions. While the socialist for over the last hundred years has believed that he is being robbed by the private enterpriser and while the politician of an underdeveloped country has believed ever since 1950 that he is being robbed by industrial nations—both beliefs being based on an abstruse theory [i.e., Marxism] of the economic process—the primitive considers himself robbed by his neighbor who through the use of black magic has been able to conjure part of his victim's crops over to his own field." I am not in a position to pronounce on the merits of Schoeck's thesis. But I find it interesting to have the range of social sciences treated in relation to sorcery.

IT WAS NOT BY CHANCE THAT THE GERMANS BECAME THE inheritors (for lack of other heirs) of the Roman Empire as christianized by Constantine, and hence Holy. A good many historians say that the Germans, in their early guise as Franks, were saddled with the Carolingian ideal first by Charlemagne himself and then by Otto the Great, neither of whom could resist the vision of the Pax Romana combined with the Pax Christiana. Scholars note that there were two preconditions to the fact of lateral transfer of the empire from the Romans to the Germans. The idea of the Roman Empire as a universal and eternal ordering factor ("Roman" meant ecumenical) was still alive even though the empire itself was not. The idea had been kept alive in the Church. For with the conversion of Emperor Constantine, not only did the Christian Church become the state church, the empire became a church-state. Prayers for the emperor and the empire were included in the liturgy of the Church and the empire was drawn into the ideology of Christianity, as the last of the world monarchies whose end would mark the beginning of the kingdom of God. Moreover, the Church was successful in promoting its view of the empire as the vehicle of God's will for the Christianization of the world. The Church has always liked a winner. It is idle to argue whether it was religious fervor or political cunning that moved Germany's rulers to assume or resume the imperial dignity. The two considerations, like the two entities they proceeded from, merged and became virtually identical. Nietzsche saw Christianity carried and corrupted by the continuing active forces of the Roman Empire. The joke about the Holy Roman Empire's being neither holy nor Roman nor an empire is merely a joke: it was all three and more —it was also "of the German Nation" as a whole until Luther split the nation and the world into Catholic and Protestant. Its last vestige was the House of Habsburg. Franz Josef exercised his veto in his capacity as apostolic emperor to prevent the election of Cardinal von Rampolla to the papacy. This was the emperor's revenge for the cardinal's refusal to allow the suicide Crown Prince Rudolf a Christian burial. Even when

[333]

institutions are disintegrating and decaying, their leading ideas sometimes live on and reemerge, often in distorted and even horrendous
forms. So it was that the Berlin-Rome axis came into being; the link was
the Church. So it was that the Concordat between the Vatican and the
Third Reich was signed. There was perhaps no basic difference between
the attitudes of Pius XII to Hitler and Leo III to Charlemagne. "Here-
sies," as Sir Thomas Browne wrote,

> do not perish with their Authors, but, like the river Arethusa,
> though they lose their currents in one place, they rise up again in
> another. . . . Opinions do find, after certain Revolutions, men and
> minds like those that first begat them. To see ourselves again, we
> need not look for Plato's year: every man is not only himself; there
> hath been many Diogenes, and as many Timons, though but few of
> that name; men are lived over again, the world is now as it was in
> Ages past, there was none then, but there hath been someone since
> that parallels him, and is, as it were, his revived self.

If this is true then can we be sure that history has written finis to what
was perhaps the grandest design ever conceived by man: the Holy Roman Empire?

It was not by mere chance that the words "of the German Nation"
came to be added to the title. Germany was the country best fitted to be
the home base of the empire. In the very center of the European land
mass it formed, then as now, the geographical, economic, and political
heart of Europe. Germany was, then as now, a network of roads and
waterways knotted together at its intersections by the great commercial
clearinghouses at Cologne, Frankfurt am Main, Leipzig, Frankfurt an
der Oder, Nuremberg, Augsburg. Inevitably, this central position meant,
through all history, pressure from all sides and the corollary of concen-
tric pressure: pivotal influence; both centrifugal and centripetal force.
Germany was naturally, and still is, at the center of all east-west and
north-south conflicts, between Habsburg and Bourbon, between Spain
and the Netherlands, between Catholics and Protestants, between capitalists and communists. It has always been clear to all concerned that the
role Germany played—or the role played in Germany by others—would
be decisive. Consequently the governments of major nations have always
tried to establish and promote their interests (whatever they might be)
in Germany. For this reason the country of the Germans has been
invaded, divided, subdivided, bought, sold, partitioned, and occupied by
foreign governments since the dawn of European history. It was because
of this situation that the lateral transfer of the Roman Empire to the

Germans was bound to be calamitous. The transfer imposed form, gave direction, and imparted thrust to the German's natural inclination to believe: it harnessed a griffin to the sacred imperial dream. Within the dream it generated the most mystical of all political concepts: the Reich.

The Reich is not a kingdom; a kingdom is a qualified Reich, a Königreich. It is not a res publica—a republic—which is best summed up in the term state. It is nothing so clearly constituted, so definite in its basis and in the articulated structure of its laws. Etymologically the word "Reich" is cognate with the English "rich." But there is nothing crassly material about the Reich: it is mantled in a vague solemn dignity that is otherwordly. To call the Reich holy (heilig) is almost repetitious. Reich is a semantic and conceptual bridge to "Himmelreich," the Heavenly Kingdom. With the lateral transfer of the Holy Roman Empire to Germany the Germans became the people chosen by God to implement the Christianization of the world, beginning with Europe. "Germany" became synonymous with the Reich, with the Kingdom of God on Earth (a development that made the confrontation between Germans and Jews all but inevitable: one chosen people versus another chosen people). This is why so much of Germany was made up of marches, which were not so much borders as approach areas to the land beyond. They were really straddle positions, some more conspicuous than others: look at the Netherlands, Flanders, Alsace, Lorraine, Switzerland, Austria, the Sudetenland, Silesia, East Prussia. Here is Müller van der Bruck's definition of the Thousand-Year Reich: "Mankind has always posed itself tasks that it cannot accomplish. It is here that the greatness of mankind resides, here is the genius that guides mankind, here is the demon that drives mankind. It is the essence of all utopias that they can never be realized. It is the essence of all chiliastic hopes that they can never be fulfilled. And it is the essence of the Thousand-Year Reich that it only lives in the proclamation of itself but can never become the lot of man."

The sacred historic mission of the Reich varies from age to age, but only superficially: the greater the variety of its changes the stronger the evidence that its basis remained the same. The concept remained that Germany must necessarily be a Reich of mediation, a great clearinghouse of the spiritual and intellectual impulses from other countries, receptive to foreign influences but not ruled by them, rather all the more capable of maintaining a dominant spiritual hegemony among them. When the Holy Roman Empire of the German Nation was pronounced extinct by Napoleon at the Peace of Luneville, the idea underlying the concept emerged untarnished. The sometime power of the Reich to annex to itself

[335]

foreign nations in the name of Christianity was now to be exercised in the name of an ideal form of higher education which, like Christianity, was not to bear the stamp of any one people but to create and cultivate the values uniting all mankind. That which constitutes the value of Germany, wrote Schiller in his poem "German Greatness," does not go lost when the Germans suffer defeat in battle. The majesty of Germany does not rest on the crowned heads of its princes; it is of a spiritual nature and, in the German scale of values, is set high above the political. It prevails even when the empire crumbles. When the fruit is ripe, it will be shown that it is German, that other peoples were only so many blossoms that wither and fall away. The German is not destined to prevail in battle, he is destined rather to achieve the highest good by striving to master the forces of nature and realize the ideal. Since the German is located in the middle of Europe's peoples, he constitutes the core of humanity. The German language, expressive of everything, the strongest and the most tender, will rule the world. Shame on the German who spurns the native excellence of his spirit and bows before the charms of France or England and seeks to go their ways. For the German has availed himself of things foreign only in order to contribute to the education and refinement of mankind. "Every people has its day in history; but the day of the German is the harvest of all time."

So the dream of the Holy Roman Empire has remained. It has bemused every generation of Germans since Charlemagne. It has beckoned and bewitched every German leader worth or not worth his salt, ranging in terms of merit and ability all the way from Barbarossa to "Kaiser Bill." The dream has proved to be an irresistible attraction and by no means only to Germans and their far-flung relatives. It has also appealed to Swedes, Spaniards, and Corsicans among others. Those captains and commanders who had no original conscious desire to travel the road to empire sooner or later discovered themselves moving along the railbed of historic progression that had been laid in the time of Charlemagne. Napoleon realized this early in his career and accepted it. Indeed, the empire was virtually thrust upon Napoleon as a matter of course by German princes. The prince elector of Mainz, Karl Theodor von Dalberg, archchancellor of the empire, wrote to the French ambassador accredited to him that the constitution of the German empire was wholly in need of renovation. This could only be undertaken by a great and magnanimous character who would reinforce the laws by concentrating the executive power in his own hands. As for the incumbent (Austrian) emperor, "he could after all become the emperor of the Orient in order to provide a bulwark against the Russians, while the Occidental Reich under Kaiser Napoleon would arise as it had under Charlemagne, consisting of Italy, France, and Germany."

When Ward Price, the English journalist, interviewed Hitler in 1934 on the subject of Austria, he asked the führer whether he aspired to restore the Holy Roman Empire. After Hitler had annexed Austria and, in conscious or unconscious imitation of the medieval German emperors, traveled to Rome with fitting pomp to negotiate with Il Duce, the German press erupted in headlines proclaiming the Holy Roman Empire of the German Nation. During Christmas 1942, when the blitzkrieg had become a protracted bloodbath, there appeared in the *Frankfurter Zeitung* an editorial under the title "The Empire Put to Proof." The point of reference was the Holy Roman Empire. "This," ran the editorial, "was a supranational European order in which a variety of culturally different peoples were subordinated to the German emperor. This empire fell apart when national states formed themselves within it. Among these Prussia developed the purest concept of the state as an institution exacting ethical behavior, as a spiritual foundation of the people, by which means it became the ordering factor of Lesser Germany [that is, without the German border states]. However, when negotiations were conducted in Saint Paul's Church [in 1848–1849] over a new Greater Germany it became clear that Greater Germany could not be an exclusively ethnic state, but would have to assume a supranational, European mission." What the men in Saint Paul's Church in Frankfurt failed to do, the führer succeeded in doing: he created the Greater German Empire. Perhaps for a moment (when he promised to be satisfied with the annexation of the Sudetenland), a closed national state seemed possible. But the immanent idea of Greater Germany forced him to go further. Greater Germany can only exist as "the core and purveyor of a new empire, it bears the responsibility before history for a new general order and for a new epoch of the European continent, an epoch free from anarchy."

It is a curious fact that according to the ancient law of the Franks the king was not the supreme ruler demanding and commanding absolute loyalty and obedience from the local nobility that made up and administered his kindgom. He was merely primus inter pares, the first among equals. The old Germans, and the Franks foremost among them, were fierce lovers of freedom—at least freedom for themselves. This was the problem that Charlemagne faced when he became ruler of a vast empire by conquest. Charlemagne recognized the closest possible association with the Church as the only way to get round the local nobles. In

short, he bypassed the traditional obstacles to secular rule by resorting
to the Church hierarchy as a parallel and equally effective administrative
command channel. In order to prevent the ecclesiastics from becoming
hereditary liege lords in their own right, the law of celibacy was introduced into the Church. (The secularization that would have inevitably
followed the development of hereditary church office would have presented the pope as well as the emperor with problems of insubordination.) These considerations led to what appears to be a complex of
coincidences: it was precisely because the Germans were not a nation and
hence not in a position to offer concerted secular resistance that the
Church instinctively chose them as the champions of the Church's empire. For the same reason the emperor chose the Church; but his aim was
exactly opposite: by using the Church hierarchy he sought to centralize
the administration of his possessions and unify his command. At one and
the same time, then, Charlemagne's coronation in Rome at the hands of
the pope involved the emperor and his successors ever more deeply in
the ecumenical pretensions of the papacy and involved the papacy to an
equal degree in the metaphysical preoccupations and political pretensions of the Germans. As a result the German people were fatally sub-
merged in the Holy Roman Empire. The title itself was the ecumenical
claim. Despite the title—or, indeed, because of it—the emperor was
merely a sort of super-king placed in honorific preeminence over the
princes and petty monarchs of the lands of Middle Europe. He was a king
whose realm was not national but notional, his authority dependent on
a superimposed idea. Big ideas are always dangerous, as any Greek who
has chased the phantom of pan-Hellenism (and what Greek has not?) can
attest. It was, all authorities agree, in the pursuit of the shadow of a
universal power that the German rulers forfeited the chance of a national
one. Of course, empire demands a Big Idea, particularly in Europe, more
particularly in Germany. The idea has to be big enough to command an
allegiance that will rise above the confines, so sharply drawn and so
deeply imbedded in Germany, of "Lokalpatriotismus." A higher patriotism is required for a higher imperial sovereignty. Hence the higher
patriotism has been preached by every European conqueror—de facto
and would-be—from Charlemagne to Jean Monnet. This is because it has
always proved impossible to put together a working linguistic majority
in Europe. But to be effective the higher sovereignty has to radiate from
a single center. In the Holy Roman Empire there were two centers of
sovereign authority: the emperor and the pope. The emperor found
himself only cocustodian of the Big Idea. The two centers became oppo-

site poles, and the spark of supreme authority—so firmly fixed in Charlemagne's time—was wont to jump fitfully from pole to pole. The result was the papal-imperial conflict which raged for more than 200 years and finally ruined both powers. The continual call to the emperor for help by popes and Italian bishops made the emperor dependent on the German princes for the men and arms necessary for such transalpine campaigns. Indeed, Otto III made the renewal of the Roman Empire the central idea of his policy ("renovatio imperii Romanorum" was the inscription on his royal seal), declaring that thenceforth Germany and Italy were to be ruled from Rome. It was in keeping with this idea that Otto set up his court at Rome. But most of his entourage, both lay and clerical, was German—particularly Saxon. By assuming a new title, servus apostolorum (servant of the apostles), Otto laid ecclesiastical claim to both Poland and Hungary, which had already come under the ecclesiastical jurisdiction of the Holy See. He was determined to rank along with the pope as an apostolic prince. He appointed Sylvester II, the first of the three German popes, and reversed the Curia Romana's concept that the pope was the emperor-maker. Otto III regarded himself as the leader of the Universal Church, the maker of popes, bishops, and prebendaries (for a consideration, of course).

The ascendancy of emperor over pope achieved by Otto did not last long. Within a generation a reform movement within the Church arose in the Abbey of Cluny in Lorraine. The main target of this reform was the practice of simony, as it was called after Simon Magus who tried to buy off the Apostles. Specifically, this applied to traffic in sacred things, the buying and selling of ecclesiastical preferments, benefices, and emoluments, a definition that reads like a job description of the Holy Roman Emperor. It took no subtle interpretation to see the whole administrative basis of the empire as simoniacal and the emperor as the foremost champion of the practice. So the champion of the reform movement, the Cluniac monk Hildebrand chose to see it. As Gregory VII, Hildebrand made demands for the suppression of simony throughout the Reich, which, if the emperor had acceded, would have meant his forfeiture of the political, administrative, and financial control of the empire. The emperor's compliance would have been tantamount to abdication. When Gregory persisted in his demands, Henry IV gathered his German bishops about him and declared Gregory's election invalid. Gregory retaliated by suspending Henry from all his offices and excommunicating him. Thereupon Henry excommunicated the pope.

At this point the merger of the religious and the political that characterizes the ecumenical nature of the empire worked to the disadvantage of the emperor. The pope's excommunication of Henry IV had the effect of releasing the princes of the empire from their oath of fealty and from all duties to the emperor. The immediate result was yet another revolt of the Saxons. Henry IV was forced by the princes to go to Canossa to beg the pope's forgiveness and plead for reinstatement. (This gave rise to the expression "to go to Canossa," meaning to undergo humiliation, to eat humble pie.) For three days and nights in the dead of winter Henry stood in the sackcloth of the penitent outside the walls of the castle of Countess Mathilde in the small Italian city of Canossa, waiting for the pope to receive him. This was the Investiture Contest, the struggle to determine who—pope or emperor—had the authority to invest candidates with the powers and perquisites of ecclesiastical office. Despite Henry's reconciliation with Gregory, the German princes elected a new emperor, Rudolf of Swabia, in Henry's stead. Thus they bore out Gregory's contention that the German monarchy was a purely electoral office and that final approval of the candidate rested exclusively with the Holy See. Henry took up arms against this contention and for a while prevailed. But neither he nor his far greater successor, Frederick Barbarossa himself, was able to reestablish the Frankish conception of hereditary monarchy, the monarchy by divine right that might have saved the empire and consolidated all the German tribes as one nation. The papacy did not fare better. The claims and counterclaims of pope and emperor wrought utter confusion. In some years there were three popes and three emperors contending for recognition.

When the pope broke with the emperor and won the German princes over to his side, it was not long before the German princes in turn broke with the pope. As a result the empire was a welter of double and divided allegiances. Gregory VII's idea of modeling the imperial election on episcopal elections was disastrous because it put something like a veto in the hand of every individual German prince. According to the uses of the ancient German folk community, the king was bound to each individual as each was bound to him by the bond of fealty. Even before the Investiture Contest—during the elections of Henry II and Conrad II —the Saxons had declared that they would not recognize or accept the elected king as their king until he had confirmed their rights. The Frankish monarchy, as formulated by Alcuin, was theocratic: Charlemagne was himself sacerdos et iudex, priest and judge. The merger of religious fervor and political cunning so ingeniously and laboriously achieved by Charlemagne and his successors proved to be less than perfect over the

[340]

centuries as a practical solution to the internal problems of the empire. "The old seats of racial opposition," says the historian Geoffrey Barraclough,

> Lotharingia and Bavaria plus the ever unruly Saxony were clamoring for independence. The lay aristocracy opposed the administrative preferment of clerics while the clerics came to resent the very idea of theocracy. The merger of the religious and the political peculiar to the empire had laid the entire system open to the charge of simony. It had also deprived the system of fixed revenues (through taxation or other means) and an official class of administrators. The empire never had a center of government: the emperor was crowned in Frankfurt, but elected by the Imperial Council which met in Regensburg, the Imperial Court of Justice sat in Wetzlar. The emperor never had a permanent residence until the Habsburgs finally settled in Vienna three hundred years later.

What was at issue from the first and has remained at issue in German history is "the whole conception of what constitutes the realm." After Hildebrand and the Investiture Contest the emperor and the German princes were never reconciled. In the absence of a fixed, recognized, and accepted conception of what constituted the realm in its extent, forms, and offices, it was always possible and usually easy for outsiders as well as insiders to play off the princes against the emperor (severally or in combinations) or the emperor against the princes. The Reich remained flawed from the reign of Henry IV. Goethe describes the scene he witnessed as a boy at the coronation of Kaiser Josef II.

> At the other end of the hall, directly at the windows, sat the emperor and the king in full ceremonial dress on thrones raised high above the floor on a dais set under baldachins. Their crowns and scepters lay on golden pillows placed at some distance behind them. The three ecclesiastical prince-electors, each with his buffet behind him, had taken their seats on separate daises: the elector of Mainz opposite their majesties, the elector of Trier to the right, and the elector of Cologne to the left. This upper part of the hall was full of dignity and gratifying to contemplate and prompted the hope that the priesthood would hold as long as possible with the ruler. By contrast the indeed beautifully decorated but totally unoccupied buffets and tables of all the secular prince-electors were reminders of the misunderstanding [Missverhältnis] which has gradually developed between them and the overlord of the empire through the centuries. The ambassadors of the secular prince-electors had already taken their leave in order to dine in an adjoining room; and if for this reason the greatest part of the hall received a spectral appearance —that so many invisible guests should be served in the most sump-

tuous way—then the great unoccupied table in the center was all the more saddening to behold, for here too so many places stood empty because all those who had every right to be seated there remained absent so as not to forfeit any of their honor on this most honorific day—out of propriety as it were, even though they happened to be in the city at the same time.

It would be rash to cite the dualism of the Holy Roman Empire of the German Nation as the original cause of the Germans' endless and unavailing struggle with definition. It is just as likely that German inability to see and set natural and rational limits was the cause of the headlong attempt to combine the empire with the papacy so closely. The inability of definition is general: it applies to territory as well as concepts. The lack of natural east-west borders was perhaps a handicap from the beginning, but then the Germans ignored the one formidable natural border they possessed—the Alps. Certainly Schrankenlosigkeit—unbridledness, the inability or disinclination to set bounds or fix limits—is the fault the Germans most often find with themselves. The Germans were so dazzled by the Big Idea of empire that they could not see the practical impossibility of realizing it. But the receptivity to such fascination is inborn. "German art is never finished," wrote one benevolent observer, "but always forming; the classical example might be Goethe's *Faust,* a masterpiece billowing vastly in the void." In any case Goethe spent a lifetime writing *Faust,* finishing it only in his eighty-second year. Not only did the emperor have no permanent residence: he possessed no sufficient power base. The various occupants of the imperial throne were never able to extend their crown lands or increase their sources of revenue sufficiently to provide such a power base. Henry IV tried to create a permanent center for his government in the Harz Mountains because he hoped to use the resources of the region's silver mines. He failed. Moreover, the continual raids of the Norsemen in the ninth century and others after them had helped to increase the power of the local magnate: men turned from the emperor who was absent to the duke who was present, from the emperor who could not protect them to the duke who would. Developments generally conspired to enhance the position of the duke. In any meaningful sense of the term, a state can be said to exist only when it is able to maintain order and administer itself. Such internal administrative autonomy, according to German tradition, was the prerogative of the duke, but not of the count. The duke was the prototype of the territorial prince.

In those sometimes lengthy interims when their lands were not occupied by foreign powers and they were more or less their own masters, the Germans have never been able to separate church from state or, more accurately, the religious from the civil. Not as the French did, not as the English did, not even to the extent that the American puritans did. This was the essential Teutonic confusion. This was the source of the dualism, the magnetic field between the two opposite poles that can be shifted on its axis to all points of the compass in any of its historical variations without losing its original force: imperialist–particularist, Catholic–Protestant, capitalist–communist. In this sense the question of what constituted the realm (the empire) was superseded by the question of what constituted Germany (Lesser Germany or Greater Germany) which, in turn, was superseded by the question of what constitutes a German. In trying to answer any of these questions it has always proved impossible to escape paradox. The most successful of the many futile attempts and most productive of durable results and disastrous consequences was realized in the German ideal of chivalry, the Knights of the Cross. Seemingly, the blending of the archetype of the German pagan hero with the Christian ideal produced the perfect combination: the knight. He had rights, privileges, social position with the prospect of advancement along the line, and he was bound by the code of chivalry, that is, placed in the service of a higher goal as characterized by the Crusades. The refinement of chivalry was something the Germans badly needed, man and woman alike.

The refining influence of the cloister and the convent and the code of courtly love on the Germans was remarkable and lasting. It produced standards of behavior as well as a code of honor, it shaped manners as well as morals. There was never any real danger in Germany that over-refinement would produce effeminacy or foppery or preciosity. Germans have a natural tendency (as do most peoples, but to a lesser extent) to overdo. But the exaggeration of the refining process, the putting of too fine a point on manners and morals in Germany usually leads to the grotesque or the macabre. It often leads to the absurd, less often to the ridiculous. In Germany the age of chivalry represented the most successful synthesis of race and culture that the German has ever known. It was the high point of the harmonious development of people, nation, state, and church. It was also a development that has left an indelible impression.

It is a commonplace that the Middle Ages determined the fate of Germany. The figure of the knight, the chevalier, has lost none of its luster to the German even today. Indeed, it is because of the German code of chivalry, I am convinced, that Germans generally make such poor athletes—that is, poor in comparison to what they could be if they were unburdened of the psychic ballast imposed by the code. The specific manifestation of "Ordnung muss sein" (we must have order) in sports is the German's punctilious fairness. The code exacts it. In any form of contest the German must above all be a decent fellow ("brav") at all times and at all costs. As a result, with very few exceptions, German athletes do not know how to cheat or foul. In team competition the art of fouling is indispensable. There is an indistinct demarcation between downright cheating on the one side and the inspired exertion of the supreme effort involved in "playing over one's head," as it is called, on the other. German athletes are given to sinning by omission, by not trying hard enough and imaginatively enough to do justice to their physical prowess and condition. They usually play a defensive game; they almost always play an apologetic game. This is not to say that they never foul—in association football (soccer), say, which is the national game. But they usually foul only after they have repeatedly been fouled against. Then they foul with a vengeance, in a towering rage, and in so unbridled and crude a manner that the foul cannot possibly be overlooked.

The diametric opposites of the Germans are the Italians who, in team sports, anyway, and in soccer especially, foul all the time. But the Italians foul cleverly, indeed almost gracefully, never crudely. It is part of their style: Italians are master foulers. For this reason it is always highly instructive to watch the Germans play the Italians. In the German Italian game in the semifinal round of the 1970 World Cup in Mexico, the German fullback Berti Vogt, a splendid athlete and a model of correctness, was so baffled (as were all his teammates) by the subtle fouling of the Italians that he committed a senseless, blatant, but totally ineffective foul on the Italian goal-getter Gianni Rivera. It was a foul that brought a penalty and perhaps cost the Germans the game. In most team sports and particularly in soccer, the Germans are so obsessed with the observance of the rules that they consider the referee a de facto member of the German team and are continually appealing to him. The German game can be characterized as either direct or indirect appeal to the referee: they turn to him with hand raised to claim a foul even while running at full tilt after the ball. Often, especially after a lost game, there is mournful speculation about what would have happened if such and such a free kick at the goal had been granted by the referee. (Inevitably in such cases there was a blatant foul committed in the defense zone that should have been penalized with a free kick but wasn't.) The result is that all too often German reportage of a championship game is far more concerned with the performance of the referee than with that of the players.

The German historian Treitschke wrote that Germans are in any case inclined to confuse "Grobheit" (grossness, coarseness) with truthfulness. But the confusion works both ways: if the truth is coarse, the coarseness has to be true—it has to be open and straightforward and clean. It is as if the primitive animal power of the Germans—the battle-lust, the "senseless, beserk wrath," the furor teutonicus of which Heine sang—must be harnessed and held in check by strict attention to exact rules. In any case the close confinement within the chivalrous code of conduct rules out imagination in the German game plan. Inter-Milan kept the German champions Borussia-München-Gladbach out of the semifinals by beating them in a replay in Berlin (after a controversial first game that ended seven to one for the Germans was annulled because a spectator had beaned the ace Italian forward Boninsegna with a Coca-Cola can after the first half-hour). Inter-Milan fought the Germans to a standstill and a scoreless tie. The Italians, professionals in every fiber of their bodies, fouled the Germans silly in a very imaginative defensive game. The German's only strategy was to lure the Italians into fouling them so severely that the English referee would grant the requisite number of free kicks or perhaps even ban a player from the field (when this happens in soccer the player cannot be replaced: his team must continue to play in its reduced condition). The referee did not oblige. He awarded only one free kick, which was muffed by the overnervous Sieloff. Apart from attempting to enlist the cooperation of the referee the Germans simply and ponderously tried to storm the Italian goal. As *La Stampa* in Turin put it: "The game was not worth much technically (but why should one consider only technical aspects in a collision between buffaloes and hyenas?). . . ." German radio and television commentators, even those on national hookups, informed the public that the Italians had won by their unfairness. German sportswriters in their evaluation of the game pointed out that the German team (and by logical extension all German soccer players) were too decent, straitlaced, and upstanding ("brav") to play so rough a game as football effectively.

This is true of Germans not only in team sports. Witness Max Schmeling in his two fights with Joe Louis: in the first he fought a carefully planned and superbly executed defensive fight, knocking Louis out in the twelfth round; in the second he was surprised by the sudden fury of Louis's immediate attack, took a crippling kidney punch (which is illegal in Germany but not so in the United States), and was himself knocked out in less than two minutes of the first round. Witness the exhibition bout between Sugar Ray Robinson and Gerhard Hecht in Berlin in 1952. Robinson knocked Hecht out with a kidney punch. The upshot was that both fighters had to take refuge under the ring from a barrage of beer bottles thrown by spectators who were outraged because of the illegal punch. In the early fifties, Peter Müller, sometime middle-weight champion, was losing badly in a ten-round fight with the new champion, Hans Stretz. In the eighth round Müller was told by the referee to stop holding. Müller turned to the referee: "He is holding, too," he said, pointing at Stretz. "You are not allowed to talk in the ring," warned the referee. At this point Müller knocked the referee down and out with a right to the chin. Müller then tried to strangle the prostrate referee, who was unconscious and remained so for several minutes. When the champion Stretz tried to restrain Müller, Müller turned on Stretz. He then struck Stretz's trainer as the trainer was climbing through the ropes to intervene. Before Müller's manager succeeded in pulling him out of the ring, the enraged boxer had made at two or three ringside spectators. It was an unprecedented scandal. Müller was barred for life by the German Boxing Association (his exclusion remained effective for less than a year). The German press did not fail to point out that Müller, in addition to being a local character, was half gypsy. He was also, therefore, by origin not truly representative of the German sportsman. What made the episode ineluctably funny is the general background of German pedantry in game rules and regulations, the prissiness of the German sports world at large. German sports announcers are forever lecturing their audiences with editorial comments like "This is very bad for the reputation of the bicycle racing sport" or "So-and-so has made no contribution to the prestige of the game today."

I have hesitated long before deciding to mention the following trait of German sportsmen: their high degree of tension. They are very often as highly strung, nervous, and antically temperamental as race horses. This is a difficult generalization; there are a number of notable exceptions (Franz Beckenbauer, far and away the best soccer player in Germany, for one), but by and large the German athlete can be depended upon to become unstrung under pressure. He is extraordinarily sensitive to outside influence, say the booing of the crowd, or the cheering of the crowd for his opponent or the opposing team. In this sense German athletes are always amateurs: they do not have, as a group, the professionals' reserve

of cunning, routine, and reflexes for emergencies. The 1971 playoff between Borussia-München-Gladbach and Inter-Milan is a prime example.
In Milan the Germans were utterly discountenanced by the hostile Italian crowd. In the return match in Berlin, the friendly German crowd
apparently only made the German team the more nervous. As for the
Italians: "The hissing of the crowd," said Bianchetti, the Inter-Milan
fullback, "was music to my ears; it spurred me on." The Italians fought
the Germans to a standstill. In victory (such as their winning the 1954
World Cup in soccer) as in defeat the Germans have been rightly characterized by the French as "metaphysical athletes."

There is one pursuit, and I use the word "pursuit" advisedly, in
which the Germans, as a general rule, are anything but chivalrous. They
are the worst drivers in Western Europe. According to a report published
by the World Health Organization in 1968, based on the number of
traffic deaths compared to the number of car owners in each of the
various countries (Communist countries were omitted for lack of data),
the Austrians and Germans, listed separately and in that order, are the
worst drivers in the world save only the Australians, who topped the list
(the Americans were fourth). I remember a brochure issued by some
automobile club for Americans visiting Europe. "Whenever you see a car
with a black license plate with white letters on it, be careful: this is a
Frenchman. He is generally a good driver but he is apt to drive too fast
and is sometimes careless. Whenever you see a car with a white license
plate with red numbers on it, be very careful: the driver does not have
a driver's license. He is a Belgian (in Belgium until only a few years ago
driver's licenses were not required). Whenever you see a white license
plate with black numbers on it be most careful: this is a German, the
most irascible driver in Europe. Whatever you do, don't pass him." For
if you pass a German on the road, there is at least an even chance that
he will pass you and cut so sharply in front of you while doing it that
you must apply the brakes to avoid a collision.

There is a saying in Germany that the German used to put on his
uniform, now he puts on his car. This is true to the extent that the
German's conduct as a driver is an aftereffect of the war, specifically a
psychological effect of the German postwar situation. Just as the German
economic miracle resulted from the channeling of all the Germans'
energies into that field—other fields for various reasons being closed to
them—so it is behind the wheel on the highway that the German com-
pensates and overcompensates for the various frustrations he bears. Hit-

ler loved to be driven out onto the highway in his big Mercedes touring car, traveling at high speeds and passing every car on the road. He particularly enjoyed passing American cars, this, too, being an aftereffect of the Allied victory over the Germans in World War I.

There is no speed limit on the autobahn except at construction sites. Two or three automobiles bumper to bumper (literally) in the pass lane at full speed, which is from 100 to 140 miles per hour, is a common sight. In Germany and in Western Europe generally, a driver signals his desire to pass the car in front of him by flashing his headlights. German drivers are much given to fixing a whole battery of powerful lights between their headlights proper. With six or more lights blazing at night, the German driver well-nigh blinds everything coming toward him. If, for whatever reason, the car in front does not immediately make way (it may be after all that he cannot cut into the right lane for the moment), the driver behind will tailgate him, coming within six inches of his rear bumper as often as not and staying there until the car in front pulls over into the right lane. Another favorite maneuver of the German driver is passing on the right, indeed even on the shoulder of the road, throwing gravel, dust, or mud in his wake. The German driver absolutely insists on his right-of-way. (I was about to add: *even when he doesn't have it,* but this would be unfair. Too often, however, the German driver falsely assumes he has the right-of-way.) German authorities have tried again and again to inculcate good road manners upon the German public—"Be a cavalier at the wheel"—as yet with a notable lack of success. The traffic death total for Germany in 1970, approximately 20,000, was uncomfortably close to half that of the United States (54,800). The United States has roughly four times the population of West Germany and at least six times as many cars on the road. (The Austrian traffic death rate is well over ten percent higher than that of West Germany.) The number of hit-and-run cases in Germany has risen sharply in recent years largely because insurance companies give special rate reductions (at times almost half) to drivers with accident-free records. The admission of having caused an accident has thus become a costly business, particularly since automobile insurance rates have tripled in the last five years. A number of insurance companies went bankrupt, being unable to make payment on the rapidly increasing number of claims, particularly the sophisticated long-term or permanent disability claims. The number of accidents in Germany, like the number of cars, doubled from 1958 to 1970. Chain crashes on the autobahn, in which anywhere from 20 to 150 cars are involved (a consequence of tailgating, especially when visibility is poor), are a German specialty.

As a result of these factors and conditions, what seems to characterize the German traffic situation is not so much the accident as the incident. Here is an account of an "auto-feud" (as it was aptly tagged by an Austrian newspaper) that occurred on the Salzburg-Vienna Autobahn in the summer of 1970. In a Peugeot loaded with baggage and carrying three passengers, a young German, Lars Frischkorn, tried to pass a Viennese, Peter Stehlik, aged twenty-four, who was driving a Mini (Morris). Instead of allowing the Peugeot to pass him, the Viennese accelerated and kept pace with the Peugeot, forcing the latter to remain in the pass lane. This neck-and-neck race was finally ended when the Peugeot managed to pass the Mini going downhill. Hereupon the Mini passed the Peugeot going uphill, cutting so sharply in front of the German that the cars scraped against each other's sides and fenders and the German was forced to pull over to the side and stop. The Viennese pulled up too. At this, the German driver's father, a city government official from the north German port of Kiel, jumped out of the car and attacked the Viennese driver with a bayonet he carried with him, ostensibly for use as a hunting knife. The Viennese was wounded in the face and in both forearms before the son was able to disarm his enraged father. Meanwhile, Frau Frischkorn had fainted and had to be taken to the hospital and treated for a circulatory collapse. Herr Frischkorn was charged with assault with a deadly weapon, a charge that might have been levied with equal justification against the Viennese driver. The Viennese driver, after having his wounds looked after, was allowed to proceed. He was charged retroactively with dangerous driving. Both parties were let off with fines.

Indeed, the number of wounds and death-wounds dealt with guns, knives, and bare fists during the altercations that follow accidents or near-accidents is so great that the traffic *incident* has come to be regarded as a peculiarly German sociological phenomenon. The traffic judge Harry Schütt was quoted by *Stern* in early 1972 as saying that "20 percent of German automobile drivers are gangsters," a conclusion that he drew from the annual average of some 1,000 court cases involving violent traffic quarrels within his jurisdiction alone. Aggressive driving has become the chief outlet for the furor teutonicus.

N JUNE 1963 I RETURNED TO BERLIN AFTER SPENDING SEVERAL months in and out of a New York hospital. I was convalescing and under doctor's orders to take it easy. I was, however, happy to accept invitations to participate in two German television panel discussions on the occasion of President John F. Kennedy's official visit to West Germany and Berlin. These televised panel discussions involved no exertion and required no preparation. Moreover, I was fascinated by the meaningfulness of the event: it was to be the first time a president of the United States, while in office, had visited Berlin. Considering the political significance of the Wall and its traumatic effect on the Germans, President Kennedy's visit was a political gesture of great international importance. It was bound to appear as a provocation to the Russians and their quislings. I arrived in Berlin the day before the great day. When I entered the office of the American Broadcasting Company I was surprised to find it jammed with people. There were, I think, thirty-six ABC employees assigned to cover Kennedy's Berlin visit: two or three producers, five or six reporters (including one from Washington and two from New York), a dozen or more assorted cameramen, sound men, engineers, and technicians, and even three or four special couriers, motorcycle riders in black leather uniforms and gum-drop crash helmets with the white letters "ABC" on a black background pasted on the front. It was the most impressive array of "electro-journalistic" talent I had ever seen assembled.

As I listened to the head producer briefing his crew on the plan of coverage I was struck by the split-second precision and the intricacy of the schedule he had set up. My staff officer experience told me that the plan was too complicated to be carried out effectively. Even with so large a staff at his disposal it seemed to me that he was trying to do too much at too many widely dispersed points along the meandering route of the president's cavalcade. But I kept my peace: I was not on active duty, as it were, but merely a guest. I had asked and received permission to come into the ABC studio the next morning and watch the event on German television.

Luckily I had my own key, for there was no one in the office when I arrived at eight the next morning. I turned on the television set, opened a can of beer, sat down, and put my feet up. President Kennedy arrived at Tegel Airport at eight-thirty and was greeted by the French commandant and Willy Brandt, then still the mayor of Berlin. The president stepped into his limousine and the cavalcade moved off. Then the phone rang. When I picked up the receiver a voice said, "This is New York. Who's there?" Taken by surprise I answered, "Nobody." "Whaddayamean 'Nobody'? Who're you?" "This is Bailey," I said. "Bailey? What are you doin' there?" "Well," I said, "the only reason I'm here is because I'm not supposed to be here—I mean I'm not on assignment; I am just sitting here watching the show on German television." "But where is everybody else?" "Oh, they're all out covering the story." "Listen," said the voice, "in five minutes we have a circuit. Can you knock out a couple of spots and feed 'em to us?" I sat down and wrote two spots—each timed to forty seconds—describing what I had seen on German television and then read them into the microphone. "Thanks a million!" said the voice. I then opened another can of beer, sat down and put my feet up, and again addressed myself to German television. At five minutes to ten the phone rang again: "Who's there?" "Still Bailey." "You mean that nobody has come in in the meantime?" "That's right," I said, "I haven't even had a phone call." "Look," said the voice, "can you do the same thing for us again?" I did so again—and again—and again: I made six or seven circuits that day, remaining in the studio until the president left Berlin at seven or eight in the evening. Nobody ever came to the studio.

At noon or thereabouts I had a phone call from Edward P. Morgan, who was wondering what he would do with a tape he had just cut at the City Hall. But there was no help for it: it was impossible to move. The crowds, unprecedented in Berlin history, were so great that no one could get through—not a motorcycle courier in a black leather uniform with ABC on the front of his crash helmet, not a policeman on horseback, not an Allied soldier in a tank—no one. Literally the entire population of West Berlin had swarmed like bees to by mere chanceb of the president's cavalcade route, which had been published in advance. Of course, the Berliners' reception of the president of the United States was extraordinary: Berlin is in effect a suburb of Washington, D.C. The Berliners were merely paying their respects to the real mayor of Berlin. This was why there was such unbridled enthusiasm for Kennedy's famous statement in front of the Shöneberg City Hall. "In ancient times," he said, "the proudest thing a man could say was 'civis romanus sum'—I am a Roman citizen. Today the proudest statement a man can make is 'Ich bin ein Berliner!' " I have never heard anything like the ocean roar of delight and gratitude that burst out with the completion of that proudest statement. But the underlying significance of that proudest statement was understood instinctively and immediately by the Berliners. When Kennedy proclaimed himself to be a Berliner, he was actually proclaiming the Berliners to be Americans—"cives americani estis"—with full rights of protection. But Kennedy's reception by the West Germans at large was not generically different from the unstinting acclaim he received in Berlin. Wherever he went in West Germany he was received as and for what the president of the United States was and is for all free Germans: protector and benefactor.

At the parade grounds in Hanau, West Germany, ABC engineers had rigged an ordinary telephone booth at the edge of the field to perform all the functions of a radio studio. After the president had reviewed the troops at Hanau, one of the star reporters, as prearranged, sprinted for the telephone booth–studio to scoop the world with his story. The trouble was that when he found himself in the booth he was facing an apparatus as complicated and bewildering as the console of a jet liner to a nonpilot. Very few reporters, and certainly not star reporters, are proficient technically. The only piece of equipment our reporter could recognize was a telephone receiver. This he picked up to find himself connected with the chief engineer in Berlin, 350 miles away. I learned of this a short while later when the engineer burst into the office and said, "Do you know, I've just had the most extraordinary conversation with somebody in Hanau. I wish I knew English. Tell me, what does the English word 'do' mean? This poor fellow on the other end of the line kept shouting, 'Vat aye do? Vat aye do?' "

Two days later, monkey see, monkey do, Nikita Khrushchev appeared in East Berlin in an attempt to offset the tremendous impact of Kennedy in West Berlin. Walter Ulbricht, the German Communist boss of East Germany, was quite frank about this aspect of the visit in his speech welcoming Khrushchev. He said that in the last few days there had been visitors in West Berlin who had raised quite a few eyebrows. But what was it, he asked, that these visitors were bringing in their luggage? Nothing that would help the West Berliners, surely. Khrushchev gave his usual bully-boy performance. The East German functionaries set up a route for his cavalcade that was approximately as long as that of Kennedy in West Berlin, and assembled every factory worker, schoolchild, and kindergarten charge they could along the length of it. This was as far as the replica went, a scraggly line of more or less unwilling spectators along the streets of East Berlin. In perfect idiocy the East German television camera crews swept back and forth along the sorry representation of a crowd. It is probable that the East German functionaries didn't care how badly they came off in the comparison. Their purpose, perhaps, was to take the edge off, to reduce somewhat the solid totality of the tremendous impression on East Germans (who had been watching the president of the United States on television even more avidly than their West German brethren had) of that day in June when John F. Kennedy came to Berlin. For here we have the guardian-ward relationship again and on a scale that is probably unprecedented in history.

Perhaps the most striking manifestation—because it is a surface one —of the great American–German guardian-ward relationship is the most popular German political discussion program, "Der internationale Frühschoppen," with six journalists from five countries. The program emanates from Cologne in the Rhineland where the Frühschoppen ("early pint"), the morning carafe of wine, is one of the most cherished traditions. The basic formula for the Sunday noon program, which is now two decades old, is the participation of four foreign correspondents, three of them representing the three Western Allies, in a forty-five-minute discussion of the major news events of the week. The other two participants are German journalists, one of whom is the program's founder and steadfast moderator, Werner Höfer. The popularity of the program is fantastic. To the best of my knowledge there is nothing like it anywhere else in the world. Almost the whole of Germany watches it —East as well as West. The program is also broadcast in Switzerland and in Belgium. The original formula of permanent seats for journalists representing the three Western Allies has been loosened somewhat over the years but it still emerges as the pattern (the French representation has perhaps suffered more than the American and British). Also, the requirement of fluent German tends to reduce the participation to a group of hardy perennials, foreign correspondents working in or near Germany. Those of them who are available enough to appear on the show three or four times a year have long since become television personalities, so intense is the limited ponim exposure ("ponim" is the Yiddish word for face). Thus, without exception, foreign correspondents who are "Frühschoppen" regulars are far more famous in Germany than they are in their home countries. Two ingredients give the program its spice: it is live, and the moderator, Höfer, makes an effort to provide a confrontation between the representatives of both sides of the issue or issues under discussion. The correspondents—except in rare cases where company policy is involved—are not limited in what they can say as are diplomats or politicians or officials in general.

This, I am convinced, coupled with the identities of the representative Western Allied journalists, is the real reason for the program's popularity. For the Allied journalists are, in effect, spokesmen in lieu of the Germans for Germany. They are the unofficial and therefore authentic voices of the guardians. They can, and do, say things the Germans themselves are burning to say but dare not say. How often have I been told by a German co-participant on the show: "I'm glad you said that; I should like to have said it, but we Germans are in no position to make such statements." Immediately after the program, if one or more of the Allied journalists have stoutly defended the German cause or roundly attacked Germany's archenemy, the Soviet Union, there are telephone calls to the studio congratulating—and thanking—them for their performance. In the spring of 1971 I appeared on the "Frühschoppen" with Eugene Grigoriev, the *Pravda* correspondent in Bonn. Since the topic of discussion was Berlin, we very soon clashed, and since my voice is very much louder than that of the mild-mannered Grigoriev, I had little difficulty in shouting him down: every time he said "West Berlin" I interrupted him shouting "Berlin." In the end he became so flustered that he himself said "Berlin" and not "West Berlin" (as the subject of the four-power negotiations). For this feat I received some twenty phone calls and as many letters during the following week. Here is one of them:

Very respected Herr Bailey!
It did us Berliners good yesterday during "Der internationale Frühschoppen" to have you make such especially strong representations on the Berlin problem vis-à-vis the Russian Eugene Grigoriev.
We Berliners are all very much concerned over our Berlin, for we wish to continue living in freedom and peace and not be given over to the barbarism of the Russians. Yesterday we had the opportunity to discuss the topic of "Frühschoppen" with Berliners who were strangers to us and we all found ourselves in agreement on this point. Also, these Berliners we met by chance expressed their gratitude to you . . . [etc. etc.].

By way of contrast here is an excerpt from the Berlin *Extra Service,* a formerly Maoist and at this writing Stalinist "underground" newspaper in West Berlin, in its issue following the same "Frühschoppen":

To get excited over the thousandth "Frühschoppen" program of Werner Höfer would at most betray senility on the part of the reviewer. In any case, vignettes such as the "Ping-Pong" between the Bonn *Pravda* correspondent Eugene Grigoriev and the American George Bailey (ABC) of last Monday should be registered. What it is that has prompted the liberal Höfer for some time now to invite genuine Communist journalists and not only renegades— although this significantly still doesn't apply to the citizens of the DDR or even Socialists from the Federal Republic—is as clear as day. But what brings a *Pravda* comrade to allow himself to be harnessed like a blockhead into a pseudo-discussion we have not yet been able to discern: faulty knowledge of the language? Insufficient practice in free debate? Misplaced courtesy? General shyness? Or simply ignorance of the subject and the motivation of his opponents? In any case the appearances of Soviet and other East European journalists on Höfer's program are gradually becoming embarrassing. They allow themselves to be teased by condescending, sneering chatterboxes like Hans Fleig [a Swiss journalist] . . . and then on top of that to be barked at by a Pentagon-Yankee like George Bailey, as though they were the representatives of the *Weekly Clarion* from Oberammergau. Before five million German televiewers surely one may expect from a Soviet journalist not only dignified facial expressions but substantial, precise, relevant exposition of the policies of the Moscow Communists, a performance that would at least hint at superiority vis-à-vis the fashion of Western anti-Soviet Kremlin-astrology. For another thing it is hardly supportable that on German television a Mr. Bailey should put his feet on the table—needless to say without being taken to task by Höfer —and Grigoriev with scarcely noticeable warmth request permission of this impudent coolie of imperialism to continue speaking. If such scenes should become the general examples of conduct by representatives of the two powers, then of course the unrelieved audacity of the American world-gendarme is not surprising. Even so, Mr. Bailey in his cowboy manner took the liberty of making the point that the Bonn government's Eastern policy is mortgaged with its self-imposed link of a solution to the Berlin problem, and therefore "we" [the United States] would have the last word on Brandt and Scheel's strategy. Such [assertions] Höfer's paladins quietly accept as though Cologne were not situated on the Rhine but rather somewhere in a banana republic of the United Fruit Company. If Soviet talk show participants in the Federal Republic have a function then it is surely to make clear—perhaps not to Werner Höfer but surely to millions of Germans watching their television screens —that the banana trees of the Yankees are not going to grow as high as heaven either in Vietnam or in Europe. Twenty-five years of the glamour of occupation à la Bailey and the inundation of billions of "rotten dollars" will soon be more than enough for Europe.

[355]

Here is a letter from the year before, dated March fifteen and obviously written in the heat of the moment:

"Very respected Herr Beily!
Unfortunately I do not know whether I have written your name correctly. Nor do I know where I could find your name in print so as to check the spelling. Please excuse me.
I simply wanted to thank you for your straightforward position on the German question on the last "Frühschoppen" of March 15. Many a German could take a leaf from your book, but there are too many scoundrels in this world; one of the biggest scoundrels, to whom you have told your opinion [he was a coparticipant on the program] is Sebastian Hafner, a German émigré, now an English citizen, and now this swine is permitted to write for the Russians, meaning Ulbricht, in Berlin. He should be thrown out. I believe we understand each other.
Respectfully, etc.

I do not believe that we understood each other. But this writer, too, has a point. Sebastian Hafner, whose real name is Pretzel, is a Berlin journalist who removed to England in 1938, took out British citizenship in 1948, and returned to Berlin as correspondent for *The Observer*. Once he was back in Berlin events gradually conspired to remove him from British journalism (where journalists are plentiful and poorly paid) to German journalism (where journalists are scarce and well paid). When the Berlin Wall went up, Hafner thought he could read the handwriting on it. He resigned from *The Observer* within ten days after construction on the Wall was begun because he felt that he could no longer work for a publication with a namby-pamby editorial policy on the Berlin question. As Willy Brandt noted during our talk the year before, Hafner was a very hard-line anti-Communist as far as Berlin was concerned. *The Observer*, on the other hand, has been tellingly described as a newspaper written by Eastern Europeans in English for Africans. Hafner then joined an outspokenly anti-Communist newspaper, Axel Springer's *Die Welt*, as a columnist. In 1963 he resigned from *Die Welt*, having meanwhile become a columnist for the German illustrated magazine *Der Stern*. More important, as a political commentator and analyst, Hafner had meanwhile done a complete about-face, having come to seeing the Wall as a triumph of the iron-willed Soviets over the irresolute West. He began pleading for a Western accommodation with the Communists in Europe and particularly, of course, in Berlin. He became one of the chief advocates of the "policy of small steps" of the Berlin Senate and, later on, an ardent apologist for the Brandt government's Eastern policy.

Hafner's status as an immigrant in the country where he was born is typical of a dilemma that is peculiar to postwar Germany. Höfer once summed up the difficulty with American participants on the "Früh-schoppen" by saying that they spoke German either not well enough or too well (America being the great haven of the German and German-Jewish immigrant). But Hafner's situation also points up a conceptual weakness of the "Frühschoppen": correspondents who are professional expatriates or, as it were, professional repatriates are often called upon to comment on events in the countries they represent. Either they have been too long away from their home country to possess anything like the basis for judgment commensurate with their legal status as American or English nationals or, like Hafner, their experience in the country they represent was limited to the duration of the war. Hafner seldom appears on "Frühschoppen" because the opinions he expresses cannot be put forth as representative or in any way typical of a British national. It is no longer possible to introduce Hafner as "the Englishman." In other words, when Hafner gave up his accreditation as a staff correspondent to *The Observer*, he deprived his opinions of their cachet. And it is the Allied cachets of the opinions expressed on "Frühschoppen" that consti-tute the basic attraction of the program. For this reason any attempt to duplicate the "Frühschoppen" formula in any country except Germany would be foredoomed to failure. The authority of the permanent mem-bers of the "Frühschoppen" could not be simulated elsewhere without the backing, however remote or indirect, of the occupying—that is to say, Allied—powers. A similar rotating discussion panel of foreign jour-nalists in Washington, say, might be interesting—if only briefly—but it would not be the "Frühschoppen."

The only time I have ever seen Werner Höfer really angry—and over the last twenty years I have seen perhaps a good half of all the "Frühschoppen" programs—was in the spring of 1965 when thirteen Arab countries broke diplomatic relations with West Germany. The break followed the discovery that the Bonn government had been supply-ing the State of Israel with arms (the arms were exclusively American: West Germany was merely acting as agent for the United States). The episode was an extraordinarily painful pratfall for the Germans. The American government induced the Bonn government to front as arms supplier to Israel because both Germany's overwhelming moral obliga-tion to the Jews and its traditional, noncolonial friendship with the Arabs (a particular point of pride with the Germans) made her appear—posi-tively and negatively—as the best candidate for the delicate undertaking.

Necessarily, all information concerning the arrangement was withheld from the public. Instead of presenting the agreement to the German Parliament for approval, the Bonn government merely informed two parliamentary members from each party retroactively. Presentation of the agreement to Parliament would have been regarded by the Americans and the Israelis as a shift to torpedo the undertaking since parliamentary approval of the agreement was virtually precluded by the inevitable Arab reaction and the prospective loss of relations with thirteen Arab countries when the Bonn government did not even have—as yet —diplomatic relations with Israel. But here again West German considerations were based on the perennial expectation of maximal support from their chief Western ally in any eventuality. In this instance the expectation seemed justified because the chief Western ally was itself the spiritus rector of the project. In the end all that the United States achieved with the project—except for the protection of its own ties with the Arab countries for another two years—was the drastic exposure of the Alliance's weakest member, West Germany, overextended as it was abroad and divided at home.

For the Communists the discovery of the West German–Israeli arms supply arrangement offered an ideal opportunity. It took one simple project—the engineering of an official invitation to Walter Ulbricht, as the harbinger of Egyptian recognition of East Germany—and the whole structure of German foreign policy in the Middle East came tumbling down like the house of cards it was. The reaction of the Bonn government to the crisis was simply headless. Chancellor Ludwig Erhard's Cabinet precipitously decided to stop the arms shipment to Israel, an act that infuriated not only the Israelis but Jews everywhere, and not only Jews. The Erhard government then went on to announce that all aid to Egypt would be stopped if the Ulbricht visit materialized. Since the Ulbricht visit was clearly a foregone conclusion (and if it had not been, threatening would have made it so), the announcement merely prompted Nasser to threaten to recognize the Ulbricht regime outright if West Germany discontinued its aid to Egypt. Thus the fuses were lit for a series of explosions that demolished an entire and vital area of Bonn's foreign policy, and with it a commensurate piece of the Hallstein Doctrine. It was a disaster.

The Germans were hopping mad at everybody, and particularly at the United States. The Bonn government spokesman, Von Hase, noted American "hesitancy" in admitting involvement in the German-Israeli arms deal. He later commented bitterly that the American government had "laboriously brought itself to consider favorably" Bonn's request for support in the Middle East. Germany's largest newspaper, *Die Bild-Zeitung,* published the story under the headline AMERICA HAS LEFT US IN THE LURCH IN THE MIDDLE EAST! As for Höfer, on the following "Frühschoppen" he turned to the American participant (Wellington Long of UPI) and made by far the most telling comment: "Mr. Long, the conduct of the Federal Republic in this crisis may be characterized as guileless, harmless, naïve, silly; but America's conduct is . . . improper!" Despite all that has happened in recent German history, despite wars of aggression with victims by the dozens of millions, despite the programmatic extermination of some six million Jews, the German word "unanständig" (improper, indecent, unethical) has retained—and I find this astonishing—much of its original muzzle velocity. It is, now as always, the strongest term of censure in the language.

THE GERMAN POLITICIAN I ADMIRED MOST FOR TWO decades after the foundation of the Federal Republic was Doctor Eugen Gerstenmaier. I admired him for his forthrightness, not to say his bluntness, for his strength of character—he was a tough, stocky little Swabian (who are the toughest, stockiest, and most hardworking of the German tribes)—and I admired him for his record. For Eugen Gerstenmaier was one of the heroes of the German wartime resistance; a compeer of Claus Schenk, Count von Stauffenberg, he had been a member of the Kreisauer circle of Count Helmuth von Moltke, a kind of inner circle of the resistance against the Nazis; he had been sentenced to seven years' imprisonment by the Nazis for complicity in the July 20, 1944, assassination attempt on Hitler. He was one of the eight children of a poor shoemaker in Kirchheim-Teck in Swabia. He had come by his doctorate in theology the hard way: going back to his studies eight years after he had left high school. He was also—as of 1954—the president of the federal Parliament (he had been a member of Parliament from its first session in 1949). Considering who he was and what he had done, his position in the West German government was an excellent advertisement for the restored health of the German body politic. He was, to all appearances and in fact, a tower of strength in the Christian Democratic Union of Konrad Adenauer.

But even more interesting than his position were his situation and his attitude. One day while I was in his office, Gerstenmaier showed me several letters accusing him of assassination. The reference was to his part in the assassination attempt on Hitler (in which several people were killed). Gerstenmaier told me that he received an average of six letters a week from young and old alike with variations of the same charge. In responding to such charges, the survivors of the plot of July 20, 1944, forced their own trial for treason by the district court of Braunschweig in 1952. They were exonerated on the ground that it is the duty as well as the right of the individual to conspire against any "illegal state." The ascertaining of precisely what constitutes legal and illegal states was ultimately left to the individual conscience, a decision boding a reform strikingly reminiscent of Luther's Reformation: every man his own supreme court judge. Whenever I tried to express my admiration of the German resistance, Gerstenmaier would remind me of two things: "We were an infinitesimally small [verschwindend klein] percentage of the population! Secondly, over ninety percent of the resistance people were aristocrats."

The charges and accusations came from all directions. Karl Barth, the Swiss theologian, lent his prestige to the vulgar charge that Gerstenmaier must have cooperated with the Gestapo in order to survive. To my mind, this throws a very strange light on Barth, who soon found himself in strange company anyway. The parachute general Ramke repeated the charge and added that Gerstenmaier had wrongfully assumed the degree and title of doctor of philosophy. The general struck Gerstenmaier's sorest point: Gerstenmaier had taken his doctor's degree at the University of Rostock in 1935 and been called to Berlin to qualify (by habilitation) to lecture at the university. He did so. But here the Nazis intervened, refusing to grant him permission to teach, and set an end to his academic career. When Gerstenmaier sued Ramke for damages, Ramke's lawyer advised his client to settle out of court, which the general and finally Gertsenmaier agreed to do. Settling out of court proved to be a mistake for Gerstenmaier: the judicial inquiry instituted by the Bonn prosecutor's office into the charge of Gerstenmaier's unauthorized assumption of academic titles continued unaffected. The state secretary in the Ministry of the Interior explained to Gerstenmaier that it was a question of interpretation as to whether Gerstenmaier possessed the venia legendi, a degree which follows the doctorate and authorizes the holder to lecture. According to Nazi law Gerstenmaier did not possess the venia legendi; according to the pre-Nazi traditional German law he did. After World War II the states of West Germany reintroduced the old, pre-Nazi law for habilitation. However, a special law had been introduced for those whose records originated and were kept outside the territory of the Federal Republic—and the University of Rostock, Gerstenmaier's alma mater, was in the Soviet zone. To sum up: Gerstenmaier, who had risked his neck in the anti-Nazi resistance, was under investigation on the charge of breaking a Nazi law which had been condemned out of hand, declared null and void by the Allies, and repealed by the Germans, but only in the area under the effective control of the Republic. Because Gerstenmaier had taken his degree in an institution beyond the effective control of the Republic no clear reading of his case could be rendered. Understandably Gerstenmaier felt that he was being discriminated against.

The importance Gerstenmaier attached to his academic degree and title was indicative of no idiosyncrasy on his part. The mainstay of the class-caste system in Germany was the effective though not actual numerus clausus of the German universities and high schools (Gymnasia). For more than fifty years—until 1955—there were twelve universities in Germany. In almost any given peacetime year in the first half of this century the number of German university students was constant: 135,000 (scarcely more than the total of university students in Greater New York in 1938) and this in a country with a population of eighty million. The number was held down by the comparative scarcity of Gymnasia, a diploma (Arbitur) from which was the prerequisite for matriculation in a German university. The number of diplomas given was restricted by the sheer weight of the workload and the severity of the examinations. Designed in large part by the educational reformer Wilhelm von Humboldt at the turn of the nineteenth century, the system was intended to produce an elite to steer the ship of state. The higher echelons of the civil service were open only to university graduates. An academic degree thus also assured the holder of social standing second only to that of the aristocracy and (in some German states) the military.

However, Gerstenmaier also harbored the fear that the state prosecutor would apply to the Ministry of Justice for the lifting of his immunity as a member of Parliament. Surely this fear was irrational. Or was it? German jurisprudence has probably suffered more from the "confusion of concepts" (Begriffsverwirrung) than any other institution in the country. In any case Gerstenmaier found it intolerable that he should be on the defensive; his role was that of the accuser, not that of the accused. In 1968, the year before his situation came to a crisis, Gerstenmaier made a speech at a ceremony commemorating the one-hundredth anniversary of the birth of the poet Stefan George, who was a sort of spiritual patron of the resistance against Hitler. "It may be," said Gerstenmaier then,

> that this blow [the assassination attempt] aimed at the head of the state and commander in chief, which was unique in recent German history and therefore also appeared incredible to many—it may be that it failed, despite all the planning and foresight, simply because Hitler was not killed. But when I think it over carefully, then I come to the same conclusion today, twenty-four years later, that I already

[362]

came to in the severe circumstances of solitary confinement when I was under arrest by the Gestapo. Regardless whether the man who was the chief target of the attempt died or escaped, Stauffenberg's deed would have become a beacon, the igniting spark of a general uprising, if—well, yes—*if* the German people, and above all the German armies and their field commanders had torn themselves from the entanglement in which they were held fast by habit, prejudice, perplexity, and—I regret having to say this—also cowardly indecision.

Gerstenmaier was not in the habit of pulling his punches.

Gerstenmaier pressed his lawyer to take whatever action was necessary to produce a court affirmation of his right to his doctorate. His lawyer, Fabian von Schlabrendorf, was himself a key figure and chronicler of the German anti-Nazi resistance. Von Schlabrendorf, protesting the difficulty of instituting such proceedings, finally returned to a suggestion he had made before and which Gerstenmaier had already rejected: to apply for restitution as a victim of National Socialist oppression. Von Schlabrendorf admitted that the process of restitution was primarily designed to provide material compensation, reimbursement for wrongs suffered and property lost. Gerstenmaier had previously rejected the idea of restitution because it was obviously unbecoming for the president of Parliament to take steps tantamount to suing the state for damages. But he now accepted restitution proceedings as a means to the end of documenting his right to a doctor's title. "In a state of suspension between belief and deception," explains Josef Nadler in his great work on the German tribes, "between the identity presumed to exist in analogy and the isolating process leading to individual existence [as distinct from that of the species, the clan, or the collective], the imagination becomes the inventor of symbols."

The moment the act of restitution (objectionable in itself) became the symbol of Gerstenmaier's vindication—the rehabilitation of his habilitation as it were—then the reservatio became the ratio, his reservation against restitution became his rationale *for* restitution: the value of the symbol outweighed all other consideration. For if restitution proceedings were the only way to come by his rights, then restitution was also a right, and a right fitting and proper to the president of Parliament. "I will have my rights," he said. "I will not bow or give way. Rather will I go down to ruin in this matter. I will not put up with something in this just, constitutional state [Rechtsstaat] that I had to put up with in an unjust, unconstitutional state [Unrechtsstaat]." A political motive ennobles what would otherwise be a dastardly deed—say murder, say particularly murder. But an economic motive, supposed or posited, can undermine a political motive. Gerstenmaier demanded his rights, *all* his rights. He received the sum of 281,107 marks and 9 pfennig, the estimated equivalent of the accumulated total of thirty-four years teaching at a university. It was unquestionably a most liberal estimate, containing as it did the cash conversion of his pension rights. Also, as part of the estimate Gerstenmaier was assigned to the rank of associate professor and given a preferential category for assignment. He was, however, with the same finding retired emeritus. Here the authorities had no choice because they had no means of fulfilling Gerstenmaier's demand for a university post. The federal government has no university: universities in West Germany are the property, and come under the authority, of the states that make up the federation (Bund). Thus, although confirmed in his doctor's title and academic dignity, Gerstenmaier was foiled in the realization of his innermost desire.

He had very little time to nurse his frustration. When the magnitude of the amount of Gerstenmaier's restitution became known publicly, the whole of West Germany seethed with indignation. I watched, fascinated, as the great, inexorable avalanche of outrage slowly gathered momentum and then swept everything before it. Gerstenmaier received thousands of letters ranging from strong disapproval to violent condemnation. The *Stuttgarter Zeitung,* from Gerstenmaier's home territory, was as strong in its reprobation as any other newspaper in the country:

> Was not restitution designed for those whom the Third Reich uprooted and whose careers it wrecked, for the university instructor in civil law who now drives a taxi in Tel Aviv because his knowledge cannot be put to use there, for those who will feel the scars on their bodies for the rest of their lives? Gerstenmaier belongs to those few persecuted who achieved high government office in the Federal Republic, and the question seems warranted as to whether he could have been expected to forgo a claim to which he had a right. For it must have been clear to him that the publication of the sum which he received would unleash resentment in the Federal Republic, resentment that could be dangerous to our democracy. Who bothers his head about the special aspects of the case? . . . The impression which this matter makes on the ordinary citizen in this country, on people who are not familiar with restitution laws and salary rights for public officials, is devastating.

If anything, this was understatement. Gerstenmaier was ruined outright. He was forced to resign as president of Parliament and his name was struck from the list of candidates for a seat in Parliament. His fellow Swabians were particularly unmerciful in their rejection of him. This says something: the Swabians generally appreciate economic motives. They have the well-deserved reputation of being the most industrious and tightfisted of the German tribes. The move to abolish the West German one- and two-pfenning pieces a few years ago foundered on the Swabian veto. In short, he was hounded out of every public office he held. He had committed no crime; he had committed a considerable indiscretion. As he said afterwards: "Why, I could have had pretty much any university chair in 1945. But I was ashamed at that time to think of my personal career." (Ah, yes, but if he had done it then it would now be over and done with, cushioned and coddled in the past.) He could find no fault with himself for what he had done—except in the article of political tact. It is true that he enjoyed the emoluments, prerequisites, honors, and invitations that his high office brought him. But why should he not have? "Oh, what a fall was there!" In my estimation Gerstenmaier's fall from political power and public grace was the most damaging single blow ever suffered by the Christian Democratic–Christian Socialist coalition and this in a crucial year (by the end of the year 1969 the conservative coalition was voted out of office after two decades of uninterrupted rule).

But I wonder if Gerstenmaier's fall did not also wreck the myth (I use the word unpejoratively) of the German anti-Nazi resistance. To be sure, the effectiveness of the myth in German postwar life was always questionable, simply because it was questioned by the majority of Germans, compromised as they had been by their support of the Third Reich. Gerstenmaier was a legitimate resistance hero; as a resistance hero, his honor and his integrity, although questioned, were unquestionable. His tragedy is that he was caught and held fast in the mentality of the resistance fighter. Even after, long after, he had become president of Parliament he remained the resistance fighter with the resistance fighter's attitude toward the state. The state had changed and so had Gerstenmaier but not enough: his relationship with the state remained disturbed. This was one of the things I found so refreshing about Gerstenmaier— his iconoclasm with regard to the state. But he was also the only conservative politician besides Adenauer that I knew who would stand up to the Western Allies. His dedication of the south wing of the restored Reichstag building in Berlin in 1963 was an act of defiance vis-à-vis the Allies who were interested then, as almost always, in playing down the presence of the Federal Republic in Berlin. Gerstenmaier's relationship with

Adenauer was not the best. As Gerstenmaier once told me: "I can't get through to him [ich kann ihm nicht zu Leibe rücken]; I can bring no influence to bear on him." At the time I thought this statement reflected on Adenauer. There was the crucial question of how the Germans—specifically their political leaders—should have acted when the Wall went up. Should the Germans have demanded Allied intervention in order to prevent the construction of the Wall? Should they have intervened if necessary? "Brandt dodged the issue. For two whole weeks Adenauer did nothing, but absolutely nothing, in this direction. As for me, I am afraid I would have done it."

So said Gerstenmaier when I spoke with him in the autumn of 1961. (I think Gerstenmaier would indeed have intervened, I mean the Gerstenmaier before the fall.) As for the Western Allied failure to intervene in Berlin: "It was a breach of treaty," he said, referring particularly to the Paris Treaty in which the Allies undertook to promote the cause of German reunification in return for West German agreement to rearm within the framework of NATO. And yet the Germans were hardly in a position to point an accusing finger at the Western Allies because their own attitude with regard to reunification was equivocal. "That—the fear of war and the way the Germans conducted the last war— is so deep in their bones that hardly more than forty percent of them could be had for any intervention involving a clear risk. . . ." And then he added, "The official language of the Federal Republic is by and large revisionist. But the conduct of the Federal Republic, its deeds, its political management, lags rather far behind its official language. The conduct coincides perfectly with the cardinal American concept of containment."

Gerstenmaier's one hero was Claus Schenk, Count von Stauffenberg, colonel in the German general staff, the leader of the wartime resistance and the man who planted the bomb in the führer's bunker, which killed five men but miraculously spared the führer. What's in a name? Stauffenberg (Stauffen-hill) and Hohenstauffen (high-Stauffen)—both were Swabian families who built on high ground as the use among aristocrats was. The family seats of Barbarossa and the modern chevalier of the lost German cause are only a few miles apart. Once in the late thirties while on a field trip from the War Academy, Von Stauffenberg enlarged on the significance of the empire of the Hohenstauffens "in whose center we should regard ourselves as standing." (The group had just climbed the Hohentwiel, a small mountain overlooking Lake Constance.) Von Stauffenberg was not a model German general staff officer because there was no model; the general staff prided itself on selecting

[366]

unorthodox, unconventional, not to say eccentric, candidates in the hope of thus acquiring original thinkers and bold, untrammeled spirits. Von Stauffenberg served with distinction in Europe and Africa, where in the spring of 1943 he narrowly escaped death by a British bombing and strafing run. He lost his left eye, his right hand, and the last two fingers on his left hand in the attack. While he was convalescing, his uncle, Count Üxküll, persuaded him to join the active opposition against the Nazi regime. Von Stauffenberg made the most of his new position as chief of staff of the commanding general of the reserve army. He conceived and staffed Operation Walküre, a masterpiece of disguise and concealment: the action to overthrow the Nazi state and party apparatus was blended into the reserve call-up plan and presented by Von Stauffenberg to Hitler, who approved it. Thus when Day X arrived, not even the troops and most of the commanders participating in the putsch would be aware of the true nature of the operation until sometime after it was all over. The putsch failed because the blast from Von Stauffenberg's bomb did not kill Hitler or even seriously wound him. Even so, the plan might have succeeded had the conspirators been willing to use the requisite amount of violence. But they—and particularly Von Stauffenberg—hoped to overthrow the Nazis, "the fiercest government since Genghis Khan," with as little bloodshed as possible. The object of the exercise was to stop the "senseless slaughter" of the war (this did not mean unconditional surrender—certainly not on the Russian front) and to "restore decency and justice." "How can we do this," asked Von Stauffenberg, "if we start with a bloodbath?"

Now the German resistance, like everything in German life, was split. The Kreisauer circle led by Count von Moltke tended to believe that Germany would have to be crushed utterly in war by the enemy in order to destroy the Nazi virus. (This strikes me as a paradoxical position for a pacifist to take: Von Moltke was a pacifist.) Gerstenmaier, the theologian, a member of Von Moltke's circle, dissented and joined Von Stauffenberg. There is a radical difference between the two points of view. One of the chief considerations of the Von Moltke view was that murdering Hitler would only make a martyr of him. The possibility of this Von Stauffenberg categorically denied. For Von Stauffenberg, Hitler was the Antichrist. The general staff officer was a Catholic who had belonged to another circle, the George circle, in which the aging poet, Stefan George, taught his disciples that tyrannicide was not only justified but a moral obligation. In his tireless attempts to recruit fellow officers for the putsch, Von Stauffenberg would quote Stefan George's poem, "The Antichrist":

There he comes from the mountain: there he stands
    in the grove!
We saw it ourselves: he turned into wine
All that water and spoke with the dead.
Oh, could you but hear my laughter by night:
Now my hour has struck: now the trap is laid,
Now whole schools of fish swim into the net
The wise men, the fools—the folk writhes in madness,
Uproots the trees: down tramples the corn:
Makes way for the train of the Arisen.

No work of heaven that I do not do for you.
By hair's breadth only do you fail to notice the trick
With your bemused senses.
I shall make for you everything that is rare
And difficult, easily: a thing like gold out of mud:
Like fragrance and juices and spices—
And all the great prophet did not dare to do:
The art of drawing from stored up forces
Without ploughing and sowing and building.

The prince of vermin expandeth his realm:
No treasure not his; no good hap evades him—
Down with the skeptics and rebels!
You exult, are entranced by the devilish show:
You squandered the sweets that remained from before
And sense your plight only when all has been lost.
Then your tongues will hang in the drying through:
And you panic like cattle in the burning farmyard
While the trumpets sound your destruction.

Von Stauffenberg has been idealized by some, like the writer Trevor-Roper, who calls him "a spirit of fire—a truly universal man, a revolutionary aristocrat careless of himself who sought to unite ethical socialism with Christian tradition." Hans Bernd Gisevius, a resistance man who met and dealt with Von Stauffenberg on occasion, takes a different view. Gisevius found him "first, last, always, and only, a soldier who was drawn into the revolutionary problematic against his will . . . a go-getter who knows what he wants, . . . what he wanted being, in the last analysis, a continuation of the 'brown-gray' [Nazi party–German army] legality." Albert Speer writes that "Von Stauffenberg had kept his youthful charm despite his serious wounds; he was peculiarly poetic and precise at the same time, formed by two apparently incompatible educational experiences: the George circle and the general staff." Von Stauffenberg was Rupert Brooke in a general staffer's uniform. In trying to sum up Von Stauffenberg, Speer quotes Hölderlin: "A highly unnatural, paradoxical character if one does not see him within the context of the circumstances which forcibly impressed a stern form on his gentle spirit." But above all, Von Stauffenberg was a failure because he had an equable view of his own people. This view may be quite mistaken. I don't know. But I do know that it is a view very few Germans have. In this sense Von Stauffenberg was truly outstanding; and in this sense he liquidated himself. But here again, the fact that he was a representative and beneficiary of hereditary privilege (including nobility of mind), a member of a disappearing caste, and, above all, a *general staff officer* rules out his being popular with German youth today.

A great many Germans indeed—and not only of Gerstenmaier's generation—have a disturbed relationship with their country. Willy Brandt was deprived of his citizenship (ausgebürgert) by the Nazi German government. Even after he had become chancellor he continued to resent the deprivation: he made mention of it in his acceptance speech at the Nobel Peace Prize ceremony. Brandt's chief lieutenant, Egon Bahr, was expelled from the German Air Force Academy in the middle of World War II when it was discovered that one of his grandparents was Jewish. "Egon," said Brandt on one occasion, "suffers severely because of this business. This wartime experience keeps boiling up in him." The third president of the Federal Republic, Gustav Heinemann, has an almost traumatic distaste of the German military and has said as much publicly. Herbert Wehner, who is perhaps fully as important as Brandt in the Social Democratic party, was a leading functionary of the German Communist party until the end of World War II. What is more, he was the resident agent of the Soviet Intelligence Service (KGB) in Stockholm during the war. This is the reason Wehner has never made a trip to the United States: he was not until comparatively recently allowed to enter the country. He now declines to visit his government's chief ally.

It is in the light or, rather, the half-light of these distortions, suffered or self-imposed, that the figure of Konrad Adenauer emerges in something approximating its true significance on the German scene. For the great majority of Germans, Adenauer was "the phenomenon." He was indeed a phenomenon. On the modern German scene he seemed a throwback, a historical freak. In fact, he embodied a cultural and historical continuity that was diverted by Bismarck, distorted by Wilhelm II, and almost destroyed by Hitler. He was the leader of the age-old spiritual underground, "the other Germany." As such he engineered a counterrevolution against both right-wing socialism (the National Socialist party

[369]

—Nazi) and left-wing socialism (the Socialist Unity party—Communist). It was this, his flat equation of communism with fascism and his success in combating them as co-evils, that earned him the undying hatred of Germany's left-wing intellectuals. This and his invulnerability to any conceivable smear campaign. His arch-heckler, *Der Spiegel,* spent years trying to get something—anything—on Adenauer.

But his most distinguishing trait was his moral stature. This was so great that he stood out like a church tower intact among Germany's ruins. Certainly his complete self-assurance and towering personal authority derived from this quality. His integrity had to be taken literally: he was all of a piece throughout, complex but uncomplicated. What I found most impressive about the man was his perception of the necessity for going so deep underground during the Nazi period that he could not be stigmatized publicly or hagridden privately for any sort of German activity, pro or anti. In spite of everything, he kept an equable view of the German people and the German case. This was a stupendous feat of what I can only call largemindedness.

Adenauer's greatness had one inherent disadvantage: the man dwarfed his party. His most striking personal traits were his warmth and his absolute candor. He was never more candid than when he explained to me in November 1963 why he had not gone to Berlin until two weeks after the Wall went up. The Americans, he said, had asked him not to go. His presence in Berlin at that time was considered inadvisable. When he asked to accompany Vice-President Johnson to Berlin a week later the Americans again refused. Then his friends and lieutenants urged him to go to Berlin on his own anyway. The Old Man refused, saying the Americans had made it plain enough they didn't want him there. To the end he was the loyal ally. In the end his loyalty cost him every practical political asset he had possessed. But in the end he was not bitter: perhaps he saw the German problem in a way that no one else saw it.

Meeting Adenauer for the first time was like meeting an old friend whom one had not seen for a very long time. An old friend whom I never knew I had. Meeting him repeatedly strengthened the conviction that he could always be reached if one really wanted to reach him. He was the most accessible politician I have ever known. I loved the man. And yet for all his humanity it was impossible to regard him as just a person. His makeup was not formed mainly by his personal experiences. He was first, last, and always the homo politicus, occupied and preoccupied with political issues. He was a kind of Marquis of Posa as Schiller represented him, the chevalier of the Cross—refreshing in his forthrightness, candor, and lust for life, but always with the dominant note of his absolute determination to persist in his quest. In short, he was a fighting man equipped with very strong aversions, for his enmities were the shadows of his goals. The significance of these extended and portended far beyond the personal.

THERE IS NOTHING MORE ASTONISHING IN GERMAN
life than the abysmal difference between the South German and the North German, between the Austrian or
Bavarian and the Prussian. They represent two diametrically opposed ways of life. It is perhaps best characterized, for a start, with the old joke about Berlin and
Vienna: "In Berlin the situation is serious but not hopeless; in Vienna the
situation is hopeless but not serious." In Austria and in Bavaria and the
Rhineland—not incidentally or coincidentally Catholic areas all—there
is that vieille sagesse, that old wisdom that preaches the importance of
not being earnest. Play is everything and everything is play: stage play,
playing instruments, play with and play on words, game play. Hans
Weigel cites Arthur Schnitzler as I have cited Hans Weigel: "We are
always playing; he who understands this is wise." Ideally the Austrian
(this must be said for him) takes nothing seriously—nothing, that is,
except his unserious way of life. If there is anything grim and unbending
about the Viennese it is their determination to be gay and carefree. If
necessary, they will work hard to live up to the ideal. Certainly this talent
is what has saved the Austrians their sanity, hard-pressed as it is. The
North German, the Prussian, on the other hand, is a very serious breed,
he is in dead earnest most of the time. That earnestness is his grand
tradition and his pride. It is the best of him and it is the worst of him.
"Order there must be!" How odd this sounds to an Austrian! Or even
a Bavarian (whom Bismarck once described as the link between mankind
and the Austrians). What is most interesting and significant is what this
"animal earnestness" (tierischer Ernst) has made of the Prussians—or
what the Prussians have made of it—for it was at least in large part
superimposed upon the people by design (the great educators and ad
ministrators such as Von Stein and Hardenberg who were out to create
a citizen for service to the state). "A lazy nation," says a footnote in my
edition of Plato's *Republic*, "may be changed into an industrious, a rich
into a poor, a religious into a profane, as if by magic, if any single cause,

though slight, or any combination of causes, however subtle, is strong enough to change the favorite and detested types of character." Speaking of lazy nations—Austria was in the front rank of such and proud of it. An Austrian proverb that might serve as the national slogan is "punctuality is a waste of time." There is the classic story of the Austrian work crew pondering the problem of how to remove a huge boulder from the road: they discussed various angles of leverage, the possibility of using block and tackle, etc. Suddenly a German work crew hove into sight, marched up to the stone, and with one great collective effort shoved it off the road. "Well, yes," said one of the Austrians, "if you want to resort to force!" On the other hand, there is no blinking the fact that Prussian sobriety and directness had a great deal to do with the German ethic of hard work—as contradistinct from the Austrian ethic of light play.

From 1901 to 1944 Germany boasted forty-four Nobel Prize winners (one-fourth of them were Jews). Perhaps more important, with few exceptions all Nobel Prize winners, not only German winners, spent at least some time studying in Berlin. For more than a century it was practically impossible to conduct a scientific discussion without mentioning Berlin. Nor did Prussian earnestness prejudice the flourishing of the German sense of humor (so widely discounted by foreigners). Above all, there is the legendary wit of the Berlin working man. "Did you knit that yourself?" ("Selbstgestrickt?") inquired a bricklayer of Rudolf Ullstein (U-4) who was walking his dog, a Scotch terrier. The nineteenth-century writer Theodor Fontana asked a Berlin grocer why he was drubbing a small boy. "Every time this rascal walks by here," said the grocer, "he pisses into the sauerkraut. Of course, it doesn't do any harm, but I ask myself, what good does it do?" I would also cite Albert Speer, Hitler's wartime minister plenipotentiary of armaments. When Speer emerged from Spandau prison after serving his twenty-year sentence, he was variously interviewed and generally admired for his refinement as well as his forthrightness. "Why, he is a courtly gentleman!" exclaimed a lady journalist after meeting Speer. So strong was the good impression Speer made that it was frequently reflected in the questions put by journalists, particularly American journalists. I took part, along with others, in one such interview:

QUESTION: Mr. Speer, how could a man of your background, upbringing, culture, and good taste have taken up with such people as the Nazi leaders?
SPEER: I was bribed.
QUESTION: But Mr. Speer! How could a man of your upbringing,

background, culture, and good taste—and above all, your wealth—
possibly have been bribed?

SPEER: I was twenty-eight years old, a struggling young architect:
my father had money, *I* hadn't. I was given the biggest architectural
commissions in recorded history. That is how I was bribed.

QUESTION: Mr. Speer, what was it that attracted you to Adolf
Hitler?

SPEER: The fact that he was chief of state.

As for the importance of creating types, Alfred Rosenberg, the one
man among the Nazi leaders hanged at Nuremberg who had no last
words to say as he stood on the scaffold, had this to say in his foreword
to the third edition of *The Myth of the Twentieth Century:* ". . . the
Roman church felt no fear of Darwinism and liberalism because she
perceived these to be merely intellectualistic [*sic*] attempts devoid of any
power to create the spirit that builds community; the National Socialist
renaissance of the Germans, however, from whom the old value associations had fallen away in the convulsion of 1914–1918, appears so dangerous because it threatens to develop into a power capable of creating
types." Spengler called Nazism "Prussian socialism." But the Prussian
state that united most of the Germanies and created the Second Reich
was the last, if also the most important, of a series of determining factors.
Before the Kingdom of Prussia there was the Duchy of Brandenburg.
The Prince of Homburg, one of the Great Elector's generals as well as
his "noble cousin," was condemned to death for disobeying an order even
though his disobedience was the act that brought about victory over the
Swedish invader. (In Austria, the Maria Theresa medal was founded for
soldiers who fought successfully without orders or in defiance of orders.
There was always, to the very end, the absolutism of the authoritarian
petty princes, the norm of absolute obedience to the Obrigkeit, the
"upper ten thousand," the "establishment." David Strauss, whose *Life
of Jesus* George Eliot translated into English, defended the overwhelming dominance of such figures as Bismarck and Von Moltke. Their
"greatness can no more be denied than it is possible to blink the prominence of their actual deeds. Then indeed must the most stiff-necked and
surly of those fellows [he is talking about Social Democrats] take the
trouble to look up a bit so as to bring into view at least as much as the
knees of those exalted figures." In the Berlin Schiller Theater's production of Schiller's *Love and Intrigue,* the story of two young lovers driven
to suicide by the machinations of the court of some dinky dukedom, the
actors and actresses play around and between the feet of a huge papier-

mâché figure of the prince which more than fills the stage, being visible only to the knees. It was a patriarchal order with the prince in loco parentis and his subjects in statu infantis.

This is the great divide between the German Germans, particularly the Prussians, and the Austrian Germans (including at least some of the Bavarians): the German Germans, as a rule, are childish; the Austrian Germans, as a rule, are not. This development was in good part determined by the Prussian military tradition—"the army is the school of the nation"—since the command structure of an army is necessarily hierarchic and paternalistic. The Prussian system put the entire nation in statu infantis, a fact that prejudiced all subsequent developments, including reforms. "Only in a state whose citizens are accustomed to discipline," wrote Prince Bernhard Bülow, "who have learned in the army unconditional obedience, who feel daily and hourly the stern pressure of the apparatus of administration, could a party organization so large and coherent as German Social Democracy originate." This was not merely militarism but the specific Prussian brand of militarism: "I have often seen children play soldiers," said a French captain watching Prussians do close-order drill, "but I have never before seen soldiers play children!" In time even Prussian leaders became childish: "Berlin, July 4, 1895. The emperor, accompanied by a brilliant suite, will leave tomorrow for a cruise in Swedish waters, where he will remain during the whole month of July. The emperor has decided to devote his leisure to designing new types of warships." The business of preparing for and waging war is an accelerating process in itself that creates premature maturity and hence permanent immaturity. Adolf, the führer, was a superannuated adolescent. His practice of adhering inflexibly to the first idea that came into his head (on the general assumption of providential inspiration) was eminently childish.

To be child*like*, however, is a point of pride and a cherished tradition of the Germans, including the Prussians. "I see today with especial pleasure my wish fulfilled, to thank your princely majesty publicly and in the most childlike way for your high favor and more than fatherly attitude." Thus Schiller to his patron. To be childlike is one of the chief enduring German ideals. Childlikeness signifies sincerity, directness, healthy simplicity, naïveté, closeness to nature, unspoiledness, genuineness, devotion, and loyalty. "Ich habe mich gefreut wie ein Kind" (I was as delighted as a child) is a German idiom much in use. Germans as like as not will address their friends in the plural as "Kinder" (children). They use the word "Kind" (child) in addressing grown-up friends and acquaintances (or enemies) far more often than Americans say "kid" to one another. "Menschenskind" (child of man), "Geisteskind" (spiritual child), as in "Wir werden sehen wessen Geisteskind er ist" (We shall see whose spiritual child—what sort of person—he is), are in use, too. The German world is the world of children. It is not by chance that the Germans are the toymakers for the world. They also traditionally make and play with big toys—like the kaiser's battleships and Big Bertha (actually "die dicke Bertha," fat Bertha, the giant cannon built by Krupp and named after his daughter) in World War I. "The most offensive relic [of baroque theater]," writes Eric Bentley in his book *In Search of Theater*,

> is the German actor's habit of screaming his head off whenever he is faced with some problematic lines: a priceless way of evading the issue. The favorite mannerism of the screaming type of actor is the sforzando [it was also Hitler's favorite mannerism as an orator]: he is talking in a slow and hushed voice, as slow and hushed as only a German actor's voice can be, when before you know it he has hit a single word or line with all the violence he can muster. The hope, apparently, is that the audience will gasp and say: "*This* is acting!"
> The ham actor is driven, one feels, by the ham director; and often he is abetted by the ham stage designer. Ham in stage design shows itself in excess of apparatus, or color, and—especially nowadays—of darkness. Jürgen Fehling's production of Sartre's *The Flies* in Berlin is a typical slice of German ham: the emotions attempted by the actors and by the designer are far bigger and more macabre than those of the play. The result is foolishness.

The cause is childishness. There are other attributes of the condition dear to the German heart and much in evidence in the past and present. "The inclination of youth to secrecy and mystery, to ceremony and big words is extraordinary," wrote Goethe in *Wilhelm Meister*, "and often a sign of a certain depth of character. In these years one longs to feel one's entire being touched and stirred. The young fellow, who has many, looming presentiments, believes that he will find much, must invest much, and can only achieve much, in the realm of mystery." For the Germans the child, and childlikeness, are closer in the sense of the condition to the source of being, unencumbered by the effects of extraneous contingent influences, still intact and part of the whole being. A child knows everything because it still is everything. It is the perfect, pure, instinctive comprehension. And so we have the total solemnity, the gravity and utter earnestness of children. They are, as Goethe points out, rigorous moralists. They expect and demand perfection in all things and beings—all must be complete and ideal and umblemished.

But to say that Germans generally are children and infantile is not to say that they are playful. Children are not knowingly playful—or if they are, play is not to them what it is to grown-ups. In its passion for the game the child is utterly serious—and that is what makes the game so much fun. For "fun" in its root meaning is deceit (in the sense of diversion—to take the mind off a line of thought and turn it toward another). To be properly deceived, one must believe, one must give credence. Children and most Germans (not only Germans) give credence readily. Austrians are—or were—indeed playful. They work—or worked—off most of their "böse Triebe" (dark impulses) in games and nonsense doings. The Austrians make a game of something serious; the Germans make something serious of a game. This is what Seyss-Inquart was getting at when he said that Hitler would never have amounted to much if he had remained in South Germany. Perhaps the Austrians are passé funsters (although the tradition is still very much alive). Probably American society—as opposed (still) to a closed or totalitarian society —incorporates the tendency to make a game of serious things. An example is the advertising of the capitalistic product: the spectacle of a group of grown men in uniform (or out) saluting and cheering and taking solemn oaths to the trivial product of some great private firm, giant corporation, or mass conglomerate. Everybody knows it's a lot of trumped-up nonsense. There is comfort in this: not the slightest constraint to believe. And yet the boisterous grown-ups saluting and cheering (for ready money) make their point and sell their product, which in a capitalistic society is the most serious thing of all.

Germans do not consider themselves to be fond of children. In West Germany, an annual average of 90 children die as a result of parental brutality. Certainly nowhere in Germany is there anything like the Latin's almost foolish fondness and indulgence of children. There is, rather, the tendency to regard them as recruits ("*My* children must obey orders!"). As for the mishandling of older children, the court record of the trial of the participants in the July 20, 1944, attempt to assassinate Hitler and overthrow the Nazi regime is quoted at some length in almost every detailed account of the German resistance. The president of the People's court, Doctor Roland Freisler, treated the defendants, who were field marshals, generals, colonels, and aristocrats, like truant schoolboys. He interrupted and insulted them, hectored, harangued, and bullied them, scarcely allowing any of them to finish his statement even when it happened to be the answer to a question Freisler himself had put. Here are two examples:

GRAF SCHWERIN (VON SCHWANENFELD): I thought of the many murders—
FREISLER: Murders?
GRAF SCHWERIN: At home and abroad—
FREISLER: You really are a low scoundrel. Are you breaking down under this rottenness? Yes or no, are you breaking down under it?
GRAF SCHWERIN: Mr. President!
FREISLER: Yes or no, a clear answer!
GRAF SCHWERIN: No.
FREISLER: Nor can you break down any more. For you are nothing but a small heap of misery that has no respect for itself any longer.

*   *   *

FREISLER: To what sort of animal would you liken yourself in your conduct of this conspiracy?
VON WITZLEBEN: What sort of animal? I don't know—perhaps a donkey.
FREISLER: No! I'll tell you the animal you resemble: a swine; you are a swine!

Here is an excerpt from the eyewitness report of the court stenographer: "Never before in German legal history have defendants been treated with such brutality and with such fanatic ruthlessness as in this proceeding. Like common murderers they were led into the courtroom, each marched along by two Gestapo agents holding them by the sleeves (and the defendants were without necktie and suspenders)." Field Marshal von Witzleben was deliberately put into a pair of outsize trousers and left without belt or suspenders so that he was obliged to hold his pants up with one hand during the time he stood before the court. I have always taken this episode to be the example par excellence of the crucial parent-child relationship in German social tradition—in this case outraged parent and subdued children.

Until a few years ago I ascribed to the vagaries of the Nazi period the fact that Freisler, as presiding judge of the court, was himself interrogating the defendants. I was wrong. The interrogation of the defendant by the judge is a basic element in German trial procedure. It is still very much in effect. The judge is in complete control of the trial and does most of the questioning. Theoretically, the prosecutor and the defense counsel are allowed to put questions to the defendant only through the judge, although in practice this rule has been gradually relaxed to the point where prosecution and defense question the defendant with the approval of the judge. The office of independent public prosecutor was introduced in Prussia only in 1849 (from France, where it appeared as an innovation of the Revolution). In the same vein, there is no habeas corpus in Germany but, in contrast, an institution called "Untersuchungshaft," investigatory detention, "U-haft" for short. "U-haft" is the province of the court, not of the prosecution or the police. It is an institution that never ceases to amaze Anglo-Saxons. A suspect can be held for investigation for as long as a year and a half and in some circumstances even longer. The prosecution or the police must convince the court—but only the court—that detention is warranted. But if detention is warranted, then why the necessity for further investigation? In actuality it is a question of being able to justify suspicion of guilt, which is one remove (and a long one) from proof of guilt. The distance of the remove can be judged by the lengthiness of the investigation, the suspect remaining in custody the while. For one of the most curious aspects of "U-haft" is the frequent coincidence of the sentence imposed with the length of time already spent in custody.

Another section of the jurisprudential corral around the status infantis of the German people was the codification of penalties for the insulting of an official while on duty—"Beamtenbeleidigung." I remember a case some years ago in an Alpine village. One of the villagers hailed another villager, a gendarme, whom he had known all his life, and who happened to be in uniform and on duty, with the words "Servus, Sepp!" (Hi ya, Joe). He was charged with "Beamtenbeleidigung," found guilty, and fined. It is not the easiest thing in the world to remonstrate with or otherwise protest to a German official. Any sort of expostulation is likely to bring the rejoinder: "My dear sir, that last remark of yours could be interpreted as 'Beamtenbeleidigung.' "

But the mass of Germans were most successfully constrained by the class-caste system (Ständensystem), which came to its highest flower in the Middle Ages and was represented in large part by the guilds. This was the sense, then, of the German flair for and preoccupation with uniforms, costumes, and trappings. The preoccupation was and is with clothes as the symbol, as the defining evidence, the stamp that fixes the value and marks the place of the individual in society. It is the legacy of medieval ceremonialism in which every estate had its uniform.

It is—it *was*—more than that. An event that took place in 1906 was neatly summed up in the *Berliner Illustrierte:*

Berlin's small neighbor-city, Köpenick, was the scene of a crime which, because of its droll attendant circumstances, has occasioned much laughter. One fine day ten guardsmen under command of a captain appeared in the courthouse there, arrested the burgomaster and the treasurer and led them to the guardhouse in Berlin while the captain took the municipal till with four thousand marks in it and disappeared. The authorities were completely nonplussed until a former convict volunteered the information that a shoemaker, Wilhelm Voigt, who had likewise left prison a short time before, had told him that he would soon like to "do a job using soldiery." Voigt was traced. The captain's uniform and the stolen money were found in a clothes closet in his rented room. Laughter resounded all over the world when it was learned that a shoemaker in an officer's uniform succeeded in duping a city government. Voigt relied on the omnipotence of the uniform and he did not deceive himself in so doing. He received a lengthy prison sentence for his impudence. He was soon pardoned. A lady, the wife of a large department store owner, set up an annuity of 1,200 marks for him.

This was the famous "Captain of Köpenick" that provided the subject of Carl Zuckmayer's play of the same name. My father-in-law Fritz Ross had two coats which I often wore: one was a splendid mohair with a wide belt and flaring pockets. Whenever I stepped into the druggist's or some other shop wearing that coat, the attendant would almost certainly say, "Ah, you'll be wishing to speak with the manager, will you not?" The other coat was a species of Hungarian trenchcoat of leather with padded shoulders and various straps and buckles. A leather coat has a very special significance in Eastern Europe. It is the uniform à choix of the political police or the Communist agitator-cum-action agent: the "iron men in the leather coat." Whenever I would appear in town wearing the Hungarian trenchcoat, policemen would eye me suspiciously and follow close behind. Germans are so sensitive to attire that a man or a woman with a large wardrobe—or the sartorial imagination to make up for the lack of one—can have a lot of fun in Germany or get into a lot of trouble, as the case may be.

In *Wilhelm Meister,* Goethe's classic educational novel, the hero discusses a problem in a letter to his brother-in-law:

> In the first place I must unfortunately confess to you that my diary was put together from various books with the help of a friend out of the need to please my father and that I certainly know the things therein written and still more such, but in no wise do I understand them nor wish to occupy myself with them. What good does it do

me to fabricate good iron when my innermost self is full of slag? And what good to put a country estate in order when I remain at odds with myself? To say it to you in one word: ever since my early youth I have had the dim desire and purpose to educate myself just as I am. I still have these same intentions but now the means which will make this undertaking possible for me have become somewhat clearer. . . . If I were a nobleman our argument would be quickly resolved; but since I am only a commoner I must take a peculiar path. . . . I do not know what it is like in foreign countries, but in Germany only for the nobleman is a certain general—if I may say personal—education possible. A commoner can turn a profit and if great need be he can train his mind; but his personality goes lost, let him turn and twist as he will. Because it is the duty of the nobleman, who is on social terms with the finest people, to give himself a refined bearing and behavior; because this comportment —since he has entrée everywhere—becomes natural to him, his being held accountable with his standing and his person, be it at court or in the army, so he has cause to respect himself and to show that he respects himself. A certain solemn grace in dealing with ordinary things, a manner of careless elegance when dealing with serious and important things clothes him, surely, because he lets it be seen that he always and everywhere keeps his balance. He is a public person, and the more studied his movements, the more sonorous his voice, the more restrained and measured his entire being, then the more perfect is he, and if he is always just the same vis-à-vis high and low, vis-à-vis friends and relatives, then there is no fault to be found in him, one has no right to wish him to be other than he is. He is cold, but understanding; insincere, but clever. If he knows how to control himself as far as appearances are concerned at every moment of his life, then no one has the right to make any further demand of him, and everything else that he has in and about himself—ability, talent, riches—all these seem to be mere supplements. Now imagine some commoner or other who intends to make any sort of claim on those privileges; he must certainly be doomed to failure, and he must needs be the more unhappy the more his natural disposition lends him ability and inclination to aspire to that manner of being.

If the nobleman knows no boundaries in ordinary life, if one is able to make a king or a kinglike figure of him, then he may with equanimity stand before his peers; he may press forward everywhere, whereas nothing becomes the commoner more than the pure, quiet feeling for the borderline that has been drawn for him. He may not ask: what are Thou? but only: what hast Thou? What insight, what knowledge, what ability, how much property? Whereas the nobleman gives everything in the very representation of his person, so the commoner through his personality gives nothing and is expected to give nothing. The nobleman may and is expected and required to exhibit himself; the commoner is merely expected to be there, and if he tries to exhibit himself he merely makes an exhibition of himself. The nobleman is expected to take action and be effective; the commoner is expected to work and be productive; he is expected to develop individual abilities in order to be useful and there is the presupposition that there is no harmony in his being, nor may there be, because in order to make himself useful in one way he must neglect everything else.

These differences are not due to the presumptiousness of the noblemen nor to the acquiescence of the commoners, but the composition of society itself is to blame; whether anything about this will ever change and what will change concerns me little; it is enough, as matters now stand, that I have myself to think of and how I should go about saving myself and achieving that which is for me an imperative need. For I have, and that is all there is to it, an irresistible inclination to exactly that harmonious development of my nature which my estate by birth has denied me. I have, since I left you, achieved much through physical exercise and calisthenics; I have shed much of my usual embarrassment and demean myself more or less straightforwardly; I have likewise trained my diction and voice, and I can say without vanity that I do not displease in society. Now I will not deny to you that my impulse to become a public person and to please and be effective in a larger circle becomes daily more overpowering. In addition there is my attraction to creative writing [Dichtkunst] and to everything connected with it, and the need to develop my intellect and taste so that gradually also in my enjoyment, which I cannot do without, I learn to take only what is really good for good and only what is really beautiful for beautiful. You will see then that all this is attainable for me only in the theater and that I can bestir and develop myself in accordance with my desires in this element alone. On the boards the cultivated man in his brilliance will make as good an appearance personally as in the upper classes; mind and body must keep pace with each other in every endeavor and I shall be able to fulfill and represent myself there as well as anywhere else. Should I feel the need of other ways to keep myself occupied, there are enough mechanical vexations in stagecraft and I can supply enough to exercise my patience daily.

For me this passage is reminiscent of the schedule and resolutions set down, purportedly, by one James Gatz, a German-American youth, in a small town in the state of Minnesota in 1906:

Rise from bed .... 6:00   A.M.
Dumbbell exercise and wall-scaling ....6:15–6:30 "

Study electricity, etc. ....7:15–8:15 "
Work ....8:30–4:30 P.M.
Baseball and sports ....4:30–5:00 "
Practice elocution, poise, and how to attain it ....5:00–6:00 "
Study needed inventions ....7:00–9:00 "

GENERAL RESOLVES

No wasting time at Shafters or [a name, indecipherable]
No more smoking or chewing
Bath every other day
Read one improving book or magazine per week
Save $5.00 [crossed out] $3.00 per week
Be better to parents

The author and practitioner of this schedule and these resolves went on to become the Great Gatsby in the novel by F. Scott Fitzgerald. There is, of course, one all-important difference between the cases of Wilhelm Meister and James Gatz: the fact that the only way open in Germany to Wilhelm Meister for the realization of his ambition to develop and fulfill himself was the theater. There are more and better actors and more and better theaters in Germany than in any other country in the world for the same reason that German music is preeminent: the lack of civil freedom. The absence of so many of the outward forms of freedom forced a turning inward. In the words of Kurt Tucholsky: "On account of bad weather, the German revolution took place in music."

The revolution also took place in the theater, contributing to—as it derived from—the German passion for make-believe. The only freedom left was the "inner freedom." There are today in West Germany alone ninety-seven state and city theaters (including opera houses; those that are not strictly speaking opera houses can and do double as such). They are all subsidized directly or indirectly by the state and city governments that make up the Federal Republic. They are either the selfsame theaters or the legacies of those state and city theaters that sprang up in the eighteenth and nineteenth centuries ("Staatstheater" and "Stadttheater") largely as a result of the particularistic emulation and vanity of the petty princes and dinky dukes. Since World War II the Germans have spent many billions of marks for the reestablishment and upkeep of their theaters and operas. Of course all this money comes out of taxes; the culture-fetishism of the Germans is adduced as the reason for their willingness to continue paying. No one in Germany questions the superiority of state-subsidized theater over private theater. The state-selected

"Intendanten" (director-producers) of the theaters consider themselves independent; if this too is a self-deception it is a harmless one as long as the machinery of the state remains in nonauthoritarian hands.

For my part I do not think it possible to exaggerate the importance of the theater, including opera, in German life. It is, as Schiller said it should be, a moral institution, both for better and for worse. The German tradition has made theater a function of society. The theater-going public has been apostrophized as the silent chorus of the German drama, as the communicating link, the conveyor belt between the stage and society. This is not in the vein of "all the world's a stage" on which each man plays a role or is disqualified therefrom by social sanction, so that Wilhelm Meister can float free and find his natural level only in the world of the theater. In Germany the theater is the interpreter of "genuine consciousness" and the exposer and destroyer of "false consciousness." By the same token it is the destroyer of "genuine consciousness" and the interpreter and promoter of "false consciousness"—there was a longish interlude there, a score of years and more, that seemed like a thousand years to a good many people, in which the Germans had "a sense of well-being while wrapped snug in the folds of a false consciousness" (Carlo Schmid, vice-president of the West German Parliament and the only bel esprit among German politicians). The function of the theater in German society is crucial—formative and normative. As such it put the artist in the key position in German society—on the sufferance, it is true, of the ruling prince. But the position was there and was still there when the ruling princes had disappeared. The Nazi leaders had no more important mandate than the one accruing to them from their self-bestowed cachet as artists. This was particularly true of the führer himself as painter and "master builder." Hitler was quick to see the value of billing himself as such. Goebbels was the author of a novel, *Michael,* and several plays (which did not see the light until they were party-sponsored but that was no considerable detraction in the eyes of the masses). Göring played Maecenas, patron of the arts and artists. He was not just a freebooter with a penchant for paintings and objets d'art: he married an actress, Emmy Sonnemann, and not merely by chance; he was the long-time patron and protector of the celebrated actor Gustav Gründgens. Alfred Rosenberg was the author of *The Myth of the Twentieth Century,* a book which sold over a million copies and would probably have been a best seller even if Rosenberg had had no connection with the Nazi party.

But the German adulation of the artist is part of the German delight in deception (die Lust am Trug). This has many roots. The center of all being is a mystery, hence the passion for black and white magic, gods and demons, riddles and runes. In Germany an unusually good actor is almost invariably referred to as "demonic," because he changes form and appearance as demons do, he is a master of guise and disguise, a magician, an enchanter. Music hath charms and is enchanting, is indeed an incantation—from "singing in" (incanto) by way of conjuring up with a magic formula. The German is not disappointed, he is "dis-enchanted" (enttäuscht); literally, he is "brought out of his deception," deception here used as a pleasant form of madness. In describing a play he saw in Verona, Goethe wrote that "it betrayed one from beginning to end." The "crazy bone" or "funny bone" in English is called "Musikanten-knochen" (musician's bone) in German. This is why Wagner is regarded in Germany as *the* artist; this is why Nietzsche broke with him: his theory of the opera, which he put to practice so brilliantly, was that music should be merely the means to the dramatic end. It was too much: an all-out attack on the senses of hearing and vision, son et lumière. Wagner's tone suspense, the endless postponement of the resolution of shifting dissonance, alarmed Nietzsche exceedingly. "The purpose which the newer music pursues," wrote Nietzsche in his essay, "Wagner as a Danger,"

in what is now intensely but unclearly described as "endless melody" can be understood by wading into the ocean, gradually losing one's foothold and giving oneself over to the mercy of the elements: one must swim. In the older music, in the graceful or solemn or fiery to and fro, quick and slow, one had to do something entirely different, namely dance. The necessary measure for this, the observance of equally qualified degrees of time and intensity exacted a continuing deliberation from the mind of the listener—in the opposition of the cooler current of air that comes from such deliberation and of the warmed-through breath of enthusiasm resided the charm of all good music. Richard Wagner wanted another kind of movement—he overturned the physiological prerequisite of all music up to that time. Swimming, floating—no longer walking, dancing . . . perhaps this is to say the decisive thing. The "endless melody" is meant to break all regularity of time and emphasis, and in so doing it ridicules itself, it has its profusion of inventiveness precisely there where it sounds like paradox and blasphemy to an older ear. From the imitation, from the prevailing of such taste there would arise a danger to music which it is impossible to exaggerate —the complete degeneration of the feeling for rhythm, chaos in place of rhythm. . . . The danger comes to a head when such music allies itself ever more closely with an entirely naturalistic method of acting and miming undisciplined by any law of form, which aims at effect and nothing more. . . . The espressivo at all costs and music in the service of, in slavery to, attitudinizing—this is the end.

The dependence of the musical intervals on certain arithmetical ratios of lengths of strings at the same tension (2:1 giving the octave, 3:2 the fifth, and 4:3 the fourth) is regarded as the greatest of Pythagoras's discoveries. The Pythagorean philosophers held that any change in the conventional structure of musical composition would be likely to have far-reaching and perhaps disastrous political consequences.

It is interesting and, I think, cogent that Nietzsche puts the responsibility for the great break in music from the ethical to the pathetic—the shift from the rational to the emotional—at the door of Beethoven. Beethoven was a "German" composer; Mozart was not. The ground for this qualitative shift was prepared by Martin Luther: by Luther personally as the composer of Protestant hymns and the discoverer of a new dimension in music to accompany his discovery of the personal relationship between the individual human being and God; by Luther representatively as the father of the Reformation, whose chorales reflected the inklings of the new dimension. In this sense Beethoven was the musical executor of Luther's spiritual estate. It is extraordinary how often one finds the figure of Luther at the beginning of characteristic German developments.

For my part, the most effective engineering of illusion I have ever seen was Wieland Wagner's production of *Parsifal* at Bayreuth in 1969. Seeing is believing: if I had not seen it I should never have believed it possible to achieve such effect as Wieland Wagner did with lights and lights alone. There were no props, no scenery, no decor—the stage was bare. An oblong pool of fairly bright light was thrown onto the center of the stage with diminishing shadings of softer lights around it. The figures of the characters materialized and dematerialized as they moved toward and stepped into the magic circle of light or stepped out and moved away. The ingenious blending of lights also set the whole stage afloat. The transitions were done with surpassing finesse: between the utter darkness and the twilight that reveals the hall of the knights in the second act, a full ten minutes passed. Parsifal's catching and throwing the magic spear was done to perfection with glancing lights. The Grail containing Christ's blood glowed and pulsed like the Koh-i-noor. The soft rain and then the torrent of crimson against the universal darkness in the third act was "Christ's blood streaming in the firmament." The performance was in the nature of a religious service of surpassing beauty (a longish one: six hours, but an unforgettable, overwhelming experience).

The opposite experience, that is, the effective dismantling of illusion, could be had by proceeding across town in Berlin to Bertolt Brecht's Theater am Schiffbauerdamm. This type of theater, sometime called "epic," was based on the Verfremdungs-effekt or "alienation effect." Brecht borrowed the idea from the Russian and Chinese theaters. This was the use of whatever technical and histrionic means were necessary to enable the spectator to ward off deception, to prevent his succumbing to the illusion generated by the story being acted out on the stage. "The actor," wrote Brecht, "must demonstrate like a bystander describing an accident," he must view and interpret the character he portrays "from a socially critical angle," he must "stand between the audience and the part" and "coldly analyze his feelings." In short, the spectator was not to be allowed "to submit to an experience uncritically by means of empathy with the characters in a play." He was to be forced to think "objectively" about the subject matter of the play through the reception of various impressions, if need be, simultaneously. Brecht's production of *Mother Courage* set me to thinking as few plays have done. But Brecht's idea of theater was basically didactic or, as he finally styled it, dialectical. Other Brecht productions impressed me as cram-course classes in night school for adult immigrants, the immigrants being en route from a bourgeois present to a proletarian future.

But one of the greatest sources of deception and illusion in Germany is surely the language. My early delight with the German language was due to its hardness, distinctness, and what I took to be clarity. The reinforced consonants, the plosives and glottal stops, gave an abrupt quality to the pronunciation that made it sound decisive. It was a language that sounded like it got things done. I suppose this is what Nietzsche meant when he claimed that German was becoming a language shaped for the utterance of military commands. But the distinctness and sharpness of spoken German is important in that it helps maintain the suspension of sense demanded by German grammatical structure. The defining article—der, die, or das—keeps ringing in the sound chamber of the mind while the procession of adjectives or adjectival clauses follows and is drilled in close order by the noun, and put at parade rest by the final verb, the accumulated sense of the sentence coming with a concerted rush at the end. For example: "The much-sung, legend-entwined, and because of heavy rains badly swollen Danube has in several places along its sinuous course while causing great damage and despite untiring efforts of local inhabitants its banks overflowed." Here is a sentence from Ernst Fischer's *Memoirs.* "Sie nannten sich Jungsozi-alisten, kürzten diesen Namen in 'juso' ab und sprachen ihn aus wie 'jusso,' scharf und hart, ein Peitschenhieb." (They called themselves Young Socialists and abbreviated this name to "Juso" and pronounced it like "Jusso," sharp and hard, a whip lash.) Note the dismantling of the verb "abkürzten" so that it surrounds the object: "kürzten . . . ab." The sense is caught between the two parts of the verb and held fast as in a vice. The "ab" winds the matter up and settles it in terms of rhythm and sound quality—all to give the impression that here was a single-minded, determined, disciplined group, whereas in point of fact—as history demonstrated—here was a motley of political derelicts stumbling around in misery and ignorance but in possession of a hard-sounding, tautly structured language.

German generally gives the impression of good, hard sense, of a situation being clearly stated or a problem definitively solved when in all probability nothing of the sort is actually happening. The frequent con-tention that German is a source of strength to an orator is a point well taken: the nature of the language itself hypnotizes both speaker and his audience. "For a person," writes Fischer, "who needs overheating and hypertension as I do in order not to fall too far behind his possibilities, rhetoric is self-deception: the as yet indistinct feeling, the as yet un-weighed thought are falsely displayed as distinct and carefully consid-ered. The abbreviated process of rhetoric hobbles the thought processes." This is true of rhetoric in any language; I submit that it is especially true of German. The period of Germany's strongest and most harmful illu-sion, the Third Reich, was the period of two orators, Hitler and Goeb-bels, hypnotizing and hypnotized, unleashed on the public at large by the new mass medium of radio.

I think I have made it clear throughout this account that what has impressed me most in my experience with Germans is the leitmotiv of deception. Germans seemed to me to be the archpractitioners as well as the chief victims of deception—at once the masters and minions of self-deception. What puzzled me particularly for so long was the com-plex of connections between deception and womankind—"the Eternal-Womanly," as Goethe called it. Benno Frank cast Adolf Hitler in the role of a marriage swindler. And indeed, Goethe's Faust was also a marriage swindler ("Heinrich! Heinrich!") and so was Goethe himself, and on a rather grandiose scale:

Frau von Stein
Went to bed at nine;
If Goethe went too,
Nobody knew.

A good many knew that Goethe went too. The marriage swindle that lurks most stubbornly in my memory is the so-called Sesenheim incident, Goethe's first throw at the game. Sesenheim is a village about twenty miles northeast of Strasbourg in Alsace. In 1770 it was the home of the Brion family and it was here that the young Goethe—in disguise, as he so often was—met Friederike Brion, the younger daughter of a country parson. It is a very simple story: boy met girl, boy fell in love with girl and girl with boy, boy left girl. When he rode up to Sesenheim from Strasbourg to say good-bye he never even dismounted, but shook hands with Friederike from the saddle. Ten years later Goethe returned to Sesenheim and found Friederike as he had left her, unmarried, and looking very much the same. He never saw her again. She never married. He carried her on his conscience, if not in his heart, for most of his life. She was the model for Gretchen. Franz Lehar commemorated the Sesenheim incident in his operetta, *Friederike*. It was Lehar's favorite—"O Mädchen, mein Mädchen! Wie lieb' ich Dich!" (The operetta was a success only so long as Richard Tauber sang the role of the young Goethe.)

Sesenheim today is a village of perhaps a hundred houses. There are two taverns, one of which has two rooms that serve as a Goethe museum, with some framed letters from the lovers' correspondence, a few poems, and a sketch or two by Goethe and a picture of Friederike's grave in a town nearby. In the center of the village there is a small Goethe memorial pavilion with three legends engraved in marble on each of the three walls: "She loved me better than I deserved"—Goethe; "Vous êtes un homme" —Napoleon (to Goethe); and "1778–1779 à la veille du génie" (at the awakening of genius). There is also a huge mural on the front wall of the school building. It depicts Goethe, dismounted, shaking hands in leave-taking with Friederike. The Sesenheim incident is clearly the greatest thing that ever happened in Sesenheim. And small wonder. Goethe was the greatest man who ever lived about whom we know so much—an important qualification when comparing him, say, with Shakespeare. He went on for almost as long as he lived, seeing a new life in a woman's face and writing poetry about it. "Gentlemen, this soul," said Goethe, tapping his chest, "is too big for this life."

Thomas Mann reflects on the Sesenheim incident in his novel, *Lotte in Weimar*, speaking through Goethe's son, August:

> Not only are his works determined and stamped by the remembrance, and not only in *Faust*, in the Maries of Götz and Clavigo and in the poor figures which their two lovers make, does the remembrance reveal itself by repetition as a fixed idea. It becomes, if I perceive rightly, the fixed idea that strives always to repeat itself also in real life. Its object, as for example, resignation, painful self-denial, or that which the confessing poet himself pillories pictorially as desertion, disloyalty, even betrayal, is the originative, the decisive, the fate-determining factor; it becomes, if I may so express myself, the motif and motive, the coining stamp that fixes the value and defines the contents of life, and all the renunciation, self-denial, and resignation that follows is only the consequence of this, only the recurring remembrance of it. Oh, I have often reflected on this, and my spirit expanded from terror . . . when I considered that a great poet is a ruler whose fate, whose work, and whose decisions in life have an effect that goes far beyond the personal and determines the development, the character, and the future of the nation. Then I sensed the fearfulness and the greatness of that picture, which we shall all never forget even though we were not present, but which two people alone fatefully represented—as the departing horseman gives his hand without dismounting to the girl who loves him from the depth of her soul and from whom his genius [daemon] decrees the cruel separation, from this daughter of the people with her eyes full of tears. These are tears, Madame, whose meaning—even when my spirit is fully extended with terror—I cannot divine.

Goethe, of course, preferred that his cast-off loves marry, settle down, and raise a family as any good, healthy bourgeois should—having served their purpose as the delightful means to a great poetic end. Friederike's ex post facto lifelong abstinence, keeping her faith after he had broken his, duly (but not unduly) bothered him. In *Lotte in Weimar*, Mann makes a plea for the recognition of, and submission to, this form of poetic license in which the poet is a sort of divine parasite whose intentions, while ostensibly dishonorable, are ultimately otherworldly. He gathers honey for the sole purpose of converting it, at some later date, into immortal verse. In his association with Charlotte Buff, who was the model of Werther's Lotte, Goethe did everything Werther did—except shoot himself. The godlike, says Mann, is not to be taken seriously insofar as it is housed in human form. The earthly bridegroom, watching

Goethe's shenanigans with the bride-to-be, can afford to tell himself, "It's all right, it's only a god." And indeed, Goethe himself did what he could to keep the story in perspective, warning the youth of the nation in later editions of the work (and after it had become fashionable to commit suicide à la Werther) not to follow his hero's example. At the same time he took the critic Friedrich Nicolai to task for belittling Werther's fatal passion:

NICOLAI AT WERTHER'S GRAVE

A young man, once—I don't know how—
  Succumbed to hypochondri-ow
  And so was duly buried;
Along did come a bel esprit
  Who moved his bowels regularly
  As suits a man unharried;
He squatted o'er the grave a while
  Depositing his little pile,
And then pronounced as up he flounced:
  "Ah how could this poor lad himself so slay!
  If he had shat as well as I he'd be alive today!"

Is this romanticism? "The tragedy of Gretchen," wrote Bertolt Brecht, "is an episode in the humanization and higher development of Faust." The Great Gatsby was a romantic lover who devoted and lost his life in the service of his lady. But if Goethe was a romantic lover then he was in the service of a higher and wider romanticism. The great difficulty facing an Anglo-Saxon or any native English speaker in comprehending the Germans is the slow start he gets from the prevailing English notion of romanticism, whether it be on the level of the love story or the "high romance" of derring-do or the lyric romance of the standard English romantic poets. The English concept is much too confined to accommodate the term as it is used in German, but it can serve as a bridge. The English romantic writers believed in general that they had greatly profited from the then modern philosophical dicta: in the first place, they believed that feeling (as contradistinct from reason) was the true realm and source of poetry; secondly, that poetry was the highest employment of which the human mind was capable; and thirdly, that poetry was an infinite power and by no means confined to verse. The German romantic writers at the turn of the nineteenth century established (to their own satisfaction) the absolute identity between poetry and philosophy. Immanuel Kant had set limits to human perception by pointing out that the act of perceiving was confined within the framework of time and space, these were the warp and the woof of cognition, the terms within which the human mind registered objects, movement, and events. But the very instruments which man used, the senses, and the framework within which he was accustomed to use them, made it impossible to penetrate to the core of reality. What man had was his own faulty, distorted concepts of the outer world as fixed a priori for each individual by immemorial usage. The thing in itself (Ding an sich), reality as it really was, could not be apprehended as long as man wore the mask of his senses and was muffled in the cloak of congenital ways of looking at things.

Kant's disciple Johann Gottlieb Fichte stood this system on its head. For the Ding an sich Fichte substituted the sich—or, rather, the Ich—ans Ding. Fichte argued that it was an illusion to believe that there was anything beyond the limits of the Ich's (ego's) perception, because whatever seemed not to belong within the scope of the ego's perception was itself a perception and therefore belonged within the scope of such. Thus the projection of the thing in itself as outside consciousness was an optical illusion: the ego itself was the thing in itself. This was the philosophical and therefore scientific legitimization of unlimited subjectivity. Fichte placed the individual in the center of the universe and made him (potentially) omnipotent. A truly Luciferian feat, it made for the Satanic element in German romanticism, a hallmark of which was the Saturnalian orgy. Like the Great Gatsby, the German romantics believed in the "orgiastic future." They were convinced of man's position at the fulcrum of creativity (for good or evil) in the center of the world.

But the romantics in Germany went beyond Fichte. An extraordinary figure, the poet Novalis, discovered that the borders of ego-consciousness lay within the ego itself, were the ego's dark underside, as it were. In this way the German romantics struck and developed the vein that led to psychiatry and psychoanalysis. It was nothing new—or, rather, was so old that it was new. Novalis took his tips from Goethe, whose play *Illis* is an exercise in group therapy. Goethe took it from the ancients. Novalis called the conscious and the subconscious, the ego and the (outer) world, the two integral halves. "Whatever I will do, I can do," said Novalis. "Nothing is impossible to man. He is a magician. But I work magic without knowing it. Therefore it is not I, but another 'I' who rules the other side of my consciousness . . . if I can gain power over this transcendental 'I' then I am a magician, only then am I truly and entirely myself."

It was the central position of the German romantics that enabled them to develop the radial sensitivity which is prerequisite to great translators, that made magicians of Schlegel and Tieck, empowering them to transsubstantiate Shakespeare into a German poet. They achieved this position through the habit of regarding the world as an extension of the individual ego, of confirming the unity of mind and matter—and this on a disciplined philosophical basis: Kant, Fichte, and Friedrich von Schelling, who reconfirmed the unity according to the strictest scientific methods. What harm does it do to believe in miracles when they are the wonders of nature? The romantics rushed straight into the natural sciences; they saw the interconnections everywhere; the study of physics for them was the most poetic of pursuits. (It is interesting and probably significant that this is the exact opposite of the Soviet Communist approach, which has so far not produced any poetry.) They saw the development of nature as a progressive coming to consciousness that was reaching its zenith in mankind. "The world," said Novalis, "is the sum of our past objectivizations—those things which we have made out and hence separated from ourselves. Even our personal God is a romanticized universe." The pitch of exhilaration inherent in the movement was altogether extraordinary. The incessant wonder at vast discoveries piling up on one another. "In that very moment," again Novalis, "when I believe in God, he exists." And "Misfortune is the call to God." "Love is without question disease; hence the wonderful significance of Christianity." And hence the morbid fascination of the romantics with disease, with the abnormal, the grotesque, the macabre. With this new departure the barriers were down on the road to decadence: "Could there not be," asked Nietzsche more than half a century later, "such a thing as a neurosis of health?" Franz Baader pointed out that the word "sin" (Sünde) comes from "sunder" (sondern)—separation. Every conscious separation from the original child state of oneness with nature is a deviation and a sin, by definition. Likewise every enhancement of one's powers is a deviation and hence a disease—a dis-ease. In order to learn the meaning of love, said Novalis, and to learn to love, to acquire the power of unification, all the sufferings, needs, and negations of life are necessary. We are lifted out of monotony by disharmony and led to harmony by love. As Paul preached, love is the bond that binds together again. The romantics reemphasized the blessedness of childhood and the desirability of childlikeness, the conscious reachieving of childhood after the necessary separation from the original state. Separation there had to be because the original state of nature undivided was subject to the compulsion of blind instinct. Sex itself was a separation of the germinat-

[393]

ing power (at one in the hermaphrodite flower) into male and female. And here the female appears in her most mysterious and mystic light— as Sophie—a name that sounds slightly ridiculous until one remembers that it comes from the Greek σοφια, wisdom, a word that also has the meaning (from the German "weisen") of guiding, of pointing out the true way to the desired goal: the "Eternal-Womanly leads us on." Goethe's Ewig-Weibliche is seen as the principle of redemption, the awakening into consciousness from unconscious being, the endless revolution, as Ricarda Huch, the literary historian, sums it up—the endless revolution begun by Eve when she plucked the apple, the first piece of forbidden fruit, from the Tree of Knowledge.

It was an extraordinarily complex development that put such indefinable and sometimes unlimited power into the hands of poets and composers, playwrights and actors—"das Künstlerpack" ("the artist-pack"), as the wiser, older Austrians call them. Plato repeatedly warned against them. Magicians all. It was not coincidence that the hero of the national poem was cast as a magician and his career based on the life of Doctor Johannes Faust (who died in 1539), a doctor of medicine, an alchemist and black magician who was famed during his lifetime for his unquenchable (and hence illicit) thirst for knowledge, who burned to explore heaven and earth, all countries and continents, the earthly and heavenly paradise and even hell itself and made a pact with the devil in order to do so. In 1587 the book entitled the *Historia of D. Johann Fausten, the Widely Famed Conjuror and Black Magician* appeared in Frankfurt am Main published by Johann Spies. In less than five years the book had gone through fourteen editions and several translations and adaptations. More than half of the book dealt with the exploration of outer space. Doctor Faust ranged the universe, traveling from planet to planet and galaxy to galaxy in a chariot drawn by dragons and in the company of his Satanic sidekick Mephistopheles, whom he inundated with questions and who lectured him after the fashion of the cosmographers of the time. A contemporary of Doctor Faust was Theophrastus Bombastus Paracelsus (1493–1541), physicist, physician, metaphysician, astrologer, anthroposophist, theologian, mystic, and magician. Paracelsus was the polyhistor par excellence. He was himself the German ideal of the universal unifier, occupying the pivotal position interconnecting all opposite extremes. It is the interconnection of extremes, the synthesis of opposites, that is forever fascinating to the German mind, the pivotal position, the shuttlecock obsession with patriotism and treason, loyalty and deceit, forthrightness and guile, faith and betrayal, wet and dry, high and low, up and down: the manful mixing of hot and cold, and the rueful discovery (every time the experimenter survives alternately burning and freezing) that the result is lukewarm.

Did it just happen that Hermann the German, Arminius himself, the first historical "national" hero, encompassed the destruction of Varus's legions by treachery? Germans are eternally (and often enough fruitfully) fussing with first principles. They cannot or they will not go beyond them; they cannot or will not assume the principles are true, accept them, and proceed from there. They are too vitally concerned with theories of cognition, with questions of the admissibility of the evidence of the senses when the criteria of admissibility, the value of value judgments, are themselves in question. "Each age," wrote the historian Leopold von Ranke, "stands in direct confrontation with God." The past is reinterpreted from the shifted standpoint of each succeeding age: history is continuously in the making and remaking; it is continually being written and rewritten—hence the preoccupation with guise and disguise, guile and beguilement, and the longing for the solid, immovable center. The primary condition of a Volk, the makings of an ethnic identity, is its rootedness in nature—an attribute that takes some time to come about.

Everywhere in the German-speaking world is the obsession with mask, the maquillage, the cosmetic face that hides reality. "There is a language here," said the Swiss author Wolfgang Steiner to a German colleague not long ago, "and in Germany that seeks to work restoratively, that makes a maquillage of a country, that builds an image. Against this I believe that the effort of writers so far consists of tearing off this maquillage, if possible to destroy this mask and bring out the naked features of the face." I do not think that very many German writers are unaware that in destroying a mask in order to reveal the true features of the face—to expose latent dogmatism in Western democracy, say—they are necessarily making a new mask. Makers and breakers of masks are interchangable roles. There is the absolute necessity in life for four-flushing. "To measure up to all that is demanded of him," wrote Goethe, "a man must overestimate his capacities." In order to be more than he seems, a man must first seem to be more than he is; to realize the ideal, one must first idealize the real. A good definition for German romanticism is heroic self-deception. Is not hypnosis a form of intense, induced deception? Hypnosis is a German discovery, a German romantic discovery (the extraordinary figure of Novalis again).

Perhaps this is one of the causative factors in a constantly recurring theme in German affairs: the phenomenon of the exchange of roles. This phenomenon has many facets: it sometimes manifests itself in what Bismarck called the renversement des alliances, the overturning of alliances, a switching of sides in battle or in readiness for battle; it is more often apparent in the heavy-duty term 'Wechselwirkung"—interaction or reciprocal action, reversing the field, turnabout, the volte face. This is in large part because the Germans have always been in the center where the tide of battle turns most easily. Along this line of reasoning, perhaps the simple geographic, demographic, schematic circumstances surrounding their centrality account for the curious fact that German subjective idealism has always been a shuttlecock on a swivel: a perimeter offense is the best perimeter defense—and how on earth is it possible to distinguish between the two? As a result the country has always been split in one way or another and usually in more ways than one. In any struggle there is always the possibility that an exchange of roles will take place. The exchange is automatic when the tide of battle turns: the attacker becomes the defender and vice versa. But there is also a psychological process involved: chinks in the consciousness that gradually grow larger until lucidity is devoured by hallucination—or vice versa. To my way of thinking the most extraordinary exchange of roles took place *before* the tide of battle turned "in the most titanic struggle in world history"—on the German eastern front in World War II. In the words of General Reinhard Gehlen in his book *The Service:* "Apart from the failure of our allies, the Russian owes his great successes to the application of German field command principles . . . the Russian converted his conduct of the war in accordance with German methods and German operational doctrine. On the other hand, we have strongly inclined toward the earlier, inflexible, firmly fixed, down-to-the-last-detail Russian method and owe many of our failures to this fact. . . ." This of course was the doing of "the greatest field captain of all time"—or "Gröfaz," as the German army command called Hitler, who had hypnotized himself into the role of generalissimus (Stalin assumed the title but not the role). Indeed, Hitler is perhaps the prime example of an exchange of roles in German history. Until the abortive Feldherrnhalle putsch in Munich in 1923, Hitler regarded himself as merely the trailblazer and forerunner "till one greater man restore us," at most a John the Baptist for the coming Messiah. There was reason for this. The adjutant of the Sixteenth Infantry Regiment in World War I, Captain Fritz Wiedemann, while citing Hitler for bravery more than once, never once considered promoting him. When asked why he had not done so, Wiedemann replied that

GERMANS

Corporal Hitler, the message runner, had "never demonstrated any qualities of leadership whatsoever." It was only during his year of confinement in Landsberg in 1923–1924 when he wrote *Mein Kampf* that Hitler hypnotized or otherwise convinced himself that he, and none other, was the predestined savior of Germany. In many ways he was a very unlikely leader: he was inordinately lazy and possessed little organizational ability; he did not have an analytical mind; he could not or would not effectively delegate authority. He very soon botched the conduct of the war as he had the preparations for war. Stalin had at least enough sense to leave the conduct of the war to Zhukov. It was a Russian, for that matter, who brought my attention to an even more striking exchange of roles. In the late fifties in Berlin an acquaintance of mine suddenly looked up during a desultory conversation and said: "A fantastic thing has happened: the Jews have become heroes and soldiers and the Germans have become businessmen and money grubbers!"

Only once in my life have I been in a place where simply being there at that time seemed like a tremendous personal achievement. The place was Israel, the time was during the Six-Day War. I had the good fortune (as a war correspondent) to observe action successively on all three fronts. The Israeli victory in the Sinai peninsula was the most awe-inspiring military feat I have ever seen. It was also the worst carnage I have ever seen: thousands of dusty Egyptian dead on either side of the road to El Arish, a place of stark beauty whose white sand dunes so delighted T. E. Lawrence that he apostrophized it as "the last clean place on earth." There were communions of corpses in the tall date palm groves that border the sea thereabouts. Many of the Egyptians were in the antic postures of instantaneous death, but others were in repose, some even seated with their backs against the palm tree trunks. All of them with their shoes off—except one, one noncom who died facing forward in his trench with his shoes on. So miserable were the Egyptians (but not the Bedouin and not the Syrians), so pitiable their slaughter that I was given to sudden paroxysms of sobbing for the next two weeks. The path of flight south to Bir Lahfan, Bir Hasana, and southwest through the Mitla Pass was littered with abandoned Soviet tanks, guns, and vehicles, about half of them undamaged. All in all on the three fronts there was over two billion dollars worth of booty.

What overwhelming contrast with the victors! The Israeli soldiers of the Six-Day War were the finest I have ever seen—lean and quick and hard, beautifully disciplined, and consummately trained. Just before the jump-off against Syria I saw a company of Israeli infantry resting in an olive grove during a break. Young gods, many of them blond and blue-eyed. An impression had formed, had built up inexorably. It received its expression at the Wailing Wall just after the capture of the old city of Jerusalem. ("We are back after one thousand years!") A small group of us journalists was standing near the Wailing Wall when a squad of Israeli infantry, complete with army chaplain, jogged up to the Wall and prayed in formation "by the numbers," as it were, the chaplain intoning and the squad giving the responses. "My God," said an Austrian journalist standing next to me, and his face was white as a sheet: "the Prussian three-minute prayer!"

It was true. The Israelis are the Prussians of today: in training, in discipline, in battle readiness, in religious fervor (comparable, if not more than comparable, to the Protestant zeal of the Prussians). Moreover, there is a startling similarity between the geographic and ethnic situation of the Jews in the Middle East and that of the Prussians in Germany in the seventeenth, eighteenth, and nineteenth centuries in Germany and Europe. Even the configuration of borders is similar. ("And indeed because of its central position Prussia was forced to take the offensive in every war." "Prussia must concentrate her power until the favorable moment . . . for her frontiers are unfavorable to a healthy body politic." —Bismarck) Israel is almost precisely in the same position among the Arabs as the Prussians were among the Germans—"unbearable as a neighbor and undesirable as an ally." To say that the Israelis have no more choice (ehn brera) than the Prussians had is also to say that the Prussians had no more choice than the Israelis have now.

For me perhaps the most fascinating postwar development has been the shift in attitudes toward the Jews that has resulted from the emergence of Israel as a necessarily dynamic, expansionist (for the Arabs are even more emotional and undivided than the non-Prussian Germans were), and militaristic nation. For example: the fact of Israel has changed the Jews from an international liberal-radical class to a nationalist, conservative, the homeland-is-holy, Blut-und-Boden, deep-roots-in-the-sacred-soil race. It has torn the archliberals out of the world "liberal" camp and forced them to enter the ranks of the conservatives. Only conservatives have understanding for such a position as the Jews now call and must call theirs. "Liberals" and leftists can have no sympathy with what is for them basically a fascist position. Communist, socialist and—for the most part—social democratic parties thus oppose Israel and side with the Arabs. The return of the Jews to their homeland after almost two thousand years is quite literally an earthshaking event. It has brought about a whole complex of role exchanges: the guardians have become the wards (the Israelis have their own minorities to look after —Arabs and Druses), the guests have become the hosts, old enemies have become new allies, and old allies have become new enemies. I have never been more surprised than when I flew to Vienna from Tel Aviv a few days after the Six-Day War to find the most notorious and hard-bitten Austrian anti-Semites out on the streets collecting money for aid to Israel. Just before he was hanged—as an anti-Semite—Julius Streicher himself expressed his admiration for the fighting in Palestine for the State of Israel.

In short, the Six-Day War merely brought public emphasis to something that had taken place as a result of the creation of the State of Israel: namely, the alignment—for the first time in history—of the conservative, nationalist German with the conservative, nationalist Jew. In keeping with this development was the attack by Robert Neumann published in (if not prompted by) the liberal-left magazine *Der Stern* against Hans Habe, William Schlamm, and Gerhard Löwenthal, all three conservative Jewish journalists. Neumann, himself a Jew, hurled a hypothetical but curiously significant charge: the three, Habe, Schlamm, and Löwenthal, he said, would have been Nazis had they been allowed to be. The charge is, of course, nonsensical: if Jews had been allowed to be Nazis there would have been no Nazis at all. With this attack Neumann in effect renounced his claim to membership in the ethical community of the Jews. We have come a long way in a comparatively short time: not so very long ago the name "Jew" in Germany (and in Europe at large) was pejorative. Now it is pejorative to tell a Jew he is not a Jew, or that he is a "poor excuse for a Jew." At the same time we have another neat exchange of concepts: the German nationalist (or French nationalist) was an anti-Semite because he felt the Jew to be a foreigner and hence an antinationalist; the Socialist or Communist is now an anti-Zionist because he feels the Jew as Israeli to be a nationalist in his own right and hence an anti-internationalist. The homeless Jew was a race enemy; the Jew at home is a class enemy.

Meanwhile, back in the Reich, the Germans have seemingly all but lost their sense of nationhood.

EPILOGUE

THE GREAT DECEPTION IN GERMAN POSTWAR HISTORY, imposed on the Germans both by the Western Allies and the Germans themselves, was the diplomatic legerdemain that made a Western collective security treaty look like a German reunification policy. There was more to the trick than the compatibility of German national goals (particularly the recovery of the territories east of the Oder-Neisse Line such as East Prussia and Farther Pomerania) with the Western Allies' anti-Communist crusade (specifically John Foster Dulles's "roll back" policy). The Treaty of Paris (called the Treaty of Germany by the Germans) committed the Allies to the German cause of reunification in return for West German rearmament within the Atlantic alliance. It also filled Germany with a bewildering tangle of overlying, undercutting, and interlocking military and administrative area designations, enclaves, corridors, and claptrap. The new alliance, NATO, and its counterpart, the Warsaw Pact, were simply superimposed upon the old wartime alliance.

The wartime alliance, meanwhile, has been kept alive symbolically in Berlin in a few vestigial institutions of the Four Power Statute like the Spandau Prison—now with one prisoner, old Rudolf Hess, who is quite mad, almost blind, and guarded by four platoons of American, British, French, and Russian soldiers in ceremonious monthly rotation. There is also a Four Power Air Control Center, a more practical operation.

In postwar Germany, crossing a line—almost any line—tended to bring about metamorphosis. NATO troops ceased to be NATO troops and became Four Power troops the moment they entered the Berlin corridor (they could be restored to their former status by simply reversing the process). Even more stupefying were the sudden sea changes that occurred during the various Berlin crises. At the beginning of these there were always mighty tidings about combined Allied initiatives and reinforcements for the new alliance. Then, inevitably, an abrupt shift would be made to the Four Power approach, that is, to the old wartime alliance. In a trice, new enemies were transformed into old allies while the newest ally reemerged as the old enemy (a convenient old enemy long since defeated and neatly trussed up in a new alliance).

The resultant imbroglio was far too complicated to allow for old-fashioned betrayal. But the imbroglio facilitated prestidigitation—"now you see it, now you don't" diplomatic sleight of hand—to the point where all parties were doing card tricks, often without even knowing it. The core of the deception was Berlin. It was fed by the umbilical cord between the Articles of Surrender (the covenant of the occupation) and the Paris Treaty (the covenant of the anti-Communist crusade). When the German federal government was granted "sovereignty with reservations" upon its accession to NATO, it was necessary—mainly because of Berlin—for the Allies to ensure that vis-à-vis the Soviet Union the original title of rights included in the Articles of Surrender remain in force. Article 2, paragraph 1, of the Paris Treaty stipulates the rights of the former occupation powers with regard to "Berlin" and "Germany as a whole." This was not only the magic formula that seemingly transformed an occupation army into the vanguard of a liberation movement. It was also, presumably, the flash point that ignited the fatal German passion for mechanistic abstraction: the reservatio became the ratio and Sam was their uncle. Because Berlin symbolized Germany, Berlin was assigned the value of Germany: West Berlin was assigned the value of Berlin. Such a feat of cerebration made the pussyfoot Allied defense of West Berlin look like a determined advance (potentially) on East Germany. It was not until the Communists built a wall right through the middle of the city, the sacred once and future capital city, that the central illusion was finally destroyed.

The Berlin Wall was the dike that turned the tide of the battle between the East and the West. Or rather, the Wall stopped the tide and altered the situation in that it foiled German nationalist aspirations (generally, reunification; specifically, freedom of movement). The Wall bottled up the East Germans and forced the West Germans (who were unsupported by the Western Allies) to treat the Wall as a "national boundary" and thus, for example, to take preventive action against Western tunnel diggers. The foiling of the German national interest inevitably led to the accentuation of class interest: divide a nation and the two separated halves will subdivide along class lines—the new split beginning with the controversy over how to heal the old one. In such cases, class and race remain essentially interconnected, ultimately convertible concepts. It was the outbreak of class warfare in 1848 in Austria-Hungary that paved the way for the racial (national) struggles that

[401]

destroyed the empire. In a national struggle a race is capable of achieving class solidarity; in a social struggle a class can achieve something like the ethnic homogeneity of a nation. Theoretically—and the Russians are acting on the theory—one-third of a German nation can become a third German nation. (Austria is the second German nation.) Thus it was hardly coincidence that after the construction of the Berlin Wall forces were set in motion that soon manifested themselves in student demonstrations, strikes, and the emergence of the extraparliamentary opposition (Ausser Parlamentarische Opposition, or APO) of Spartacus, the Communist student organization. Spartacus has since succeeded in taking over the student administrations of several German universities. For its part, the West German electorate was slowly but steadily swayed to increased support of the Social Democratic party (Sozialdemokratische Partei Deutschlands, or SPD) to an extent that first made possible the formation of a grand coalition in 1966 and the return in 1969 of a Social Democratic government (albeit in a minor coalition with the quicksilver Free Democrats) for the first time in forty years. (In West Berlin the Social Democrats achieved an absolute majority in the 1971 elections and chose to govern for the first time in twenty years without a coalition.)

It was this development that laid the foundations of the Brandt administration's Eastern policy (Ostpolitik). It also set the stage for the Four Power Agreement on Berlin. The price of this détente was the renunciation of the German claim to the territories east of the Oder-Neisse Line, the acceptance of all state borders in Eastern Europe as "inviolable" (including those of East Germany), and the renunciation of the German Federal Republic's claim to West Berlin as a part of its territory. In return the Soviet Union undertook the establishment of a contractual guarantee of access between West Germany and West Berlin subject to certain rules and regulations worked out between the East and West German governments. Part of the same complex of agreements was the arrangement whereby West Berliners were allowed to visit East Berlin and East Germany for as many as thirty days a year, again in keeping with certain rules, regulations, and procedures. Subsequently the East German government agreed to discuss the possibility of allowing East German citizens to visit relatives in West Berlin and West Germany on other than an emergency basis. (It appears that relations in general between the two German states will be worked out in bilateral negotiations and that eventually the two states will apply for admission as individual members of the United Nations.) Thus Brandt as chancellor presided over the destruction of an illusion, the illusion that Germany

GERMANS

would somehow manage to salvage its territorial unity from the shambles
of World War II and the cold war that followed. In so doing he may have
created another illusion in its place, the illusion that Germans will accept
the division. Whether Brandt deliberately set about doing this or merely
accepted the ultimate consequences of the toleration of the Berlin Wall
by the Western Allies is of no great import.

One of the greatest paradoxes wrought by the selective persecution
of the Third Reich was the emergence of the Social Democratic party
as *the* German nationalist party. This was in good part because the Social
Democrats emerged from the debacle of World War II as the only
Germans who could afford to be nationalist. Nobody—but nobody—can
denounce Willy Brandt as a "militarist," a "neo-Nazi," or a "clerico-
fascist." It is worth remembering that the Social Democratic party voted
against rearmament and the European Defense Community. Social
Democratic opposition to NATO remained steadfast until 1960. (It was
Kurt Schumacher of the SPD who branded Konrad Adenauer "chancellor of the Allies!") The Social Democrats advocated détente and disen-
gagement in Europe, accepting neutrality for Germany. For above all,
this was the party of reunification by direct means (going East instead
of West). In the late fifties the Social Democrats finally realized that their
foreign policy, particularly their opposition to NATO, was generating
resistance against their party within the electorate. In 1960, with the
adoption of the Godesberger Program (in which the party virtually
renounced Marxism and embraced the principles of the market
economy), the SPD accepted the American rules of the game; only by
doing so could they hope to win (and so end) the game. Moreover, the
party foresaw the coming of the Democratic administration of John F.
Kennedy and shaped its program accordingly.

Win they did and they ended the game. For the first time in more
than half a century the Germans had a government that was morally
unassailable. Thus the nationalism of the Social Democrats was important because it could be acted upon. Brandt, because of his party's history
of persecution by the Nazis, was in a far better position to define and
promote the national interest than his predecessors had been. But socialists in general make poor nationalists (because their class orientation is
international by definition). The Social Democrats were not open to
moral blackmail, but they were open to tactical blackmail if they went
on, as they did, to accept the Soviet rules of the game. Having done so,
they also had to accept the rigidities of political geometry. Brandt acknowledged the division of Germany both to appease Germany's neigh-

[403]

bors and to make the division less painful for the Germans. There is not one country in Europe that would like to see Germany reunited; most countries, including West Germany's allies, actively oppose reunification. The Ostpolitik was realizable, then, only as the cornerstone of the European security treaty so fervently desired by the Soviets as the means of consolidating the status quo. All countries concerned have agreed to hold a preparatory European security conference and the necessary arrangements are under way. The European security treaty will be based on the division of Germany. The division of Germany will not guarantee the peace of Europe, but the peace of Europe will guarantee the division of Germany.

One of the ironies of postwar history is that the emergence of West Germany as the most powerful industrial nation of Western Europe was made possible by the institution of the Common Market. If Germany had not been divided, her neighbors would have taken infinite care lest they be drawn into her toils again. In this regard, as Adenauer divined, partition was a boon because it made Germany look harmless; it lulled her neighbors into a sense of security (and a security system) whose only proviso was that Germany remain divided. The military alliances on either side—NATO to the West and the Warsaw Pact to the East— guaranteed the division. To ensure durability these alliances were buttressed with economic systems—the Common Market to the West and COMECON to the East. In this way the American and Soviet spheres of interest were secured, magnetic fields with the two superpowers as opposite poles whose forces of attraction were calculated to be strong enough to keep the two halves of Germany apart indefinitely.

As a result of the Allied occupation, the Marshall Plan, the European Coal and Steel Community, and finally the Common Market (granting access to markets in a community area with disappearing tariff walls), West Germany was installed at the center of a new preferential system. "What I had in mind," wrote Adenauer in his memoirs, "was to use the means of competition and the increasing integration of the German into the world economy to provide a systematic corrective against the structural defects of the German economy." To this end the Basic Law of the Federal Republic contains an article (number 24) providing for the transfer of sovereign powers to international institutions. To achieve integration the Adenauer government and the majority of Germans were prepared to make any and all sacrifices—financial, political, and even ethnic (as in the Saar conventions which incorporated the Saarland in a politico-economic union with France). Adenauer was genuinely distressed when a plebiscite returned the Saar to Germany. He said that the gaining of the Saar for Germany was the loss of the Saar to Europe. He was right. Kurt Schumacher, then head of the Social Democrats, who always denounced NATO for what it was and harbored deep-seated suspicions of Western Europe anyway (he called it "the breeding ground of capitalism, clericalism, and cartels"), accused Adenauer of having put German industry in the service of French diplomacy. Schumacher might indeed have perceived, as Adenauer did, that the proposition could be turned around. The French bid for leadership in Western Europe was made possible only by the German need to have the universally most acceptable nation front diplomatically for the universally most unacceptable nation.

There is no question of who has profited most from the relatively free flow of goods, services, and investment capital within the Common Market area. In an arterial system of trade it was only a question of time before German economic influence came up flush with the linguistic borders of the old Reich—the whole of Alsace, about half of Lorraine, and Eupen et Malmédy. To quote a 1970 edition of a Strasbourg newspaper, "Twenty-five years after the liberation, the old Alsace-Lorraine issue, long ago pronounced dead, has risen again!" In February 1969 a Strasbourg economist, Etienne Juillard, gave a lecture for the Industrial Chamber of Commerce of the Lower Rhine. The title of the lecture: "Is Alsatia Being Drawn into the German Economic Sphere?" There are now more than a hundred German factories operating in Alsace and over thirty in Lorraine. Juillard spoke of "an indirect German reconquest" of the eastern provinces of France through "dynamic industrial and commercial enterprises" and "the saturation" of these provinces with German residential housing projects. "Saturation" with German residential housing projects (the most visible form of economic penetration) is also bemoaned by the Dutch, the Swiss, and the Austrians; all of these groups are clearly members of the German linguistic confraternity.

Some thirty thousand Alsatians and some ten thousand Lorrainers commute to the Federal Republic as dayworkers. Also, ninety percent of the population of Alsace and about thirty percent of the Lorrainers speak German as a first language. An added attraction to German industry is of course the contiguity of these provinces with German heartland. Alsace represents an extension of the Rhine River flatland that forms a natural economic unit in itself. In addition, the reception of Germany's three television channels is especially good in the flatland area (France has only two channels). Today in Alsatian cities there are almost as many

German magazines and newspapers on the stands as there are French. There was a time—only five or six years ago—when Federal Republican Germans noted with gratification how stubbornly the Alsatians persisted in speaking their unholy dialect despite such French pressures as the exclusion of German from schools and the printing of all sports news in French. That time has passed. "Anybody who wants a job in Alsace today," one hears throughout the region now, "has to speak German."

The French outcry and campaign against the alienation of the region because of German economic influences has prompted some pious expostulation from the Germans. "Have not the French the same opportunities in the neighboring German areas?" asked a major German newspaper. (Obviously not: the French have no linguistic overlap in the Federal Republic.) "And is not economic penetration the sense and purpose of the European Economic Community?" Indeed, hardly three years ago the French government was still inviting, nay, exhorting the Germans to contribute to the industrial development of Lorraine. The French even made a point of reminding the Germans that a good part of the population of the Lorraine area (specifically the department of Moselle) was bilingual in French and German. The Germans accepted the invitation with alacrity. The French abruptly shifted ground. Wouldn't the Germans like to invest in, say, the Bordeaux region? They would not. The Germans seem to be interested only in those areas where the bilingual population can be put into the service of the German economy, both as sales force and consumers.

Before the Six had become the Ten (expanding to include Britain, Ireland, Denmark, and Norway), the European Community Information Service published a map of the Common Market area in which all national borders had been expunged to make way for the lineaments of fifty-three administrative regions, the largest of which is Bavaria. If the founders of the Common Market did not fully appreciate the ramifying significance of what they were doing, the Bavarian politician Franz Josef Strauss did. "Whoever wishes to be a German," he said, "must see to it that he becomes a European while there is still time. We must have patriotism in an entirely new understanding of the word." A higher patriotism for a higher sovereignty. The words had a familiar ring.

There is a reason for the recurring need of a higher patriotism. It has always proved impossible to put together a linguistic majority in Europe. The cement of medieval Europe was Church Latin. It is ironic but in keeping with the times that now even the Latin liturgy of the Roman Catholic Church has been abolished in favor of national languages. Indeed, in the face of the dissolving fabric of Western society, nationalism has become the only bulwark against the growing menace of the loss of identity. De Gaulle turned his perception of this fact to political advantage.

By contrast, the majority of Germans under their Christian Democratic leaders made no attempt to conceal that their prime interest in renouncing sovereignty was to slough off their oppressive national identity and blend into a larger allegiance—the European Community. Other Europeans are inclined to take German self-renunciation as protesting too much, as a kind of negative nationalism—Deutschland unter alles —another aspect of the same old bogey and a deceptive one at that. The Germans under the Christian Democrats were on the treadmill of the vicious circle. It was only by producing evidence of having outgrown nationalism that they could draw the strength they needed to achieve the national aim. The postwar Germans became Europe's most prolific producers of synthetic common causes. But the moment the label "Made in Germany" came to light, the product was rejected.

Strauss was often hailed in the German press as the first German politician to announce that the question of German reunification could be solved only within the context of Europe as a whole. So the drive to create a united Europe was suspect from the outset as a German shift to achieve reunification, and reunification, however achieved, would inevitably mean a Europe united under German domination. The demonstration of this inevitability is the Common Market's great and perhaps self-defeating achievement.

I wrote a letter to Axel Springer from Szombathely, Hungary, in late October 1956 during the Hungarian Revolution. In it I told Springer that what was going on then in Hungary proved wrong his prescription for the German people as historical convalescents, simply because events were showing that there was no time for such convalescence. The German people would have to engage themselves, despite their past, despite their invalid condition, despite their pariahdom, in the great struggle that was now unmistakably in progress between communism as championed by the Soviet Union, and the non-Communist world. (Once again Germany's geographic position simply made it impossible for her to recover in any sort of prescibed or otherwise effective convalescence. Germany has always been an area under contention, an armed camp or a place d'armes, with German or foreign standing armies on its soil.) I do not know whether Springer received the letter (considering that it was posted from Hungary at that time, it is unlikely that he did). I have never asked him about it because not long after that Springer made a trip to Moscow for his fateful interview with Khrushchev and returned a different man (Khrushchev having read him the riot act on German reunification).

Would it not be more reasonable, Springer was asked by a lady journalist during a television interview in 1970, to take cognizance—without illusions—of the reality of the existence of an East German state? Said Springer: "The word 'reality' kills me. . . . This business of acknowledging terrible realities is actually the excuse of the weak. The world is changed by dreams, by hard work." And then he quoted an authority he described as "an important man": "If you really want it, then it is no fairy tale." Springer might have quoted Josef von Sternberg ("reality consists of a thousand illusions") or Lenin, for whom reality was "not what is, but what should be," or any major German philosopher, say Kant or Schopenhauer. Instead he quoted Theodor Herzl, the founder of Zionism. It was very like Springer to do so.

It was very like Springer, on another occasion, to quote a passage from a speech delivered by the novelist Ernst Wiechert to German youth just after the war:

> We once had a fatherland, and that was Germany. It was a country like other countries. In it people worked and laughed, loved and suffered as they do in other countries. From its cathedrals the bells tolled, and in its fields the swish of the scythe was heard, in its coal mines the call "Luck [on the way] up!" There was affliction and quarreling in it, envy and hate, but in the evening here and there a girl would sing the Song of the Rising Moon, and a fiddle would exult in the sunset glow.
>
> Many thought it was a better country than the others and some thought it was a worse country. But most of the people were of good will and when they returned from abroad they complained a bit about its signs prohibiting this and that, but they made themselves as comfortable as they could, put flowers in their windows, argued about everything under the sun ["um Gott und die Welt"—"about God and the world"] and were loyal servants in the vineyard of the Lord.

I have often wondered why it is that Axel Springer reminds me of the Great Gatsby. It is not only because Springer's conspicuous display of wealth, like Gatsby's, is a degraded form (necessarily degraded because modern) of medieval courtesy. It is not only because Springer's private noblesse vis-à-vis his public enemies is also an equivalent (and in no way a degraded one) of medieval courtesy. It is rather because

Springer, like Gatsby, is the last of the courtly lovers. His lady is Germany. He loves her with a passion the seriousness of which is utterly out of date. Springer is an old-fashioned German patriot, the only one I know who is not ashamed or afraid or otherwise indisposed to proclaim his patriotism publicly. "What Springer says is true," a prominent German editor confided to me recently, "but what he says and keeps saying is a declaration of principle, not an editorial policy or a political program." In other words, "Sure, we all love the old girl but um Gottes Willen we just can't come out like that and say it! Think of her past!" Most of the editorial positions Springer adopts are only natural, normal commonplaces (Selbstverständlichkeiten), such as the insistence on reunification, on freedom of movement, on the rescinding of the Communist order to open fire on escaping refugees, etc.—that is to say, they would be perfectly reasonable commonplaces in any other country. But Germany is not any other country. And besides, the wench is dead.

DD
76
B15

Bailey, George, 1923–
    Germans: the biography of an obsession. New York, World Pub. ₁1972₎

    409 p. 24 cm. $10.00

266338

    1. Germans. 2. Germany (Territory under Allied occupation, 1945–1955. U. S. Zone)   I. Title.

DD76.B19   1972   914.3′03′87   72–81465
ISBN 0–529–04814–0   MARC

    Library of Congress   72 ₄₎